Kierkegaard, Literature, and the Arts

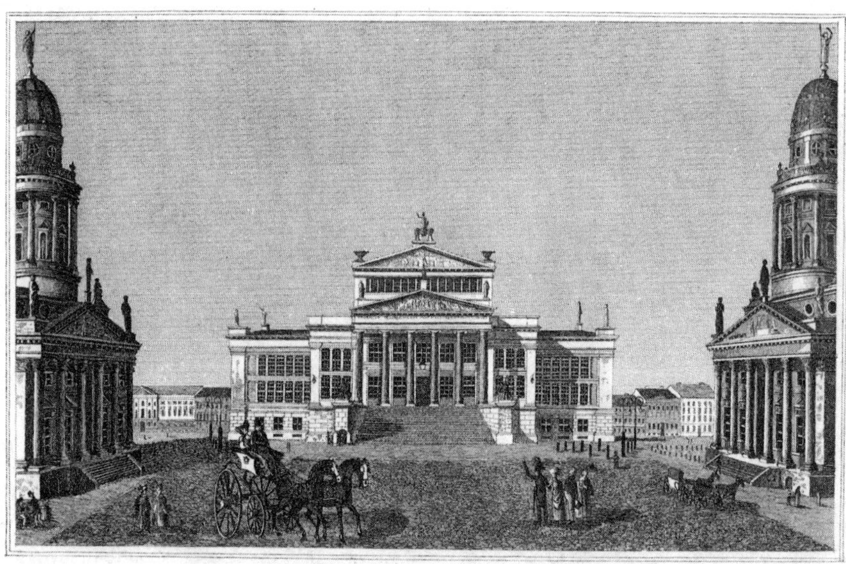

Engraving, ca. 1837, by Carl Strahlheim showing the Gendarmenmarkt in Berlin, with what was then the Schauspielhaus, or Theater (*center*)—now the concert house of the Konzerthausorchester Berlin—flanked by the German Cathedral (*left*) and the French Cathedral (*right*). Pictured in the background to the immediate right of the theater is the building, still standing today, in which Kierkegaard lodged during his four stays in Berlin, in 1841–42, 1843, 1845, and 1846. It was there, as noted by a plaque outside, that Kierkegaard wrote the first drafts of *Either/Or*, *Repetition*, and *Fear and Trembling*.

Kierkegaard, Literature, and the Arts

Edited by Eric Ziolkowski

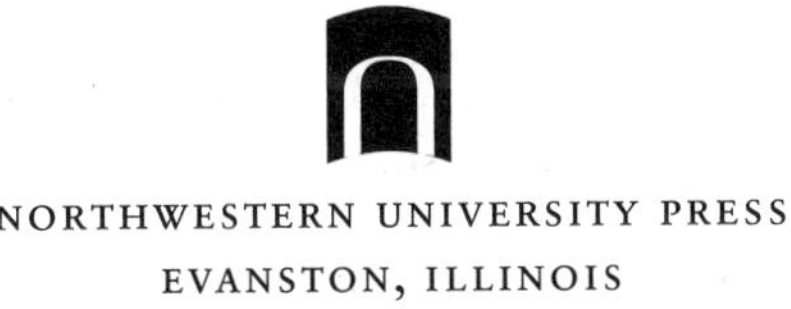

NORTHWESTERN UNIVERSITY PRESS

EVANSTON, ILLINOIS

Northwestern University Press
www.nupress.northwestern.edu

Printed in the United States of America

10 9 8 7 6 5 4 3 2 1

Library of Congress Cataloging-in-Publication Data

Names: Ziolkowski, Eric Jozef, 1958– editor.
Title: Kierkegaard, literature, and the arts / edited by Eric Ziolkowski.
Description: Evanston, Illinois : Northwestern University Press, 2018. | Includes
    index.
Identifiers: LCCN 2017029795 | ISBN 9780810135970 (cloth : alk. paper) | ISBN
    9780810135963 (pbk. : alk. paper) | ISBN 9780810135987 (e-book)
Subjects: LCSH: Kierkegaard, Søren, 1813–1855. | Kierkegaard, Søren, 1813–
    1855—Aesthetics. | Literature—Philosophy. | Music and philosophy. | Art and
    philosophy. | Performing arts—Philosophy.
Classification: LCC B4377 .K4558 2018 | DDC 198.9—dc23
LC record available at https://lccn.loc.gov/2017029795

CONTENTS

ILLUSTRATIONS

ACKNOWLEDGMENTS

A number of people deserve my heartfelt thanks for having helped to make possible this volume, which draws together essays by fourteen authors from five different countries. Andrew Burgess and Sylvia Walsh, former co-chairs of the Kierkegaard, Religion, and Culture Group of the American Academy of Religion, encouraged this project from the outset, and they facilitated my initial contact with several authors from whom I solicited revised versions of papers originally presented on panels sponsored by that AAR Group.

At every stage of its consideration, review, and production at Northwestern University Press, the volume has benefited from the expertise, meticulousness, and generosity of the individuals involved there: Henry Lowell Carrigan Jr., Maggie Grossman, Liz Hamilton, Marianne Jankowski, Nathan MacBrien, Gianna Francesca Mosser, and J. D. Wilson. The published volume is also stronger as a result of the helpful comments and suggestions made by the anonymous reviewers of its manuscript.

Malene Anthon and Ingrid Langhoff of the Ordrupgaard Collection in Copenhagen are to be thanked for granting the permission for, and providing the digitized reproduction of, Johan Thomas Lundbye's 1841 landscape *Søbyvang*, which Marianne Jankowski has incorporated so handsomely into this volume's cover layout.

Here at my own institution, Lafayette College, I remain always thankful for the dedication and efficiency of both Laura McKee, secretary of the Department of Religious Studies, and the entire staff of the David Bishop Skillman Library.

To Lee Upton, my gratitude is in perpetual and ceaseless competition with my boundless admiration for her.

ABBREVIATIONS

A	Georg Wilhelm Friedrich Hegel. *Aesthetics: Lectures on Fine Art.* 2 vols. Trans. T. M. Knox. Oxford: Clarendon, 1975.
ASKB	*Auktionsprotokol over Søren Kierkegaards Bogsamling* (*The Auctioneer's Sales Record of the Library of Søren Kierkegaard*). Ed. H. P. Rohde. Copenhagen: Royal Library, 1967. Citations by list-numbers: e.g., *ASKB* 3567 (= *ASKB* + volume list number 3567).
BA	Søren Kierkegaard, *The Book on Adler*. Ed. and trans. Howard V. Hong and Edna H. Hong. Princeton, N.J.: Princeton University Press, 1998.
BB	See *SKS*.
CA	Søren Kierkegaard, *The Concept of Anxiety*. Ed. and trans. Reidar Thomte in collaboration with Albert B. Anderson. Princeton, N.J.: Princeton University Press, 1980.
CD, CCLA	Søren Kierkegaard, *Christian Discourses* and *The Crisis and a Crisis in the Life of an Actress* [and "Addendum: Phister as Captain Scipio" ("PCS")]. Ed. and trans. Howard V. Hong and Edna H. Hong. Princeton, N.J.: Princeton University Press, 1997.
CDP	*The Collected Dialogues of Plato, Including the Letters*. Ed. Edith Hamilton and Huntington Cairns. Bollingen Series 71. Princeton, N.J.: Princeton University Press, 1961.
CI	Søren Kierkegaard, *The Concept of Irony* and "Notes on Schelling's Berlin Lectures." Ed. and trans. Howard V. Hong and Edna H. Hong. Princeton, N.J.: Princeton University Press, 1989.
Cor.	Søren Kierkegaard, *The Corsair Affair*. Ed. and trans. Howard V. Hong and Edna H. Hong. Princeton, N.J.: Princeton University Press, 1982.
CUP	Søren Kierkegaard, *Concluding Unscientific Postscript*. 2 vols. Ed. and trans. Howard V. Hong and Edna H. Hong. Princeton, N.J.: Princeton University Press, 1992.
CWA	*The Complete Works of Aristotle: The Revised Oxford Translation*. 2 vols. Ed. Jonathan Barnes. Bollingen 71, no. 2. Princeton, N.J.: Princeton University Press, 1984.
DD	See *SKS*.
EO	Søren Kierkegaard, *Either/Or*. 2 vols. Ed. and trans. Howard V. Hong and Edna H. Hong. Princeton, N.J.: Princeton University Press, 1987.
EPW	Søren Kierkegaard, *Early Polemical Writings*. Ed. and trans. Julia Watkin. Princeton, N.J.: Princeton University Press, 1990. Contains *From the Papers of One Still Living*.

EUD	Søren Kierkegaard, *Eighteen Upbuilding Discourses*. Ed. and trans. Howard V. Hong and Edna H. Hong. Princeton, N.J.: Princeton University Press, 1990.
FSE, JFY	*For Self-Examination* and *Judge for Yourself!* Ed. and trans. Howard V. Hong and Edna H. Hong. Princeton, N.J.: Princeton University Press, 1990.
FT, R	Søren Kierkegaard, *Fear and Trembling* and *Repetition*. Ed. and trans. Howard V. Hong and Edna H. Hong. Princeton, N.J.: Princeton University Press, 1983.
GWFHW	*Georg Wilhelm Friedrich Hegel"s Werke*. 18 vols. Ed. Philipp Marheineke, Johannes Karl Hartwig Schulze, Eduard Gans, et al. Berlin: Duncker und Humblot, 1832–45. *ASKB* 549–65, 1384–86.
JFY	See *FSE*.
JJ	See *SKS*.
JP	*Søren Kierkegaard's Journals and Papers*. 7 vols. Ed. and trans. Howard V. Hong and Edna H. Hong, assisted by Gregor Malantschuk. Bloomington: Indiana University Press, 1967–78.
KBHA	Kongelige Bibiliotek, Håndskriftssamlingen
KJN	*Kierkegaard's Journals and Notebooks*. 9 vols. Ed. Niels Jørgen Cappelørn, Alastair Hannay, David Kangas, Bruce H. Kirmmse, George Pattison, Vanessa Rumble, and K. Brian Söderquist. Princeton, N.J.: Princeton University Press, 2007–.
LD	Søren Kierkegaard, *Letters and Documents*. Trans. Henrik Rosenmeier. Princeton, N.J.: Princeton University Press, 1978. Each letter is assigned the same number (no.) it appears under in vol. 1 of *Breve og Aktstykker vedrørende Søren Kierkegaard*. 2 vols. Ed. Niels Thulstrup. Copenhagen: Munksgaard, 1953–54.
MLW	Søren Kierkegaard, *"The Moment" and Late Writings*. Ed. and trans. Howard V. Hong and Edna H. Hong. Princeton, N.J.: Princeton University Press, 1998.
NB	See *SKS*.
Notesbog	See *SKS*.
NRSV	Bible, New Revised Standard Version
P	Søren Kierkegaard, *Prefaces* and *Writing Sampler*. Ed. and trans. Todd W. Nichol. Princeton, N.J.: Princeton University Press, 1997.
Pap.	*Søren Kierkegaards Papirer*. 16 vols. Ed. P. A. Heiberg, V. Kuhr, and E. Torsting (I–XI). Copenhagen: Gyldendal, 1909–48. 2nd., augmented edition, ed. Niels Thulstrup (XII–XIII). Copenhagen: Gyldendal, 1968–70. Index, ed. Niels Jørgen Cappelørn (XIV–XVI). 1975–78. A Roman numeral indicates the volume (*bind*); a superscript Arabic numeral (following some but not all volume numbers) indicates the volume's separately bound part (*afdeling*): e.g., XI^1 (= vol. 11, pt. 1), which is bound separately from XI^2 (= vol. 11, pt. 2).
Papir	See *SKS*.
PC	Søren Kierkegaard, *Practice in Christianity*. Ed. and trans. Howard V. Hong and Edna H. Hong. Princeton, N.J.: Princeton University Press, 1991.
"PCS"	See *CD*.

PF	Søren Kierkegaard, *Philosophical Fragments* and *Johannes Climacus, or De omnibus dubitandum est*. Ed. and trans. Howard V. Hong and Edna H. Hong. Princeton, N.J.: Princeton University Press, 1985.
PL	Patrologiae cursus completus. Series latina. 222 vols. Paris: J.-P. Migne, 1844–55, 1862–64.
PV	Søren Kierkegaard, *On My Work as an Author: The Point of View for My Work as an Author* and *Armed Neutrality*. Ed. and trans. Howard V. Hong and Edna H. Hong. Princeton, N.J.: Princeton University Press, 1998.
R	See *FT*.
SK	Søren Kierkegaard
SKS	Søren Kierkegaard, *Søren Kierkegaards Skrifter*. 28 vols. Ed. Niels Jørgen Cappelørn, Joakim Garff, Jette Knudsen, Johnny Kondrup, Alastair McKinnon, and Finn Hauberg Mortensen. Copenhagen: Gads Forlag, 1997–.

    BB, DD, JJ = among the titles by which Kierkegaard designated ten of his journals, written 1833–46.

    Notesbog 1 through 15 = titles by which Kierkegaard designated fifteen notebooks written 1839–49.

    NB, NB2, NB3, etc., to NB36 = titles by which Kierkegaard designated thirty-six of his journals, written 1839–49.

    Papir = Loose paper.

SKS K	*Kommentar til Søren Kierkegaards Skrifter*. 28 vols. Søren Kierkegaard Forsskningscenteret. Copenhagen: Gads Forlag, 1997–.
SLW	Søren Kierkegaard, *Stages on Life's Way: Studies by Various Persons*. Ed. and trans. Howard V. Hong and Edna H. Hong. Princeton, N.J.: Princeton University Press, 1988.
SUD	Søren Kierkegaard, *The Sickness unto Death: A Christian Psychological Exposition for Upbuilding and Awakening*. Ed. and trans. Howard V. Hong and Edna H. Hong. Princeton, N.J.: Princeton University Press, 1980.
SV[1]	Søren Kierkegaard, *Samlede Værker*. 14 vols. 1st edition. Ed. A. B. Drachmann, Johan Ludvig Heiberg, and H. O. Lange. Copenhagen: Gyldendal, 1901–6.
TA	Søren Kierkegaard, *Two Ages: The Age of Revolution and the Present Age. A Literary Review*. Ed. and trans. Howard V. Hong and Edna H. Hong. Princeton, N.J.: Princeton University Press, 1978.
TDIO	Søren Kierkegaard, *Three Discourses on Imagined Occasions*. Ed. and trans. Howard V. Hong and Edna H. Hong. Princeton, N.J.: Princeton University Press, 1993.
UDVS	Søren Kierkegaard, *Upbuilding Discourses in Various Spirits*. Ed. and trans. Howard V. Hong and Edna H. Hong. Princeton, N.J.: Princeton University Press, 1993.
WA	Søren Kierkegaard, *Without Authority*. Ed. and trans. Howard V. Hong and Edna H. Hong. Princeton, N.J.: Princeton University Press, 1997.
WL	Søren Kierkegaard, *Works of Love*. Ed. and trans. Howard V. Hong and Edna H. Hong. Princeton, N.J.: Princeton University Press, 1995.

Kierkegaard, Literature, and the Arts

Here, an immediate qualification is in order. Despite the concentration of this volume on the relation of Kierkegaard to literature and the arts, he himself cannot be categorized as a poet, novelist, or story writer in any conventional sense. Nor was he a practitioner of any of the other arts. For all his and his pseudonyms' manifest love of music, particularly of Mozart, Kierkegaard played no musical instrument, nor sang, nor does he or any of his pseudonyms, when discussing music, broach the sorts of questions that musicologists and music theorists conventionally treat—that is, concerning key, harmony, rhythm, and so forth; indeed, there is no evidence that he could read music. Dance and the visual arts, as the essays by Anne Margrete Fiskvik and Ragni Linnet demonstrate, likewise bear significantly upon Kierkegaard's writings (in ways unappreciated heretofore). Yet he wrote relatively little about dance and visual arts and set forth no theory of them. Moreover, his artistic skill, in Pattison's words, "seems to have been limited to some rather primitive caricatures in the margins of the journals," and he never performed ballet. As Fiskvik suggests, despite his personal acquaintance with the ballet master August Bournonville, it would be difficult even to imagine Kierkegaard on the ballroom floor.

As for his pervasively literary nature,[4] his self-image as "only a singular kind of poet [*en egen Art Digter*]" (*SKS* 12:281 / *WA* 165) or "hardly anything but a poet [*næsten kun en Digter*]" (*SKS* 13:25 / *PV* 18), and his predilection for the theater, which led him to contemplate "transform[ing] [his personal] struggle into literary works, even present[ing] it on the stage as straight drama" (*SKS* 24:193, NB22:164, n.d. 1851 / *JP* 6:6718), his compulsion to engage in "creative writing" is undeniable. His journals and papers up through the 1840s record any number of ideas and plans for, and occasionally sketches or drafts (none of them completed) of, stories, novels, dramas, and various other literary-artistic writing projects, the most fully developed of which is an Aristophanic burlesque play (*SKS* 17:280–97, DD:208, n.d. 1837 / *KJN* 1:272–89).[5] Consistent with certain hints by the pseudonyms, some of the pseudonymous writings have previously been read as novels,[6] and in the present volume Pattison and Joakim Garff read *Either/Or* and *Practice in Christianity* as Bildungsromane; Howard Pickett ascribes a "theatrical form" to the entire pseudonymous corpus, especially *Concluding Unscientific Postscript*; and Martijn Boven finds the whole authorship, especially *Repetition*, functioning as a "theater of ideas." However, the fact remains, none of Kierkegaard's published works was written for the stage, and none presents itself as a *traditional* novel. In the final analysis, if there could ever be such an analysis of Kierkegaard, we would have to agree with Mooney: "Kierkegaard did not deliver novels or plays or poems, but he easily *could have*. He had other fish to fry. Something diverts his attention from becoming *only* a literary figure."

There is another point to acknowledge before examining Kierkegaard in his relation to literature and the arts. Ultimately, those writings, let alone that relation, cannot be considered in isolation from the life of Kierkegaard, a life that was overtly none too exciting. To be sure, there were his painful break on August 11, 1841, from the single love of his life, Regine Olsen, and then, five years later, his publicly humiliating, yearlong imbroglio with the local tabloid, *The Corsair* (*Corsaren*), whose cartoonist caricatured him as both a cruel cad and a skinny hunchback, a kind of foppish Quasimodo in a top hat, overcoat, and trousers with uneven legs.[7] Closing out the twilight of his relatively brief life, there was also his fierce, bold attack upon his nation's established church, homing in on Denmark's twin ecclesiastical icons at that time, the recently deceased bishop Jakob Peter Mynster and his episcopal successor, Hans Lassen Martensen. Still today, imposing, larger-than-life busts of these two clerics flank the north side of Copenhagen's Church of Our Lady (Vor Frue Kirke), statuary centurions on guard, as if to assure their flock of protection against the likes of Kierkegaard. The latter's own most conspicuous memorial, a full-body statue of him seated and writing, is situated blocks away, in the somewhat secluded, innocuously secular, tree-shadowed space of the Royal Library garden.

Nonetheless, Kierkegaard's life seems rather undramatic, unless one perceives in it, as Mircea Eliade did (rightly or wrongly), the recurrence of an ancient mythic pattern. The Romanian-born novelist, story writer, and historian of religions likened Kierkegaard to, of all people, Achilles, on the grounds that both men were lifelong bachelors. In Eliade's view, Achilles resisted the happy, fruitful life that had been predicted for him, had he married, because in that case he would have given up his becoming a hero and his uniqueness and immortality that came with that status: "Kierkegaard passes through exactly the same existential drama with regard to Regina [*sic*] Olsen: he refuses marriage in order to remain himself, 'the unique,' to be able to hope for the eternal, by rejecting the modality of a happy existence in the 'general.'"[8] Otherwise, aside from the highly public *Corsair* debacle and assault on Christendom, Kierkegaard's life offers little external drama, nor even much physical movement outside the chambers of the successive Copenhagen houses and apartments he inhabited over the years. Aside from his daily walks about the city, his random chats with people on the streets (his "people baths," as he called them), his theater and concert-going, his occasional carriage rides through the nearby countryside, and his five trips abroad (once to Sweden, in 1835, and four times to Berlin, in 1841–42, 1843, 1845, 1846), what confronts us is a most unconventional drama of intensely private, introspective, and yet obsessively recorded, inscribed, and transcribed existence that revolved around incessant reading, reflecting, and writing. The sheer verbosity of Kierkegaard, a basic and at times perhaps irritating aspect of his work, justifies Garff's diagnosis of him as a graphomaniac, a sufferer of hypergraphia.[9] This led Johan Ludvig Heiberg to characterize the "two big, thick volumes" constituting *Either/Or* as "a monster [*Monstrum*] of a book,"[10] introducing several size-related associations—*bigness, thickness, monstrosity*—that became standard tropes in reviews and critical discussions of Kierkegaard's published writings. Martensen harked back to these associations in an article published in 1854, where he dismissed "the whole prolix [or longwinded, *vidtløftige*] Kierkegaardian literature,"[11] averring that Kierkegaard produced more books, both signed and pseudonymous, than was divinely warranted.[12]

The indissoluble link between the personal existence of Kierkegaard and his literary art is suggested by an observation made by the Swiss writer Denis de Rougemont in 1934, that heyday of fascism, Nazism, communism, and what he disparaged as mass rule. Among the writers whose thought had transformed "the data of [people's] lives" by that time, Rougemont distinguished two main "families." The first, to which Hegel, Marx, and Georges Sorel belong, "acts only by the objective content of its theories, not by its indifferent style. On the other hand," wrote Rougemont regarding the second "family," the one by which he claimed to have been personally inspired: "a Pascal, a Kierkegaard, a Rimbaud act less by virtue of their conclusions than by that of *their personal drama made 'flesh' by the turns of their language, the movement of their thought*."[13] We might add, not only are aspects of the persona of Kierkegaard incarnated into his writings, but also material objects from his immediate physical surroundings are reflected, sometimes betraying his attraction to other arts. For example, as Roger Poole has shown, several of the *Discourses at Friday Communion* (1849, 1851), at least two of which Kierkegaard evidently delivered in the Church of Our Lady, allude to Bertel Thorvaldsen's celebrated statue of Christ, which stands at the altar there, facing Thorvaldsen's sculptured renditions of the twelve disciples, six on each side of the nave. In several instances in his delivery of those discourses, it seems probable that Kierkegaard even gestured with his hand toward the Christ statue, connecting his words directly with it. Moreover, the inscription from Matthew 11:28 above the statue, "Come here, all you who labor and are burdened, and I will give you rest" (*SKS* 12:13 / *PC* 5), is the text for the entirety of *Practice in Christianity*, which Kierkegaard published in 1850 under the pseudonym Anti-Climacus: "All those mediations are full of implicit and often explicit reference to the figure of Christ, standing in marble at the altar of Vor Frue Kirke."[14] Another, earlier example occurs in Kierkegaard's *Repetition*, published in 1843 under the pseudonym Constantin Constantius, whose account of his arrival back in Berlin for a return visit places him in the same apartment building, Jägerstrasse 57, on the corner with Charlottenstrasse, where Kierkegaard had resided on his first sojourn in Berlin (see Kierkegaard to Emil Boesen, January 1, 1842, *SKS* 28:156, Brev 83 / *LD* 116, letter 60)—and where, in fact, he wrote *Repetition* on his second visit, in 1843.[15] "So I arrived in Berlin," writes Constantin Constantius: "I hurried at once to my old lodgings to ascertain whether a repetition is possible. May I assure any commiserating reader that the previous time I managed to get one of the most pleasant apartments in Berlin; may I now give even more emphatic assurance. . . . Gensd'arme [*sic*] Square is certainly the most beautiful in Berlin; *das Schauspielhaus* [the theater] and the two churches are superb, especially when viewed from a window by moonlight" (*SKS* 4:27 / *R* 151). Later in life, Kierkegaard would satirically analogize the contemporary church to the theater as an institution, likening priests to "stage performers" (*Skuespillere*; *SKS* 24:71, NB21:119, n.d. 1850 / *KJN* 8:67). Priests, he suggested, would be the first to condemn any believer who dared to act in accord with the New Testament; they would regard it "as ridiculous as if a person were to act according to what he sees or hears in the theater" (*SKS* 23:485, NB20:172, n.d. 1850 / *KJN* 7:493). Further, in a statement quoted in part by Pickett, he wryly noted, "In the theater, if one notices the prompter [*Souffleuren*]," that is, the hidden person who whispers forgotten lines to actors onstage, "the illusion is disturbed. In church, the illusion would be perfect only if the prompter were present" (*SKS* 24:252, NB23:88, n.d. 1851 / *KJN* 8:251). Nonetheless, the scene evoked above of "*das Schauspielhaus* and the two churches" is emblematic of the life of Kierkegaard in a way that even he may not have recognized. This can be appreciated by anyone familiar with the Gendarmenmarkt, whether from visiting there today (as its basic layout remains the same as in Kierkegaard's time, despite the severe damage it suffered during the Second World War) or by perusing the frontispiece of this volume, an engraving from about 1837 that shows the Gendarmenmarkt in the decade prior to Kierkegaard's first Berlin stay, with Kierkegaard's building visible in the background.[16] As though concretized upon that celebrated square to mirror materially and architecturally one of the basic tensions in his own existence, *aesthetic existence* (in the form of the theater Kierkegaard attended, now the concert house for the Konzerthausorchester Berlin) is literally flanked on either side by *institutional religion* (in the form of the German Cathedral and the French Cathedral). When viewed at night by moonlight, Constantin Constantius goes on to comment, this whole scene "is transformed into a stage setting [*en scenisk Decoration*]. A dream world [*En drømmende Virkelighed*] glimmers in the background of the soul" (*SKS* 4:28 / *R* 152).

The linguistic, reflective incarnating of Kierkegaard's personal drama is rendered immeasurably more complex by what Pattison, in his essay herein, calls the "moving kaleidoscope of [Kierkegaard's] works, styles, and genres." Any reader of Kierkegaard's so-called aesthetic writings published under exotic, often amusingly Latinate noms de plume is acquainted with the vertiginous array of pseudonymous voices that speak from them. As much as any literary artist ever, Kierkegaard exists, as I have put it elsewhere, "largely in, or even *as*, a dialectic between his (and his pseudonyms') reading of literature and his (and their) production of literature—literature, that is, in the conventional sense of poetic or literary art."[17] Thus, we know, to borrow Mooney's words, that Kierkegaard "inherits genetic material from his ancestors": Socrates, Plato, Kant, Hegel, and other philosophers, as well as, no less profoundly, Aristophanes, Shakespeare, Cervantes, Goethe, Hamann, and German Romantics such as Friedrich Schlegel, Jean Paul, Novalis, Ludwig Tieck, E. T. A. Hoffmann; the post-Romantic Heinrich Heine; and Adam Oehlenschlæger, Jens Baggesen, and other Danish writers. The extensive, standard-setting series of several dozen volumes edited by Jon Stewart at the Kierkegaard Research Centre in Copenhagen, "Kierkegaard Research: Sources, Reception and Resources," offers what is as close as possible to a comprehensive scholarly accounting of the manifold major thinkers, writers, poets, and others who influenced Kierkegaard, and also of those around the globe whom he in turn influenced. His works are, to echo Mooney again, "like lively biological specimens . . . self-replicating," passing on their "genes" to Ibsen, Kafka, Rilke, and countless others up through John Updike and Woody Allen.

Yet even the notion of "influence" becomes problematic when applied to Kierkegaard, given his insistence on distinguishing himself from his pseudonyms: "That is, I am impersonally or personally in the third person a *souffleur* [prompter] who has poetically produced the *authors*, whose *prefaces* in turn are their productions, as their *names* are also. Thus in the pseudonymous books there is not a single word by me. I have no opinion about them except as a third party [*Trediemand*], no knowledge of their meaning except as a reader, not the remotest private relation to them, since it is impossible to have that to a doubly reflected communication" (*SKS* 7:569–70 / *CUP* 1:625–26). Such a severance of author from authorship, a feature of his that has endeared Kierkegaard to postmodernists, among others, was not entirely new with him. For example, Kant, in his first critique, where he suggests that our understanding of Plato's expression "idea" may differ from Plato's understanding of it, observes "that it is by no means unusual, upon comparing the thoughts which an author has expressed in regard to his subject, whether in ordinary conversation or in writing, to find that we understand him better than he has understood himself. As he has not sufficiently determined his concept, he has sometimes spoken, or even thought, in opposition to his own intention."[18] Kierkegaard, in claiming to relate to his pseudonyms as a "third party" or reader, in effect—whether wittingly or not—takes Kant's point a step further, distancing himself as author from his own pseudonyms whose works Kant would have us believe we might understand "better than" they (and also "better than" Kierkegaard).

In a number of places in his journal, Kierkegaard characterizes the relationship between his pseudonymous and signed writings with a memorable analogy to one of the great rivers of the Iberian peninsula, renowned since ancient times for the geologically peculiar fact that, not far from its source, the river dives below the earth's surface and follows a subterranean course before resurfacing some ten miles farther. "Just as the Guadalquibir [*sic*] plunges underground at one point and then emerges later," writes Kierkegaard, "I must now plunge into pseudonymity; but I have now also understood where I will emerge again in my own name" (*SKS* 22:70, NB11:123, n.d. 1849 / *KJN* 6:65). It is a marvelous analogy, almost surely derived from his reading of *Don Quixote*, but there is a problem: Kierkegaard cites the wrong river—that is, the Spanish waterway famous for its subterranean plunge is not the Guadalquivir (which never goes underground) but the Guadiana, as mentioned in Cervantes's novel.[19] Aside from this confusion of the rivers, Kierkegaard's analogy can also seem misleading, for it might distract us from remembering that all of Kierkegaard's numerous Guadiana-like plunges "into pseudonymity" were accompanied by the *surfacing and, quite often, resurfacing* of his various literary personae, all of whom must be regarded as separate, distinct *writers* as well as separate, distinct *readers* in their own right, with attitudes, convictions, worldviews, and interpretive proclivities that cannot necessarily be equated with Kierkegaard's own or with those of each other.

The question of how to construe Kierkegaard, especially in relation to literature and the arts, becomes more complicated if we consider him in the light of two seemingly opposed conceptualizations of the human being: Ellen Dissanayake's notion of *homo aestheticus* and Eliade's, of *homo religiosus*. These two notions encapsulate the human being, or what Dissanayake and Eliade posit to be two essential aspects of the human being, within the two categories that stand opposed as the first and third of Kierkegaard's and his pseudonyms' existential stages: the aesthetic and the religious. Although the cognitive distinction between art and religion is a relatively recent, peculiarly Western development,[20] Kierkegaard and his pseudonyms separate the aesthetic stage and the religious stage so radically as to locate the ethical, as well as the transitional phases of irony and humor that border it, as a separate stage in between (e.g., *SKS* 7:455 / *CUP* 1:501–2). Dissanayake takes art to be "a biologically evolved element in human nature," that is, "a natural, general proclivity that manifests itself in culturally learned specifics such as dances, songs, performances, visual display, and poetic speech"—hence her coinage, *homo aestheticus*.[21] At the same time, although Eliade applies the term *homo religiosus* in some instances to "the man of the traditional societies,"[22] as opposed to modern, "secularized" humans, it is evident that he conceives of *homo religiosus* also, perhaps even primarily, as an essentialist description of the entire human race at any and all times and places.[23]

Are Dissanayake's and Eliade's conceptions of the human being reconcilable with the Kierkegaardian conception of the aesthetic and the religious? On the one hand, whatever else Kierkegaard might have thought of the Darwinian theory of biological evolutionism had he lived to be acquainted with it, he would have recognized the affinity between Dissanayake's view of human beings as "inherently aesthetic and artistic creatures"[24] and his (and his pseudonyms') own association of the aesthetic stage with natural, instinctual existence and the arts. For Dissanayake, the human being is *homo aestheticus* because it is in human nature to be so; likewise, Kierkegaard and at least some of his pseudonyms seem to recognize that the movement of the individual into the ethical stage or even, finally, into the religious can never entail an absolute transcendence of, or evolvement from, the aesthetic. He allows that the poetic and aesthetic dimensions of life are not confined to the aesthetic stage but, in Sylvia Walsh's words, "are crucial to and may be integrated with an ethical or religious orientation."[25] As Christopher Barnett observes in the present volume, echoing a suggestion made also by C. Stephen Evans, all three Kierkegaardian stages—the aesthetic, ethical, and religious— "are permanent domains within the self, which, like a Venn diagram, overlap one another at certain key junctures." On the other hand, Eliade's understanding of the human being as inherently religious cannot be squared with Kierkegaard's portrayal of the religious as an existential stage into which only the ethically qualified individual might enter by means of a decision and "leap" that is, as Fiskvik reminds us, expressly conceived by Kierkegaard as ballet-like.

Notwithstanding the allowance by his pseudonym Johannes Climacus for the presence of Religiousness A "in paganism [*i Hedenskabet*]" (see *SKS* 5:506 / *CUP* 1:557), Kierkegaard's primary association of religion with Abrahamic faith and Christianity does not square with Eliade's recognition of "archaic"—that is, pre-Christian and also "pagan"—peoples as epitomizing *homo religiosus*. If the notion of *homo aestheticus* seems to suit Kierkegaard's anthropology more closely than does that of *homo religiosus* (because for Kierkegaard, whereas the individual may conceivably retain residual aesthetic traits after entering the ethical or the religious stage, a person can bear no trace of the religious stage before having entered it), there would seem in turn a natural affinity between this aesthetic anthropology and the bourgeois, "post-Romantic" age Kierkegaard inhabited, an age described by Pattison as "permeated through and through by the Romantics' valorization of art as a, if not the, central mode of human beings' self-experience and self-understanding."

Still, there is yet another category in which Kierkegaard, his literary and aesthetic proclivities, and his aforementioned graphomania might most suitably be construed. In a little book published not much over a decade ago in Cali, Columbia, Diego Gil Parra submits that in the same way as there exists *homo ludens* (the human who plays), *homo faber* (the human who makes), and *homo sapiens* (the human who thinks), and, we might add, *homo religiosus*, whom Gil Parra does not mention, there are legitimate reasons to speak of the existence of *homo litterarius* (the literary human), who is human inasmuch as he or she writes and reads.[26] This idea gives pause because, for an obvious reason, the argument could never be made, as Dissanayake and Eliade do make it for *homo aestheticus* and *homo religiosus*, that the condition of *homo litterarius* is inherent or essential to the human race. Why? Because as Dissanayake reminds us in a different context, "literacy is a recent human invention and an even more recent widespread accomplishment. It can be reasonably claimed that 99 percent of the humans who ever existed could not have read the Great Books, or any books, indeed anything at all."[27] Thus, for Gil Parra, who seems aware of this consideration, *homo litterarius* "is not a permanent condition . . . a professional attribute, for example," but rather "a *moment*, a stage [*un estado*], perhaps a trance" that is "purely an infinitive verb, purely to make, purely to grasp."[28] Epitomes of *homo litterarius* include Homer, Dante, Cervantes, Shakespeare, Dostoevsky, Flaubert, Baudelaire, Kafka, and Borges, while Don Quixote is the consummate *homo litterarius* of "living flesh and body."[29] Kierkegaard, who fancied himself a latter-day Don Quixote (*SKS* 22:199, NB12:103, n.d. 1849 / *KJN* 6:199) and who reportedly dubbed himself "the greatest prose stylist Denmark had produced,"[30] should naturally be added to Gil Parra's list.

With the aspects of the *litterarius*, *aestheticus*, and *religiosus* in Kierkegaard as its three main focal points in approaching his writings, the present volume is structured to consider his relation and pertinence to literature and the arts from a broad range of angles.

This volume of fourteen essays divides into four main parts, the first two of which consist of four essays each, and the last two parts, three essays each. The essays in part I focus on Kierkegaard in relationship to literature, his own main medium of expression; part II, to the performing arts, including theater, music, and dance; part III, to visual arts and film; while the essays of part IV are comparative in nature, considering Kierkegaard in juxtaposition with a Romantic poet, a modern composer, and a contemporary musician, singer, and songwriter.

The first two essays offer overarching perspectives on Kierkegaard's whole literary project, each with a different emphasis. The opening essay, George Pattison's "The Bonfire of the Genres: Kierkegaard's Literary Kaleidoscope," pursues the twofold task of examining Kierkegaard as reader or recipient in relation to literature and other arts contemporaneous with him, and then of gauging his contribution as a writer to his cultural world. The second essay, Edward F. Mooney's "Kierkegaard's Disruptions of Literature and Philosophy: Freedom, Anxiety, and Existential Contributions," considers Kierkegaard likewise in relation to literature, but then also to philosophy as well as to his native city, Copenhagen.

Pattison stresses "the sheer scale and variety of [Kierkegaard's] engagement with literature and the arts," ranging from the early, extensively informed interests Kierkegaard developed in Faust, Don Juan, the Wandering Jew, folk literature, the troubadours, and children's stories, to mention but a few of the more prominent of those interests, onward through his deep engagements with drama and opera and his evident fascination with guitar playing and ballet. It is only with the visual arts, both classic and contemporary, that Kierkegaard seems "lacking an all-round and in-depth familiarity"—although, as Ragni Linnet's essay will reveal, there runs throughout Kierkegaard's writings a detectable "ontology of pictorial art." Most important, Pattison urges us to resist the temptation to view Kierkegaard's relation to literature mainly within the context of all the many authors we know he read. Not to be overlooked is the fact of Kierkegaard's regular and frequent attendance at the theater, both in Copenhagen and in Berlin during his stays there: "Kierke-gaard is not just sitting at home or in the library reading books: he is out there in the theater and writing not just on what he has read but on what he has seen and heard." This point resonates in self-evident ways with the focus of more than one other essay in this volume, most notably Martijn Boven's, on Kierkegaard's oeuvre as a "theater of ideas" and the roles of performance and performativity particularly in *Repetition*, and Nils Holger Petersen's, which extends the discussion to Kierkegaard's ideas on specifically *musical* theater and opera. Likewise, Pattison's further comments on Kierkegaard's fascina-tion with the phenomenon of "live performance, which, in an age before film and sound reproduction, was by definition an ephemeral art," anticipate the essay by Ronald M. Green, who, in bringing several of Kierkegaard's writings to bear on Denis Villeneuve's film *Incendies*, expresses his conviction that Kierkegaard would have appreciated the cinematic medium.

Setting the tone, in a sense, for this entire volume is the titular metaphor Pattison offers to sum up Kierkegaard's oeuvre: "a kind of moving kaleido-scope of works, styles, and genres," the only sufficient representation of the "present age" described in Kierkegaard's *Two Ages*, a time whose many and diverse self-representations are perpetually "on the edge of falling away into incoherence." Pattison invokes Mikhail Bakhtin's theory of the modern novel, with its ability to incorporate multiple genres, as an analogue to Kierkegaard. Accordingly, we might look to that novelist whose works Bakhtin deemed the peerless epitome of the novel's "polyphonic" potentialities, Dostoevsky, for an expression of that same sense of the telltale contemporary uncentered, cultural multifariousness that Pattison ascribes to Kierkegaard. I have in mind the scene in Dostoevsky's *The Idiot*, published in 1869, less than a decade and half after Kierkegaard's death, where the rogue Lebedev enrages the other guests at Prince Myshkin's birthday party by sharing his drunken cogitations about the current age's lack of a "binding idea" like that which "bound and guided men's hearts and fructified the waters of life" in medieval Europe.[31] Later, Myshkin reiterates Lebedev's theory when he distinguishes between the "one idea" by which people were "animated" during the reign of Peter the Great and the ideological diffusion—and, some might say today, increasingly compulsive and frivolous "multitasking"—of modern humans: "In those days people seem to have been animated by one idea, but now they are much more nervous, more developed, more sensitive—they seem to be animated by two or three ideas at a time—modern man is more diffuse and, I assure you, it is this that prevents him from being such a complete human being as they were in those days."[32] In negotiating his way through the same era of ideological diffusion, Kierkegaard, as Pattison puts it, "held a kaleidoscope to a kaleidoscopic time" and thereby "gamble[d] . . . that his efforts would be kept from falling into formlessness by the 'great, uplifting, simple, elementary thoughts' [*SKS* 8:286 / *UDVS* 189] that he sought to keep in constant view." In this regard, perhaps the closest musical analogy to Kierkegaard's writings is found in the symphonies and song collections of Mahler. Although regarding his work, as Leonard Bernstein noted, there is much "carping about how derivative the music is of Mozart, Schubert, Wagner and the lot"[33] (including Beethoven and Bruckner, we might add), it has become platitudinous to observe that Mahler extended the conventional key system of tonality to the edge of atonality.

Another of Pattison's points, about Kierkegaard's literary penchant for satire, pastiche, and spoofing, and the attendant question about whether the pseudonymous works are to be taken "seriously," overlap with a concern taken up in Mooney's essay. Mooney considers whether Kierkegaard, in establishing his "disordered" or "hybrid status," is "just playing around" and at times "pulling our leg" in his writings, making them "just flippant, a wisecrack," or "all a joke." Whatever the case, as Mooney points out, the effect of the writings on readers can be seducing, stinging, and confusing all at once, as Kierkegaard stops, interrogates, and often abandons his audience "without answers." This applies even to the question of what Kierkegaard, as "a kind of philosophical poet," *really was*. Pursuing the *via negativa*, Mooney observes that Kierkegaard is *not* a dramatist, an essayist, a "man of letters," a journalist, a historian, or a biographer, though his writings yield examples and elements of the sorts of works produced by all those different types of writer. Complicating this quandary, Mooney notes, is the fact that in Kierkegaard, not only a philosophical vocation but a religious vocation as well competes with the literary one, making his writer's identity a "three-part" one "in the trifold identity of his works: religious, aesthetic, and philosophical—*all* of the above, and hence not *simply* any of the above." At the same time, Mooney contends, the refusal by Kierkegaard to "settle" exclusively "into" any one of those three areas, that is, philosophy, theology, or "literature" per se, has the "existential rationale" of allowing him—and presumably his readers—to remain free for "new life." Thus Mooney distills from Kierkegaard the lesson that reading is, as an activity, "an ethical venture" by which "we expose who we are—I expose who *I* am (existentially) in 'the what' and 'the how' of my writing and reading."

No less so than Mooney's essay, the third essay in part I, Marcia C. Robinson's "Kierkegaard's Existential Play: Storytelling and the Development of the Religious Imagination in the Authorship," is concerned with the effect of Kierkegaard's writings on readers. Robinson aims both to demonstrate how Kierkegaard and his pseudonyms cultivate a religious imagination in readers by "heighten[ing] their abilities to 'feel' and to 'know' the ideality and actuality of faith" and to show that the development of this imagination through stories in particular is not a one-time process, any more so than reading the Bible is for a devout religious person. Drawing upon Pattison's

2002 monographic study of Kierkegaard's *Upbuilding Discourses*,[34] she agrees with Pattison that Kierkegaard's imagery has an ethical purpose and she further attempts to develop a kind of dialectic of the image that balances the kataphatic/phenomenal and the apophatic/noumenal. Her suggestion is that an ever developing or maturing religious imagination is essential for a vibrant and engaged spiritual and ethical life because such an imagination makes sense of the divine in its power to be compelling.

Robinson is especially interested in how the tempering of imagination with actual experience in Kierkegaard occurs through his carefully worked-out method of "faith-oriented storytelling," which presupposes a deep understanding of his readers' "actual circumstances, values, fears, concerns, and conceptions of and attitudes toward faith." While acknowledging the usefulness of Pattison's construal of Kierkegaard's authorship as a "magic theatre" (an image drawn from Kierkegaard's Constantin Constantius) and Martin Thust's construal of it as a "marionette theatre," Robinson, inspired by Fellini's 1954 film, *La Strada*, proposes that we view it as a "'funhouse' of existential activity"—albeit a funhouse that "is not a simple matter of fun and games, but more like a fairy tale that uses the comic, the charming, the seductive, or the magical, in order to draw the reader into the anxiety, the suffering, the terror, and the death that dog human existence." Robinson demonstrates the crucial role played by works of the German Romantic Johann Ludwig Tieck in helping to shape the understanding at which Kierkegaard arrived during his student years of the inseparability of the moral-religious ideal from the feeling it instills or from the aesthetic medium through which it is communicated. Of all the cast of pseudonyms Kierkegaard later developed to act on this understanding, Climacus, that "dialectical poet" of both *Philosophical Fragments* (or *Philosophical Crumbs*) and *Concluding Unscientific Postscript*, is the one whom Robinson identifies as his most exemplary storyteller.

The last essay of part I, Joakim Garff's "Kierkegaard's Christian Bildungsroman," and the first essay of part II, Howard Pickett's "Beyond the Mask: Kierkegaard's *Postscript* as Antitheatrical, Anti-Hegelian Drama," have in common that they each single out a specific one of Kierkegaard's pseudonymous writings to examine it as exemplifying a particular literary genre: in Garff's case, *Practice in Christianity*, as a Christian Bildungsroman; in Pickett's case, as his subtitle indicates, *Concluding Unscientific Postscript*, as what Pickett calls an antitheatrical drama.

Connecting provocatively with Linnet's essay on Kierkegaard's treatment of visual art later in this volume, Garff suggests that Kierkegaard's philosophical discourse, with its constant oscillation between concept and image, is a "discourse of *visualization*," while his theological discourse, with its effort to suspend the eighteen hundred years that separate the modern reader from Jesus, is a "discourse of *autopsy*." Appealing to the Kantian distinction between the beautiful, as that which merely pleases, and the sublime, as that which "arouses satisfaction, but with dread [*erregen Wohlgefallen, aber mit Grausen*],"[35] Garff further observes that the aim of each of Kierkegaard's writings is precisely to "imitate or mimic the sublime by shaking its reader rhetorically." Of the innumerable instances of this tendency in the authorship to evoke the sublime, which dovetails with Kierkegaard's "frequent appeal to the reader's readiness to visualize," Garff holds up for analysis as a perfect example Anti-Climacus's chronicling of the lingering, gradually transformational effect that the strange and horrifying sight of the crucified Jesus, as represented in a picture, has on the unnamed youth in *Practice in Christianity*.

This crystallizes the aspects of *Practice in Christianity* that make it what Garff calls Kierkegaard's *billeddannelsesroman*, literally an "image formation novel" but more accurately, albeit loosely, as Garff prefers to render it, "visualizing Bildungsroman." The Bildungsroman (novel of education, educational novel, or, more precisely, novel of cultivation), a term coined by Karl Morgenstern in the early 1820s for a genre that portrays the mental and intellectual development of the protagonist from childhood to maturity and thus contributes to the reader's own education or cultivation (*Bildung*), finds its prototype in C. M. Wieland's *Geschichte des Agathon* (1766–67, *The Story of Agathon*) and reaches its literary apogee with Goethe's *Wilhelm Meisters Lehrjahre* (1795–96, *Wilhelm Meister's Apprenticeship*). As developed in such masterpieces as these, the Bildungsroman as a genre is not distinctly Christian in orientation. Yet, whereas Wieland's novel is set in ancient (pagan) Greece and Goethe's is wholly secular in it ambience, Kierkegaard departs from, or innovates upon, that literary tradition in two main ways in his oeuvre as a whole and in Anti-Climacus's *Practice in Christianity* in particular: first, by making specifically "*Christian* identity-formation," to borrow Garff's terms, the crux of the narrative; second, by not so much focusing on the moral, intellectual, and psychological development of the protagonist as seeking to actualize the individual reader's own relationship to self and to the God of the New Testament narrative. (In this regard, we might note, the story of the youth's Christian identity-formation in *Practice in Christianity* inverts the little narrative that closes the fourth and final chapter of Kierkegaard's unpublished "Book on Adler," drafted between the fall of 1846 and January 1847: namely, what might be described as the mini-Bildungsroman of the upbringing of a pseudo-Christian within Christendom; *SKS* 15:287–95 / *BA* 134–42.)

Thus, as Garff points out, while the conventional Bildungsroman traces "a process of individuation, the sequential structure of which follows the topography of the formation journey and can therefore be reproduced with the phrases *at home—homeless—home*," the visualizing Bildungsroman alters this sequence by "add[ing] a dialectical Christian qualification to the second phase, and postpon[ing] the third phase to a . . . metaphorical eternity." In this way, through Garff's analysis, an unexpected connection becomes perceptible between the aim of Christian edification underlying Kierkegaard's (or Anti-Climacus's) *billeddannelsesroman* and the medieval mystical sensibility of Hugh of St. Victor. At that phase in the narrative when the youth has developed the sense of being "a *stranger* among people, but . . . nonetheless *at home* because he was at home with the image he so passionately wanted to resemble," we might be reminded of Hugh's adage from the late 1120s: *Perfectus vero cui mundus totus exsilium est* (He is perfect to whom the entire world is as a foreign land [or place of exile]).[36]

With the transition from Garff's essay to the first of the four essays of part II, our focus shifts from the relation of Kierkegaard to literature to his relation to the performing arts. While Garff also found *Practice in Christianity* as a visualizing Bildungsroman to reflect "Kierkegaard's highly ambivalent relationship toward *art*" (my emphasis), a relationship that Linnet's essay will later explore in depth, Pickett investigates an equally intense ambivalence toward *theater* reflected in *Concluding Unscientific Postscript*, a text Pickett regards as "essentially theatrical" in form but "also *anti*theatrical" in content. Climacus disparages and dismisses the abstract, speculative thought of Hegelianism as a mere *Schattenspiel*, or "shadow play" (*SKS* 7:323 / *CUP* 1:353). As Pickett points out, Hegel himself, in his *Lectures on the Philosophy of History* (*Vorlesungen über die Philosophie der Geschichte*, delivered in Berlin in 1821, 1824, 1827, and 1831; published posthumously in 1837), routinely deploys theatrical terminology to describe the Spirit's concrete self-manifestation "on the stage [*auf dem Theater*]" of "Universal History." Schelling, we might add, likewise posits human history as "a play" (*Schauspiel*) in which the deity "reveals and discloses himself successively,"[37] and this idea—known also as the *theatrum mundi*—evidently struck Kierkegaard. In *Either/Or, II*, Kierkegaard's pseudonym speaks of the person who "feels himself present as a character in a drama the deity is writing [*der føler sig med som en Person i det Skuespil, Guddommen digter*]" (*SKS* 3:136 / *EO* 2:137). Perhaps hovering in the background of all such conceptions, albeit not in a lineage of direct influence, is Calvin's notion of the cosmos as "a dazzling theater [*theatrum*]."[38]

Kierkegaard's stance toward the theater, as Pickett points out, sets him and Climacus in very different relationships to two of the most seminal thinkers of the ancient West. While Climacus is bothered that actual ethical agents are ethically obliged to engage in actuality, not possibility, it was Aristotle who, in valuating possibility above actuality, viewed the theater positively as dealing in possibility. At the same time, Kierkegaard, in viewing theater negatively, joins Augustine, who in his *Confessions* (3.2.2) lamented that the audience at a theater play (*spectaculum theatricum*) is encouraged to enjoy observing the sufferings of characters onstage without feeling an inclination to assist them.[39] Further, Climacus charges Hegelian philosophers not only with hypocrisy and charlatanry for pretending to be merely spectators (looking on outwardly and as though they had God's vantage) in the theater of the world, rather than actors (engaged inwardly) within the world, but also with being naively theatrical in their tendency to act as though they can envision life and the world as a total, complete "system."

On the other hand, despite his having cast the theater and the theatrical Hegelian subject in so negative a light, Climacus also elaborates his own theatrical metaphor for "becoming subjective." Whereas the Hegelian "shadow play," in relying upon an objective form of thought that Kierkegaard and Climacus viewed as artificial and illusory, amounts in Pickett's words to "a 'philosophy of the spectacle' focused on detached spectators and mere external appearances," Climacus favors "an inward, subjective 'philosophy of the actor,' with its defining emphasis on action and internal effort." Despite his denunciation of the theatrical Hegelian subject, Climacus comes to construe the individual's ethical development as a "private theater" (*Privat-Theater*) in which not only God is the "spectator" (*Tilskuer*) but the individual, too, is a spectator and is also supposed to be an "actor" (*Skuespilleren*), albeit "not . . . one who deceives [*bedrager*] but one who discloses" (*SKS* 7:146 / *CUP* 1:157; quoted by Pickett). To be sure, *Postscript* lacks the typical features of a theatrical play, such as acts, scenes, stage directions, and dialogue. Yet Pickett demonstrates that *Postscript* "signals its theatricality," with Climacus himself emerging as its "most theatrical feature" as he delivers one long soliloquy. In this way, Pickett concludes, Kierkegaard's theatrical technique in *Postscript* counters Climacus's antitheatrical rhetoric, and the spectacle of *Postscript* distinguishes itself from its counterpart in Hegel by "admit[ting] its own theatricality." By transcending the bipolarity of antitheatrical versus pro-theatrical to the point of being what Pickett calls metatheatrical, and by anticipating the *Verfremdungseffekt*, or alienation effect, cultivated in the theater by Brecht, Climacus's work "awakens its readers to the challenges posed by their own inward subjectivity."

Part II's second essay, Martijn Boven's "A Theater of Ideas: Performance and Performativity in Kierkegaard's *Repetition*," in a sense picks up where Pickett's essay left off, though Boven concentrates his attention on *Repetition*, which appeared a little more than two and a half years before *Postscript*. Submitting that Kierkegaard's whole oeuvre, and *Repetition* in particular, may be viewed as a "theater of ideas," Boven first establishes a theoretical framework on the distinction between "performative writing strategies" and "categories of performativity," an approach informed by the theory of J. L. Austin and the earlier investigations of Kierkegaard by Sylviane Agacinski, Samuel Weber, and Gilles Deleuze. For Boven, Kierkegaard is a writer who diverges from the Aristotelian tradition of mimetic representation by developing his oeuvre as a conceptual "theater" in which performance, rather than representation, of philosophical and existential problems occurs: "His works not only *say* something; they also attempt *to do* something, to have a performative effect."

Boven's next step is to demonstrate that the titular concept of Constantin Constantius's *Repetition* is a category meant to trigger the reader's subjectivity into action by compelling the reader to confront a vaguely articulated, confusing, contradictory, "unresolved" existential problem. Here, we might be reminded of Mooney's wondering whether Kierkegaard's writings might be ultimately a "wisecrack" or "joke." Yet, as Boven suggests, there is method to the seeming madness, as Constantius achieves this active effect in the reader by means of a performative writing strategy involving a "dialectic of advance and withdrawal," whereby the reader is confused by the constant oscillation in the senses of the term *repetition* that are evoked in the text—between repetition in the "ordinary" sense of "an event that occurs for a second, a third, or any other time," as with a rehearsal, and repetition in the "existential" sense of an occurrence that "will always emerge as a unique event." This latter notion points to Boven's reminder that Kierkegaard regarded subjectivity itself as repetition, inasmuch as he viewed subjectivity—somewhat, we might note, as Buddhists regard the individual self—as lacking any essential, unchangeable, or unchanging core. Finally, considering *Repetition* as "philosophical theater," Boven uncovers three specific "clues" left by Constantin Constantius, each of which hints at his consciously developed performative writing strategy: the subtitling of his book as a "venture," which implies an outcome that cannot be known in advance; his indication in his letter to his book's "real reader" that he is seeking a reader willing to make an effort to understand the book; and the digressive mise en abyme that reveals how to perform the book we are reading through two examples of kitsch, one involving a Nürnberg print (of the sort discussed also by Linnet) and the other, a type of popular play, a *Posse* (or farce, burlesque, or vaudeville). Perhaps, we might add, a fourth "clue" to the compositional plan behind *Repetition* as "philosophical theater" is the mention by Constantius of the *Schauspielhaus* on the Gendarmenmarkt, visible by moonlight from his Jägerstrasse apartment, together with his elaborative description shortly afterward of the three theaters in Berlin at that time: the Gendarmenmarkt *Schauspielhaus*; the opera house for ballet and opera, that is, the Staatsoper, or the State Opera, located on the boulevard Unter den Linden, not far from the Gendarmenmarkt, and still operative; and the Königsstädtisches Theater, or Königstädter Theater, which stood on Alexanderplatz, a fair distance from the Jägerstrasse lodgings of Kierkegaard/Constantin Constantius.

Another aspect of the deep-seated concern of Kierkegaard with the theater, his theatrical aesthetics, together with his theory of music, is the focus of the next essay, by Nils Holger Petersen, "Kierkegaard's Notions of Drama and Opera: Molière's *Don Juan*, Mozart's *Don Giovanni*, and the Question of Music and Sensuousness." Petersen's interest is in the treatise on Mozart's *Don Giovanni*, "The Immediate Erotic Stages or The Musical-Erotic," in *Either/Or, I*, ascribed to the aesthetical pseudonym "A." In probing "A's" understanding of drama and the medium of music and how that understanding relates to more general questions of worldview, Petersen considers closely the distinction "A" draws between language as the authentic medium of the idea, absolutely qualified by spirit, and music as the medium through which sensuous immediacy finds expression and which exists only while it is being performed. Petersen suspects that "A's" ranking of language above music, viewing language as more precise and reflective than music, may express Kierkegaard's polemical attitude toward the early Romantics, such as Wilhelm Heinrich Wackenroder and E. T. A. Hoffmann, who exalted music as the loftiest of the arts. This conception of music underlies "A's" discussion of Molière's *Don Juan* and Heiberg's version of that drama, to both of which Petersen devotes considerable attention. Yet the theological implications of "A's" aesthetics are what most intrigue Petersen, who draws from Ettore Rocca's reading of "The Immediate Erotic Stages" as a Christian text. Rocca challenges "A's" argument that music, as the medium of the sensuous erotic, is the "devil's work" and that music is therefore excluded from Christianity. For Rocca, the function of music is to act under the power of the spirit. As Petersen points out, this same function carries over to Mozart's *Don Giovanni*, inasmuch as the idea of this work is so intimately linked with its form. In Mozart's opera, the conflict between the spirit and the sensuous is encapsulated in that between the Commendatore qua spirit and Don Giovanni qua sensuous immediacy.

The Don Juan–like seductiveness of "A's" rhetoric could make it easy for the reader to lose sight of precisely that aspect of "The Immediate Erotic Stages" about which Petersen reminds us when he cautions about the need "to be careful about drawing overly strict musical-philosophical implications out of a treatise that, after all, is written in a literary, associative style rather than based on a consistent theoretical construction." On this point, Petersen, like Boven, might almost seem to approach Mooney's view of Kierkegaard/"A" as engaging in a sort of joke. Nonetheless, Petersen takes "A's" music philosophy seriously enough to consider the implications of its being "based on notions of ephemerality and of music being silenced by reflection and memory," especially as the memory of Don Giovanni's past sins and wrongs is brought by the statue of the Commendatore. Through further appeals to Augustine's deconstruction of the present moment of a musical tone in book 11 of the *Confessions*; to the late Danish thinker K. E. Løgstrup's argument that perception of time occurs through comparison with at least momentarily unaltered objects, or fictional space; and to Theodor Adorno's notion of music as the condensing of suffering into a moment—through these and other appeals, Petersen demonstrates that "A's" music philosophy collapses, or "annihilates itself," through its own inherent contradictions (e.g., by finding that Mozart's opera expresses "what cannot be retained") and also as the result of our taking it at face value.

A fitting segue to the final essay in part II is afforded by "A's" own summation of Don Giovanni's life, a summation whose latter portion is referenced several times by Petersen, as having developed "in the dancing strains of the violin [*i de dandsende Violintoner*], in which he lightly, fleetingly . . . dances over the abyss [*dandser han over Afgrunden*], jubilating during his brief span" (*SKS* 2:131 / *EO* 1:130). In her essay "'Let No One Invite Me, for I Do Not Dance': Kierkegaard's Attitudes toward Dance," Anne Margrete Fiskvik examines the surprising number of allusions to dance and movement in *Either/Or* (both parts), *Fear and Trembling*, *Philosophical Fragments*, *The Concept of Anxiety*, and *Works of Love*, analyzing the concern these works express with both the ballroom dancer and the ballet dancer; the contrasts between male and females dancers; the dancing master who choreographs and designs the ballet; the expressionistic, emotive aspects and potentialities of dance; the question of what sorts of plots and subjects are suitable for ballet; as well as the use made of dance as a metaphor or allusion for the enrichment of the philosophical or theological discussions in these works. This essay is groundbreaking, for Fiskvik has no scholarly precursor in considering these various uses of dance in Kierkegaard's writings together in any sort of systematic way.

Just as Garff and Pickett found Kierkegaard ambivalent toward art and theater in *Practice in Christianity* and *Concluding Unscientific Postscript*, respectively, so Fiskvik finds Kierkegaard betraying an ambivalence toward dance, despite his admiration of it as an art form and despite his personal acquaintance with the ballet master August Bournonville, whom he admired as a dancer—though not so much as a choreographer or poet. Although, as Petersen reminds us, *Either/Or*'s "A" stresses that it is through the *audial* medium of music that the demonic being of Don Juan is best captured ("*Listen to* the beginning of his life . . . *hear* the whisper of temptation, *hear* the vortex of seduction, *hear* the stillness of the moment—*hear, hear, hear* Mozart's Don Giovanni"; *SKS* 2:106–7 / *EO* 1:103, my emphasis), Fiskvik calls attention to passages in *Concept of Anxiety* as well as in Kierkegaard's journal that explicitly reflect the deep and favorable *visual* impression left on Kierkegaard by the dramatic leaps he had seen Bournonville execute on stage, especially in the role of another, even more explicitly demonic character: Mephistopheles. Still, while briefly entertaining the thought that the best way to portray Don Juan's story might be to stage it as a ballet, "A" then rejects that idea (*SKS* 2:109 / *EO* 1:106) because, in Fiskvik's words, he clearly "feels that the deepest and most profound thoughts of humans cannot be portrayed through bodily movement." The fact that "A" conveys this attitude in what Fiskvik characterizes as a didactic manner is but one more symptom of what Boven describes as the "performative" strategy of Kierkegaard's pseudonymous writings. Their aim, to paraphrase Boven, is not only *to say* something but also to try *to do* something, to have a performative effect—in this case, to cause the reader, as Fiskvik puts it, "to contemplate balletic plots and the usefulness of bodily movement and dance as aesthetic expressions."

It is indicative of Kierkegaard's irrepressible habit of transforming the materials of both art and life into philosophically or theologically useful images and metaphors that he or one of his post–*Either/Or* pseudonyms will often convey thoughts through dance metaphors, thus seeming to contradict the uncomplimentary remarks made in *Either/Or* about Bournonville's choreographic skill or the dramatic capacities of ballet. Among the dance-related metaphors in Kierkegaard's writings that Fiskvik considers in demonstrating this point are those having to do with loneliness in mortal life (= refraining from dancing with anyone, hence the title of Fiskvik's essay); the concealment by Kierkegaard of his own efforts as an author (= the balletic ideal of the concealment by the dancer of his or her panting and exertion); the "leap" of faith (= the dancer's leap) and the constant flux of faith (= the twisting of a tightrope dancer); lost love (= the dancer who remains in the stance expressive of bowing toward one who is not seen); and so forth. In the case of Johannes de Silentio's use of the ballet dancer as a metaphor for the "knight of infinity," the pseudonym's point that the dancer's momentary wavering upon landing from a leap "shows that they are aliens in the world" (*SKS* 4:135–36 / *FT* 41; quoted by Fiskvik) might again call to mind Anti-Climacus's discussion of the developing Christian youth who "walks like a stranger, and yet . . . seems to be at home" (*SKS* 12:188 / *PC* 189)—a discussion which, in connection with Garff's notion of Anti-Climacus's "visualizing Bildungsroman," I earlier related to Hugh of St. Victor's adage about the perfection of the person to whom the whole world is as a foreign land. As Kierkegaard puts it in "The Book on Adler," the young person who hopes earnestly to live a Christian life must stand in solitude "like an alien," totally aloof from "the glad gospel that is proclaimed on the dance floor of youth [*Ungdommens Dandseplads*]" (*SKS* 15:294, Cap. IV, §5 / *BA* 141).

The "high" art of ballet is one thing; the social realm of the "dance floor," or the ballroom, is quite another. Mooney, in his own application of a dance metaphor to Kierkegaard, may be right to conclude that the Dane's "writings bring us to the dance, and perhaps demonstrate some steps, but the rest is up to us—to *me*." In contrast, Fiskvik points out that, with regard to the ballroom, Kierkegaard seems to have held a conservative view that belies his role otherwise as an "intellectual rebel." He apparently believed that a gentleman should dance well, but not so well as to be confused with a professional ballet dancer.

Like the relationship of Kierkegaard to dance, the subjects of this volume's third part, his relationships to visual arts and film, have heretofore remained largely unexplored. The first of part III's three essays, Christopher B. Barnett's "Painting with Words: Kierkegaard and the Aesthetics of the Icon," opens with a discussion of the "rupture" between Kierkegaard's religious and aesthetic commitments, with references to the contrasting assessments of that rupture by Pattison, who sympathizes with Kierkegaard's vision, and by Hans Urs von Balthasar, who does not. Despite the seeming unlikelihood that a favorable appraisal of aesthetics might be developed from Kierkegaard's writings, Barnett detects an "'aesthetics of the icon' . . . implicit in

Kierkegaard's own copious employment of aesthetic imagery," his contention being that Kierkegaard does not rupture the two spheres but rather "has a dialectical view of the matter: aesthetic imagery can function either in the manner of icons or in that of idols." Barnett pursues this thesis in a threefold manner. First, he examines the variety of ways, both positive and negative, in which the concept of *Billede* (image or picture) is employed in Kierkegaard's writings. For example, on the one hand, Kierkegaard and his pseudonyms regard *Billede* as a dangerous concept, knowing all too well that an image can entice someone to become fatally enraptured, like Narcissus, with what is not real. On the other hand, in some places, especially his upbuilding discourses, Kierkegaard characterizes certain biblical heroes, such as the prophetess Anna (Luke 2:36–38) and the woman who was a sinner (Luke 7:37–50), as "images." Second, Barnett argues that this dialectic use of *Billede* enables Kierkegaard potentially to integrate the aesthetic and the religious in his thinking, in that he not only applauds but employs the aesthetic to draw readers to seek the religious in their concrete existence. Third, Barnett demonstrates that the distinction drawn by Jean-Luc Marion between the idol, which absorbs the observer's gaze, and the icon, which redirects it, can illuminate the "pictures" that crop up throughout Kierkegaard's oeuvre. The "aesthetics of the icon" that emerges from Barnett's analysis of Kierkegaard's writings thus "points beyond itself, viewing art not as an end in itself but as a means toward religious and, with it, existential fulfillment."

This positive aesthetics, in enabling Kierkegaard to present images of holiness, is a far cry from his wariness of the negative, dangerous aspects of *Billede*, epitomized by the representation of Johannes the Seducer's preference for fantasizing about Cordelia rather than being in a relationship with her. Such wariness, ingrained in the Jewish, Christian, and Islamic traditions through the second Mosaic commandment (Exodus 20:4) and the messages against *shirk*, or idolatry, conveyed by the prophet Muḥammad (Qur'ān 13:13 and 31:13, to mention but two of the many pertinent qur'ānic verses), is not limited to cultures conditioned by those moral teachings. Perhaps no work of literature outside Kierkegaard's writings illustrates more vividly the perceived danger of image making, whether through art or through the purely mental processes of the imagination, than Yukio Mishima's *The Temple of the Golden Pavilion* (*Kinkakuji*, 1956). Set in Kyoto in the period leading up to, during, and following the Second World War, the novel recounts the life of the young Zen acolyte Mizoguchi, a deeply traumatized and suffering neurotic but also a consummate aesthete in the Kierkegaardian sense of the term, whose obsession with the image of the celebrated temple named in the novel's title passes through a series of modes, each one more divergent from reality than the one preceding it. The image is first formed for him, before he ever sees the temple, from his father's exalted descriptions, but then is challenged by his disappointment with the sight of the actual temple when he first visits it; later it is restored when the thought that the temple might be destroyed by an Allied bombing leads

> my image of the Golden Temple gradually . . . to be superimposed on the real temple . . . just as the copy that one has made through a piece of drawing-silk comes to be superimposed on the original painting: the roof in my image was superimposed on the real roof, the Sosei on the Sosei that extended over the pond, the railings and the windows of the Kukyocho on those railings and windows. The Golden Temple was no longer an immovable structure. It had, so to speak, been transformed into a symbol of the real world's evanescence. Owing to this process of thought, the real temple had now become no less beautiful than that of my mental image.[40]

In the end, to rid himself once and for all of the problem posed by the temple, its beauty, and its image, Mizoguchi burns it down. Given the merely coincidental but manifest impact that the pyrophobia from which Kierkegaard suffered from childhood had on his writings, there can be little doubt that he would have read Mishima's novel with great interest.[41]

The second essay of the third part offers a kind of counterpoint to the focus of Petersen's essay on Kierkegaard's notion of music as the demonic, sensual medium expressive of passion, as embodied by Mozart's antihero, Don Giovanni. Ragni Linnet's "Kierkegaard's Approach to Pictorial Art, and to Specimens of Contemporary Visual Culture" takes as its subject Kierkegaard's much less often discussed understanding of pictorial art as emblematic of the reflective aesthetic, which she finds represented by *Either/Or*'s "A" and Johannes the Seducer, who considers this passion detachedly from a distance. Linnet observes that *Either/Or*'s opening sentence, in broaching the question of the relationship between the "inner" and the "outer," pinpoints "the essence and nature, and the limits and potentials, of the concrete image, because a picture, if anything, is the medium of 'the outer'—that is, the external presentation of its subject." She also notes how important this definitive aspect of pictorial art was for Kierkegaard, because only "academic, idealistic painting," as opposed to "popular pictorial art," is assessed by a congruence of the "inner" and the "outer." And whereas "The Immediate Erotic Stages or The Musical-Erotic" was the obvious text for Petersen to concentrate on as an exposition of "A's" (and implicitly Kierkegaard's) theory of music, Linnet turns to another, short essay in *Either/Or*'s first part, "Silhouettes," for an exposition of what she calls the "beautiful image."

Much like Fiskvik in her exploration of the place of dance in Kierkegaard's thinking and writings, Linnet is, for the most part, unprecedented in exploring the multifaceted bearing of the visual arts upon them.[42] Kierkegaard's pseudonym Inter et Inter might even seem to discourage such exploration when he speaks disparagingly of the art critic's profession: "Most people's art criticism [*Konstkritik*] has categories and thought-patterns essentially in common with every butcher's assistant, national guardsman, and store clerk, who talk enthusiastically about a damned pretty and devilishly pert wench of eighteen years. These eighteen years, this damned prettiness and this devilish pertness—this is art criticism" (*SKS* 14:94 / *CD* 305). Yet, while acknowledging that Kierkegaard set forth no cohesive pictorial theory and made relatively few references to statues, pictures, and artists, Linnet finds that "Silhouettes" presents the primary means for reconstructing "the pictorial theory that remains by and large unchanged throughout all Kierkegaard's work: the picture's relation to time, including the past (recollection), the present (presence), and the future (self-appropriation), and to the spirit, the body, existence, the self and subjectivity, and love." "Silhouettes," she shows, bifurcates into halves Kierkegaard's own pictorial thinking over two questions: the question of the relation between the inner and the outer, and of whether the inner can be objectified into an outer, visible manifestation; and the question of the nature of sight. For Kierkegaard, the inner and the outer are fundamentally incommensurable, and the picture is capable not of encompassing but of affecting the individual's innermost being. As for the relation between form and appropriation, "Silhouettes" carefully exposes the limitations of pictorial art. Invoking the examples of the three jilted women in "Silhouettes," Goethe's Marie Beaumarchais, Mozart's Donna Elvira, and Goethe's Margaret, "Silhouettes" suggests that once their immediate sorrow becomes reflective, it ceases to be expressible through pictorial art—a suggestion that counters the famous theory of Lessing in his *Laocoon* (*Laokoon*, 1766) that, because art depicts repose while poetry depicts motion, the subject of artistic portrayal must have, as "A" puts it, "a quiet transparency so that the interior rests in the corresponding exterior" (*SKS* 2:167 / *EO* 1:169).

The bulk of Linnet's essay consists of a systematic analysis of a selection of seven "appropriations" of pictorial artworks and specimens of visual culture that figure in various writings of Kierkegaard, whether ekphrastically or as the grist for theoretical discussions, ranging from Veronica's Veil, Ferdinand Piloty's lithograph of Romeo and Juliet's "kiss," and an "ancient" painting of Ariadne and Theseus, to the popular one-sheet prints of the time known as *Neuruppiner Bilderbogen* or *Nürnbergs* (mentioned also by Boven) and a reproduction of Raphael's *Sistine Madonna*, to mention but some of Linnet's examples. In contrast, Ronald M. Green's essay "Kierkegaard's Concept of Inherited Sin: A Cinematic Illustration," which completes the third section, uses the discussions of hereditary sin in three pseudonymous writings by Kierkegaard as lenses through which to analyze a single work in "the most modern of all the arts,"[43] cinema.

Those writings are the essays "The Tragic in Ancient Drama Reflected in the Tragic in Modern Drama" and "The Balance between the Esthetic and the Ethical in the Development of the Personality" by *Either/Or*'s "A" and Judge William, respectively (*SKS* 2:137–62; 3:155–314 / *EO* 1:137–64;

2:155–333), and *The Concept of Anxiety*, "written by" Vigilius Haufniensis. The theory of original sin that Green distills from these texts is threefold: we are shaped by our past and the actions of our predecessors; we participate in and are responsible for those actions, both good and bad, and therefore, in choosing ourselves, we must repent for our predecessors' wrongful deeds; and our moral and psychological links to our parents are ineluctably bound up with sexuality. The film to which Green applies this theory is the Quebec director Denis Villeneuve's *Incendies* (2010, literally "Fires"), an adaptation of the Lebanese Canadian playwright Wajdi Mouawad's 2003 drama of the same title, known in English as *Scorched*.[44] Before turning to that film, after noting Kierkegaard's pioneering employment of fictional materials such as operas, plays, and novels in the development of philosophical and theological concepts, Green makes an extraordinarily pregnant claim to support the use of a film to illustrate Kierkegaard's ideas: "If Kierkegaard were alive today, there is no doubt in my mind that he would be entranced with contemporary cinema, and that *Incendies*, if he viewed it, would be among the creative works that would draw his interest." The first part of that claim is worth considering for a moment.

Despite the significant influence he has exerted on film directors ranging from Carl Theodor Dreyer to Woody Allen, the bearing of Kierkegaard's writings upon the film medium is rarely considered.[45] Yet it seems certain that, in support of Green's claim, the theory and underlying technology of cinematography would have fascinated Kierkegaard. Bona fide "series photography," which paved the way to the first projection of motion pictures for public viewing in December 1895, was not developed until over a decade and a half after his death. Yet, inspired largely by discussions of the illusory "persistence of vision" for which Peter Mark Roget had proffered a seminal—albeit, we now know, false—explanation in 1825,[46] the inventing of the various oddly named machines and devices designed to create the illusion of moving pictures began during Kierkegaard's lifetime.[47]

Although there is no evidence that Kierkegaard knew of Roget, or of the Thaumatrope, the "Wheel of Life," the Phenakistoscope, the Stroboscope, or the Daedalum,[48] there are remarkable affinities between certain interests of Kierkegaard's and various developments whose eventual coalescence made possible the birth of cinema. In one of his polemics against Christendom in 1854, Kierkegaard urges, "Away, away, away with all optical illusions [*Øienforblindelse*], forward with the truth . . . : We are incapable of being Christians in the New Testament sense" (*SKS* 14:159 / *MLW* 34). Here, his use of the analogy of an optical illusion corresponds to Roget's concern, expressed in a different context, with a "curious optical deception" or "visual deception"[49] that involved the spokes of a rolling carriage wheel appearing curved when glimpsed through a series of vertical apertures such as venetian blinds. It is also not impossible that Kierkegaard was to some extent aware of the two separate but parallel lines of development on which, as Jack C.

Ellis points out, the discoveries and inventions leading to motion pictures occurred: first, the notion, stemming from the discussion of persistence of vision, that a succession of related still images could create an illusion of movement; second, the invention of a process of still photography and, later, of a technical means by which to take and show photographs fast enough to employ fully the image-succession theory.[50] Regarding the first of these developments, Kierkegaard notably characterized his own times as "an age of movement" (*Pap.* VII[1] B 195:373 / *MLW*, Suppl., 384). His enduring preoccupation with "illusions," "imaginary constructions," and—as noted by Fiskvik in connection with dance—"movements" and "motions"[51] entitles us to suspect that he would have been captivated by the ability film grants us "to see a series of static images as a single continuous movement," which makes cinema the first form of art "to rely solely on psycho-perceptual illusions generated by machine."[52]

Like the developments that led to the invention of film, the beginning of the second line of development mentioned by Ellis coincided with Kierkegaard's youth, as photography finds its earliest precursors in the invention of heliography by the Frenchman Nicéphore Niépce in the 1820s and of the daguerreotype by his countryman Louis Daguerre toward the end of the next decade. As Linnet points out, the daguerreotype arrived in Denmark in 1840, and by 1844 there were three "photo" studios, two of which were already there in 1842. Kierkegaard's own awareness of the technology behind the daguerreotype, she notes, is reflected in Judge William's estimation that the daguerreotype process took a half-minute to record an image.

There are still more reasons why the cinema would likely have entranced Kierkegaard. For example, the theatrical quality that Green, like Pattison, Pickett, and Boven, perceives in some of Kierkegaard's writings, together with Kierkegaard's and some of his pseudonyms' musings upon the existential pertinence of theater, is noteworthy because the incorporation of pictorial and realistic staging in the popular nineteenth-century theater "offered extraordinarily precise models for what . . . films would become."[53] Moreover, given his disdain for "rabble-barbarianism" (*Pøbelagtighed*; see *SKS* 20:19–20, NB7 and 7d, March 1846 / *Cor.*, Suppl., 213–14; *Pap.*VII[1] B 123, n.d. 1845–46 / *TA*, Suppl., 136; *SKS* 20:258, NB3:28, n.d. 1847 / *CD*, Suppl. 360; *SKS* 16:45, 47 / *PV* 64, 67) and for the "crowd" (*Mængde*), which he equated with cowardliness (*Feigheden*) and untruth (*Usandheden*; see, e.g., *SKS* 16:88 / *PV* 108), Kierkegaard would supposedly have been wary of the association Walter Benjamin perceived between the cinematic medium and the increasingly emergent "masses" (*die Masse*).[54] Nonetheless, although the "discreet but decisive role" that Kierkegaard is found to have played "in Benjamin's thought in general"[55] seems not to have extended to that German thinker's pioneering theory of film, two other aspects of cinema that Benjamin identifies as definitive of the medium correspond with some of Kierkegaard's central preoccupations. First, Kierkegaard, the consummate dialectician, might be expected to feel an affinity with the "dialectical structure" of film, whereby "discontinuous images replace one another in a continuous sequence."[56] Second, as "the first art form whose artistic character is entirely determined by its reproducibility," film might seem—in its capacity not only to be "technologically reproducible"[57] but to be replayed, rewatched or re-viewed, and hence experienced over and over—to bring about an experience akin to what Constantin Constantius unsuccessfully sought to achieve upon returning to Berlin to take up lodgings in his former quarters next to Gendarmenmarkt: *repetition*.

The natural affinity Green discerns between the film *Incendies* and the several Kierkegaardian texts he considers on hereditary sin might seem strengthened when we consider that repetition, that technical hallmark of cinema, is a category invoked in one of those texts, *The Concept of Anxiety*, whose pseudonym, Vigilius Haufniensis, repeatedly draws upon Constantin's *Repetition* (see *SKS* 4:324fn.–325, 340, 351, 393fn., 408, 415, 449fn., 451fn. / *CA* 17fn.–18, 34, 46, 90fn., 106, 113, 149fn., 151fn.). As it happens, the plot of Villeneuve's film, like the plots of so many great movies, hinges not so much on repetition as on what Constantin and hence Vigilius construe as a category that complements repetition: *recollection*, a notion crucial to ancient Greek, and particularly Platonic, epistemology. "Repetition and recollection," Constantin observes, "are the same movement, except in opposite directions, for what is recollected has been, is repeated backward, whereas genuine repetition is recollected forward" (*SKS* 4:9 / *R* 131; compare *SKS* 4:393, including 393fn. / *CA* 89–90, 90fn.). Even more to the point is yet another category crucial to the Greeks, and especially the exposition of tragedy by Aristotle in his *Poetics*. This other category, *recognition* (ἀναγνώρισις), is discussed by the pseudonym of Kierkegaard's *Fear and Trembling*, Johannes de Silentio.

Although neither Johannes de Silentio nor Constantin nor Vigilius ever discusses all three of these terms together in relation to one another, recognition—which always presupposes and dispels some "prior hiddenness" (*SKS* 4:174 / *FT* 83)—clearly must precede both recollection and repetition inasmuch as each of the latter, in order actually to occur, would have to presuppose some form of recognition: that is, what remains "hidden" and is not first recognized can be neither meaningfully recollected nor meaningfully repeated. The focus of *Incendies* switches back and forth between contemporary Montreal and an unnamed Western Asian country in the past, torn by interreligious warfare and savagery (presumably Lebanon during its civil war), as the film employs successive flashbacks—a cinematic form of recollection—to link scenes from the life of a now deceased Western Asian woman who had immigrated to Canada with the lives of her three offspring. Through a series of tragic recognitions, one of these offspring is revealed to have been unwittingly the torturer and rapist of his own mother and the father of her other two children, his siblings. In turn, these recognitions touch

upon what Green deems a fundamental point in the Kierkegaardian analysis
of hereditary sin: "We must all ask to what extent, by accepting, affirming,
and sexually reproducing our identities within warring families, ethnicities,
and communities, we are complicit in the crimes of our ancestors."

The fourth and last part of this volume comprises three essays that consider
Kierkegaard in juxtaposition with several other creative figures in literature
and the arts: the English poet and visual artist William Blake (1757–1827)
in "The Moravian Origins of Kierkegaard's and Blake's Socratic Literature,"
by James Rovira; the German composer Arnold Schoenberg (1874–1951) in
"*Don Giovanni* and *Moses and Aaron*: The Possibility of a Kierkegaardian
Affirmation of Music," by Peder Jothen; and the contemporary American
singer, songwriter, and 2016 Nobel laureate (for literature), Bob Dylan (b.
1941) in "Kierkegaard, Dylan, and Masked and Anonymous Neighbor-
Love," by Jamie A. Lorentzen. Kierkegaard, as I have elsewhere discussed,[58]
disparaged the act of comparison (*Sammenligning*) as dangerous and misguided, arguing that it distracts the individual from focusing on eternal truth.
The overriding assumption of each of these three essays, however, is that
thoughtful comparison, equally attentive to similarities and differences, and
with "a clear articulation of purpose,"[59] can enhance our understanding of
both figures (and their works) under consideration.

Regarding Kierkegaard's relation to Blake, Schoenberg, and Dylan, the
three essays acknowledge that Blake, who died when Kierkegaard was fourteen, could not have known of him; that there is, by the same token, no
evidence that Kierkegaard knew of or was influenced by Blake, though it is
not impossible that he encountered some of his poetry in German translation; and that there is no reason to suspect that Schoenberg, who was born
almost twenty years after Kierkegaard's death, or Dylan, was influenced by
Kierkegaard, or even that either of them read him. So what is the purpose
of these three comparisons by Rovira, Jothen, and Lorentzen? For Rovira,
Kierkegaard and Blake, despite their obvious national, vocational, and other
differences, "are mutually illuminating figures not only because they similarly appropriated Socratic thought but also because their works respond
to very similar, and mutually influential, cultural milieux." In both cases, an
upbringing by Moravian parents had the probable consequence that Blake
and Kierkegaard were influenced in their views of Socrates by that found-
ing Moravian figure and self-styled Socratic figure Count Nikolaus Ludwig
von Zinzendorf and as a result regarded Socrates with "some ambivalence."
Because the "literary qualities" of Kierkegaard stem from the Socratic nature
of his philosophical enterprise, which "favors dialogic contemplation of significant questions over the systematic, discursive presentation of conceptual
truths," Rovira contends that a comparison of him and Blake in their engagements with Socrates can shed light on Kierkegaard's literary qualities.

Jothen, too, is concerned with a particular ambivalence in Kierkegaard,
but with regard to music rather than to Socrates. Arguing that Kierkegaard's

musical aesthetic has less to do with music itself than with the formative role music plays in relation to desire, thought, and the form of one's life, particularly in the aesthetic stage, Jothen does two things. First, he shows that whereas music serves for *Either/Or*'s "A" to disclose sensuous, abstract immediacy rather than clear, comprehensible truth to the listener, Kierkegaard himself elsewhere suggests that music, especially gospel-related hymns, can valuably serve to guide the listener to cultivating a self-consciousness shaped by Christian truth. Then, pursuing the implications of this ambivalence, Jothen uses his comparison of Schoenberg's *Moses and Aaron* and Mozart's *Don Giovanni* to demonstrate that the atonal, de-sensualizing subversion by Schoenberg's opera of the harmonic tradition epitomized by Mozart's opera, which so allured "A," exposes both the limitations of "A's" conception of music (as did the analysis of it in Petersen's essay) and the possibility of regarding music as an aid to Christian self-cultivation.

This last point is especially suggestive when considered in relation to Bob Dylan, for whom music, and songs in particular, are not so much aids to religious self-cultivation as constitutive of a kind of religion itself. In a statement quoted by Lorentzen, Dylan denies heeding rabbis, preachers, evangelists, or any other religious clerical figures. Instead, he declares "songs" to be his "religion," his "lexicon," and the objects of his belief, as he finds "the religiosity and philosophy" exclusively "in the music." Lorentzen's comparison of Kierkegaard with Dylan is therefore a fitting subject on which to close this volume. For Dylan's equation of religion with songs, a medium that fuses word and music, offers a possible resolution to the hierarchizing by Kierkegaard's "A" of poetry over music and the other arts—a hierarchizing done under the influence not only of the Lutheran axiom *sola scriptura*, as Jothen points out, but also of Lessing's *Laocoon*, as touched upon by Linnet. "A's" suggestion is that art grows more perfect the more it grows free of space and turns to time, transitioning from sculpture to painting, as Lessing already indicated; then to music, whose element is time, but which exists only in the moment; and ultimately to poetry, "the highest of all the arts and therefore also the art that best knows how to affirm the meaning of time" (*SKS* 3:135 / *EO* 2:136).[60] That the composer and singer of "The Times They Are a-Changin'" suggests otherwise is all the more provocative in view of Lorentzen's observation that one of the affinities shared by Kierkegaard and Dylan lies in Kierkegaard's deeply informed, long-standing fascination with the medieval troubadour tradition and Dylan's musical-ethical ambition "to serve as a performing artist qua modern troubadour."

Considered together, the essays by Green and Lorentzen point to a tension, if not ultimately an impasse, in Kierkegaard's thinking when considered in the light of *Incendies* and Dylan's songs. With Dylan, as Lorentzen points out, Kierkegaard shares the sense that becoming fully human requires loving the neighbor and the development of the "self-as-relational phenomenon."

As Judge William tells "A," "You are a nonentity and are something only in relation to others, and what you are you are only through this relation" (*SKS* 2:157 / *EO* 2:159). Yet, as Green demonstrates through the lens of *Incendies*, Kierkegaard and his pseudonyms also expose the formidable if not fatal impediment posed to neighbor-love by the perpetuation and accentuation of human sin through human sexuality and procreation. It is perhaps this conceptual tension or impasse in Kierkegaard that makes contemplating his relation to literature and the arts so fascinating and yet challenging. For surely no other thinker casts the stage of existence epitomized by Johannes the Seducer in so seductive a light, revealing its ultimate rootedness in the inherently erotic, sexual disposition of the human being, while at the same time indirectly cautioning against the fatal danger of what Bakhtin termed— arguably under Kierkegaard's influence—the "temptation of aestheticism."[61] If this notion of temptation seems to hark back to the biblical myth of the Fall, despite the definitive lack of a sense of guilt consciousness in the aesthetic stage, it is not surprising that, as Tatiana Shchyttsova has suggested, Bakhtin should have followed Kierkegaard in associating the preference for the aesthetic mode of existence with sin, or in Bakhtin's words, with "a fall (a lapse into sin) that is immanent to being."[62] Though not an overriding theme of this volume, this implicit association of the aesthetic with sin in Kierkegaard's thinking perhaps lies somewhat in the background of the following essays on Kierkegaard, literature, and the arts.

Notes

1. Nathan A. Scott Jr., *The Poetics of Belief: Studies in Coleridge, Arnold, Pater, Santayana, Stevens, and Heidegger* (Chapel Hill: University of North Carolina Press, 1985), 11.

2. Ibid., 11, 171n50. See also Scott's *Negative Capability: Studies in the New Literature and the Religious Situation* (New Haven, Conn.: Yale University Press, 1969), 26.

3. Hans Urs von Balthasar, *Herrlichkeit: Eine theologische Ästhetik* (Einsiedeln: Johannes, 1960–), 1:47; *The Glory of the Lord: A Theological Aesthetics*, 7 vols., trans. Erasmo Leiva-Merikakis, ed. Joseph Fessio (San Francisco: Ignatius, 1982–89), 1:50.

4. See Eric Ziolkowski, *The Literary Kierkegaard* (Evanston, Ill.: Northwestern University Press, 2011).

5. See ibid., 28–29; Pattison's essay in this volume.

6. See Ziolkowski, *The Literary Kierkegaard*, 29–30.

7. Reproductions of these cartoons are found in vol. 6 (1979) of Uffe Andreasen, ed., *Corsaren: M. A. Goldschmidts årgange*, 7 vols. (Copenhagen: Det danske Sprog-og. Litteratureselskab, C. A. Reitzel, 1977–81); *Cor.*, Suppl., 109–37, intermittently throughout.

8. Mircea Eliade, *Traité d'histoire des religions* (Paris: Payot, 1953), 368 (§149), my translation.

9. Joakim Garff, *Søren Kierkegaard: A Biography*, trans. Bruce H. Kirmmse (Princeton, N.J.: Princeton University Press, 2005), 458.

10. Johan Ludvig Heiberg, "Litteræ Vintersæd" (Literary Winter Grain), in *Intelligensblade* (ed. J. L. Heiberg), 2, no. 24 (1843): 288; trans. in *Cor.*, 273n40. See also the discussions of this review in George Pattison, "The Initial Reception of *Either/Or*," in *International Kierkegaard Commentary: Either/Or, Part II*, ed. Robert L. Perkins (Macon, Ga.: Mercer University Press, 1995), 295–96; Alastair Hannay, *Kierkegaard: A Biography* (Cambridge, U.K.: Cambridge University Press, 2001), 182–83.

11. Hans Lassen Martensen, "On the Occasion of Dr. S. Kierkegaard's Article in *Fædrelandet*, no. 295," *Berlingske Tidende*, 302 (December 28, 1854), in *SV*[1] 14:13 / *MLW*, Suppl., 364.

12. In Martensen's words, Kierkegaard as author had failed to consider that a servant of God "must not only guard against suppressing anything of what he is sent to say to people but likewise must guard against saying more than he is sent to say, which includes also that he must guard against saying more than he in particular is sent to say according to the specific gift of the Spirit that is place in his soul" (*SV*[1] 14:13 / *MLW*, Suppl., 363). Had this "golden rule" been heeded, adds Martensen, "much untruthful and exorbitant talk about the heights and depths of the Christian life, for example, about dying to the world . . . would be avoided; indeed, many upbuilding discourses and books would be unwritten" (*SV*[1] 14:13 / *MLW*, Suppl., 364). Four years earlier, Martensen had alluded to the Kierkegaardian authorship as a "prolix literature [*vidløftige Litteratur*]" with which he admitted to being only meagerly and fragmentarily acquainted. Hans Lassen Martensen, *Dogmatiske Oplysninhger: Et Leilighedskrift* (Copenhagen: C. A. Reitzel, 1850), 13; trans. in *MLW* 624n20. After the appearance of Martensen's 1854 article, Kierkegaard would remind readers of that admission, with the obvious intent of questioning Martensen's integrity; see *SKS* 14:129fn. / *MLW* 9fn.; compare *Pap.* XI[3] B 82, p. 125, 1854 / *MLW*, Suppl., 491. Later, Kierkegaard repeated Martensen's own phrase, claiming to have "managed to get my whole 'prolix literature' situated in literature until its time comes" (*Pap.* XI[3] B 89, p. 141, n.d. 1855 / *MLW*, Suppl., 503). For further discussion, see Eric Ziolkowski, "Kierkegaard, Fire, and the Prolixity of Filling Time," *Toronto Journal of Theology* 29, no. 1 (2013): 19–36.

13. Denis de Rougemont, "Kierkegaard" (1934), in *Les personnes du drame* (Neuchâtel: Baconnière, 1944), 18–19; *Dramatic Personages*, trans. Richard Howard (New York: Holt, Rinehart and Winston, 1964), xi, emphasis mine.

14. Roger Poole, *Kierkegaard: The Direct Communication* (Charlottesville: University Press of Virginia, 1993), 245.

15. Today, on the outside wall of this building on Jägerstrasse, a plaque commemorates Kierkegaard's four stays in that building (1841–42, 1843, 1845, 1846), indicating that it was there that he wrote the first drafts of *Either/Or I*, *Repetition*, and *Fear and Trembling*.

16. Engraving by Carl Strahlheim (pseud. for Johann Konrad Friedrich) in Carl Strahlheim, *Die Wundermappe oder sämmtliche Kunst- und Natur-Wunder des ganzen Erdballs*, vol. 5: *Nord-Deutschland* (Frankfurt a.M.: Im Comptoir für Literatur und Kunst, 1837). The picture, a copy of which I possess, appears between pp. 82 and 83, although the list of illustrations on p. vii states that this

engraving, labeled "Ansicht des Gensd'armen-Marktes mit dem Schauspielhaus," appears on p. 72. (I am grateful to Stefan Lankuttis and his associates at the Kultur und Bibliotheken–Wissenschaftliche Stadtbibliothek, Landeshauptstadt Mainz for providing me a digitized photocopy of that list and for confirming the location of the Gendarmenmarkt illustration within the original volume, a copy of which I was unable to obtain.) On the volume's title page, the following statement is found: "Treu nach der Natur abgebildet und topographisch-historisch beschrieben von C. Strahlheim."

17. Ziolkowski, *The Literary Kierkegaard*, 37.

18. Immanuel Kant, *Kritik der reinem Vernunft*, ed. Jens Timmermann (Hamburg: Felix Meiner, 1998), 421 [B 314]; *Critique of Pure Reason*, trans. Norman K. Smith (London: Macmillan, 1956), 310.

19. See Eric Ziolkowski, "Guadalquivir: Kierkegaard's Subterranean Fluvial Pseudonymity," in *Kierkegaard's Literary Figures and Motifs*, Tome 1, ed. Jon Stewart, Kierkegaard Research: Sources, Reception and Resources, vol. 16 (London: Ashgate, 2014), 279–96. On Kierkegaard's reading of *Don Quixote*, see Ziolkowski, *The Literary Kierkegaard*, 127–81.

20. See Ziolkowski, *The Literary Kierkegaard*, 8–12.

21. Ellen Dissanayake, *Homo Aestheticus: Where Art Comes From and Why* (1992; Seattle: University of Washington Press, 1995), ix, xii.

22. Mircea Eliade, *The Sacred and Profane: The Nature of Religion. The Significance of Religious Myth, Symbolism, and Ritual within Life and Culture*, trans. Willard R. Trask (New York: Harcourt Brace Jovanovich, 1959), 15.

23. This point is convincingly demonstrated by Bryan Rennie, *Reconstructing Eliade: Making Sense of Religion* (Albany: State University of New York Press, 1996), 41–46 (chap. 5: "Homo Religiosus"). Though space is obviously lacking here for a full rehearsal of the evidence Rennie marshals on this point, suffice it to quote Eliade himself from two different works of his (each quoted by Rennie as well; ibid., 44): "Nonreligious man *in the pure state* is a comparatively rare phenomenon, even in the most desacralized of societies. The majority of the 'irreligious' still behave religiously, even though they are not aware of the fact" (Eliade, *Sacred and the Profane*, 204, italics in text); "In the last analysis, we discover that the latest activities and conclusions of scientists and technologists—the direct descendants of *homo faber*—reactualize, on different levels and perspectives, the same fears, hopes and convictions that have dominated *homo religiosus* from the very beginning" (Mircea Eliade, "*Homo Faber* and *Homo Religiosus*," in *The History of Religions: Retrospect and Prospect*, ed. Joseph Kitagawa [New York: Macmillan, 1985], 11).

24. Dissanayake, *Homo Aestheticus*, ix.

25. Sylvia Walsh, *Living Poetically: Kierkegaard's Existential Aesthetics* (University Park: Pennsylvania State University Press, 1994), 4.

26. Diego Gil Parra, *El homo litterarius* (Cali, Colombia [?]: Fundación Literaria Botella y Luna, 2004), 1. Gil Parra was not the first to coin the term *homo litterarius*. It also occurs in the title of Reto Ferrari's dissertation "Ermanno Cavazzoni e le tentazioni del 'homo litterarius': Un discorso sul bisogno di inventare storie o di farsele narrare nelle opere 'Il poema dei lunatic' e 'Le tentazioni di Girolamo'" (Lic. phil., I Univ. Zürich, 1996). My effort to obtain a copy or photocopy of this work proved futile, as I was informed that Zentralbibliothek

Zürich, which owns the sole catalogued copy, will not lend or scan it and that it is not available for purchase.

27. Dissanayake, *Homo Aestheticus*, 3.

28. Ibid., 107.

29. Ibid., 21, 111.

30. Quoted in Bruce H. Kirmmse, ed., *Encounters with Kierkegaard: A Life as Seen by His Contemporaries*, trans. Bruce H. Kirmmse and Virginia R. Laursen (Princeton, N.J.: Princeton University Press, 1996), 113.

31. Fyodor Dostoevsky, *The Idiot*, trans. David Magarshack (1955; repr. with new pagination, Middlesex, U.K.: Penguin, 1986), 391 (pt. 3, chap. 1).

32. Ibid., 528 (pt. 4, chap. 5).

33. Carnegie Hall Speech, 1960, quoted by Egon Gartenberg, *Mahler: The Man and His Music* (New York: Macmillan, 1979), 367.

34. George Pattison, *Kierkegaard's Upbuilding Discourses: Philosophy, Theology, Literature* (London: Routledge, 2002).

35. Immanuel Kant, *Beobachtungen über das Gefühl des Schönen und Erhabenen* (1764), in *Werke in sechs Bänden*, ed. Wilhelm Weischedel (Wiesbaden: Insel, 1960), 1 (1960): 826 (sec. 1); *Observations on the Feeling of the Beautiful and Sublime and Other Writings*, ed. Patrick Frierson and Paul Guyer (New York: Cambridge University Press, 2011), 14.

36. Hugh of St. Victor, *Didascalicon de studio legendi* [a.k.a. *Eruditionis didascalicae*] 3.20, in PL 176 (1854): 778B; *The Didascalicon of Hugh of St. Victor: A Medieval Guide to the Arts*, trans. Jerome Taylor (New York: Columbia University Press, 1961), 101, quoted (with slight variance in spelling) by Erich Auerbach, "Philology and *Weltliteratur*," trans. Maire Said and Edward Said, *Centennial Review* 13, no. 1 (1969): 1–17, here 17.

37. Friedrich Wilhelm Joseph von Schelling, *System des transzendentalen Idealismus (1800)*, in *Werke*, 3 vols. (Leipzig: Fritz Eckardt, 1907), 2:276; *System of Transcendental Idealism*, trans. Peter Lauclan Heath (Charlottesville: University Press of Virginia, 1978), 210.

38. John Calvin, *Institutes of the Christian Religion*, 2 vols., ed. John T. McNeill, trans. Ford Lewis Battles, Library of Christian Classics, vols. 20–21 (Louisville, Ky.: Westminster John Knox Press, 1960), 1:61 (1.5.8). Compare *Institutes*, 1:72 (1.6.2): "this most glorious theater"; 1:179 (1.14.20): "this most beautiful theater"; 1:341 (2.6.1): "This magnificent theater"; and in other works of Calvin.

39. For further discussion see Eric Ziolkowski, "'I Came to Carthage'; 'So I Arrived in Berlin': Autobiographical Memory in Augustine's *Confessions* and Kierkegaard's *Repetition*," in *Kierkegaard as an Author*, ed. Joseph Westfall (Burlington, Vt.: Ashgate, forthcoming).

40. Yukio Mishima, *The Temple of the Golden Pavilion*, trans. Ivan Morris (New York: Random House, 1994), 45.

41. See Ziolkowski, "Kierkegaard, Fire, and the Prolixity of Filling Time."

42. There are exceptions, of course, one of which is Poole's aforementioned analysis of the role Thorvaldsen's statues of Christ and his apostles in Copenhagen's Vor Frue Kirke play in two of Kierkegaard's *Three Discourses at the Communion on Fridays*. Also considered has been Anti-Climacus's thought experiment in Kierkegaard's *Practice in Christianity* contemplating how a modern

child unfamiliar with the story of Jesus would react to being shown an image of the crucified Christ juxtaposed with pictures of Alexander the Great, Napoleon, and other famous heroic figures (*SKS* 12:176–79 / *PC* 174–77; compare *SKS* 21:154, NB8:20, n.d. 1848 / *KJN* 5:160). See Eric Ziolkowski, "A Picture Not Worth a Thousand Words: Kierkegaard, Christ, and the Child," *Religious Studies and Theology* (Edmonton, Canada) 17 (1999): 4–19; Eric Ziolkowski, *Evil Children in Religion, Literature, and Art* (Houndmills, U.K.: Palgrave, 2001), 137–38.

43. David Parkinson, *History of Film*, 2nd ed. (New York: Thames and Hudson, 2012), 7.

44. Wajdi Mouawad, *Incendies* (Montreal: Leméac, 2003); *Scorched*, trans. Linda Gaboriau (Toronto: Playwrights Canada Press, 2005).

45. On Kierkegaard's influence on Dreyer, especially his film *Ordet* (1955, *The Word*), see Ziolkowski, *The Literary Kierkegaard*, 293–309. Judith Thurman asks, "Without [Kierkegaard], where would Woody Allen be?" "Søren K.'s Two-Hundredth Birthday," *New Yorker*, May 20, 2013, http://www.newyorker.com /books/page-turner/sren-k-s-two-hundredth-birthday, accessed August 24, 2016. For a satirical statement by Allen himself on Kierkegaard's primacy among philosophers for him, see the opening of Woody Allen, "My Philosophy," in *Getting Even* (New York: Random House, 1971), 27–28. In October 2013, to commemorate Kierkegaard's bicentennial, there was held at the Village Recoleta multiplex in Buenos Aires, hosted by the Danish Embassy, a Søren Kierkegaard Film Festival, featuring "three Scandinavian masterpieces centring on or somehow discussing the themes present in Kierkegaard's most relevant works": Dreyer's *Ordet*, Roy Andersson's *En kärlekshistoria* (1970, *A Swedish Love Story*), and Ingmar Bergman's *Smultronstället* (1957, *Wild Strawberries*). See Julio Nakamurakare, "Kierkegaard Festival: Through a Film Darkly," *Buenos Aires Herald*, October 15, 2013, http://www.buenosairesherald.com/article/142896 /kierkegaard-festival-through-a-film-darkly, accessed August 24, 2016. I am grateful to Rhonda Burnette-Bletsch for calling this website to my attention.

46. See P. M. Roget, "Explanation of an Optical Deception in the Appearance of the Spokes of a Wheel Seen through Vertical Apertures" ["read December 9, 1824"], Royal Society of London, *Philosophical Transactions*, 115 (London: Nicol, 1825), 131–40. On the concept of "persistence of vision" as "an inaccurate and inadequate explanation for the apparent motion found in a motion picture," see Joseph and Barbara Anderson, "The Myth of Persistence of Vision Revisited," *Journal of Film and Video* 45, no. 1 (1993): 3–12; here 3; a sequel to the same two authors' "The Myth of the Persistence of Vision," *Journal of the University Film Association* 30, no. 4 (1978): 3–8.

47. The invention of "series photography" is generally credited to the English photographer working in the United States, Eadweard Muybridge (born Edward James Muggeridge), with the unveiling of his Zoögyroscope in 1879 (later renamed the Zoöpraxiscope in 1881), and the French scientist, Étienne-Jules Marey, with his invention of the *fusil photographique* (photographic revolver or gun) in 1882. These inventions were preceded—during Kierkegaard's life—by the Thaumatrope, developed in the 1820s; the Wheel of Life, invented by the English scientist Michael Faraday in 1831; the Phenakistoscope, by the Belgian Joseph Plateau in 1832; the Stroboscope, by the Austrian Simon Ritter von Stampfer in

1831; and the Daedalum, by the English mathematician William George Hoerner in 1834 (marketed as the Zoetrope in the 1860s); and—after Kierkegaard's life—by the Praxinoscope, invented by the Frenchman Charles Émile Reynaud, in 1876. See Jack C. Ellis, *A History of Film* (Englewood Cliffs, N.J.: Prentice-Hall, 1979), 14–21; Parkinson, *History of Film*, 8–14.

48. Additional information on these designs can be found in our previous note.

49. See Roget, "Explanation of an Optical Deception," 131, 132; compare 139.

50. Ellis, *A History of Film*, 13.

51. See the fulsome entries on these terms in *Cumulative Index to Kierkegaard's Writings*, prepared by Nathaniel J. Hong, Kathryn Hong, and Regine Prenzel-Guthrie, series eds. Howard V. Hong and Edna H. Hong (Princeton, N.J.: Princeton University Press, 2000), 162–63, 219–20.

52. Parkinson, *History of Film*, 8.

53. Ellis, *A History of Film*, 13.

54. Walter Benjamin, "Das Kunstwerk im Zeitalter seiner technischen Reproduzierbarkeit—Zweite Fassung" (1936), in *Gesammelte Schriften*, 7 vols. [in 15], ed. Rolf Tiedemann and Hermann Schweppenhäuser (Frankfurt a.M.: Suhrkamp, 1972–89), 7, pt. 1:355, 369–70; "The Work of Art in the Age of Its Technological Reproducibility—Second Version," in *Selected Writings*, 4 vols., ed. Marcus Bullock and Michael W. Jennings (Cambridge, Mass.: Belknap Press, 1996–2003), vol. 3: *1935–38* (2002), 105, 113.

55. Rainer Nägele, "Body Politics: Benjamin's Dialectical Materialism between Brecht and the Frankfurt School," in *The Cambridge Companion to Walter Benjamin*, ed. David S. Ferris (Cambridge, U.K.: Cambridge University Press, 2004), 174n8, quoted by Joseph Westfall, "Walter Benjamin: Appropriating the Kierkegaardian Aesthetic," in *Kierkegaard's Influence on Philosophy*, Tome 1: *German and Scandinavian Philosophy*, ed. Jon Stewart, Kierkegaard Research: Sources, Reception and Resources, vol. 11, Tome 1 (Farnham, U.K.: Ashgate, 2012), 51.

56. From an unpublished fragment of 1935, Benjamin-Archiv, MS 1011, in Walter Benjamin, *Gesammelte Schriften*, vol. 1, pt. 3 (1974): 1040; "The Formula in Which the Dialectical Structure of Film Finds Expression," in *The Work of Art in the Age of Its Technological Reproducibility, and Other Writings on Media*, ed. Michael W. Jennings, Brigid Doherty, and Thomas Y. Levin, trans. Edmund Jephcott et al. (Cambridge, Mass.: Belknap Press, 2008), 340.

57. Benjamin, "Das Kunstwerk im Zeitalter seiner technischen Reproduzierbarkeit—Zweite Fassung," 361; "The Work of Art in the Age of Its Technological Reproducibility—Second Version," 109.

58. Ziolkowski, *The Literary Kierkegaard*, 45.

59. Jonathan Z. Smith, *Drudgery Divine: On the Comparison of Early Christianities and the Religions of Late Antiquity* (Chicago: University of Chicago Press, 1990), 53. For elaboration on this oft-cited statement by Smith, see Ziolkowski, *The Literary Kierkegaard*, 46.

60. Compare, e.g., Gerardus van der Leeuw, *Vom Heiligen in der Kunst* (Gütersloh: Carl Bertelsmann, 1957), 162, 292; *Sacred and Profane Beauty: The Holy in Art*, trans. David E. Green (Oxford: Oxford University Press, 2006), 156, 288–59.

61. Mikhail Bakhtin, *Toward a Philosophy of the Act* [*K filosofii postupka*, written 1920–24, first published 1986], trans. Vadim Liapunow, ed. Vadim Liapunow and Michael Holquist (Austin: University of Texas Press, 1993), 18.

62. Mikhail Bakhtin, *Author and Hero in Aesthetic Activity* [*Avtor i geroi v esteticheskoi deiatel'nosti*, written ca. 1920–23], trans. Vadim Liapunov, in *Art and Answerability: Early Philosophical Essays*, ed. Michael Holoquist and V. Liapunov (Austin: University of Texas Press, 1990), 124. See Tatiana Shchyttsova, "Mikhail Bakhtin: Direct and Indirect Reception of Kierkegaard," in *Kierkegaard's Influence on Literature, Criticism and Art*, Tome 5: *The Romance Languages, Central and Eastern Europe*, ed. Jon Stewart, Kierkegaard Research: Sources, Reception and Resources, vol. 12, Tome 5 (Farnham, U.K.: Ashgate, 2013), 111–12. Shchyttsova quotes the same two passages from Bakhtin, though directly from Russian editions, and hence her wording for the second quotation differs slightly from the wording of its rendering in Liapunov's translation.

Part I

✦

Literature

The Bonfire of the Genres

Kierkegaard's Literary Kaleidoscope

George Pattison

In reflecting on Kierkegaard's relation to literature and the arts, two tasks immediately present themselves. The first is to see how he himself related to the literature and other arts of his own time as reader or recipient. The second is to see how he then contributed to his cultural world, specifically as a writer. It is to these two tasks that this essay offers a preliminary contribution.

That Kierkegaard might be read in the perspective of literature and the arts is no new discovery. An early reviewer of *Either/Or* commented that its message would be clear to those "who have followed the many branchings of modern literature, not so much in the realm of pure academic study, but in the sphere of belles-lettres," while another compared it (favorably) with the novels of Edward Bulwer-Lytton and Eugène Sue.[1] Subsequent commentators in the Danish and German traditions have always been well placed to recognize that many of the questions addressed in various of Kierkegaard's writings were precisely the kinds of questions that constituted the core agendas of Romanticism and literary modernism in their own traditions, and it was no accident that the first significant monograph on Kierkegaard, Brandes's 1877 "Critical Presentation," was the work of a literary critic rather than of a philosopher or theologian.[2] In English, too, the earliest articles about Kierkegaard situated him in relation to literary modernism, primarily Ibsen and Nietzsche, but with references also to Flaubert, Renan, Carlyle, Emerson, Dostoevsky, and Wagner.[3] This last name reminds us of the importance of music to Kierkegaard, evidenced not least by the essay in *Either/Or* on *Don Giovanni*, which, recent research has shown, was curiously influenced by none other than Richard Wagner![4] Subsequently, Kierkegaard has not only been compared with one or another literary figure or claimed for one or another literary movement but has himself entered into the symbolic world of several major modern novelists, including Franz Kafka and Thomas Mann. (In the latter's *Doctor Faustus*, it is while the composer Adrian Leverkühn is reading Kierkegaard's essay on *Don Giovanni* that Mephistopheles first appears, and Kierkegaardian themes of angst and the demonic permeate the novel.) Several major poets too have been receptive to a certain Kierkegaardian influence, notably W. H. Auden and R. S. Thomas.[5]

Kierkegaard's Response to the Arts of Denmark's Golden Age

Turning to Kierkegaard himself, what gradually become more and more apparent are the sheer scale and variety of his engagement with literature and the arts. The early studies on Faust, Don Juan, the Wandering Jew, and folk literature are well known, but the same journals also witness extensive notes on the poetry of the troubadours[6]—among the longest reading notes anywhere in the journals. He also offers an extensive essay on how to tell stories to children (*SKS* 17:122–33, BB:37, n.d. 1837 / *KJN* 1:116–25). Although there are few significant discussions of contemporary Danish poetry, notes suggest he took a keen interest in this and was especially admiring of Christian Winther (*SKS* 20:34, NB32, n.d. 1846 / *JP* 5:5909).[7] Eric Ziolkowski has recently drawn attention to the importance of Aristophanes—an enthusiasm Kierkegaard shared with Early Romanticism[8]—while Thomas Miles has written of Horace as "one of the earliest and longest lasting of Kierkegaard's influences."[9] Kierkegaard's first publication was essentially a review of a novel by Hans Christian Andersen (*SKS* 1:15–57 / *FPOSL* 61–102), while another contemporary Danish novelist, Madame Thomasine Gyllembourg, was the focus for the review known by the title of the novel in question, *Two Ages* (*To Tidsaldre*, 1845). There are also notes for a review of one of Scandinavia's first feminist novels, *Clara Raphael*[10] (*SKS* 24:136–38, NB22:63, n.d. 1850 / *KJN* 8:133–34). Drama, too, was central to his writing about literature. As well as the essay on Scribe's *The First Love* in *Either/Or* and the justly celebrated eulogy of Mme Heiberg's stagecraft (*SKS* 14: 93–107 / *CCLA* 301–25), the journals contain a more or less complete celebration of another contemporary giant of the Danish stage, J. L. Phister, in the comic role of Captain Scipio, a tipsy Vatican police captain (*SKS* 16:125–43 / "PCS" 327–44). Published and unpublished works also contain a vast number of brief allusions, full-blown references, and occasional extensive discussions of plays and playwrights. The great Danish playwright Ludvig Holberg is among the most cited of all Kierkegaard's sources, and such contemporaries as Johan Ludvig Heiberg are also frequently mentioned.[11] Sophocles and Shakespeare provide occasions for extensive reflections on the nature of tragedy, as well as images and scenarios with which to explore psychological traumas that may have been Kierkegaard's own.[12] In a quite different register, the farces of the Austrian writer Johann Nestroy provide the pseudonym Constantin Constantius with an opportunity to test whether repetition is possible (*SKS* 4:29–43 / *R* 154–69). The essay on *Don Giovanni* has already been mentioned, but Kierkegaard published a further short review of a contemporary performance of the opera, and there are passing references to, for example, guitar playing and ballet.

It is only in the case of the visual arts that Kierkegaard seems to have been lacking an all-around and in-depth familiarity with classic and contemporary material. When pictures do enter his work, they are not, for the most part, examples of great art. We might think of the use of the trick picture of Napoleon's grave in *The Concept of Irony* (*SKS* 1:80–81 / *CI* 19; see *SKS* K1:169 for illustration) or the reference to a copperplate print of sea-maidens (i.e., waves that seem to take the shape of female figures) in the essay on *Don Giovanni* (*SKS* 2:97 / *EO* 1:92; see *SKS* K2:129 for illustration). Of course, the Church of Our Lady, where he regularly worshipped and occasionally spoke, housed a collection of statues of the apostles by Europe's greatest living sculptor, Bertel Thorvaldsen, but although many passages of his later religious writings seem unmistakably to allude to the all-dominating statue of Christ, this is never commented on with regard to its artistic quality.[13] Here, however, we should be mindful of André Malraux's caution that, until the advent of quality color reproductions in the mid-nineteenth century and of easier travel access to the great sites and museums of Western art, even the most influential critics and theorists were, by our contemporary standards, familiar with only a few great works or with black-and-white reproductions.[14] Had Kierkegaard, like many of his artist contemporaries, traveled to Italy, we might have had some very different visual records from his pen.[15] His keen observation of scenes from daily life, his ability to conjure forth word pictures, and the extraordinary plasticity of his style in both aesthetic and religious works are well known, while notes from 1846 offer a remarkable meditation on the nature of color (*SKS* 27:369, Papir 344:3 / *JP* 3:2844). It is therefore clear that he was not lacking in visual intelligence, only that, in this case, he did not find a corresponding range of artistic works through which to develop, express, and interpret what and how he saw.

It is very tempting to scholars to see Kierkegaard's relation to literature primarily in terms of reading, and the roll call of writers whom he read is impressive. He cites Holberg, Goethe, Shakespeare, and other great dramatists at will. But we must also remember that he was an avid theatergoer. When, as he describes in *The Point of View*, he let himself be seen nightly at the theater so as to give the impression that he was nothing but a *flâneur* and lounger, the ruse could work only in a context in which he was known to be a regular member of the audience at Copenhagen's Royal Theater, and it is in relation to performances at this theater that the review of *The First Love*, the note on the seduction of Zerlina, the commentary on Madame Heiberg's stagecraft, and the portrayal of Captain Scipio by Herr Phister were all written. This theater therefore deserves special mention in relation to Kierkegaard's experience of literature and the arts.[16] By modern standards, it staged an extraordinary range of productions. In the 1831 season, from September 1 to May 31, there were approximately one hundred different productions, from across the whole range of theatrical genres, including both works by "the greats" and contemporary light entertainments. Performances were held on Sundays and public holidays, with rest days only on Christmas Day, Easter, and Whit Sunday. A Copenhagen resident such as Kierkegaard could therefore soon build up a rather rich stock of theatrical experiences.[17]

As in the case of the visual arts, theater, too, was in a golden age. Frederikke Bremer, a Swedish novelist who visited Copenhagen in the late 1840s (but was rebuffed by Kierkegaard when she proposed calling on him; see *SKS* 28:467–69, Brev 308–10 / *LD* 286–88, letters 201, 203–4), wrote of Danish theater:

> It is the Danes' most favored form of enjoyment. And, in truth, here we find fresh life: there is life in what is put on, life in the acting, life in the audience's participation. It is only small, this theater, where so many great plays have been played and so many artists have trodden the boards in recent times, but how friendly, how lively it is! There is life in these boxes full of people, and the public involuntarily reveals its involvement by a rapid buzz and a sympathetic movement. And there we see the front stalls, where the poets sit, where people can see their favorites, where Thorvaldsen died while listening to a Beethoven symphony and where, each evening still, people whisper to each other "Look! There's Øhlenslæger, Hertz, Hauch, Andersen . . ." etc.
>
> "Not just for pleasure" is written above the entrance to Copenhagen's Temple of Thalia. And those who have seen Øhlenslæger's tragedies, the comedies of Holberg, Hertz, and Overskou, who have seen them played by Nielsen and his wife, Rosenkilde, and his daughter, Phister, the young Wiehe, and the enchanting Mme Heiberg, the pearl of the Danish stage (talents that are rare in any land), those who have seen Bournonville's ballets, consummate works of art of their kind—they will have to acknowledge that the moral spirit of the North has ennobled the magical powers of the stage and that here the theater is indeed "not just for pleasure." We do not merely enjoy ourselves here, we become better while we enjoy ourselves, and the mind is raised to a noble longing for higher, more noble dramas than those of everyday life, to intimations of what human glory is, both in its greatest sufferings as well as in its greatest pleasures.[18]

In a work of exceptional scholarly microscopy, Peter Tudvad has tracked possible references in Kierkegaard's writing to live theater by working through the performance schedules of the Theater Royal for the period of Kierkegaard's possible theatergoing life.[19] There is some uncertainty as to when this began. Children under ten were not allowed in the Danish theater until 1849, and Tudvad consequently guesses that Kierkegaard, having been born in 1813 (and coming from a rather conservative family), is unlikely to have started attending the theater until the late 1820s, which, as Tudvad suggests, makes it just possible for him to have seen Mme Heiberg's reputation-making performance as Juliet in the 1828–29 season (when he would have been fifteen or sixteen years old). The first clear reference to a contemporary performance is from September 1834—among the earliest of all Kierkegaard's journal notes—to a comedy by Scribe, *Fra Diavolo*.

In a small but significant way, Tudvad's work changes or at least shifts our view of Kierkegaard's own creative writing process. To take one example among many: a journal note from November 1834 contains references to yet another play by Scribe,[20] to Goethe's *Egmont*, and to a comedy by Holberg. It might seem natural to assume that these references were based on Kierkegaard's private reading, but since Tudvad shows that these were all performed at the Theater Royal earlier in the year, Kierkegaard is as likely as not drawing on his memories of live theatrical performances. In other words, Kierkegaard is not just sitting at home or in the library reading books: he is out there in the theater and writing not just on what he has read but on what he has seen and heard. Even in Berlin, it is actual performances that are the focus of his interest in theater.[21] And while notes on Hegel's *Aesthetics* and on a German translation of *Antigone* from his first Berlin visit indicate the seeds of the essay on ancient and modern tragedy that would be included in *Either/Or* (*SKS* 2:137–62 / *EO*1:137–64), it is probably not coincidental that a much-publicized production of *Antigone*, with music by Mendelssohn and the translation used by Kierkegaard in his notes (*SKS* 19:286–87, Notesbog 10:2–4 / *KJN* 3:282–83), was staged at Potsdam in the days after his arrival. As in the case of the visual arts, we therefore need to take the material context of Kierkegaard's relation to literature and the arts rather more seriously than earlier scholarship has done. Further testimony of a rather different kind to the kinship between Kierkegaard and the theater is the fact that he was even represented as a character, the theology student Søren Kirk (later changed to Søren Torp), in the musical comedy *The Neighbors* (*Gjenboerne*) by J. C. Hostrup, first performed in 1844 in Copenhagen's Court Theater and later going on tour to Norway, where, in December 1847, it was greeted with "rapturous applause," one Mr. Smith playing the Kierkegaard character (*SKS* K27:776–77).

In this bourgeois age that is "post-Romantic" in the specific sense of having been permeated through and through by the Romantics' valorization of art as a, if not *the*, central mode of human beings' self-experience and self-understanding, the world of the arts is not just a matter of intellectual inquiry but is, effectively, the living body of both individual and social self-representation. When Kierkegaard describes his age as "aesthetic," he is not just alluding to the proliferation of dreamy poetic types (such as his own "A") but pointing to the most immediate testimony to how the age and its people feel about themselves or to who and how they experience themselves as being. It is not just about a professed faith in beauty, truth, and goodness (which was often lacking) or the "aesthetic" values of later nineteenth-century aesthetes, but—as idealist theory in fact emphasized—the immediate and spontaneous self-expression of lived life. Or, to look at it from a different theoretical angle, the aesthetic provided a symbolic order or semiosphere that could be collectively and individually appropriated and enacted as showing how life in this emergent modern world felt.

It is for this reason—not in the sense of some carefully calculated program, but as the "reason" in his own intuitive relation to his age—that Kierkegaard's own writing about literature and the arts engages as often with what posterity has judged to be ephemeral and minor as with the great. Of course, there are discussions of Aristophanes, Sophocles, Shakespeare, Lessing, Mozart, and Goethe as well as of the great figures of Romantic literature. But Kierkegaard is just as ready to write about light comedies by contemporary writers such as Scribe and Vernoy de St. Georges (author of *Ludovic*, in which the character of Captain Scipio appears), popular women's novels (*Two Ages*), and commonplace book illustrations as he is capable of analyzing and extolling "classic" works. Even the humble art of the street musician was not outside his range of interest (*SKS* 2:39 / *EO* 1:30).[22] And, as his writings about theater show, he was also fascinated by the phenomenon of live performance, which, in an age before film and sound reproduction,[23] was by definition an ephemeral art that could live on only in the memories and memoirs of those who had, as it is said, "been there."[24]

Kierkegaard's reception of literature and art, then, was marked by an openness to a more than usual range of sources, genres, and styles, and he was no less willing to engage what we might regard as low art than the kind of "fine art" that was the subject of, for example, Hegel's lectures on aesthetics. Like Hegel, however, Kierkegaard seems to have subscribed to an "end of art" thesis, in the sense that, to use Hegel's words, "the peculiar nature . . . of works of art no longer fills our highest need,"[25] a development indicated by the fact that, as in ancient Athens, art had abandoned the task of representing gods and heroes and turned instead to depictions of everyday social reality. Indeed, this was precisely one of the aims of J. L. Heiberg's promotion of contemporary musical comedies (or "vaudevilles," as Heiberg called them) instead of the historical costume dramas favored by the previous Romantic generation.[26] Kierkegaard himself would say that the task of a modern religious writer was to show what the Christian life would look like if lived today, on any weekday, "on Amagertorv [Amager Square]" (*SKS* 12:72 / *PC* 59), a conception that correlates closely with his receptiveness to the whole range of literary and artistic forms in which the ongoing self-interpretation of "the present age" took shape. I have elsewhere written of the carnivalesque aspect of Kierkegaard's authorship, and that is relevant here too.[27] For what is at issue is precisely, as Kierkegaard complains in *Two Ages*, that the present age lacks any single defining form or great idea and is in the process of disintegrating into an ever-increasing multiplicity of diverse and disconnected forms, ideas, and values.[28] Consequently, the only adequate representation of the age will have to be a kind of moving kaleidoscope of works, styles, and genres, which is also to say that there is no single adequate representation of the age and that its manifold self-representations are therefore always on the edge of falling away into incoherence. Mikhail Bakhtin, writing in a distinctively post-Hegelian idiom, saw the emergence of the modern, nineteenth-century novel as the most faithful means available of representing such an age to itself, precisely because the extreme flexibility of the novel allows it to incorporate a whole range of genres and even carnival elements, as well as to become a forum for the political, sexual, and theological debates in which the nineteenth century struggles to find and articulate its own identity. The novel does not merely represent life but becomes a player in life, attacking, shifting, and remaking opinions and sensibilities.

What Bakhtin sees occurring in the novel applies fairly directly to Kierkegaard. Again, the early reviews of *Either/Or* were alert to just this "engaged" aspect of the book, comparing and contrasting it with works by Young Germany that promoted sexual liberation, political radicalism, and emancipation from established religion. *Either/Or* did not just set up opposing life views in order to adjudicate between them on their philosophical merits; it offered a set of choices about personal, cultural, and religious values that related to the life situation of its likely readers. And, of course, few books have been as genre-busting as this debut work, bested only by the succession of other extraordinary pseudonymous works, journalism, and religious writings that followed.

Kierkegaard as Writer

I have been considering Kierkegaard's relation to his own sources and how he absorbed the hugely varied range of cultural forms in which his age not only sought to *express* its identity but, simply, *sought its identity*, preeminently in literature, theater, and music. But I have already made a start on the second task of this essay, namely, to see how what Kierkegaard himself wrote might be regarded as a contribution to the world of literature and the arts.

Here, we immediately note a significant narrowing of the field. It is true that, as a writer, Kierkegaard worked in an exceptionally carnivalesque multiplicity of styles and genres, and I shall be exploring further how this is manifested in the works collected under his name. But where I have been emphasizing how his reception of literature and the arts was not just a matter of reading but of going to the theater and experiencing live drama, opera, music, and ballet, and, perhaps, albeit in a much lesser degree, of looking at paintings and book illustrations, Kierkegaard himself never acted or performed ballet and he did not play the piano or guitar, while his artistic skill seems to have been limited to some rather primitive caricatures in the margins of the journals. Even within literature, his writing falls within the admittedly broad parameters of conventional prose. Appreciative of poetry as he is, he never writes and seems never to have attempted to write poetry, although his writing is often intensely poetic, rising to moments of intense lyrical concentration.[29] As a student he wrote a draft for an Aristophanic spoof on contemporary speculative philosophy, "The Conflict between the

Old and New Soap-Cellar" (*SKS* 17:280–97, DD:208, n.d. 1837 / *KJN* 1:272–89), which, despite being treated rather disdainfully by many commentators, does show some potential for comic dramatic writing, although this is never further developed. At various points in the journals he writes short dialogues, including the famous encounter between Socrates and Hegel in the underworld (*SKS* 27:323, Papir 315:1–3 / *JP* 3:3306, n.d. 1845). He writes up the public response to his encounter with *The Corsair* in a short dramatic scene (*SKS* 27:376–77, Papir 347, n.d. 1846),[30] and in a scene running to several pages he lampoons a priest who, despite being employed by a Temperance Society, is partial to a schnapps or two—or, in fact, three or four (*SKS* 27:465–68, Papir 391, n.d. 1849 / *JP* 3:3138). However, after "Soap-Cellar" he never attempted a full-blown work in this genre.

Yet if the prose literature that Kierkegaard himself produced represents a certain narrowing in relation to all that fed into his creative process, this still leaves him with an unusually broad range of literary possibilities. Several times I have mentioned his work of literary and dramatic criticism, of which the review articles on Andersen's novel *Only a Fiddler*, *The First Love*, Mme Gyllembourg's *Two Ages*, and the eulogies of Mme Heiberg and Herr Phister are the best-known. Although several of these stretch the limits of the genre in terms of content (Heiberg, translator and director of *The First Love*, thought Kierkegaard's praise was entirely out of proportion) and size (both the Andersen and the Gyllembourg review had been intended as articles, not free-standing books), they are, nevertheless, recognizable for what they are. Similarly, the upbuilding discourses, though generally much longer than the published sermons that were a major part of nineteenth-century religious literature, were accessible to early readers, and no less an authority than Bishop Mynster refused to accept Kierkegaard's disclaimer that they were *not* sermons.[31] As a thesis submitted for the degree of Master of Philosophy, *The Concept of Irony* was constrained by the requirements of academic discourse, even though there are clear signs of how awkward this was for Kierkegaard, as he himself seems to concede in craving the reader's indulgence in his eulogy of Plato (*SKS* 1:89 / *CI* 27–28), while the panel of examiners was not slow to censure his tendency, as the classicist J. N. Madvig put it, to "a self-indulgent search for what is piquant and witty" that can sometimes end up in "simple tastelessness" (*SKS* K1:134). *The Concept of Anxiety* comes close to the form of an academic treatise, and there is some evidence for the view that Kierkegaard had originally planned to publish it under his own name (*SKS* K4:323). Here too, however, the work as written, though drawing on contemporary works of psychology, veers away from academic rigor.

Nevertheless, even if several works are closely affiliated with one or another recognizable genre, *Either/Or* and subsequent works proved bewildering to many readers. To be sure, *Either/Or* itself was, as we have seen, perceived as belonging to an influential stream of contemporary literature. It had many of the features of the contemporary Bildungsroman, or novel of formation,[32] even if it lacked a clear narrative structure and resolution. From Goethe's *Wilhelm Meister* (generally regarded at the time as the paradigmatic work of the genre) through works like Tieck's *Kater Murr* or Jean Paul's humorous novels, it had become acceptable, if not universal, for novels to incorporate other genres, including criticism, poetry, and, in the case of later versions of *Wilhelm Meister*, scientific treatises. Remoter models from the eighteenth century, notably Swift and Hamann, also provided points of orientation for bemused readers. What was overwhelming in Kierkegaard's case was the sheer multitude of kinds of writing and the scale of it all—"monstrous," as J. L. Heiberg observed of *Either/Or*.[33] Individual elements were familiar enough. Kierkegaard borrowed freely from the repertoire of mysteriously discovered or misappropriated manuscripts (*Either/Or, Stages on Life's Way*), the epistolary novella (*Either/Or*, part 2 of *Repetition*), and the diary ("The Seducer's Diary," *Stages on Life's Way*), and *Either/Or* famously concludes with a sermon.[34] "The Seducer's Diary" and Quidam's Diary do tell a story, and the latter also incorporates an urban "Gothic tale" anticipating Baudelaire's Parisian prose poems. *Philosophical Fragments* has a five-act structure borrowed from the theater, complete with interlude, but while some inspiration from Plato[35] and even Descartes may be discernible, it is "philosophy in a new key" (to borrow Suzanne Langer's phrase)[36] if it is philosophy at all. The same could be said with perhaps even greater force of the *Concluding Unscientific Postscript to the Philosophical Fragments*. Here, Kierkegaard inserts both reflections on how philosophical writing might benefit from including humorous or other nonscholarly elements, referring to his own teacher Poul Martin Møller's treatise on immortality and providing plentiful illustration as to how this might be done in the *Postscript* itself (which also includes a lengthy survey and discussion of all his own pseudonymous and signed writings from 1843 onward). And how might one even begin to classify *Fear and Trembling*?

Kierkegaard could, it seems, write in many different genres and many different styles, and often did so in the compass of a single book. But this also points to another feature of his literary persona: a penchant for satire and pastiche. I have already referred to the student satire "The Conflict between the Old and New Soap-Cellar," and later work such as *Prefaces* and the incomplete *Writing Sampler* are explicitly parodic, spoofing different aspects of contemporary literary culture. *Either/Or*'s aesthete, of course, ended his *Diapsalmata* with the plea that he might always have laughter on his side (*SKS* 2:52 / *EO* 1:43), although, apart from the essay on boredom, *Either/ Or* as a whole is one of his least funny books. Johannes Climacus is certainly witty and has a surer and lighter touch than "A." Satire—including, as it is wont to include, satirical misrepresentation—is a key weapon in his battle against what he sees as the comically self-forgetful fantasies of speculative thought.[37] So pervasive is this satirical tone that some have seen what others regard as Kierkegaard's most rigorously Hegelian work, *The Sickness unto Death*, as a spoof.[38] One might say that, irony being irony, this is as things should be, although one might also claim that, on the whole, we know irony when we see it—at least in literature. (Life, being a bit more fast-moving, can make it more difficult to spot: "I found your essay interesting," says the professor, and the student goes away smiling.)

But Kierkegaard's virtuosity in writing in multiple styles and genres brings with it what for some is the disturbing question of whether or how far we are to take "seriously" any of the pseudonymous works. "Seriousness" is, of course, urged not only by Assessor Vilhelm (Judge William) and Vigilius Haufniensis but also by Kierkegaard himself, as in the discourse "At a Graveside" (*SKS* 5:442–69 / *TDIO* 69–102), often taken as anticipating if not inaugurating the "seriousness" of twentieth-century existential philosophy's pursuit of authenticity.[39] Is Kierkegaard just having fun at our expense, or does he mean it? And if he means it, which bits of it does he mean? All? Much? Some? A little? Would it, for example, be right to partition the works according to whether they are "aesthetic" or "religious," assigning the aesthetic works to humor and irony and the religious and Christian to seriousness? But that does not seem quite right either, since, even as a Christian writer, Kierkegaard writes as one "without authority" and practices a kind of self-effacing Socratic irony aimed at keeping the reader's own spiritual needs at the center of the process. Even the final attack on the Church, what some might see as the "most direct" piece of communication in Kierkegaard's entire authorship, marks a powerful return to the satirical mode, as well as a condensing of the voluminous prolixity of much earlier work into the "short and sharp" focus of the polemical pamphlet.[40]

I suggest that the first half of this essay has some implications for how we might consider such questions. The exuberant and often excessive carnivalesque play of genres and styles that is constitutive of Kierkegaard's authorship is not just a sign of its author's quirkiness, though it may be that as well. It is also a sign of how he experienced the culture of his present age in its aesthetic self-manifestation, a manifestation that was postaesthetic in Hegel's sense of having passed from the sphere of the beautiful and ideal into the prose of everyday life. As such it was also a culture in which the clear contours of classical forms were chronically unable to hold the creative and destructive forces of the age in check, with the result that often—and I am continuing to speak of Kierkegaard's experience—it seemed on the edge of falling away from the kind of moral seriousness that could still inform Mme Gyllembourg's *Tales of Everyday Life* into the meaningless "chatter" that he saw as more characteristic of his own generation, a process carefully analyzed in his review of her *Two Ages*. Carnival collapses into chaos, and chaos into formlessness—and formlessness means a kind of proneness to any new form-giving power no matter how arbitrary or violent, a will to power, for example. The aesthete's invocation of a blind vortex as the ground of cosmogenesis (*SKS* 2:166 / *EO* 1:168) plays out in the violence of the Seducer and, in Kierkegaard's view, the revolutionary politics of 1848.

The Point of View signals Kierkegaard's intention to meet his age on its own ground, "the aesthetic." And this seems broadly to make sense both of the work itself and of how it was perceived by contemporaries, even if there is much to question regarding the "directness" of this work. Yet, parodying his time's wastage of inherited literary forms, Kierkegaard also constantly risks collapsing into "chatter," into endless and pointless verbiage. As is often the case, the satirist and those he satirizes are interdependent, and Kierkegaard sometimes seems too close to what he attacks. This is not only in the sense that his portrayals of the aesthetic life have often been more appealing to many readers than the admonitions of Assessor Vilhelm, but also because, as he often complains of his contemporaries, he too does not always seem to know when to stop.[41] Some readers, at least, have found it so.[42] But then again, what is a serious authorship that does not take any risks? Kierkegaard had to go into the literary equivalent of the "human swarm" if he was to speak to those within it. Loss of form was then the risk he had to take.

Kierkegaard, Heidegger, and Everydayness

These comments invite a concluding reflection on one of the most significant twentieth-century responses to Kierkegaard, namely, the philosophy of existence of Heidegger. For many twentieth-century readers, Heidegger was to be understood as having rendered Kierkegaard's carnivalesque and sometimes chaotic engagement with his age into the somber prose of phenomenological philosophy, using Kierkegaardian insights in order to reopen the ancient metaphysical question as to the meaning of Being. As Heidegger portrays the situation, modern human beings are congenitally incapable of attending to this question, which would require them to cease fleeing from the acknowledgment of their own mortality and anxiously and resolutely to "run toward" death, accepting their ineluctable temporality. There is undoubtedly much Kierkegaard in this, both pseudonymous and "edifying."[43] And precisely by starting with average everydayness rather than (like Plato) with the philosopher or (like Nietzsche) with the artist, Heidegger repeats Kierkegaard's Socratic willingness to plunge into the human swarm. Yet, in the end, Heidegger and Kierkegaard prove to be authors of two very different kinds. Heidegger turns away from the concrete issues of how people are to commit to specific life options in order to meditate on the basic relationship between Being and beings. Kierkegaard, however, no less critical than Heidegger of the inauthenticity of the average everydayness of his own time, accepted that this—"Amager Square"—was where the decision for or against Christ had to be worked through. Consequently, Heidegger writes in the rigorous "scientific" (*wissenschaftlich*) style of fundamental phenomenology. Kierkegaard's strategy, I am suggesting, was virtually the opposite. Instead of wresting a contrary interpretation of existence from the chatter of the age, he expends all the lavish wealth of his literary talent on plunging into that same chatter so as to engage those incapable of philosophy, "the common man" whom he claimed as his intended reader. Literature is sometimes said to hold a mirror to its time, but Kierkegaard held a kaleidoscope to a kaleidoscopic time. His gamble was that his efforts would be kept from falling into formlessness by the "great, uplifting, simple, elementary thoughts" that he sought to keep in constant view and that, he hoped, his contemporaries and, no less importantly, posterity[44] would also see—at first in their fragmentary reflection in the literary kaleidoscope, but then more and more clearly in their own continuing rediscovery of "the glory of being human."[45]

Notes

1. For discussion of contemporary reviews of *Either/Or*, see George Pattison, *Kierkegaard, Religion and the Nineteenth-Century Crisis of Culture* (Cambridge, U.K.: Cambridge University Press, 2002), chap. 7: "The Reception of *Either/Or*," 137–53.

2. Georg Brandes, *Søren Kierkegaard: En Kritisk Fremstilling i Grundrids* (Copenhagen: Gyldendal, 1877); Ger. translation ("Autorisirte deutsche Ausg."): *Sören Kierkegaard: Ein literarisches Charakterbild* (Leipzig: J. A. Barth, 1879). For discussion, see Steen Tullberg, "Denmark: The Permanent Reception—150 Years of Reading Kierkegaard," in *Kierkegaard's International Reception*, Tome 1: *Northern and Western Europe*, ed. Jon Stewart, Kierkegaard Research: Sources, Reception and Resources, vol. 8 (Farnham, U.K.: Ashgate, 2009), 12–17.

3. See George Pattison, "Great Britain: From 'Prophet of the Now' to Postmodern Ironist (and After)," in Stewart, *Kierkegaard's International Reception*, Tome 1, 237–70.

4. See Elisabete de Sousa, "Kierkegaard's Musical Recollections," in *Kierkegaard Studies Year Book 2008*, ed. Heiko Schulz, Phillip Schwab, and Karl Verstrynge (Berlin: De Gruyter, 2008), 85–108. (On the treatment of Mozart's *Don Giovanni* in *Either/Or*, see also the essays by Nils Holger Petersen and Peder Jothen in this volume.—Ed.)

5. See Leonardo F. Lisi, "Kierkegaard and Modern European Literature" and Hugh Pyper, "Kierkegaard and English Language Literature," in *The Oxford Handbook of Kierkegaard*, ed. John Lippitt and George Pattison (Oxford: Oxford University Press, 2013), 550–69, 570–90; George Pattison, "Music, Madness and Mephistopheles: Art and Nihilism in Thomas Mann's *Doctor Faustus*," in *European Literature and Theology in the Twentieth Century*, ed. David Jasper and Colin Crowder (Basingstoke, U.K.: Macmillan, 1990), 1–14.

6. See also in this volume the essay by Marcia C. Robinson, who likens Kierkegaard's role to that of "a Socratic troubadour," and the essay by Jamie Lorentzen, who relates Kierkegaard's fascination with the troubadours to Bob Dylan's ambition "to serve as a performing artist qua modern troubadour."—Ed.

7. He also presented Winther with a copy of *Either/Or.*

8. Eric Ziolkowski, *The Literary Kierkegaard* (Evanston, Ill.: Northwestern University Press, 2011), 55–86.

9. Thomas Miles, "Horace: The Art of Poetry and the Search for the Good Life," in *Kierkegaard and the Roman World,* ed. Jon Stewart, Kierkegaard Research: Sources, Reception and Resources, vol. 3 (Farnham, U.K.: Ashgate, 2009), 39–52.

10. J. L. Heiberg, ed., *Clara Raphael: Tolv Breve* [*Clara Raphael: Twelve Letters*] (Copenhagen: C. A. Reitzel, 1851). The author, who published the book anonymously, was Mathilde Fibiger (1830–72).

11. In the context of his polemics against Hegelianism, Kierkegaard usually treats Heiberg rather roughly. However, he uses illustrations from Heiberg's dramatic work on their own merits and as they serve the point he is trying to make.

12. See "The Tragic in Ancient Drama Reflected in the Tragic in Modern Drama" in *SKS* 2:137–62 / *EO* 1:137–64; the discussion of Hamlet in *SKS* 6:417–19 / *SLW* 452–54; and "The Great Earthquake" journal entries: *SKS* 27:291–94, Papir 305:1–5 / *JP* 5:5427–32. On the debate about these last see George Pattison, "The Year 1838," *Revista Portuegesa de Filosofia* 64, nos. 2–4 (2008): 750–53.

13. Though see what is probably a description of the interior of the Church of Our Lady in the discourse "Watch Your Step When You Go to the House of the Lord," in *SKS* 10:175–77 / *CD* 163–65.

14. André Malraux, *Le Musée Imaginaire* (Paris: Gallimard, 1965), 10–12.

15. Of course, he was himself living through the golden age of Danish painting, and artists such as C. W. Eckersberg, J. T. Lundbye, and Christian Købke were producing work of international quality, even if their achievement is only relatively recently getting recognition outside Scandinavia. *Either/Or* suggests that he was familiar with the spring exhibition (*SKS* 2:310–13 / *EO* 1:319–23), but it has left little trace in his writing other than as the location for a seductive opportunity. Kierkegaard did, of course, visit Berlin, where he could have seen more than was possible at home, but we know nothing of his visits, if any, to museums there. The art historian Ragni Linnet has written about connections between Kierkegaard and J. T. Lundbye in her essay "Golden Tears: Johan Thomas Lundbye and Søren Kierkegaard," in *Kierkegaard and His Contemporaries: The Culture of Golden Age Denmark,* ed. Jon Stewart, Kierkegaard Studies, Monograph Series, vol. 10 (Berlin: De Gruyter, 2003), 406–26. (In the present volume, see also Linnet's essay on Kierkegaard's approach to pictorial art and visual culture.—Ed.)

16. On this point see the essay by Martijn Boven in this volume.—Ed.

17. See Peter Tudvad, *Kierkegaards København* [Kierkegaard's Copenhagen] (Copenhagen: Politiken, 2004), 233.

18. Frederikke Bremer, *Liv i Norden* [Life in the North] (Copenhagen: F. H. Eiber, 1849), 18–19, my translation. Bremer's roll call of great actors significantly overlaps with those discussed (and also praised) by Kierkegaard.

19. Tudvad, *Kierkegaards København,* 238–91.

20. Largely forgotten today, Scribe was at the time Europe's most successful dramatist. J. L. Heiberg translated many of his plays for the Danish stage as part of his campaign to remodel the Danish theater according to French rather than German models.

21. On the special interest expressed by *Repetition*'s Constantin Constantius in the performances he attended of the actor Friedrich Beckmann in Berlin's Königstädter Theater, see the essay by Anne Margrete Fiskvik in this volume.—Ed.

22. See also, in Peder Jothen's essay in the present volume, the quotation from Kierkegaard on the appeal of hand organ music, which represents for him "a kind of poetry on the street corner."—Ed.

23. Apropos of this observation is the suggestion by Ronald M. Green, in his essay in this volume, that if Kierkegaard were living today, "he would be entranced with contemporary cinema."—Ed.

24. It is not accidental that in his memoir *Sixteen Months in the Danish Isles* (London: Richard Bentley, 1852), 269, Andrew Hamilton, giving the first known English-language reference to Kierkegaard, says that, despite the difficulty of his books, he aspires to be known as a popular writer. As I argue in *Kierkegaard, Religion and the Nineteenth-Century Crisis of Culture*, it is as important to see him in relation to the world of the feuilletons to identify his connections to formal philosophical aesthetics.

25. G. W. F. Hegel, *Einleitung* [introduction] to *Vorlesungen über die Aesthetik, in GWFHW* 10, ed. Heinrich Gustav Hotho, pt. 1 (1835): 14; *A* 1:10.

26. This aversion was probably a factor in Heiberg's having declined to stage Henrik Ibsen's *Hærmændene paa Helgeland* (1858, *The Warriors at Helgoland*) in 1859.

27. See George Pattison, *Kierkegaard and the Quest for Unambiguous Life* (Oxford: Oxford University Press, 2012), chap. 2: "The Carnival Is in Town," 30–57.

28. The complaint is analogous to Nietzsche's lament concerning the lack of greatness in contemporary music and his pointed switch from Wagner to Offenbach. See Friedrich Nietzsche, *The Will to Power*, trans. Walter Kaufmann and R. J. Hollingdale (New York: Vintage, 1968), 439 (aphorisms 833 and 834).

29. As, for example, in his 1849 discourses on the lilies and the birds; see, for example, the evocation of nature's silence in the first of these (*SKS* 11:18–19 / *WA* 13) or the call to be joyful in the third (*SKS* 11:43–44 / *WA* 39–40).

30. I am aware of no published English translation of this scene.

31. In a treatise on the art of preaching Mynster had argued that the designation "upbuilding discourse" was the most appropriate way of referring to contemporary sermons, which, he thought, needed to be neither evangelizing nor didactic. For discussion, see George Pattison, *Kierkegaard and the Theology of the Nineteenth Century: The Paradox and the "Point of Contact"* (Cambridge, U.K.: Cambridge University Press, 2012), 172–79.

32. Compare Joakim Garff's essay in the present volume, which interprets Kierkegaard's *Practice in Christianity* as a "Christian Bildungsroman."—Ed.

33. J. L. Heiberg, "Litterær Vintersæd," *Intelligensblade* 24 (March 1843): 288.

34. He had also experimented with the epistolary and diary forms in his early journals, especially the Gilleleie Journal and the so-called Faustian letters (*SKS* 17:7–30, AA:1–12 / *KJN* 1:3–25; *SKS* 17:198–208, CC:12–24 / *KJN* 1:189–99).

35. Also, of course, the model for the banquet in "In Vino Veritas" in *Stages on Life's Way*.

36. Susanne K. Langer, *Philosophy in a New Key: A Study in the Symbolism of Reason, Rite, and Art* (1941), 3rd edition (Cambridge, Mass.: Harvard University Press, 1957).

37. See John Lippitt, *Humour and Irony in Kierkegaard's Thought* (Basingstoke, U.K.: Macmillan, 2000).

38. For a (qualified) Hegelian reading, see Jon Stewart, "Kierkegaard's Phenomenology of Despair in *The Sickness unto Death*," in *Kierkegaard Studies Yearbook 1997*, ed. N. J. Cappelørn and H. Deuser (Berlin: De Gruyter, 1997), 117–43. For the "spoof" hypothesis, see Roger Poole, "'My Wish, My Prayer': Keeping the Pseudonyms Apart," in *Kierkegaard Revisited: Kierkegaard Studies Monograph Series 1*, ed. N. J. Cappelørn and J. Stewart (Berlin: De Gruyter, 1997), 166–68.

39. See, e.g., Charles Guignon, "Heidegger and Kierkegaard on Death," in *Kierkegaard and Death*, ed. P. Stokes and A. Buben (Bloomington: Indiana University Press, 2011), 184–203.

40. "Short and Sharp [*Kort og Spidst*]" (rendered by the Hongs as "Brief and to the Point") is in fact the title of one of the articles in *The Moment*, no. 6, in *SKS* 13:257–59 / *MLW* 203–5.

41. Although he is capable of extraordinary concision, as, for instance, *Fragments* and the 1849 discourses on *The Lily of the Field and the Bird of the Air* (*SKS* 11:7–48 / *WA* 1–45) demonstrate.

42. Compare the comment by Walter Lowrie on the tedium of translating large swaths of *Stages on Life's Way*. See his "Translator's Introduction" to Søren Kierkegaard, *Stages on Life's Way*, trans. W. Lowrie (Oxford: Oxford University Press, 1940), 13.

43. On the importance of the edifying literature, see Martin Heidegger, *Being and Time*, trans. J. Macquarrie and Edward Robinson (Oxford: Blackwell, 1962), 494 (note to p. 235 of Heidegger's text).

44. On Kierkegaard's writing as an appeal to posterity and beyond posterity toward a universal resurrection, see Pattison, *Kierkegaard, Religion and the Nineteenth-Century Crisis of Culture*, 221–24.

45. The phrases "great," "uplifting," "simple," "elementary thoughts," and "the glory of being human" are from his 1847 discourses on the lilies and the birds of Matthew 6. See *SKS* 8:281–96, esp. 286 / *UDVS* 183–200, esp. 188–89. My English translations here vary slightly from the Hongs'.

Kierkegaard's Disruptions of Literature and Philosophy

Freedom, Anxiety, and Existential Contributions

Edward F. Mooney

I will address Kierkegaard's anomalous relations to literature and to philosophy. In addition, I consider Kierkegaard's relations, as a Socratic philosopher, both to his community and to specific individuals, the readers whom he meets one by one and challenges to effect an existential resolution, given the impersonal drift of their lives. It is not easy to disentangle these matters of literature, philosophy, and existential challenge. Each knits into the others. As a *literary figure* and as a *philosopher*, Kierkegaard disrupts the *conventions* of literature and philosophy, and as a person he enacts a kind of disordered, anomalous, hybrid status for himself. He becomes, simultaneously, a literary philosopher (or philosophical *littérateur*) and a cultural and existential *provocateur*.

Kierkegaard is precariously poised in Copenhagen in the way that Socrates is precariously poised in Athens: obeying the law, yet, through interrogations, challenging the law; a good citizen, yet not a good citizen. Socrates models a kind of existential heroism. He resolves the issue of *who he will be* in Athens, an issue with no conventional answer. This prods his admirers to resolve who *they* shall be. The full title of Kierkegaard's *Postscript* crescendos toward an enigmatic finale: the tome, we read, makes "an Existential Contribution." The contribution is to awaken me to the urgency of resolving who I will be.

Socrates disrupts Athens. Kierkegaard disrupts Copenhagen, its staid patterns of literature, philosophy, and personal life. Through face-to-face encounters, Plato's Socrates, especially in the early dialogues, makes *existential, philosophical* interventions. He stings his listeners, stops to interrogate them, and as often as not, abandons them—seduced but confused and without answers. Kierkegaard's pseudonymous texts are crafted to replicate the sting of Socratic face-to-face encounters. *Postscript* or the earlier *Philosophical Crumbs*,[1] comes close to being *overtly* Socratic, yet the apparently more *literary* works (*Either/Or, Fear and Trembling*, and *Repetition*, for instance) are also Socratic. I begin with Kierkegaard as a disruptive *littérateur*.

A Kind of Philosophical Poet?

Kierkegaard is not a novelist, though "The Seducer's Diary," from the first volume of *Either/Or*, reads like a novella. He is not a dramatist, though *Stages on Life's Way* restages Plato's drama, the *Symposium*. Kierkegaard's not an essayist, a "man of letters," a journalist, nor a historian or biographer with a remarkable literary flair. His reputation does not rest on producing aphorisms or inventing pseudonyms under which he writes.[2] There is a tradition that claims Kierkegaard as a kind of poet, though we would be hard-pressed to find a poem in his work.[3] That seems to exhaust the usual ways of being a literary figure.

If a field biologist is lucky enough to encounter strange plants or insects that are neither this nor that, that do not fit existing taxonomies, she might get to name her finds as a new species. We do not like to leave quirky things off the map, without a name, especially if they are terribly interesting. The brilliance of Kierkegaard's sentences and paragraphs and the endlessly innovative and ever-increasing bulk of his publications make his specimens terribly interesting. His works, like lively biological specimens, are even self-replicating. One strange invention spawns successors with family resemblances to earlier family specimens, and the extended family spawns successors. Kierkegaard's genes reappear in Ibsen and Kafka, for instance. Literature has an evolutionary history.[4] Kierkegaard becomes an Ur-text for Ibsen, Rilke, Auden, Dinesen, Kafka, and (perhaps in a different league) Ingmar Bergman, John Updike, and Woody Allen. And it is clear that Kierkegaard inherits genetic material from his ancestors, Dante, Plato, Aristophanes, Cervantes, and Goethe (to name a few).[5]

Kierkegaard did not deliver novels or plays or poems, but he easily *could have*. He had other fish to fry. Something diverts his attention from becoming *only* a literary figure, and a clue lies in the fact that he has sprouts, or siblings, in the gardens of Heidegger and Wittgenstein, Ortega and Sartre. A philosophical vocation competes in his breast with a literary one, making him both (and neither). To complicate matters, he has a religious vocation, too. The result is an anomalous mix, evident existentially in the writer's three-part identity and in the trifold identity of his works: religious, aesthetic, and philosophical—*all* of the above and hence not *simply* any of the above.

Kierkegaard is his anomalous, hyphenated, elusive yet irresistible progeny. We face the riddle of the *Mona Lisa* or the Socrates who primarily tells us he knows nothing, leaving us smitten but empty-handed. It is hard to do philosophy, and harder to do *Socratic* philosophy. The Socratic task requires that you forgo the "objective" rigors of adding new paragraphs to the history of the subject, even paragraphs that are a critique of the subject. It requires that you "become subjective," that you place the quite particular human being that you are smack in the middle of the picture. If you are Socrates, you are not an objective QED machine, and you question other "subjectivities" in your path. You battle, sting, and nurse these into birth. Socrates is a midwife, not an expositor of old, or inventor of new, philosophical results. He sees us naked, in labor, and steps in to help, however painful the process. Kierkegaard sees us naked, too, and would push and pull us toward birth.

Having a Kierkegaard book arrive at our door is like having Socrates arrive there. If in beard and sandals he knocked and announced that he was a midwife come to assist, and you had expected an Amazon.com delivery, his arrival would be anomalous, out of bounds. Kierkegaard knows he cannot announce himself directly as our local midwife. He sticks to delivering strange books, half-philosophy, half-literature (and the religious ones sing from the side).[6] We do not need an encyclopedia salesman hawking books of knowledge and wisdom, nor do we need a literary dilettante hawking film scripts or novels. We need his anomalous, pseudonymous books because, like Socrates, they administer to our souls, and our souls yearn.

Of course, the whole thing can backfire. We want to know what brand of writing confronts us, and if the answer evades us, we will be anxious, perhaps unbearably anxious, and we may just shut down. We are creatures who like to know what's going on. Responding to the knock at the door, if a Socratic voice spoke up—"I'm here as a midwife. . . . You didn't notice you were in difficult labor?"—we would slam the door. Or perhaps humor him a bit, hoping he'd move on. And if that failed, call psychiatric services.

Can Philosophy Abide Poetry?

After completing an apprenticeship in the university, earning the equivalent of a modern Ph.D., Kierkegaard never put his training to work in a recognized profession or career. He did not become a parson, professor, or lawyer, an editor, journalist, or dramatist. If he became a writer, it was perhaps in the style of a "freelancer" (it is the self-ascription Johannes de Silentio adopts in *Fear and Trembling*). But what, exactly, is that, other than a refusal to be tied down as a dramatist, novelist, poet, or critic? He might have become a professor and the author of philosophical tracts.

Now you might counter that Kierkegaard *has* a genre: he is a poet, at least "a kind of poet" (of course, not a straightforward poet, someone who writes poetry). Calling him one lets him be figurative, evocative, allusive, elusive, and enigmatic in a way denied to a standard essayist or philosopher. Yet being "a kind of poet," however alluring, can also be off-putting, much in the way Kierkegaard's texts can be.[7] We might envy the freedom that comes with release from the demands of strict philosophical categories and a consequent permission to explore the unknown in a carefree way, with imagination and passions given plenty of line. On the other hand we might *resent* a careless way with cultural requirements of discipline and order. Plato warned against this hybrid, banishing poets from the state ordered by philosophy (or so it *seems*: he did not rule out of order his *own* poetry). Logical positivists wanted to exile nonsense, and that nonsense included all that we call "poetry. For them, a poetic philosopher was an oxymoron: Nietzsche's aspiration to be a "Music Playing Socrates" was madness.[8]

On the other hand, Jamie Ferreira finds two writers who *prefer* a volatile mix, and she cites them to introduce Kierkegaard—Robert Frost: "a poetic philosopher or . . . a philosophical poet, my favorite kind of both,"[9] and then Wittgenstein: "philosophy ought only to be written as a poetic composition."[10] If poetry loosens straitlaced philosophy, philosophy can focus poetry beyond the everyday, transient, and local. Why not *enjoy* disruption of expectations, *enjoy* hybridity, its ambiguity and amorphousness? Border crossing and border erasing are attractive for they are daring, even if we dread the attendant insecurity.

Should We Suffer Misfits?

A book titled *Prefaces* that contains nothing but prefaces is not poetry or short story or political polemic. Odd creatures, like *Prefaces*, *Either/Or*, and *Postscript*, are full of brilliant writing bent on breaking up literary cubbyholes. They are Socratic irritants that can teach us Socratic ignorance, bafflement viscerally conveyed in a mix of annoyance, helplessness, and allure. Socrates's interlocutors are left puzzling over missing definitions. Kierkegaard's readers are left puzzling over texts missing their identifying labels and purposes. The job of sorting new arrivals for the library shelves was to have been simple and straightforward. But how did I come to expect that all proper books have proper places, simple niches, on my shelves? Perhaps I expect too much order from the world, or the wrong *kind* of order.

Books that are evasive about their genre can be evasive about their authorship. Neither *Prefaces* nor *Either/Or* has a straightforward author. They are pseudonymous: we both do and do not know who authors them. Is *Middlemarch* to be filed under George Eliot or Mary Anne Evans? Evans used a pseudonym so her work would be taken seriously. Kierkegaard used pseudonyms for less evident reasons. One might see them alternately as fluffy devices to provoke public interest, as suspect means to deflect personal responsibility for opinions or positions, or as tools to incite Socratic self-awareness and interpretative alertness. And apart from the motivations for using pseudonyms, there remains the issue of *power*. Can "Kierkegaard" overrule the claims to authorship made by Climacus, Johannes de Silentio, or Nicolaus Notabene?[11]

If you wanted to shelve by genre, would the books end up under literature, philosophy, essays, or personal meditations? Perhaps (heaven forbid!) Kierkegaard is just "playing around" as an afternoon's amusement. He says that his *Prefaces* are "like tuning a guitar, like talking with a child, like spitting out of the window" (*SKS* 4:469 / *P* 5). But I suspect he is pulling our leg. After all, we might equally think that the *Postscript* or *Fear and Trembling* was not entirely serious, was like "tuning a guitar." In fact, an early section of *Fear and Trembling* is called—exactly—"attunement."[12] His feints, his intimating that it is all a joke, provoke our anxious parries. He calls *Prefaces* the work of "a light-minded ne'er-do-well [*en letsindig Døgenicht*]" (*SKS* 4:470 / *P* 6). But that's just flippant, a wisecrack.

Fear and Trembling is perhaps Kierkegaard's best-known book. We think of Abraham bringing his son to Mount Moriah. Kierkegaard must be defending Abraham's shocking and even servile compliance, we suppose. But why assume this book is out to make a case for Abraham (or against him)? Does it *look* like a book with a thesis to defend? The first part looks like a set of fables or mood swings and nightmarish dreams, and the second, like logical machinations of a deluded scholastic.[13] Well, if it is not *that* disjointed, perhaps it is another hybrid, defined apophatically by what it is *not*: neither essay nor fable, nor sermon nor poem, nor polemic—but just possibly a dash of each of these in a strange stew.

Kierkegaard calls the book a "dialectical lyric," which is a stab at two of its stylistic features. But it is also pure unprecedented invention, a collage of fable, biblical exegesis, social commentary, dialectical investigation of concepts like "the ethical," "the tragic," and barely concealed farce. It is burlesque, or what Bakhtin calls "the carnivalesque."[14]

Kierkegaard is a *literary* genius, not just an astute philosopher, a withering social critic, and a profound diagnostician of the soul. He endlessly invents countergenres, parabooks, unclassifiable publications that question our sense of what forms a piece of writing can take. He gives us the vertiginous sense that there may be *no end* to such inventiveness—that under his spell, we live and read in infinite possibility.

What Is a Postscript?

Like *Prefaces*, the title *Postscript* names a *section* of a book's interior and can only anomalously fit as a title. Why do we divide interiors into prefaces, acknowledgments, chapters, postscripts, indexes, and so forth? If Kierkegaard gives us *Prefaces* or *Postscript*, will the next book be *Footnotes*? Or *Epigraphs*, or *Dedications*? Note that this tome, numbering nearly six hundred pages in its standard English edition, dwarfs the slim volume to which it is an appendage.

The slim parent-book is *Philosophical Crumbs, or a Crumb of Philosophy*. What is it to publish philosophical *crumbs*,[15] trifles, or crumbling remains, especially in an age of philosophical structures and systems? The full title utterly dwarfs the shorthand *Postscript*: *Concluding Unscientific Postscript to "Philosophical Crumbs": A Mimic-Pathetic-Dialectic Compilation—an*

Existential Contribution.[16] Open it, and you'll discover what looks like a scholarly tome, full of sections and subsections, appearing systematic and self-important, hardly "mere crumbs" or "fragments." In his masterful biography, Alastair Hannay suggests "Concluding Unscholarly Addendum."[17]

However we render the title, Kierkegaard is bending literary expectations to a breaking point. Is this title (not to mention what follows) some sort of insider's joke?[18] Kierkegaard ensures—or hopes to ensure—that *if* we go on reading, we cannot be blasé, as if canvassing this sort of thing were routine, an everyday encounter. Unfortunately for many readers, I suspect, the shock of the title has ceased to make trouble. We dash on, ever eager to get to the business at hand: What positions are advanced or attacked, and with what arguments? Unfortunately, *Postscript* is not just about QEDs. The heart of its mission is forecast in the rest of the title. What is a "mimic-pathetic-dialectic compilation—an existential contribution"? (This does not sound like a promise of arguments.) A "postscript to crumbs of philosophy" seems troubling enough, and a "mimic-pathetic-dialectic compilation" only ups the ante. To mime or mimic is to engage in the comic, while to evoke pathos engages the tragic, and "dialectic" brings philosophy on stage. What sort of book, or genre, lets tragedy, comedy, and philosophy play equal and simultaneous parts?

Why Get off the Map?

Thoreau and Nietzsche were unreservedly literary writers *and* philosophers. Kierkegaard is not alone in being *both* philosopher *and* literary figure, working out a collaborative, hyphenated cultural and personal identity—off the map of standard vocational cubbyholes. There is a tradition, as it were, of defying traditions. Kierkegaard's Socratic, existential motivations *drive* him to defy classification. He artfully dodges our trapping moves. He has no wish that a *new* genre be inaugurated in his honor, and no wish to found a new philosophical style. To focus on classification—natural enough for orderly persons—distracts from our deeper needs and yearnings. Knowing where Kierkegaard belongs on philosophical or literary maps does not answer our existential anxieties about who we are and where we are going. The subtitle declares that the author makes an *existential* contribution. Mapping his oeuvre onto larger conventional cultural frameworks is a nonexistential *objective* project.

The *Postscript*'s author contributes, if he does, by leading me away from classifications to the quality of my singular life, here and now, a life ready to be shaped, as I alone can shape it. Failing to settle objective matters of genre spins me out of objectivity toward emptiness. The books *refuse to tell me* which way to turn. I'm thrown into existential space wherein I anxiously realize that any resolution, any step forward is a step taken *on my own.* As if to highlight this abandonment to my own devices, and the withdrawal of helping hands, in its final pages, *Postscript* invites me to leave it, relinquish it, as if its six hundred pages, like *Prefaces*, were the work of "a light-hearted do-nothing."[19] Like Socrates, the book stings and sings and departs.

Kierkegaard is attractive-unattractive, ordered-disordered, sober-comedic, and discomposes with a passion. He is an enfant terrible, a misfit who took pleasure in not fitting in and was just as nonconformist when it came to the shape of his literary production. He does not trade in the coin of the land.[20] If he eludes standard literary cubicles, he does no better when it comes to standard ways of writing philosophy. He can hold forth on the philosophical themes of subjectivity and objectivity, the individual and the crowd, the anguish of faith and the false assurance of careerism and church. But the faux genres he adopts are amusingly bizarre. Kant gives us titles without banners and whistles: *The Critique of Pure Reason* and *Prolegomena to Any Future Metaphysics*. In full-dress regalia, Kierkegaard gives us *Concluding Unscientific Postscript to "Philosophical Crumbs": A Mimic-Pathetic-Dialectic Compilation—an Existential Contribution*, authored by Johannes Climacus, with S. Kierkegaard responsible for publication. He won't settle into a literary, philosophical, or theological scene, or into essays or poetry, novellas, treatises, or history. *These refusals have an existential rationale. They serve freedom and new life.* He creates *anxiety*, that forerunner of change of self or recovery of soul.

To follow routine expectations is to idle one's freedom. We know from *The Concept of Anxiety* that freedom requires passage through "*a sympathetic antipathy* and *an antipathetic sympathy*" (*SKS* 4:348 / *CA* 42, emphasis in text). The amorphous nonshapes of his literary products induce and replicate the anxiety that is part and parcel of freedom. As Gordon Marino slyly dubs him, Kierkegaard is a "doctor of dread."[21] We undergo mild, or screaming, vertigo, and controlled, or terrifying, prescribed doses of "*sympathetic antipathy* and *antipathetic sympathy*." Of course the doctor has our deep yearnings, our true interests at heart. This is all a forerunner and companion to my freedom.

What Is an Existential Contribution?

Postscript has a final tag in its amusing-disquieting subtitle. This "mimic-pathetic-dialectic compilation," we are told, is "an existential contribution." This is the first time in European philosophy, to my knowledge, that the adjective "existential" is used to signify a concern for one's personal existence.

Kierkegaard wants his literary philosophy to address readers intimately, existentially, to call out from them their sense of the meanings and directions of their life. Persons have complex social identities, but that is not the end of the matter. One may be identified as a judge or an aesthete, a shopkeeper or a priest, an uncle, a hero, or a rogue. Kierkegaard's literary genius in its *first* phase is to give compelling portraits of social ways of being, as a public might construe and misconstrue them.

There are different ways to describe the role of a parson or professor. Kierkegaard critiques commonplace ways of taking these social identities, but he typically moves from social critique to soul diagnostics. Even as he provides provocative sketches of how a parson might appear on Sunday (for just one example), he moves simultaneously into more private landscapes of identity. In the *second* phase (or level) the question "How does *one, in general,* exist as a proper parson, or *typically* lose one's soul as a parson?" becomes quite another question. I now ask, "Have *I*, as a parson, lost my soul?" In this second phase of questioning, a general query about social identity gets transformed. I modulate the question, hearing it *existentially*, hearing it as addressing *me* and requiring *my* answer or response (and general questions drop away).

How do we know if Climacus has fulfilled his promise to provide an "existential contribution"? Well, I have to ask whether the register of my questioning has shifted. I have to ask whether I have modulated from the excellent but nonintimate, objective question "What is it to *exist* as a soul in love?" to another question, perhaps light years away. Do I find myself wandering toward or right in the middle of the question "Am *I* in love?" If that modulation takes place, Johannes Climacus has pushed or pulled me to consider an identity *I might assume* that is deeper than an array of possible social identities, generally considered. *That* is his "existential contribution."

A judge may play out his courtroom role, making brilliant legal points (or being only banal and routine), performing (or not performing) his social role. We might ask, if he falters, if he has his heart in his work, has sold his soul to the devil, or finds anything august in the office he holds. But these are not yet existential questions. They are still evaluations of social identity. To perform a *role* adequately can require that one put one's heart into it. A Socratic existential contribution does not ask us to assess whether someone fulfills a social identity, even fulfills the requirement that one does what one does with passion. Instead, the Socratic contribution elicits *from a particular someone, from this very judge in question, a self-evaluation.* An existential intervention succeeds when *this very judge* is startled or unnerved or disquieted by the existential address of another, and is then moved decisively to resolve or close down a just-opened field of possibilities. *This very judge* decides to reform, or resign, or prefer to do nothing, and then cashes out the decision in action.

I can now bring out subphases within this phase of considering my existence. I no longer focus on what someone in my circumstance does to achieve an identity, say, as a judge. I focus on what I alone must do to achieve this identity, and that cannot be a matter of rote imitation of what is generally done in that role. I move to the brink of existential commitment, my own forging of what that role uniquely will be *for me*, and then move through the resolutions and actions that secure (however precariously) that unique existential identity, *my* reality. I move to the brink of the pond, dive into the pond, and come up swimming (or not). At the brink I no longer attend to existential reality *in general*. Diving in means leaping from a pond's-edge *view* of what an existential reality requires (say, that I must choose myself, dive in or not, as every human must)—to full immersion in *another* question. Who will *I, in particular*, be? And in the midst of immersion, I must settle the matter. Will I rise to the surface (or stay under longer, or forever)? Subsurface, how will I move, with what speed, and to what end? Will I rise to the occasion to do what I must do to be the minister or parson I must be? How, and with what style, and to what end?

Kierkegaard makes an existential contribution that only *I* can complete. *His* contribution is to offer me an existential space distinct from social space. If I accept this offer, I accept the open space where existential possibilities are vividly acknowledged, and then I *close* that radical openness through decisive resolution and action. Kierkegaard cannot complete the process he initiates. He can offer possibilities, but he cannot determine which of these will become mine. A contribution to charity is *realized* only when it is accepted, and Kierkegaard's existential contribution is *realized* only when I resolve first-personally to accept it by taking *this* step rather than *that*, thus resolving my anomalous situation *this* way rather than *that*. Accepting an existential contribution allows me to become who I *am* by allowing me to become who I *will be*.[22]

It is hard to grasp the uncanny *magnitude* of the *Postscript*'s intention. The comic, dialectic, and tragic are in the service of an infinite demand. It is a demand that can be fulfilled or rejected in any number of ways, and there are no guidelines included. So I can refuse the Climacus offer. I might be entertained by his comic wit, impressed by his dialectical finesse, or moved by the pathos of his descriptions. But his contribution is realized only if I am transformed, turned around. It is realized only if I am undone and then do myself up again (or find myself graciously restored—and not reject *that*).

You might reasonably think that it is enough for a literary figure to make a significant contribution to the canon or to stretch the canon or to win acclaim in her age. You might think it enough for a philosopher to better understand a classical philosophical puzzle or text or to win acclaim as a critic of the arts or politics, of gender relations or religious intolerance, or become a critic of insensitivity to the natural world. But none of this, laudable as it is, would be enough for Socrates, or for Kierkegaard.

Socrates engaged in enigmatic, unfinished conversations. Kierkegaard writes enigmatic, unfinished books. The aim is not to advance philosophy or literature as a discipline but to *alter listeners and readers* existentially, one by one. Both Socrates and Kierkegaard want to make headway toward the salvation of souls, or at least to remove vanities that obstruct that venture. Kierkegaard is the Socrates who "makes [those in his presence] ill at ease, and inflicts upon them the unpardonable offense of making them doubt themselves."[23] Kierkegaard writes late in life that his mission has always been Socratic.[24] His pseudonymous authorship especially is an endlessly unsettling Socratic installation of self-doubt offered as a preliminary to self-transformation.

Do We Need Cultural Credentials?

Kierkegaard is nonconforming. He will resist falling into conventional slots, and even a set of slots custom-made for him. Let me consider this indeterminacy of identity by reflecting on Henri Bergson in the last days of his life.[25] His life is not exactly a text, but he has an identity at stake; he lives out the inadequacy of social identity and the necessity of existential identity. The question he faces in his last days is not unlike the question facing Socrates in his last days in Athens, under trial and under arrest.

When Jews in Paris were required to wear yellow armbands after the Nazi takeover, Bergson was not exactly *required* to identify himself as such, ethically or religiously or existentially. He was close to converting to Roman Catholicism, as his friends had known, years before the Nazi invasion. His world renown as a philosopher would have earned him the exemption from persecution offered to Freud or negotiated by Wittgenstein for his sisters. (The Nazis were not entirely deaf to the onus of appearing to be cultural barbarians.) Yet Bergson, now a frail man in his eighties, chose to line up outside in a cold drizzle, wearing the armband marking his identification with the Jews already facing a horror that would only grow. He determined his identity, an existential identity, at that moment, when his social identity was indeterminate.

As outsiders we could wonder whether Bergson fit into social reality as a Jew, as a world-famous intellectual, as a soon-to-be-Catholic convert, or as a frail old man. Of course he was all of these. But social identity merely poses the question of his existential identity. Bergson's final days bring into prominence the need for an *existential* determination: Will he resolve to have it end this way or that, in keeping with *these* of his espoused values and commitments, or *those*? Will he skirt the tempting but ultimately self-betraying alternatives?

Kierkegaard's corpus stands to us roughly as Bergson's life does. We recognize that the corpus or the life could be focused this way or that. The big difference is that we can revel in the choice Bergson made. He lined up in a cold drizzle. But the large Kierkegaard community has not yet resolved the field of possibilities that interpreters of Kierkegaard's must work. It is relatively easy to make the case that Bergson is a hero. Is it as easy to make the case that Kierkegaard is Socratic and passes the existential task of response to *me*? My reading of his corpus can have *this* sort of life, *this* sort of identity, rather than that. The focus is up to me (and to *you*). If I am right, Kierkegaard intends to put the ball in my court, if I exercise only my scholarly resources in order to find his cultural niche that will silence his voice—his *Socratic* voice.

We might say, "Look, Bergson had a moment of existential anguish, and thank God he came out of it a hero. *That's* what matters, not the array of possibilities that we see preceding his decision to walk into the rain and line up." Likewise, we might say, scanning the possibilities for shelving Kierkegaard's texts, "Look, here I am in a moment of anguish, and thank God I now come out of it taking the author as a serious, Socratic philosopher (not as a perpetual adolescent misusing great talent)." Thus I cease searching in the grid of objective possibilities for his literary-philosophic niche. Kierkegaard enacts Socratic parries and feints, delivering texts that escape our nets. Slipping our nets is more than an exhibition of skill, as if his contribution were to excel at child's play, hide-and-seek, or magical tomfoolery.[26] Having an objective cultural slot for him would defeat his aim. By repeatedly slipping our nets, he hopes to make *a Socratic, existential contribution.*

How Does a Socratic Sting Change Me?

If I am the recipient of an existential contribution, I should gather more than the information that *people like me* can be stung. I am humbled. I realize that *what* I make of the text is up to *me*. I can throw it aside, be slapdash, or struggle with it. If I decide to struggle, there are options. One possibility is a strategy of suspicion or resentment. Another is to follow what Kierkegaard calls "love, that lenient interpreter." That is, I can adopt a strategy of charity.[27] Which way I resolve this crux shapes the interpreter I will be. If I interpret generously, I am being generous and will be grateful for insights bequeathed. If I interpret suspiciously, as a master unmasker, I will feel myself proud, above being fooled, and grateful for little. If I interpret resentfully, I will take offense that someone has attempted to pull the wool over my eyes. I will not be grateful that texts or words or images have come my way. A grateful person is different from an indifferent or self-righteous or haughty and condescending one.

A reader willing to praise the beauty and worth of a range of appearances or partial realities is different from one who filters all appearances through an ideological lens that reduces them, deflating them to a status where they are helpless pawns in a play of power or money, or pawns in a war of genders or ethnicities or classes or religions or sexual orientations. A debunker enjoys domination over appearances, texts, or partial realities at hand. I might learn from such a lordly hermeneuticist that museums are extensions of colonial aggression (nothing more), that concert halls are monuments to wealth extracted from the poor (nothing more), that writing is a sublimation of sexual desire (nothing more), that Kierkegaard's oeuvre is a vain attempt to assuage guilt (nothing more), that because his stature was unimpressive, his writing is working out a Napoleon complex (nothing more), that his father's confession of guilt made him an emotional cripple. Things are dispraised for what they mask rather than praised for any gift they might bring and for any occasion they might provide for thanksgiving.

I am a different person depending on the interpretative approach I accept and follow. How much of the world of texts is a world I can love? Is it within my purview to love many or few? How large is the world I must despise or wish dead? What powers my writing? Is it wonder or competitive adrenalin, tender, sympathetic appreciation, or disgust and resentment? I can (to some extent) tilt different interpretative postures this way or that, thus constituting an interpretative personality. Do I face texts or art or historical periods and events with indifferent royal aplomb? How much do I value my own halting or imperious voice?

I become *this* sort of interpreting person or *that* as I take my cues for interpretation this way or that. In the broadest sense, reading is an ethical venture, an activity that reveals something of what I take to be good and take to be part of the good life and take to be beyond the pale, and my quickness to find fault with texts can be a stain on my reading character just as my quickness to find fault with persons can be. We are our labor, and if our labor is writing and reading, we expose who we are—I expose who *I* am (existentially) in "the what" and "the how" of my writing and reading.

Kierkegaard's Words

It is of interest to Socrates how *he* lives, how he relates to *the truth*, and how his life and his connection to the truth can have a *saving effect* on his interlocutors. Kelly Jolley writes, "[Philosophy] does not exist [for Socrates] as a sort of idol of which [Socrates] would be the guardian and which he must defend. It exists rather in its living relevance to the Athenians."[28] Just so, the literature Kierkegaard produces in varied profusion does not exist as a tribute to "the literary life" or as a gift to "the great tradition of literature" or to "the great tradition of philosophy." These are not temples in which he wished to enshrine his texts and himself. On the best interpretation, his words were to exist in their "living relevance" to his townsfolk or, more accurately, in their "living relevance" to *single individuals* in whose souls they lodged as a provocation, judge, and inspiration. Although he writes in veins that are in turn literary or aesthetic, ethical or philosophical, religious or counterreligious, and writes to bring these into conflict and repose, these are not *ultimate* categories of exploration or veneration for him.

Kierkegaard is Socratic. First and last he worships at no single shrine but inaugurates, for each reader, a trial of self-knowledge, self-resolution, self-realization, and selflessness. (The trial both is and is not "all about me.") He conducts trials of existence, where his subjectivity meets mine around love and responsibility, urgency, delight, and suffering. It is a trial of my existence, and yours, or in another of his favorite images, an invitation to sweep onto the floor for a solo dance before God, before such presence as can be pleased or displeased with the tilt of my soul. Kierkegaard's writings bring us to the dance, and perhaps demonstrate some steps,[29] but the rest is up to us—to *me*. So *his* manner of writing is in *our* service, in *my* service. In its poetry and philosophy, its comic mimicry and tearful pathos, it is a great gift, an existential contribution.

Notes

1. For years the Danish *Smule, Smuler* was translated "Fragments." This suggests we might assemble the fragments into a larger system, or that a larger system or structure has been broken up. "Crumbs" or "trifles" are throwaways first and foremost. This suggests a lowly *place* in orders of *significance* rather than something in the order of parts-to-whole. It might also be translated "smidgens."

2. See Edward F. Mooney, "Style and Pseudonymity in Kierkegaard," in *Oxford Handbook to Kierkegaard*, ed. John Lippitt and George Pattison (Oxford: Oxford University Press, 2013), chap. 10.

3. Louis Mackey titles his study *Kierkegaard: A Kind of Poet* (Philadelphia: University of Pennsylvania Press, 1971).

4. A measure of literary genius is the capacity to spawn *further* genius and to prompt inquiry into its own ancestral progenitors.

5. Eric Ziolkowski, *The Literary Kierkegaard* (Evanston, Ill.: Northwestern University Press, 2011).

6. Living with the anomaly of a literary-philosophical output is difficult enough. If it is also a *religious* output, this may be juggling too many categories. To keep the scope of my inquiry manageable, I will leave the *purely* religious texts (like the *Discourses*) to one side. Some texts are in limbo. *Fear and Trembling* takes up Abraham's near sacrifice of Isaac, but that does not automatically make it a religious text. The pseudonym Johannes de Silentio is silent about many things, for instance how his outpourings *bear* on religiosity. Perhaps he narrates a horror-show *spectacle* that is highly *irreligious* or a parody of religious texts or a parody of philosophical texts. See Edward F. Mooney, *On Søren Kierkegaard: Dialogue, Polemics, Lost Intimacy, and Time* (Aldershot, U.K.: Continuum, 2007), chaps. 2–4, where I argue that Kierkegaard can have a collaborative Christian-Socratic identity, and chap. 8, where I treat parts of *Fear and Trembling* as an irreligious spectacle.

7. Henry David Thoreau has a capacious sense of "the poetic." He writes, "Yet poetry, though the last and finest result, is a natural fruit. As naturally as the oak bears an acorn, and the vine a gourd, man bears a poem, either spoken or done." *A Week on the Concord and Merrimack Rivers*, ed. Carl F. Hovde, William L. Howarth, and Elizabeth Hall Witherell (Princeton, N.J.: Princeton University Press, 1980), 91. Kierkegaard balks at a general endorsement of "poetic living" for fear it would endorse the life only of the aesthete or dandy.

8. See Friedrich Nietzsche, *The Birth of Tragedy*, trans. Douglas Smith (Oxford: Oxford University Press, 2000), 85 and 93 (in secs. 15 and 17).

9. Robert Frost, "On Emerson," in *Selected Prose of Robert Frost*, ed. Hyde Cox and Edward Connery Lathem (New York: Holt, Rinehart, and Winston, 1959), 112, quoted by Jamie M. Ferreira, *Kierkegaard* (Oxford: Wiley-Blackwell, 2009), 1.

10. Quoted by Ferreira, *Kierkegaard*, 1.

11. Others in this gallery of pseudonyms include Victor Eremita, Constantin Constantius, Vigilius Haufniensis, and Anti-Climacus. See the discussion in Edward F. Mooney, "Pseudonyms and Style," in *Oxford Handbook of Kierkegaard*, ed. John Lippitt and George Pattison (Oxford: Oxford University Press, 2013), chap. 10.

12. Johannes de Silentio's (Kierkegaard's) term here, "Stemning" (*SKS* 4:105), is translated by the Hongs as "Exordium" (*FT* 9).

13. Lengthy accounts of the enigmas of *Fear and Trembling* are given in Edward F. Mooney, *Knights of Faith and Resignation: Reading Kierkegaard's Fear and Trembling* (Albany: State University of New York, 1991), and in Mooney, *On Søren Kierkegaard*.

14. Mikhail Bakhtin, *Problems of Dostoevsky's Poetics* (Minneapolis: University of Minnesota Press, 1984). I do not want to invent or borrow a genre to cover Johannes de Silentio's creation. It is more important to emphasize an author peddling strange goods that challenge what writing should look like.

15. See n. 1.

16. The full title—including the subtitle—as rendered by the Hongs is slightly different: *Concluding Unscientific Postscript to "Philosophical Fragments": A Mimical-Pathetical-Dialectical Compilation: An Existential Contribution* (CUP 2:xiii).—Ed.

17. Alastair Hannay, *Kierkegaard: A Biography* (Cambridge, U.K.: Cambridge University Press, 2001), 315. It can be called an "unscholarly" postscript insofar as its content often satirizes academic treatises and scholarly frames of mind, not just "scientific thinking" of the sort done in science labs.

18. For every smitten disciple of Socrates there were plenty who thought he was "only a sophist" and still others who thought his tomfoolery was a threat to the state. Kierkegaard's disquieting challenge to expectations might be seen as a threat to the city's moral-religious fiber. It exposed too much.

19. The final unnumbered pages push the pseudonym aside: now "S. Kierkegaard" claims to be its author. All that has been written seems to be revoked, thrown away, like Wittgenstein's ladder. See chapter 12, "*Postscript*: Humor Takes It Back," in Mooney, *On Søren Kierkegaard*.

20. Kierkegaard's appreciation of Mozart's *Don Giovanni* can count as an essay, even though it is folded into an unwieldy nonessay titled *Either/Or*, published under a pseudonym. His social analysis of nineteenth-century Copenhagen in *Two Ages* could also count as an essay. But these instances of straightforward "essay exposition" are rare in his oeuvre. George Steiner, a "man of letters," writes, as Kierkegaard might write, on love and desire, art and philosophy, mysticism and moral vision, self-deception, and goods. However, Kierkegaard would never be mistaken for a man of letters. Socially, he has no use for the literary clubs that could grant him the laurel "man of letters," and he insists on irking his public, thus attracting (at least in his lifetime) mainly disapprobation.

21. See Gordon Marino, "The Danish Doctor of Dread," *New York Times*, March 17, 2012.

22. See Robert Pippin, "On 'Becoming Who One Is' (and Failing): Proust's Problematic Selves," in *Philosophical Romanticism*, ed. Nikolas Kompridis (London: Routledge, 2006), 113–40.

23. See Maurice Merleau-Ponty, *In Praise of Philosophy*, trans. John Wild and James M. Edie (Evanston, Ill.: Northwestern University Press, 1988), 31–39. Kelly Dean Jolley develops Merleau-Ponty's discussions of Bergson's decision to stand up as a Jew and links it to the Socratic nature of philosophy in a discussion I encountered while floundering. A draft of his lecture, "Merleau-Ponty in Praise of Philosophy" (given August 31, 2012, Auburn University) is available at "Draft of MMP Talk," *Quantum Est in Rebus Inane*, August 31, 2012, http://kellydean-jolley.com/2012/08/31/draft-of-mmp-talk/. It was of immense help.

24. From his deathbed, looking back on all that lay behind, Kierkegaard writes, "The only analogy I have for what I am doing is Socrates. My task is the Socratic task of revising the definition of what it means to be a Christian" ("Min Opgave," *SKS* 13:405 / "My Task," *MLW* 341). The remark was penned in 1854. See my discussions in Mooney, *On Søren Kierkegaard*, chaps. 1–3.

25. Merleau-Ponty, *In Praise of Philosophy*, 36, quoted in Jolley, "Merleau-Ponty in Praise of Philosophy," 12.

26. Especially in the early dialogues, Socrates can seem less than serious, raising all sorts of questions and refusing to give answers. He says that his wisdom is to know nothing, and he seems to be in a persistent hunt for definitions, refusing to propose any himself, and to be content to refute the efforts of others—attracting and exasperating, equally.

27. See chapter 5, "Love, That Lenient Interpreter," in Mooney, *On Søren Kierkegaard*.

28. Merleau-Ponty, *In Praise of Philosophy*, 36, discussed by Jolley, "Merleau-Ponty in Praise of Philosophy," 12.

29. For a full discussion of this point, see Anne Margrete Fiskvik's essay on Kierkegaard's attitudes on dance in the present volume.—Ed.

Kierkegaard's Existential Play

Storytelling and the Development of the Religious Imagination in the Authorship

Marcia C. Robinson

Søren Kierkegaard's polyphonous authorship is replete with imagery. From the early polemical writings to the late attack on the established Church, analogies, figures, and stories of all sorts pervade his reflections on God and human existence. Indeed, the prominence and prevalence of stories as biblical, mythical, fictional, or historical accounts of human situations suggest a deliberate desire to make religious philosophy poetry. Kierkegaard does not use all of this imagery, however, just to create philosophical or theological art. Rather, as George Pattison rightly notes, Kierkegaard uses imagery for rhetorical and ethical purposes.[1] That is, in good Ciceronian fashion, he offers his modern cultured readers an imaginative philosophy in a narrative and conversational style in order to persuade them to become persons of faith or "selves before God" (*SKS* 11:129–32, 143, 225–27 / *SUD* 13–16, 26–27, 113–14)—an attitudinal ethic that Pattison convincingly presents as a "regulative ideal."[2] This suggests that for Kierkegaard, faith not only has intrinsic value—as a way of seeing and being in the world that defines human being as human being, which is precisely what makes it the ethical purpose driving his rhetorical aesthetic—but as such, faith also has the capacity to incite deep feeling and desire, and so to serve as its own incentive for action.[3] In other words, faith addresses itself to the whole person—head, heart, and soul, not just head; therefore, the presentation or communication of faith must do likewise. For Kierkegaard, this means that faith requires artistry, not just prose.

Kierkegaard's logician-humorist pseudonym Johannes Climacus confirms this in the *Concluding Unscientific Postscript*, where he discusses "the subjective thinker" or person of faith "as an artist" and faith as an "existence-communication" (*SKS* 7:317–20, 346–47 / *CUP* 1:348–51, 379–80). There, after presenting faith as "an objective uncertainty" on which to stake one's whole life, Climacus says that the person of faith or subjective thinker realizes that "imagination and feeling," not just "dialectical thinking," are needed to exist in, and to communicate, faith because such an existence involves "passion . . . difficulty and contradiction" (*SKS* 7:186–87, 317–20, 346–47 / *CUP* 1:204, 348–51, 379–80). In other words, reason and prose are not sufficient for addressing or relaying passion and life's challenges and paradoxes as they are experienced; poetry *is* sufficient—that is, a dialectical poetry that speaks to head, heart, and soul. Climacus concludes, then, that "to exist is an art" and to communicate the art of living is also an art because the whole person must be involved and addressed in both.

Storytelling and Human Nature

All of this suggests that Kierkegaard's rhetorical strategy depends upon some kind of holistic conception of human nature, a conception that goes hand in glove with the ethical-religious ideal he promotes. This understanding of human nature, though, should not be viewed primarily as a formal or fully developed anthropology or ontology, concerned with objective certainty. Rather, it should be viewed, as Pattison observes, as a practical or "experimental" anthropology, concerned primarily with faith and life.[4] As such, we might see Kierkegaard sketching this "experimental" anthropology in order to identify aspects of human nature that he thinks are central to becoming and being a faithful self and that he thinks must be engaged in order to persuade his readers to pursue such selfhood. That is, with both his own experience and the long Western tradition of conceiving human nature in mind, including the Idealist and Romantic anthropologies of his day, we might see Kierkegaard setting out a working conception of human nature for his "art of living" that considers humans to be sentient, rational, and free beings ("feeling, knowing, and willing"), defined by time, place, and circumstance ("finitude"), yet able to transcend and transform these limitations in problematic situations, at least to some degree, by means of imagination's "infinitizing reflection" (*SKS* 11:145–47, 154–57 / *SUD* 29–31, 38–41). If we take this perspective, we might then see Kierkegaard to be assuming that if his readers possess sufficient imagination, as his premier Christian pseudonym, Anti-Climacus, puts it, he might be able to awaken and develop this capacity in them by presenting narratives of moral and religious conflict that would allow them to envision life's potentiality or ideality in direct relation to its problematic or difficult actuality (*SKS* 12:186 / *PC* 186; *SKS* 11:146–47 / *SUD* 30–31). The tension created by these opposites might in turn "intensify" or sharpen his readers' abilities to "feel" and to "know" the issues at stake and, if they are receptive to the paradigm shift introduced, "to long for" and "to seek" the moral and religious ideal presented (*SKS* 11:147 / *SUD* 30–31). This in effect would make their imaginations' capacities "instar omnium" since their whole persons would be "transformed" by its vision (*SKS* 11:147 / *SUD* 30–31).[5]

With regard to faith, this would mean that Kierkegaard tells stories because he assumes they can awaken his readers' imaginations and heighten their abilities to "feel" and to "know" the ideality and actuality of faith itself. If they are receptive, they will fall in love with faith's goodness and beauty, in spite of its challenges and risks, and be moved to "seek" its possibility and plenitude in the midst of life's difficulties, just as Anti-Climacus's earnest youth does in *Practice in Christianity* (*SKS* 11:146–47 / *SUD* 30–31; *SKS* 12:186–94 / *PC* 186–96). The capacity of the imagination to do this, however, suggests that for Kierkegaard, it cannot be awakened just once. As the capacity for a high level of ethical and religious reflection that influences how one views and responds to existential challenges, the imagination must be cultivated throughout a person's life, indeed always in relation to a person's experiences (*SKS* 12:186–88 / *PC* 187–88). We might conclude, then, that Kierkegaard tells stories about faith and life throughout the authorship, from multiple perspectives, and particularly with actual experiences in mind in the religious discourses, because he wants to help his readers to develop mature religious imaginations, controlled powers for envisioning divine possibility that can keep them "awakened" to, in love with, and thankful for life as divine gift, grace, and task (*SKS* 11:146–47 / *SUD* 30–31; *SKS* 12:186–88 / *PC* 187–88; *SKS* 10:73–75, 138–40, 142–43, 209–10 / *CD* 64–66, 127–129, 131–33, 200; *SKS* 1:312–16 / *CI* 276–80).

Kierkegaard's tempering of imagination with actual experience in this careful union of storytelling and faith suggests that his rhetorical strategy assumes more than a broad, working conception of human nature. His faith-oriented storytelling also assumes that he possesses a good understanding of his audience's actual circumstances, values, fears, concerns, and conceptions of and attitudes toward faith, since these kinds of particularities are the "premises," as he puts it in *The Concept of Irony*, of any type of effective communication (*SKS* 1:313 / *CI* 277).

Audience and Storytelling Method

As is well known, in *The Point of View for My Work as an Author*, Kierkegaard indicates that his primary audience is modern Danish Christians, who, he believes, live in illusions about faith and life (*SKS* 13:15–17; 16:23–38 / *PV* 9–11, 41–56). According to him, ecclesiastical and cultural leaders such as Hans Lassen Martensen and Johan Ludvig Heiberg are largely to blame. As advocates of a right-wing or conservative Hegelianism, a popular intellectual and cultural movement of the day, Martensen and Heiberg encourage their bourgeois followers to believe that the difficulties of faith and the anxieties of modern life are easily resolved in institutional expressions of a divinized reason and in triumphs of artistic genius. In other words, as Kierkegaard sees it, Martensen and Heiberg wrongfully encourage their followers to bury their anxiety and despair in the false security of the Church, the state, the university, and the arts community—a democratized absolutism, or "leveling," as

Kierkegaard puts it—rather than face life in earnest as genuine "selves before God" who learn to be faithful "out over 70,000 fathoms" (*SKS* 20:187–88, NB2:119, n.d. 1847 / *KJN* 4:186–87; *SKS* 8:74–89 / *TA* 77–93; *SKS* 11:117–18 / *SUD* 5–6; *SKS* 7:131, 187, 212, 263 / *CUP* 1:140, 204, 232, 288). For Kierkegaard, Martensen's participation in this activity is particularly disturbing because he is a minister of the Gospel (*SKS* 20:205, NB2:160, n.d. 1847 / *KJN* 4:204; *SKS* 23:179–80, NB17:23, n.d. 1850 / *KJN* 7:182–83; *SKS* 25:28–29, NB26:21, n.d. 1852 / *JP* 6:6807). As such, says Kierkegaard, he should be helping modern Danes to deal with their troubles and to find more honest and authentic ways to live in a disorienting, frightening, uncertain, and fragmented world, not to sneak out of it or to deceive themselves into thinking that all is well (*SKS* 7:402–403 / *CUP* 1:443).[6]

Kierkegaard sees it as his task, then, to call Martensen, Heiberg, and their followers back to a serious engagement of faith and life. He does not do this with loud protestations or direct and vociferous attacks—at least not at first (*SKS* 16:24–29 / *PV* 42–47; *Pap.* X[6] B 171, n.d. 1851 / *JP* 6:6748; compare *SKS* 14:123–217; 13:127–68 / *MLW* 3–126). Rather, realizing the power of Martensen's and Heiberg's eloquence, he pursues an indirect or aesthetically sophisticated course that he believes is appropriate for, and immediately attractive to, his art-loving, theatergoing audience—an approach that he maintains is driven by Socratic purpose and Christian love (*SKS* 16:25–28, 35–36 / *PV* 43–46, 53–55; compare *SKS* 27:334, Papir 323:1, n.d. 1845 / *JP* 1:631; *SKS* 25:83, NB26:80, n.d. 1853 / *JP* 1:824; and *SKS* 23:322, NB18:99, n.d. 1850 / *KJN* 7:328–29). Kierkegaard testifies to this in a journal entry on his now famous tangle with the editor of the *Corsair*, where he refers in Hamlet-fashion to a vision of his dead father: "It seemed to me that my dead father put this demand to me: You must present Christianity in its utmost *rigorousness*, but you must keep it *poetic*, you may attack no one, and on no account may you make yourself out to be better than the most insignificant person" (*Pap.* X[6] B 171, pp. 264–65, n.d. 1851/ *JP* 6:6748, p. 397, my emphasis).

Thus, styling himself "a peculiar kind of poet" (a dialectical poet, we might say), Kierkegaard takes on the role of a Socratic troubadour or court jester, a master storyteller leading a troupe of "actors," or pseudonyms, representing a wide array of lifestyles and perspectives. This allows him to meet his avowedly Christian audience where they take their cultured, and not so cultured, ease in illusions: at Our Lady Church, at the Royal Danish Theater, in the halls of the university, in the galleries of Charlottenborg and the Thorvaldsen Museum, and at Copenhagen's mass attractions and distractions, namely, Tivoli, the Deer Park, and the pages of popular newspapers and scandal sheets (*SKS* 12:281 / *WA* 165; with *SKS* 7:569–73 / *CUP* 1: 625–30; *SKS* 22:250, NB12:178, n.d. 1849 / *JP* 6:6498; *SKS* 25:44, NB26:38, n.d. 1852 / *JP* 6:6809; *Pap.* XI[3] B 53, n.d. 1854 / *JP* 6:6943). In doing so, he not only accommodates them by creating his own eloquence, as Erasmus (Aristotle) says a good orator should (*SKS* 18:236, JJ:305, n.d. 1845 / *KJN* 2:217).[7] But he also sets the stage for "deceiving" them in a "godly" way, as M. Holmes Hartshorne notes, a way that allows his readers to recognize privately what faith truly is and who they truly are, so that they might acknowledge, or perhaps even become receptive to, faith as a risky, but healthy way of living (*SKS* 16:25–29, 35–36 / *PV* 43–47, 53–55).[8]

Pattison's characterization of Kierkegaard's authorship as a "magic theatre," an image he borrows from Kierkegaard's pseudonym Constantin Constantius, is quite apropos (*SKS* 4:30 / *R* 154).[9] For by qualifying his characterization with Martin Thust's older interpretation of the authorship as a "marionette theatre," Pattison not only indicates how Kierkegaard deploys the poetic by appropriating nineteenth-century dramaturgical theory in constructing the pseudonyms and other figures—that is, by making them personifications of ideas, attitudes, or perspectives rather than three-dimensional characters, something familiar to his cultured Christian audience.[10] But he also illuminates the nature of Kierkegaard's role as a Socratic poet. With Thust's assistance, he helps us to see Kierkegaard as a master manipulator of existential dialogue, a "puppeteer" who gives his figural "assistants" or "marionettes" the right words, sensibilities, and timing so that they might engage the reader in just enough Socratic conversation to make themselves and their ethical and religious issues personally compelling.

However, in order to understand more about the rhetorical impact that Kierkegaard makes on his reader, it might also help us to view the authorship as a veritable funhouse of existential activity, teeming at every turn, like a Fellini film, with opportunities for self-exploration, self-examination, and self-assessment.[11] Such a funhouse is not a simple matter of fun and games but more like a fairy tale that uses the comic, the charming, the seductive, or the magical in order to draw the reader into the anxiety, the suffering, the terror, and the death that dog human existence. By viewing Kierkegaard's artistry in this way, our analytical focus shifts away from what he does behind the scenes to the impact of his manipulations on the psyche of the reader experiencing them. This allows us to be attentive to the often strange but attractive nature of his personified ideas, attitudes, and perspectives, something that makes them akin to clowns who know how to unite levity and earnestness. Viewing the authorship as a funhouse also allows us to be attentive to the way he uses imaginative existential situations to induce a free and personally invested response from his readers.[12] Hence, as we follow Kierkegaard's receptive, nineteenth-century Danish readers, running like children through the creative corridors of his literary, yet interactive, Christo-Socratic theater, we too are put in a position to respond to the uncanny voices, strange sounds, and unexpected happenings emerging and reverberating around every corner. All of this puts us in a better position to see the significance of the psychological and experiential for illuminating, enlivening, and instantiating Kierkegaard's ethical or regulative ideal "before God." For such an imaginative situation tells us that the moral and religious ideal cannot be separated from the feeling it induces or the aesthetic form through which it is communicated, since this very feeling and this very form are what allow the reader to be alive to the compelling power of this ideal.[13] The German Romantic poet and playwright Johann Ludwig Tieck helped Kierkegaard to see this early on in the 1830s and early 1840s, while he was developing ideas about good writing and a life view.[14]

As with other Romantics, Kierkegaard was both openly critical and quietly appreciative of Tieck. In his dissertation of 1841, he openly criticizes Tieck for failing to deploy his insights about poetry for moral and religious purposes (*SKS* 1:330–31, 337–39 / *CI* 296–97, 304–6).[15] In his journals and papers from the mid- to late 1830s, though, he appreciates and appropriates Tieck's insights about allegories and fairy tales because they help him to see that storytelling is a kind of Socratic play in which a master storyteller weaves existential themes and issues into the magic and immediacy of a narrative's details, so that an audience might have an entertaining, engaging, yet nonthreatening way to deal with their fears and questions about life and to develop morally and religiously.[16] Tieck's remarks in several works to which Kierkegaard refers, cites, and/or responds make this apparent.

For example, in *The Old Book and the Voyage into the Blue* (*Das alte Buch und die Reise ins Blaue hinein*, 1835), a novella to which Kierkegaard refers in tongue-in-cheek fashion (*SKS* 1:133 / *CI* 74; *SKS* 3:246 / *EO* 2:258), Tieck writes, "The true fairy-tale . . . opens up with its child-like tone and its play with the wondrous, an area of our spirit into which other kinds of art and poetry cannot find their way."[17] In doing so, Tieck continues, it allows us to experience—that is, to see, to sense, to feel, to know—matters that pertain to "our first, and most sacred, relations with nature and the invisible world, the basis of our faith, the elements of our perception, birth, and grave . . . and . . . the origin of good and evil," all things that "cannot be resolved into what we call rational or consequent."[18] This, though, is not the only thing that fairy tales do for us, says Tieck in a fascinating passage from the *Phantasus* (1812–16), a self-selected collection and interpretation of his works that Kierkegaard quotes at length in an 1836 journal entry. As an "allegory" attending to the "double phenomenon" of "good and evil," a fairy tale (*Märchen*) "moves us anew . . . appeals to us in the most diverse forms in every enigma, and . . .—through a struggle—wants to disclose itself to the understanding" (*SKS* 17:76, BB:6 / *KJN* 1:69, as translated at 1:388). Kierkegaard underscores these remarks himself in another journal entry from 1836, where he says, "Does not 1 Corinthians 13:12 . . . imply a recognition of the necessity of *allegory* for our present condition . . . since the whole idea [of life] cannot be contained in the . . . expression.—metaphor—[?]" (*SKS* 27:108, Papir 77 / *JP* 3:3807).[19]

Kierkegaard absorbs all of this in an 1837 journal entry, where he basically credits Tieck for pointing out the significance of storytelling. "Not telling children tales and legends capable of occupying their imaginations," he declares, "leaves room precisely for an anxiety that, not moderated by such narratives, returns with all the greater strength. (Cf. 'Die Verlobung,' short story by Tieck, Dresden 1823, pp. 63 below, 64 and 65. . . .)" (*SKS* 17:131n10, BB:37, n.d. 1837 / *KJN* 1:124n10, continued from previous page). In other words, as products of the imagination (the storyteller's in concert with the readers'), fairy tales deal with life's problems, absurdities, and paradoxes, and seek to unite sense, head, and heart in a magical exploration of these experiences that is at first both wondrous and unnerving, as they re-present them; then cathartic, as they facilitate working through them; and ultimately educative, as they encourage respect for the mystery, fragility, and beauty of life.[20]

It comes as no surprise, then, that in the same journal entry, Kierkegaard immediately puts this insight to work sketching a procedure for telling children stories. Indeed, we can already see in this appropriation of Tieck a way for him to address an adult audience that is equally reticent about growing up spiritually. The procedure of storytelling, writes Kierkegaard, "should be *Socratic*. One must awaken an appetite in [children] to *ask questions*. . . . What matters is to bring *the poetic to bear on their lives in every way*, to exert a magical influence; when least expected, suddenly to let in a glimpse and then to have it vanish again . . . so that the child's soul is electrified by it" (*SKS* 17:124–25, BB:37 / *KJN* 1:118, 119). In other words, as Tieck indicates, "the poetic," as the tale "capable of occupying [children's] imaginations," should naturally and powerfully evoke the "Socratic," as existential questions. Yet "the poetic," as Kierkegaard indicates in this same passage, should also be the exploratory space around the tale that the storyteller creates in order to set the right tone and to keep the audience in the right frame of mind to identify with the story's issues. Tieck helps Kierkegaard to see, then, that "the poetic" and "the Socratic" are of a piece in good storytelling, for the creation of an ethical-religious situation within an inviting, exploratory space gives an audience the opportunity, confidence, and distance it needs to deal with life's difficulties (*SKS* 1:338–40 / *CI* 306–7).[21]

Johannes Climacus, Dialectical Poet: Kierkegaard's Model Storyteller

Kierkegaard immediately puts these insights to work, along with his ideas of good writing and a life view, in the construction of a polyvocal authorship, in which he creates narrative situations that make both his pseudonymous and his signed writings function individually and cooperatively as poetic confessionals, so to speak—that is, as a series of imaginative spaces able to metamorphose into private places for assessing self and life (*SKS* 16:26, 35–36 / *PV* 43–44, 53–55; *Pap.* X^6 B 171, n.d. 1851 / *JP* 6:6748).[22] Johannes Climacus's king and maiden story in the *Philosophical Fragments* (or

Philosophical Crumbs) is particularly exemplary of this unique appropriation of Tieck's storytelling theory.[23] This is not only because Climacus is easily recognizable as the most Socratic of all of Kierkegaard's voices. It is also and primarily because Climacus's king and maiden story functions as the very dialogical poetry or expository-interactive drama of divine love that is needed to awaken the moral and religious imaginations of his Hegelian-Christian audience and to guide them effortlessly into the self-examination and confession needed to develop those imaginations for authentic living.

Climacus takes on the role of Kierkegaard's Socratic-Tieckian storyteller in the preface and first two chapters of the *Fragments*. There "the poetic" becomes both the farce of philosophy and theology that he puts on to relax and to entertain his urbane audience, and the fairy tale that he deploys at the center of this farce in order to get that same audience to question the meaning of God and faith existentially or "Socratically." Climacus stages his farce by offering only "crumbs" of philosophy and "scraps" of theology in comparison to the intellectual "feast" that his Hegelian colleagues Heiberg and Martensen provide. This bit of fun is his way of entering their intellectual and cultural space and establishing himself as someone in need of their expertise so that they will not feel threatened by the questions about God and faith he will ultimately raise. That is, Climacus knows that he cannot disabuse Heiberg, Martensen, and their followers of their "superior" knowledge about God and faith all at once, so he takes the indirect road that Kierkegaard sketches in *The Point of View*, a path that requires a little deception, as indicated earlier (*SKS* 16:24–26, 32, 35–36 / *PV* 42–44, 50, 53–54). Knowing that neither Heiberg nor Martensen considers farce to be a particularly refined form of comedy, he starts appropriately with its unrestrained joking and laughter so that he can appear to be lower than they and they can appear to be higher than he—that is, where aesthetics, not to mention philosophy and theology, are concerned.[24] Farce is also particularly appropriate for Climacus's purposes because, as his pseudonymous colleague Constantin Constantius explains, it requires an audience to participate; precludes it from responding conventionally, particularly in a refined manner; and leaves open-ended the audience's resulting mood (*SKS* 4:34–35 / *R* 159–61; *SKS* 4:218–42 / *PF* 9–36; *SKS* 7:263–64 / *CUP* 1:289). Climacus's strategy is to make the members of his audience comfortable in their intellectual and cultural superiority, in spite of his little taunts, so that they will not suspect there is a personal tragedy hidden in the comedic form of the medieval fairy tale at the heart of his play.[25]

Climacus starts his farce and sets the tone and the context for his storytelling in chapter 2 by characterizing the *Fragments* in the preface as a ridiculous "pamphlet" with no "claim to being a part of the scientific-scholarly endeavor in which one acquires legitimacy . . . as a co-worker, . . . volunteer attendant, . . . a hero or . . . an absolute trumpeter" (*SKS* 4:215 / *PF* 5). This bit of fun and games, with an edge, continues into chapter 1, where he presents the doctrine of the incarnation as the central moral problem of his "thought-project"

(*SKS* 4:218 / *PF* 9). There he appropriates the language of Hamlet's soliloquy in a punning manner, reminiscent of Shakespeare's comedies, in order to offer his audience "crumbs" from Plato's dialogues and "scraps" from doctrinal Christianity, before plagiarizing outright the God-man of the Gospels (*SKS* 4:218–30 / *PF* 9–22). Anticipating his audience's irritation at his flippant treatment of Socrates's reflection on how one knows the truth, and at his even more flippant treatment of Christianity's doctrines of the incarnation and of salvation, Climacus immediately releases the tension by admitting in a self-deprecating manner that he is "the most ludicrous of all project-cranks" for trying to pass off the figure of Jesus Christ and the standard conversion narrative as his own inventions (*SKS* 4:229–30 / *PF* 21–22). This allows him in all of his ineptitude to start again, in chapter 2, with a "poetical venture" (*SKS* 4:230–31 / *PF* 23)—a step down perhaps from trying to be a philosopher of religion to trying to be a simple poet of the religious.

Taking on the role of poet, however, does not preclude Climacus from continuing to be a comic or a logician, for he opens chapter 2 of the *Fragments* with the same jocularity and questioning as in the preface and chapter 1, by teasing his Hegelian audience about their assumption that everyone has surpassed or "goes further" than Socrates (*SKS* 4:231 / *PF* 24) with their God's-eye view of existence and "world historical knowledge" (see *SKS* 7:124–28, 146, 176 / *CUP* 1:133–37, 157–58, 192; compare *SKS* 4:219–20, 227–28 / *PF* 10, 19). This time, however, his teasing sets the stage for delving more deeply into Christ's unique plight as teacher-savior. That is, Climacus figures that if he can get his readers to see the difficulties involved in Socrates's role as teacher, particularly in regard to Socrates's attempt to create a situation of equality with his students, he might also get his audience to see the challenges involved in the God-man's attempt to achieve equality with human beings.

Climacus begins by giving a kind of pseudo-historical account of Socrates as an ordinary man who has nothing on his followers where the truth or the divine is concerned (*SKS* 4:230–31 / *PF* 23). In fact, he says, it is the duty of Socrates as teacher to help his pupils see that they must help each other to long for and seek the truth (*SKS* 4:231–32 / *PF* 24). The situation becomes comical, though, when Plato and Alcibiades attempt to "idolize" Socrates, who, although a lover of his overzealous followers, must display "cold irony [*kolde Ironi*]" (*SKS* 4:231–32 / *PF* 24). With a smile still on his face, Climacus shifts the focus to the God-man by rehearsing—or, as he will later suggest, "plagiarizing" (see *SKS* 4:241 / *PF* 35)—another story familiar to his nineteenth-century audience: the ballad of King Cophetua and the beggar maid (*SKS* 4:233–37 / *PF* 26–30). The point in recounting this story is to provide a Christian parallel to the Socratic one that challenges his audience's identification of God with power—that is, as absolute Spirit or Mind.

The ballad of King Cophetua and the beggar maid is a medieval English tale of an unconventional, idealized, romantic love between an African prince and an impoverished girl variously called Penelophon or Zenelophon.[26] In appropriating it from Shakespeare, who himself appropriated it from earlier troubadours, Climacus knows that he is fooling no one. Indeed, he expects his Hegelian audience to roll their eyes at this, since he is obviously being just as much a *poet crank* as a *thought-project crank*.[27] Climacus, nevertheless, asks them to indulge him because he knows that the best way to challenge their conceptions of God as incarnate power and knowledge is to take the psychological and moral road of "dialectical" poetry, which does not "foreshorten" the difficulties of faith by providing a "reassuring conclusion" (*SKS* 4:229–30, 233–34, 241 / *PF* 20–21, 26, 35; *SKS* 7:263–64, 317–21, 399–403 / *CUP* 1:289, 347–51, 439–43).

Climacus begins innocently enough by encouraging his sophisticated audience to act like children. "Suppose," he says, "there was a king who loved a humble maiden" (*SKS* 4:233 / *PF* 26).[28] That is, imagine that God is a lofty and awe-inspiring king like Cophetua in the ballad, who loves human beings passionately and wants to be their equal in love. Then, in order to give them a sense of human inferiority before God, that is, human sin, which, for Climacus, is more a moral matter than an ontological one, Climacus says: Imagine that human beings are like a poor, dirty, but beautiful, young, peasant woman like Penelophon who has, amazingly, garnered the king's favor. Is this not something to wonder at? Does this not create a huge dilemma for both parties? Is it not impossible for unequals to be happy in love (*SKS* 4:233–34 / *PF* 26–27)? By setting up such a situation and asking questions that highlight the opposition, Climacus immediately creates tension and brings his audience's now awakened imaginations into concert with his own. He then outlines the problem for his readers' consideration, as though it were their job to solve it. By doing so, Climacus gives his audience both intimacy with and distance from the king's and the maiden's dilemma. That is, in accord with the storytelling procedure that Kierkegaard discusses in the aforementioned journal entry from 1837, Climacus gets his audience on board by demonstrating that he has confidence in their intellectual abilities to help him to solve this intriguing but vexing problem since he is "only a poet" (*SKS* 4:233 / *PF* 26; see also *SKS* 17:124–25, BB:37 / *KJN* 1:118–19). However, as it is a "poetical" problem, he initially treats it as though it were a particularly interesting parlor game or salon discussion—something with which Heiberg and Martensen were thoroughly familiar (*SKS* 4:233–42 / *PF* 26–36; compare *SKS* 10:135–36 / *CD* 124–26).

Climacus continues by maintaining that the barrier between the divine king and his beloved maiden-creation rests in the probability that she will not understand him (*SKS* 4:234–37 / *PF* 28–29). In other words, as in the medieval ballad, Climacus's concern is to foreground the psychological anguish and anxiety of both parties. And like the medieval storyteller, Climacus starts with God the King's initial problem of getting the human-maiden to come to him in love, which in itself is no mean feat, since regal power is awe-inspiring, and so off-putting. Once the human-maiden is under the sway of the divine power, though, the real problem emerges for the king, namely, what kind of relationship will facilitate genuine intimacy between them. Climacus immediately divides this second problem into two problems because he realizes that there are only two things that God the King can do to help the human-maiden to understand him and be truly intimate with him. Either God the King must raise her to his regal status or he must lower himself to her humble status.

Assuming that his audience is predisposed to value power, Climacus starts with the former option, but he realizes immediately that it poses a serious problem. He does not get ponderous about it, however; instead, he keeps everything light by gently exposing the contradiction with a bit of levity. That is, picking up the relationship of the God-man to his disciples as set out in chapter 1 of the *Fragments*, Climacus maintains that the disciple-maiden can become "most terribly deceived" only if God the King raises her to his level, because she cannot help but be "spellbound by a change of costume" (*SKS* 4:236 / *PF* 29). That is, like Penelophon and, for that matter, Plato and Alcibiades, she cannot help but to overidentify with God's absolute power to the point of rejecting herself as created, since the costume basically reveals that she is "nothing" for divine power without it (*SKS* 10:138–40 / *CD* 127–29). She does not realize this immediately, though, because at the moment, she is caught up in a dream. Her "prince has come; swept her off her feet; and carried her off in style."[29] According to Climacus, the learner-maiden's forgetfulness of herself does not satisfy God the King because he wants her glorification, not his own, and delights in her as "something" for his love, not his power, as Kierkegaard says elsewhere (*SKS* 10:138–40 / *CD* 127–29; compare *SKS* 7:224 / *CUP* 1:246). Therefore, he must tell her that the benefits of monarchical power are not real benefits—something that can only seem like foolishness as long as power is the definition of divinity—and the perceived means for well-being. Herein, however, is the crux of the matter, for it is difficult for human beings even to recognize God as tenderness and vulnerability when the very concept of divinity is synonymous with domination and power (*SKS* 4:236–37 / *PF* 29–30).

Climacus concludes that this option will not lead to genuine intimacy; therefore, the path of humility must be considered. On this second path, Climacus divests divinity of the very power that ordinarily defines and makes it attractive by showcasing the suffering of the God-man and by bringing his audience closer to the God-man's "wise and unwavering eyes," as Kierkegaard puts it in his discussion of Tieck's fairy-tale figures in *The Concept of Irony* (*SKS* 1:339 / *CI* 306). That is, in this instance, God the King becomes a lowly and despised human being so that he might be the equal of all human beings. Yet, by doing so, he subjects himself to even graver misunderstanding than before, for this time misunderstanding brings with it rejection, abuse, and death (*SKS* 238–40 / *PF* 31–34). God the King suffers all of the risks of trying to be the equal of his beloved but fragile human creation, while also working desperately not to crush or offend them (*SKS* 4:238–39 / *PF* 32). This makes God an "unhappy," even tortured "consciousness," to use Hegel's terms,[30] particularly when one gazes at him, in all of the vulnerability of his love, as he is brutally beaten and executed by the very ones from whom he seeks love (*SKS* 4:232–33, 238–39 / *PF* 25–26, 32–33). It is futile, however, says Climacus, to try to dissuade this king to give up this position of despised and condemned servant, even out of sincere concern for him, for doing so will only make one his adversary, so that he will say, "To think that you could become so unfaithful to me and grieve love in this way; so you love only the omnipotent one . . . not him who humbled himself in equality with you" (*SKS* 4:239 / *PF* 33).

With this subtle shift to the personal pronoun "you," Climacus brings the tension in the story to its climax, for his "imaginary [re]construction" of the gospel story has not "slacken[ed] the tension of the conflict in a reassuring conclusion, but by means of its teasing form [has made his readers] even more contemporary [with it]" (*SKS* 7:263–64 / *CUP* 1:289), so that they are now confronted with a decisive or "transformative" moment.[31] They must now admit to themselves how they truly feel about the Christian God. Will they view Climacus's conception of the divine as a thoroughgoing nightmare and denounce Climacus for disrupting their dream? Or will they allow his little existential play to be the beginning of a new life of faith, fueled by a grace-imbued imagination? As Kierkegaard the dialectical poet sees it, these are some of the weighty questions that a little storytelling can facilitate.

Notes

1. George Pattison, *Kierkegaard's Upbuilding Discourses: Philosophy, Theology, Literature* (London: Routledge, 2002), 93–106, 113–18, 125–32, 141–42, 145, 147–67. Compare *SKS* 16:72 / *PV* 93. See also Grethe Kjær, "The Role of Folk and Fairy Tales in Kierkegaard's Authorship," in *Kierkegaard on Art and Communication*, ed. George Pattison (Basingstoke, U.K.: Macmillan, 1992), 78–87.

2. Pattison, *Kierkegaard's Upbuilding Discourses*, 93–117, esp. 95–106, 112–16.

3. Compare Immanuel Kant, *Critique of Practical Reason*, trans. Lewis White Beck (New York: Macmillan, 1985), 30–33, 74–92, 128–36.

4. Pattison, *Kierkegaard's Upbuilding Discourses*, 68–78, esp. 75–76, 78.

5. See M. Jamie Ferreira, *Transforming Vision: Imagination and Will in Kierkegaardian Faith* (Oxford: Clarendon Press, 1991), 62–84, 87–97, 116–25; John Lippitt, *Humour and Irony in Kierkegaard's Thought* (New York: St. Martin's Press, 2000), 104–20.

6. Kierkegaard also blames a family friend and one-time family pastor, Bishop Jakob Peter Mynster, for deceiving Danish cultured Christians into thinking that Christianity is soft, secure, and comfortable.

7. See Marjorie O'Rourke Boyle, "Evangelism and Erasmus," in *The Cambridge History of Literary Criticism*, ed. Glyn Norton, vol. 3: *The Renaissance* (Cambridge, U.K.: Cambridge University Press, 1999), 49nn30–32, for a brief discussion of the idea of accommodation in Erasmus with reference to his *Ratio verae theologiae* and *Paraclesis*; compare 1 Cor. 9:19–22; Desiderius Erasmus, *Paraclesis*, in *Readings in Christian Humanism*, ed. Joseph M. Shaw et al. (1982; Minneapolis, Minn.: Fortress Press, 2009), 293–94.

8. M. Holmes Hartshorne, *Kierkegaard, Godly Deceiver: The Nature and Meaning of His Pseudonymous Writings* (New York: Columbia University Press, 1990), 6–7.

9. George Pattison, *Kierkegaard: The Aesthetic and the Religious, from the Magic Theatre to the Crucifixion of the Image*, 2nd edition (London: SCM Press, 1999), 95–124.

10. Ibid., esp. 95–96, 120–21; Pattison, *Kierkegaard's Upbuilding Discourses*, 162.

11. I have in mind here Fellini's film *La Strada* (1954). See also Pattison's Bakhtinian reading of the carnivalesque nature of Kierkegaard's works in *Kierkegaard and the Quest for Unambiguous Life, between Romanticism and Modernism: Selected Essays* (Oxford: Oxford University Press, 2013), 30–57. (In addition, see Pattison's essay in this volume.—Ed.)

12. Compare Edward F. Mooney, *On Søren Kierkegaard: Dialogue, Polemics, Lost Intimacy, and Time* (Aldershot, U.K.: Ashgate, 2007), 10–11, 178–79, 186–87, 205–10, 225; Edward F. Mooney, "Pseudonyms and 'Style,'" in *The Oxford Handbook of Kierkegaard*, ed. John Lippitt and George Pattison (Oxford: Oxford University Press, 2013), 207, 208–9; Joseph Westfall, *The Kierkegaard Author: Authorship and Performance in Kierkegaard's Literary and Dramatic Criticism* (Berlin: De Gruyter, 2007).

13. This does not mean there is only one aesthetic form through which faith might be presented and experienced. It just means that whatever aesthetic form the religious ideal takes, and whatever feeling it induces, must match or be appropriate to the ideal itself.

14. Marcia C. Robinson, "Tieck: Kierkegaard's 'Guadalquivir' of Open Critique and Hidden Appreciation," in *Kierkegaard and His German Contemporaries: Literature and Aesthetics*, Tome 3: *Literature and Aesthetics*, ed. Jon Stewart, Kierkegaard Research: Sources, Reception and Resources, vol. 6 (Aldershot, U.K.: Ashgate, 2008), 295–310.

15. See also ibid., 278–82.

16. See also ibid., 282–95.

17. Ludwig Tieck, *Das alte Buch und die Reise ins Blaue hinein*, in *Das alte Buch und die Reise ins Blaue hinein: Der Alte vom Berge. Eigensinn und Laune. Die Gesellschaft auf dem Lande* (Berlin: G. Reimer, 1853), as translated in Roger Paulin, *Ludwig Tieck: A Literary Biography* (Oxford: Clarendon Press, 1985), 310.

18. Ibid.

19. 1 Cor. 13:12, NRSV: "For now we see in a mirror, dimly, but then we will see face to face. Now I know only in part; then I will know fully, even as I have been fully known."

20. Robinson, "Tieck," 288–93.

21. Ibid., 284–85.

22. Ibid., 295–310.

23. Ibid., 295, 309. Note also that Kierkegaard's *Philosophical Fragments, or A Fragment of Philosophy* is now, with the lead of Alastair Hannay, Edward F. Mooney, and Marilyn Piety, being alternatively translated as *Philosophical Crumbs, or A Crumb of Philosophy*. See, for example, Søren Kierkegaard, *Repetition and Philosophical Crumbs*, trans. M. G. Piety, Oxford World Classics (Oxford: Oxford University Press, 2009). (For further discussion of this retranslation of Kierkegaard's title, see Mooney's essay in this volume.—Ed.)

24. Robert Leslie Horn, "Positivity and Dialectic: A Study of the Theological Method of Hans Lassen Martensen," Th.D. diss., Union Theological Seminary of New York, 1969, 121–23, 150–61.

25. The reference here is to comedy in the classical sense, as a situation or story in which a conflict resolves favorably or happily. However, I have mainly used references to the comic to mean anything that is funny, which is how Kierkegaard used the category of "the comic," as noted by Lippitt, *Humour and Irony in Kierkegaard's Thought*, 63.

26. See n. 4 on v. 70 of "King Cophetua and the Beggar-Maid," in Thomas Percy, *Reliques of Ancient English Poetry: Consisting of Old Heroic Ballads, Songs, and Other Pieces of Our Earlier Poets; Together with Some Few of Later Date*, 2 vols., ed. J. V. Prichard (London: George Bell, 1876), 1:138 [bk. 2, ballad 6].

27. See, e.g., Pattison, *Kierkegaard: The Aesthetic and the Religious*, 16–26, 122.

28. In this instance, I use David F. Swenson's more succinct translation, as found in Robert Bretall, ed., *A Kierkegaard Anthology* (1946; Princeton, N.J.: Princeton University Press, 1973), 165. The Hongs render "en ringe Pige" as "a maiden of lowly station in life."

29. These lines are from Disney's animated feature-length films *Snow White and the Seven Dwarfs* and *Robin Hood*, which were released in 1937 and 1973, respectively.

30. G. W. F. Hegel, *Phenomenology of Spirit*, trans. A. V. Miller (Oxford: Oxford University Press, 1977), 126–31, 456–57.

31. See Ferreira, *Transforming Vision*, 114–25.

Kierkegaard's Christian Bildungsroman

Joakim Garff

> He walks like a stranger, and yet he seems to be at home, for
> through the imagination he is always at home with this image,
> which he desires to resemble. (*SKS* 12:188 / *PC* 189)

"When it was a matter of boldness, enthusiasm, zeal, almost to the border
of madness, what was this pen not able to present!" So exclaims Kierkegaard, with joyous breathlessness, in *The Point of View for My Work as an
Author* (*SKS* 15:52 / *PV* 72). As one can see, it is not intractable paradoxes
he falls into a swoon over, not the silent plains of the conceptual or the infinity of combinations, but rather the pen's artistic appeal to the senses in a
thoroughgoing and not insignificant sense. It is hardly a risky claim to make
that it is precisely thanks to this eminent command of the rhetorical register
that Kierkegaard *is* Kierkegaard. Just as Hegel's thought characteristically
operates on such a high level of abstraction that association and imagination must rush to the rescue of readers when they are just about to succumb
under the strenuousness of the concept, so almost the opposite is the case
with Kierkegaard.[1] No sooner have you been set down in the midst of a
complicated dialectical operation than you are sent off on a rejuvenating
jaunt into a text that expounds itself expressively, brightly, and breezily, as all
the while the compact mass of the concept transforms into images, expands
allegorically, or dons the down-to-earth form of the fable. One could therefore fittingly call Kierkegaard's philosophical discourse, which continually
oscillates between concept and image, a discourse of *visualization*, while his
theological discourse is a kind of discourse of *autopsy*, insofar as it attempts
to suspend the time between Jesus of Nazareth and the modern reader.

Kierkegaard's aesthetic practice associates him with a famous pair of concepts in the aesthetic tradition: namely, the concepts of the beautiful and
the sublime, which, particularly since the appearance of Kant's *Critique of
Judgment* (*Kritik der Urteilskraft*, 1790), have been a constant part of the
curriculum in modern aesthetic theory.[2] The beautiful, according to Kant, is
everything that merely *pleases* but never *affects* the viewer in a deeper sense,
and thus awakens neither anxiety nor desire in the viewer but instead engenders a contemplative state that may very well look a little like happiness.
This experience of beauty stands in contrast to the experience of the sublime,

which has an almost violent effect upon the imagination. The sublime is the catastrophic, the awesome and anxiety-inducing: mountains in sudden motion, a foaming sea, earthquakes, fatal phenomena that completely breach the familiarity of civilization and momentarily throw humanity's self-evident place in the world into doubt.[3]

For obvious reasons, a text cannot be sublime in the Kantian sense, but it can imitate or mimic the sublime by shaking its reader rhetorically. Countless examples could be used to demonstrate that this is what the Kierkegaard-ian texts aim to do, but let me just cite a journal entry from 1845, where Kierkegaard, speaking of the ideal of the art of preaching, remarks, "If no earthquake, no volcanic eruption, no plague, war, etc., teaches people about the uncertainty of everything, then daily use of the religious discourse ought to have the same effect" (*SKS* 18:275, JJ:407 / *KJN* 2:254). With this, Kierke-gaard is not merely far-removed from the values of enlightened humanism and the norms of cultivated society; he has also announced the discourse of sublimity that he practices in his writing. And just as the text mimics the sublime, so must the reader mimic the text.

This is confirmed, almost to excess, by the third section of *Practice in Christianity*, which Kierkegaard published on September 27, 1850, and, at the last minute, attributed to Anti-Climacus. The work consists of three sections or numbers, with three separate title pages and three separate but identical prefaces, all of which are signed "S.K." The third of these sections is presented on the chapter title page as "Christian Development" and thereby calls to mind formation and the Bildungsroman. In this third section, which is divided into seven chapters of varying length, the third chapter is introduced with the following prayer:

> Lord Jesus Christ! How various are the many things to which a per-son can feel drawn, but there is one thing to which no one ever felt naturally drawn, and that is to suffering and abasement. We human beings think that we ought to flee from that as long as possible and in any case must be forced into it. But you, our Savior and Redeemer, you the abased one, who will not force anyone, and least of all into what must be a person's highest honor: to dare to want to be like you—would that the image of you in your abasement might stand before us so vividly, so awakening and persuasive, that we will feel ourselves drawn to you in lowliness, drawn to want to be like you in lowliness, you who from on high will draw all to yourself. (*SKS* 12:170 / *PC* 167)

The prayer is not just a prayer. It also contains elements of the tactic with which Kierkegaard intends to overcome the resistance with which the so-called natural person meets suffering and abasement. And just as such resistance is natural, so too is the resistance of the text to the artistic, the artificial, the cunning. As the text demonstrates, the natural person's resistance to suffering and abasement is overcome precisely through an "image," one that makes such suffering and humiliation not merely "vivid" and "awakening" but also so "persuasive" that the reader is drawn into wanting to resemble the abased one.

Although it is imperative for Anti-Climacus to maintain the "prototype's" radical and fundamental difference from an epoch that aestheticizes the Christian categories, the countermove he initiates against such an aestheticization is itself utterly aesthetic, insofar as his text persistently addresses the reader's powers of visualization. Symptomatic in this respect is the marked tendency, to which Anti-Climacus is prone, of appealing often and excessively to the eyes and the gaze. "Is this sight not able to move you?" (*SKS* 12:173 / *PC* 171; compare *SKS* 12:174 / *PC* 171) he declares after an account of the debased savior, an account that is accompanied on its passage through the text by persistent comments on the impact this particular "sight" has upon the reader. "So look at him once again, him the abased one! What effect does this sight produce? Should it not be able to move you in some way to want to suffer in a way akin to his suffering?" (*SKS* 12:176 / *PC* 174; compare *SKS* 12:176, 180 / *PC* 173, 178). With this *iconography* the reader will be moved—"not," it should be noted, "to tears" (*SKS* 12:174 / *PC* 171) and other sentimentality but rather *away from* the text and thence to action *outside* the text. Only there, on the outside, is this particular reading concluded in earnest.

In parallel with this frequent appeal to the reader's readiness to visualize, the text sets out to exclude our well-known, all-too-well-known image of Christ. Sounding almost like a hypnotist's patter, it says, "If possible, forget for a moment everything you know about him; tear yourself away from the perhaps apathetic habitual way in which you know about him; approach it as if it were the first time you heard the story of his abasement" (*SKS* 12:176 / *PC* 174). Even if this gesture does not have the desired effect, the text promptly offers a radical alternative: "Or if you think you are not able to do that, well, then, let us help ourselves in another way, let us use the help of a child, a child who is not warped by having learned by rote a simple school assignment about Jesus Christ's suffering and death, a child who for the first time hears the story—let us see what the effect will be, if only we tell it fairly well" (*SKS* 12:176 / *PC* 174). One notes how Anti-Climacus carefully maintains that the child is not spoiled by the hackneyed interactions with the divine that follow from the mechanical rote learning in schooling but, on the contrary, that the child possesses the "primitivity" that is the alpha and omega of the religious condition. Anti-Climacus continues, "Imagine a child, and then delight this child by showing it some of those artistically insignificant but for children very valuable pictures one buys in the shops" (*SKS* 12:177 / *PC* 174).[4] Various pictures are laid out in front of the child—one of Napoleon, one of William Tell, and so forth—which the adult accompanies with lively, horizon-broadening explanations. Just as the child, with "unspeakable delight," lets its gaze leap from picture to picture, its eye is suddenly caught by one "that you have deliberately placed among the others; it portrays the one crucified" (*SKS* 12:177 / *PC* 174–75). At first the child cannot relate to the picture, which it puzzles over and asks "why he is hanging from such a tree" (*SKS* 12:177 / *PC* 175). When the adult explains that the picture depicts an execution, the child becomes greatly affected, to such a degree that it becomes "anxious and afraid for his parents and the world and himself" and forgets all about the other pictures, for "as it says in the ballad, they will all turn their backs, so different is this picture" (*SKS* 12:177 / *PC* 175).

The sight of one crucified is, in a Kantian sense, a sublime moment, filled to the brim with strangeness and horror, and thus capable of carrying the child away from the familiar, well-known world that Anti-Climacus has broken down. Special emphasis is placed on the way this breakdown brings about immense alienation within the child, whose shock, understandably enough, increases when one tells it "that this crucified one is the Savior of the world" (*SKS* 12:177 / *PC* 175). Once this one *picture* (*billede*) has pushed itself in front of all the others and has thereby wholly concretely made itself into a *prototype* (*forbillede*), the adult must then furnish the child with the "prototype's" more specific religious character:

> See, now is the moment; if you have not already made too powerful an impression upon the child, then tell him now about the one who was lifted up, who from on high will draw all to himself. Tell the child that this one who was lifted up is [the crucified]. Tell the child that he was love, that he came to the world out of love, took upon himself the form of a lowly servant, lived for only one thing—to love and to help people, especially all those who were sick and sorrowful and suffering and unhappy. Tell the child what happened to him in his lifetime, how one of the few who were close to him betrayed him, the few others denied him, and everyone else insulted and mocked him, until finally they nailed him to the cross—as shown in the picture. . . . Tell it very vividly to the child, as if you yourself had never heard it before or had never told it to anyone before; tell it as if you yourself had composed the whole story, but do not forget any feature of it that has been preserved, except that you may forget as you are telling it that it is preserved. (*SKS* 12:178 / *PC* 176)

Anti-Climacus's recurring imperatives ("Tell! Tell!") signify that the occasion is no longer—as with Climacus in *Philosophical Fragments*[5]—a laconic, world-historical *nota bene* but rather a dramatically presented narrative sequence, which takes shape through the narrative's almost feverish engagement in what is narrated. Whereas for Climacus the moment was a paradoxical point that evades both comprehension and vision, with Anti-Climacus it becomes expressive and plastic: the moment (*Øieblikket*, "the glance of an eye") unites with the eye's glance when it is exposed to an image that works by grasping, and grasps by making itself present. At the sight of this bloody image the child loses its sense of "time and place" (*SKS* 12:186 / *PC* 186) to such a degree that it quite forgets that the event itself, the crucifixion, took place "over eighteen hundred years [ago]" (*SKS* 12:179 / *PC* 177).

Bildungsroman and Visualizing Bildungsroman

The experiment with the child constitutes the first part of the sequence that I, in a hybrid translation, call Kierkegaard's *billeddannelsesroman*. The hybrid is formed by combining the word *billeddannelse*, which can be translated as "image formation," with the word *dannelsesroman*, which in English is rendered by the German term *Bildungsroman*. Perhaps one could render *billeddannelsesroman* as "image formation novel" or "picture creation," but in what follows I prefer to use the term "visualizing Bildungsroman." The point is that the images that are formed transform the one who forms these images. Hence it is no coincidence that the word *Bild*, "picture," occupies such a prominent place in *Bildung*.

Formation novels and visualizing formation novels are both in the business of bringing an identity-formation to consummation. Such an identity-formation normally depends upon a productive exchange between individualization and socialization. A person never becomes herself *by* herself and *for* herself but always via detours, by historical, cultural, and many other detours, in other words, via the world. It is this process that the Bildungsroman presents in epic fashion, when it has its protagonist—typically a young, intellectual man—go out into the world in order to fulfill his own, natural talents and little by little bring himself into balance with himself and his surroundings. The Bildungsroman is a diverse and folkloristic undertaking, with an extensive gallery of personae—artists, jugglers, magicians, sensual women, and other captivating figures—wherein the protagonist (and the reader!) can see themselves reflected.[6] After an enthusiastic odyssey through foreign milieux and cultures, the protagonist returns home as a *clarified* version of himself and has, through his return, carried out the three-phase compositional scheme *at home—homeless—home* by which the Bildungsroman is guided and with which it consolidates its capacity to edify.

Kierkegaard never wrote a Bildungsroman; indeed, it is a matter of debate whether any text among the mountains of written paper he left behind can meaningfully be called a *novel*. It is indisputable, however, that Kierkegaard thinks in character types and populates his work with *textual characters* that he either imports from the rich stock of world literature or single-handedly conjures up from the magical darkness of the ink bottle. The presence of these textual characters in Kierkegaard's discourse is not merely due to Kierkegaard's wanting to *illustrate* his philosophical or theological concerns in them but goes considerably further and reveals the long-neglected fact that Kierkegaard understands the person as a being that, in its encounter with stories—be it in myth, Greek tragedy, or biblical accounts—is endowed with a *narrative identity*, which it is inscribed into and is being interpreted through. This is true of the young man in *Repetition*, whose self-understanding is fundamentally altered after reading the book of Job; it is true of a number of characters in *Fear and Trembling*, where the account of Abraham's willingness to sacrifice Isaac is maintained in the most varied ways, but it is true also in the upbuilding production, where the reader is exposed to and enclosed by the New Testament narrative, inasmuch as the exposure reflects "the law" and the enclosure corresponds to "the gospel."

The conception of *Christian* identity-formation that is developed and radicalized, work by work, throughout the authorship is also inextricably bound up with the New Testament narrative: in Christian identity-formation, one receives one's identity by placing oneself as a narrative possibility at the disposal of the God that came into being in Jesus of Nazareth and has sealed his fate. In the comprehensive program of formation that Kierkegaard offers in his authorship, there thus stands a *theological* aim of actualizing, within the individual person, the relationship to self and to God given in the Christian narrative.

There is thus a double identity-formation in Kierkegaard: first, *human* identity-formation, which implies that the person must relate to himself or herself as a more or less realized self-relation; second, *Christian* identity-formation, which entails that the person in such a self-relationship must also relate to himself or herself as a not-yet-actualized narrative possibility. Vigilius Haufniensis and Anti-Climacus represent the double formation in their respective programmatic declarations; the former, when he demonstrates in *The Concept of Anxiety* that the task is to make a person into "the true and the whole man" (*SKS* 4:325 / *CA* 18); the latter, when he decrees in *The Sickness unto Death* that "the self must be broken in order to become itself" (*SKS* 11:179 / *SUD* 65).

The New Testament narrative is the prism through which this breaking of the subject takes place, and Anti-Climacus has thereby, with brilliant, anachronistic precision, announced the deconstruction of the subject as practiced in the late Kierkegaard's upbuilding discourses and the late production overall. This deconstruction is practiced in various ways, but if one turns one's gaze toward the next phase in the visualizing Bildungsroman, one will, I think, be able to get an impression of this theological praxis.

"The Image of Perfection"

With this background in mind, let me return to the third section of *Practice in Christianity*, whose fourth chapter portrays the child's further development.

The chapter does not refer expressly to the previous one, but it seems evident that the two chapters belong together in narrative terms and fall under the category "Christian Development" announced by the section heading. The child is no longer a child, but a youth. From the stage directions that introduce him, it appears that the earlier "vision" of the abased savior continues to work as an indelible *afterimage* and lies behind the life view the youth goes by in the world. The child, hypnotically thrown into his state of contemporaneity with Jesus of Nazareth, had certainly expressed his astonishment that God did not step in and prevent the horrors of the crucifixion, but when the adult, by way of response, had spoken of the resurrection on the third day, the account made no particular impression on the child, who is absorbed by the story of Jesus's suffering and death to such a degree that it simply "will not feel like hearing about the glory that followed" (*SKS* 12:179 / *PC* 177). After a period of wishing to avenge Jesus and put his tormentors to death, the child regained his composure, but he has by no means forgotten that impression from childhood; now he simply interprets the impression in a different way (see *SKS* 12:180 / *PC* 178).

Before the next phase of the visualizing Bildungsroman unfolds, Anti-Climacus inserts an anthropological statement into his text: "Every human being possesses to a higher or lower degree a capability called the power of the imagination, a power that is the first condition for what becomes of a person" (*SKS* 12:186 / *PC* 186). One understands that the youth in the visualizing Bildungsroman we are considering is in possession of precisely such an imaginative capacity, thanks to which he is able to comprehend "some image of perfection (ideal)," which can *either* be "handed down by history" and thereby have "the actuality of being" *or* be "formed by the imagination itself" and thus be a nonactual entity, a mere "thought-actuality" (*SKS* 12:186 / *PC* 186–87). Anti-Climacus informs us, "To this image . . . the youth is now drawn by his imagination, or his imagination draws this image to him. He becomes infatuated with this image. . . . He does not abandon it, even in sleep, this image that makes him sleepless" (*SKS* 12:186 / *PC* 187).[7]

One of imagination's strengths is that it is able to suspend time and space, but its weakness is that it places the youth at a distance from the sufferings that are in fact associated with wanting to actualize the ideal. Anti-Climacus explains, "In one sense the imagination's image or the image that the imagination depicts or maintains is still nonactuality; with regard to adversities and sufferings, it lacks the actuality of time and of temporality and or earthly life" (*SKS* 12:187 / *PC* 187). How it comes about that the nonactual "image" or "picture" depicted by the imagination nonetheless does impose the sufferings of actuality upon the youth is described in the following passage, in which the youth experiences a decisive metamorphosis:

> His appearance shows it; his eyes see nothing of what lies closest around him, they seek only that image; he walks like a dreamer, and

yet one can see by the fire and the flame in his eyes that he is wide
awake; he walks like a stranger, and yet he seems to be at home, for
through the imagination he is always at home with this image, which
he desires to resemble. And just as it so beautifully happens with
lovers that they begin to resemble each other, so the young man is
transformed in likeness to this image, which imprints or impresses
itself on all his thought and on every utterance by him, while he,
to repeat, with his eyes directed to this image—has not watched his
step, has not paid attention to where he is. He wants to resemble this
image; he is already beginning to resemble it—and now he suddenly
discovers the surrounding world of actuality in which he is standing
and the relation of this surrounding world to himself. (*SKS* 12:188 /
PC 189)

It is a subtle fact in the visualizing Bildungsroman that as a result of his
infatuation with the image, the youth loses his orientation in the empirical world and is thereby exposed to the very suffering that his "imaginary
image" had kept at a safe distance from him. Like the lovers who over time
come to resemble each other, the youth is little by little transformed by his
"imaginary image," which has occupied him to such an extent that the image
visibly "imprints or impresses itself" in his whole appearance, his thought
and speech: the *iconic fixation* has brought about his own *iconification*.

As already mentioned, the typical Bildungsroman brings to fruition a
process of individuation, the sequential structure of which follows the topography of the formation journey and can therefore be reproduced with the
phrases *at home—homeless—home*. The visualizing Bildungsroman deconstructs this schema, inasmuch as it adds a dialectical Christian qualification
to the second phase and postpones the third phase to a more or less metaphorical eternity. We thus came to know of the youth that he went about
as a *stranger* among people but was nonetheless *at home* because he was at
home with the image he so passionately wanted to resemble (compare *SKS*
12:188 / *PC* 189). Precisely this modality, being *a stranger and yet at home*,
is the authentic, Christian modality in this world, a world in which only
the inauthentic Christian can feel at home: "So the youth goes out into the
world with this image before his eyes. He does not need to do what piety
felt the urge to do—to walk the long way to the Holy Land in order to put
himself back in time, because this image is so vivid to him that in another
sense he still can be said to have journeyed abroad, although he remains in
his customary place in the old surroundings—but occupied solely with wanting to resemble this image" (*SKS* 12:192 / *PC* 193). This allegorization of the
pilgrimage, which is carried over from the outer, real world to the subject's
interiority, corresponds to suspension instituted by the "imaginary image" of
the time between the youth and Jesus of Nazareth. The youth shall *not* set out
on the long journey to the Holy Land, *not* give himself over to homelessness,

because he already *is* homeless in this world—precisely thanks to the image whose existential configuration he increasingly takes on. With a paradoxical logic of its own, the youth also undergoes a metamorphosis into an "old person," "although not many years have passed" (*SKS* 12:194 / *PC* 195). The visualizing Bildungsroman's ontogenetic final stage is a reality, and Anti-Climacus can conclude:

> In a certain sense the youth's imagination has deceived him, but indeed, if he himself *wills*, it has not deceived him to his detriment, it has deceived him into the truth; by means of a deception, it has, as it were, played him into God's hands. . . . A shudder, it is true, may go through him for a moment as he now considers the matter, but abandon the image—no, that he cannot persuade himself to do. On the other hand, if he cannot persuade himself to abandon the image, he cannot escape the suffering either. . . . So he does not abandon the image but cheerfully enters the suffering into which he is being led. . . .
>
> He perseveres until he dies: then he passed his test. He himself became the image of perfection he loved, and the imagination has truly not deceived him any more than Governance. (*SKS* 12:189–91 / *PC* 190–91)

Exit: Brushes, Palette, Pen, Paper

Kierkegaard's critique of the cultivated society, a critique that gathers strength over time and becomes one of the essential preconditions for the so-called struggle with the Church, is a chapter in itself but is rooted in a Christian quarrel with every nonreligious body of thought that assumes the person *herself* has at her disposal the crucial conditions for emancipating herself from her more or less self-imposed immaturity and becoming herself—and thus, under her own power, escaping her existential *homelessness* and coming *home*, as the terminology of the formation novel would have it. Kierkegaard wishes to keep existence open, such that every time is accessible for God, who is the person's creator and therefore reserves the sovereign right to compose poetically with his creation—terrible, joyful, sublime.

That it is the iconic representation of Christ that is transposed into the youth's imitation should have made it clear how the aesthetic (image) is active in the religious (prototype) or, if you will, how deeply *mimesis* is connected with *imitatio*. So it is not for nothing that the difference between the words "picture" (*billede*) and "prototype" (*forbillede*) is only the little prefix *for-*, which Anti-Climacus never remarks upon. Nor does he note that the difference between the words "draw" or "attract" (*drage*) and "deceive" (*bedrage*) is only *be-*, and that there is thus only a hair's breadth between the redemptive activity carried out by the divine and the manipulative practice characteristic of a seducer.

However, in his portrayal of the movement of the icon-fixated youth toward the sufferings of actuality, Anti-Climacus himself presumably senses how his portrayal has suddenly acquired an alarming resemblance to a seduction story. In any case, he finds himself compelled to include this reassuring remark: "If the power that governs human life were a seductive power, then at this moment it would mockingly say of this youth: Look, now he is trapped" (*SKS* 12:188 / *PC* 189). Yet Governance does not mock in this way, so long as "the power that governs human life is love" (*SKS* 12:189 / *PC* 189). This is of course an upbuilding thought, but—one may well object—in itself it is absolutely no guarantee that the *text* in which the dangers of seduction are repudiated does not *itself* have seduction within its power and perhaps practices it most effectively precisely by downplaying it. And perhaps, when all is said and done, that is the only way one can seriously play the reader "into God's possession."

The visualizing Bildungsroman testifies to Kierkegaard's highly ambivalent relationship toward art, reminiscent of the "sympathetic antipathy" that in *The Concept of Anxiety* is a fundamental determination of anxiety's ambiguous essence. Later in *Practice in Christianity* this tension between aesthetic theory and aesthetic practice becomes dramatically exposed. In the work's penultimate section, Anti-Climacus mocks the sermon that gives in to something as aesthetic as "contemplation" and thereby holds itself at an existential distance from "the prototype": "by observing I go into the object (I become objective)," with the result that "I leave myself or go away from myself (I cease to be subjective)" (*SKS* 12:228 / *PC* 234). It is precisely these characteristics that the experiment with the child's gaze, which got lost in the image of the crucified one, refutes in the starkest terms. If he were not so wrapped up in the image, the youth would never have wished to have become subjective.

The opposition between, on the one hand, "observation" or "admiration" as the merely objective, and, on the other hand, "imitation" as the subjective, true attitude toward the "prototype" gives Anti-Climacus the opportunity to speak about "Christian art" (*SKS* 12:246 / *PC* 254). In this regard he stresses how impossible it would be for him to portray Christ; indeed, as he explains further:

> [It is] incomprehensible to me from whence an artist would gain the calmness, or incomprehensible to me is the calmness with which an artist has sat year in and year out occupied in the work of painting Christ—without having it occur to him whether Christ would wish to be painted, would wish to have his portrait, however idealized it became, depicted by his masterly brush. I do not comprehend how the artist would maintain his calm, that he would not notice Christ's

displeasure, would not suddenly throw it all out, brushes and paints, far, far away, just as Judas did with the thirty pieces of silver, because he suddenly understood that Christ has required only imitators [i.e., disciples]. . . . I do not comprehend it; the brush would have fallen out of my hand the very second I was about to begin; very likely I would never have been the same again.

I do not comprehend this calmness of the artist in this kind of work. . . .

Yes, this is incomprehensible to me; I repeat, it is incomprehensible to me. (*SKS* 12:246–48 / *PC* 254–56)

Perhaps what is most incomprehensible is that it all seems so incomprehensible to Anti-Climacus. If the painter must throw out his paints and palettes, then Anti-Climacus, too, should throw out his pens and papers, for they are both producing "Christian art." Nonetheless, or perhaps especially because of this, he continues indignantly, "Soon it will have gone so far that people must make use of art in the most various ways to help get Christendom to show at least some sympathy with Christianity" (*SKS* 12:248 / *PC* 256).

Anti-Climacus is right. Except that the moment will not come soon, but has already long since arrived and has come thanks, among others, to Anti-Climacus, who drills Christianity into his unchristian reader.

As art, indeed, can do.

Notes

Translated by Patrick Stokes.

1. Compare Jørgen Carlsen, "'Her rulles,'" *Slagmark*, no. 4 (Aarhus 1985): 28–45; see 33.

2. Compare Jørgen Dehs, "Ikke Phantasiens Kunstrige Væven, men Tankens Gysen," *Slagmark*, no. 4 (Aarhus 1985): 46–59.

3. Compare ibid., 48–49.

4. On this passage, see also the essay by Ragni Linnet in this volume.—Ed.

5. "Even if the contemporary generation had not left anything behind except these words: 'We have believed that in such and such a year the god appeared in the humble form of a servant, lived and taught among us, and then died'—that is more than enough. The contemporary generation would have done what is needful, for this little announcement, this world-historical *nota bene*, is enough to become an occasion for someone who comes later, and the most prolix report can never in all eternity become more for the person who comes later" (*SKS* 4:300 / *PF* 104).

6. Compare Johnny Kondrup, *Levned og tolkninger: Studier i nordisk selvbiografi* (Odense: Universitetsforlag, Odense, 1982), 85.

7. Possibly something about this insomniac, this life vision in this chapter of *Practice in Christianity* is an aesthetic marker, the permanently seeing eye that cannot be closed.

Part II

✦

Performing Arts

Beyond the Mask

Kierkegaard's *Postscript* as Antitheatrical, Anti-Hegelian Drama

Howard Pickett

Several problems take center stage as a reader enters the thick of Søren Kierkegaard's *Concluding Unscientific Postscript* (1846). Perhaps none is as daunting or as decisive for the rest of the work as the one Johannes Climacus, pseudonymous author of this follow-up to *Philosophical Fragments* (1844), announces near the start of an early section entitled "The Subjective Issue": "The difference between subjective and objective thinking must . . . manifest itself in the form of communication" (*SKS* 7:74 / *CUP* 1:73). This problem of form—how can one communicate outwardly a subjective existence characterized by "the isolation of inwardness"?—animates *Postscript* from beginning to end (*SKS* 7:74 / *CUP* 1:73). It also animates the present essay, which asks: What exactly is the form of *Postscript*, and how well does that form manifest the difference between subjective and objective thought? Alternatively, how well does the form of *Postscript* avoid the problems that arise when describing outwardly and abstractly (that is, *objectively*) the inward and particular existence of a *subjective* individual?

Taking my cue from "A First and Last Explanation" (Kierkegaard's signed addendum to *Postscript*)—in particular, Kierkegaard's comparison of himself to both a dramatic poet and a stage prompter (*SKS* 7:569 / *CUP* 1:625)—I argue that *Postscript* is essentially theatrical in form, a point sometimes intuited but rarely tied to the text's own explicit theatricality.[1] Yet *Postscript* is also *anti*theatrical, at least in content. Tellingly, Climacus condemns abstract, speculative thought ("Hegelianism") as a mere *Schattenspiel*, or "shadow play" (*SKS* 7:323 / *CUP* 1:353). Consequently, a theatrical approach is the last thing *Postscript* ought to adopt in its quest to take seriously actual, subjective individuals. Nevertheless, by Kierkegaard's own admission, a thoroughly theatrical method is precisely what one finds on display not only in Hegel's works but also in pseudonymous works like *Postscript*.

As I will argue, *Postscript*'s ambivalence toward the theatrical is neither carelessly inconsistent nor naively self-contradictory. For one thing, a reader might observe that Climacus rejects only certain aspects of theatricality while affirming other aspects. As I show, Climacus rejects a Hegelian "philosophy of the spectacle" focused on detached spectators and mere external appearances in exchange for an inward, subjective "philosophy of the actor," with its defining emphasis on action and internal effort. In short, Climacus adopts a form of theatricality (and a theatrical view of the subject with it) purged of Hegelian detachment and deception. For another, Kierkegaard's use of an antitheatrical theatrical persona (Climacus) suits a treatment of the subject especially well, since it dramatizes the inexpressibility of the essentially inward subject, while also highlighting its inevitable theatricality and insincerity. In effect, Johannes Climacus's reader learns that the subject is not amenable to direct external communication; subjective existence is not an outward spectacle to contemplate and display but an inward performance to enact. Yet, from "S. Kierkegaard," signed "editor" of *Postscript* and spokesman of its final epilogue ("A First and Last Explanation"), the reader learns that the theatrical is inescapable for a philosophy of the subject. The best a published work like *Postscript* can do, then, is not to unmask itself but rather to draw attention to its mask *as* mask, exposing and confessing (metatheatrically, as it were) its own inadequacy and hypocrisy.

Hegel's Philosophy of the Spectacle

While debate continues over Kierkegaard's precise relationship to Hegel, *Postscript*'s attack on systems, on the identity of thought and being, and on a preoccupation with the world-historical poses a substantial challenge to ideas found in the writings of both Hegel and Danish Hegelians (e.g., N. F. S. Grundtvig, J. L. Heiberg, and H. L. Martensen).[2] Climacus's repeated use of theatrical (more accurately, *anti*theatrical) metaphors not only offers a persistent critique of Hegelianism but also borrows the terms of that critique from Hegel's own mouth, in particular, his *Lectures on the Philosophy of History*, posthumously published in 1837, nine years before *Postscript*.[3] There, theatrical terminology serves to describe Hegel's central concept, the self-manifestation of Spirit in history: "On the *stage [auf dem Theater]* on which we are observing it,—Universal History—Spirit displays itself in its most concrete reality."[4] So central is this metaphor, the so-called *theatrum mundi* (theater of the world) topos, that it appears repeatedly throughout the lectures, in references to "Spirit; which has the History of the World for its theatre [*Schauplatze*, literally 'scenes,' 'theaters']," "the real theatre [*Theater*] of History," and "the theatre [*Theater*] which was on the point of becoming the centre of History"—that is, Europe.[5] Hegel also uses related metaphors from the theater to describe the human observation of Spirit's self-exhibition. Prior to his religiously inflected "slaughter-bench [or altar] of history" analogy, Hegel imagines himself, the Spirit-contemplating philosopher, in theatrical terms, as one who "stands on the quiet shore, and thence enjoys in safety the distant spectacle [*Anblicks*] of 'wrecks confusedly hurled.'"[6] The philosopher is, as Hegel says in the same passage, the one who studies the "actions of men . . . in this scene [*Schauspiel*] of activity."[7]

For Johannes Climacus, however, both the outward visibility (even hypocrisy) of a theatrical spectacle and the detached, inactive orientation of its spectator are ill-suited to the inwardly engaged, subjective ethical agent. In effect, Hegel's theatrical descriptions of his own philosophy quietly confess the superficiality and irresponsibility his thought fosters.

Theater's Illusion

What Climacus wants is a philosophy of actual, subjective existence. Consequently, what he condemns in Hegelian thought is the artificiality and illusoriness of objective thought, which bear too strong a resemblance to the theatrical arts. In part 2 of *Postscript*, he complains, "The dubiousness of 'the method' is already apparent in Hegel's relation to Kant. . . . To reply to Kant within the fantastical *Schattenspiel* of pure thinking is precisely not to reply to him.—The only *an sich* that cannot be thought is existing, with which thinking has nothing at all to do" (*SKS* 7:299–300 / *CUP* 1:328). While Climacus emphasizes the actuality of the existing subject, Hegel, in contrast, emphasizes the phantasm of pure thinking, compared here not only to the fictitious illusions of the stage (themselves, in some sense, unreal) but also to the insubstantial shadows cast by the mere puppets of a *Schattenspiel*. Moreover, with that analogy, Climacus links Hegelian speculation not only with shadow theater's thoroughly insubstantial illusions but also, because his analogy recalls Plato's allegory of the cave (*Republic* 7.514a–520e, *CDP* 747–52), with the West's archetypal image of illusory, erroneous thought.[8] As Climacus later observes, the centerpiece of a philosophy of the subject is not "humanity in general, subjectivity in general, and other such things, whereby everything becomes easy inasmuch as the difficulty is removed and the whole matter is shifted over into the *Schattenspiel* of abstraction" (*SKS* 7:323 / *CUP* 1:353). Rather, what matters is the particular lived reality of the existing individual: "The difficulty is to exist in them, not abstractly to think oneself out of them and abstractly to think about, for example, an eternal divine becoming" (*SKS* 7:323 / *CUP* 1:354). Simply put, a particular, lived existence is real; abstract thought is not.

More to the point, ethical engagement is real; the object of detached contemplation, a theatrical illusion. In Climacus's words, "Only in the ethical is there immortality and eternal life; understood otherwise, world history is perhaps a play, a show [*Skuespil*]" (*SKS* 7:143 / *CUP* 1:154). This antitheatrical distinction between actuality (the ethical) and theatricality (the aesthetic) also appears in Kierkegaard's journals, which highlight "the tension of actuality: that here—unlike the theater—actual hum. beings are playing" (*SKS* 23:106, NB16:18, n.d. 1850 / *KJN* 7:106). Accordingly, Climacus seems unlikely to adopt a theatrical approach to his own subjective, existential philosophical project. His is, after all, a philosophy of real existence, not the walking shadows of the stage.

Theater's Detached Spectator

The Hegelian spectacle's unreality also rests in no small part on the disengaged or detached relationship one has with it. The posture of a spectator is wholly unsuitable to the ethical-existential. Again, the ethical has to do with the "tension of actuality," that *actual* human beings are playing here, not as in the theater." Yet, as already mentioned, the Hegelian philosopher of history stands back and observes, as would a spectator at the playhouse, the spectacle of Spirit's self-manifestation. Climacus voices his ethical objections to the objective and the aesthetic by noting, "Esthetically it is altogether appropriate that I as a spectator [*Tilskuer*] am enchanted by the stage scenery, the theatrical moonlight, and go home after having spent a very pleasant evening, but ethically it holds true that there is no change other than my own" (*SKS* 7:358 / *CUP* 1:393). Whether fair to Hegel or not, Climacus condemns the Hegelian for obsessing over the outwardly observable events taking place at a distance from oneself and from one's own inmost, passionately engaged decisions.

No matter how powerful onstage examples may be, observable others (in their superficial visibility and externality) serve for spectators as mere possibilities. Yet those spectators, insofar as they are living, breathing agents, remain ethically obligated to engage not in possibilities alone but in actuality—not to spectate but to act.[9] In contrast to Aristotle's (alleged) view that "possibility, poetic and intellectual, is superior to actuality" (*SKS* 7:290 / *CUP* 1:318), Climacus contends that actuality is superior. As a result, Aristotle's notion, found influentially in the *Poetics* (9.1451a, *CWA* 2:2322–23) and repeated here by Climacus—namely, that theater deals in possibility—urges Climacus's ready rejection of dramatic metaphors for the ethical (at least, initially). In short, the genre of the possible seems altogether unsuitable for the task of the actual and the ethical.

Kierkegaard's journals second that complaint. Specifically, Kierkegaard reiterates St. Augustine's disgust with theater, complaining, in an echo of *Confessions* 3.2.2, that "tragedy is supposed to awaken compassion, 'but what sort of compassion is it in which the spectator is not called upon to rush to provide assistance, but is only invited to enjoy the pain [?]'" (*SKS* 24:282, NB23:156, n.d. 1851 / *KJN* 8:282).[10] Like modern-day psychologists who worry that TV violence might desensitize spectators to the suffering of others, Augustine condemns the fundamentally unethical, irresponsible habits encouraged by the theater. Kierkegaard shares Augustine's fears both here and in a separate, but no less Augustinian, journal entry from 1848: "To want to spectate [*betragte*] and to spectate . . . is essentially sinful and culpable lasciviousness, just as any other lasciviousness—to be uplifted as a spectator instead of coming out into the tension of true actuality, spectating upon suffering as a good thing instead of suffering, etc. . . . In spectating one wants the enjoyment and bids goodbye to earnestness" (*SKS* 21:13, NB6:4 / *JP* 1:1051; compare *KJN* 5:9).[11] What makes spectatorship so bad is its passivity, its aesthetic side, its failure to take seriously the actuality (the "earnestness") of lived experience, in which subjects ought to be engaged. What is wrong with Hegelian speculation is that it is, in effect, Hegelian "spectaculation."[12] Because the human is called not simply to know certain things about the world but to participate fully and ethically in that world, the adoption of an aesthetic view denies our ethical calling. It also denies our true humanity, since it focuses us on an image (mental or theatrical) rather than on the thing itself: "One thing continually evaded Hegel: what it is to live; he knew only how to *reproduce a copy* of life" (*SKS* 20:44, NB42, n.d. 1846 / *KJN* 4:42).

Theater's Outwardness and Hypocrisy

The theater is not only ill-suited to Climacus's interest in actuality and ethics—"the very home of existence," as he says (*SKS* 7:116 / *CUP* 1:121)—because it involves both shadowy illusions and inactive, disengaged spectators. It is also unsuitable as a paradigm for the ethical-existential insofar as it fetishizes the visible. Because, in Climacus's view, subjectivity, ethics, and inwardness all align with one another, outward spectacles are, at best, morally irrelevant. Even if "Governance [i.e., Providence] arranges things so that a person's inner striving is reflected magically in the shadow play of world history [*verdenshistoriske Skyggespil*]," there would be no "merit" in that externality (*SKS* 7:130 / *CUP* 1:139–40). What matters is the inward decision, not its outward appearance. Worse, this Hegelian emphasis on the external spectacle is not just morally indifferent; it risks being morally illicit as well, since it smacks of *hypocrisy* (not incidentally, from the Greek for "stage actor"). In effect, the contagion of theater's hypocritical side bleeds over into the Hegelian philosopher, who, like an actor, also hypocritically pretends to be something he or she is not. Making that criticism explicit, Kierkegaard's journals regularly associate Hegel with the "hypocrisy of the understanding" (*SKS* 24:443, NB25:7, n.d. 1851 / *KJN* 8:449). Kierkegaard complains, in particular, of the "frightful hypocrisy that has been promoted" by Hegelians, namely "that the objective . . . is everything—the subject is a matter of indifference" (*SKS* 24:260, NB23:109, n.d. 1851 / *KJN* 8:259).

As that passage implies, Hegelian philosophers pretend to be something they are not when they obsess over the objects out there rather than the subjects they are within. The Hegelian is, then, most hypocritical when pretending to be a mere spectator in the theater of the world rather than its actor. Therefore, one might say, the Hegelian is most actor-like when being least *actor*-like. By Climacus's estimation, the Hegelian philosopher is not just theatrical and hypocritical, but also comical: "Now, all in all, there are two ways for an existing individual: either he can do everything to forget that he is existing and thereby manage to become comic (the comic contradiction of wanting to be what one is not . . .), because existence possesses the remarkable quality that an existing person exists whether he wants to or not; or he can direct all his attention to his existing" (*SKS* 7:116 / *CUP* 1:120). In wanting to see existence from a vantage point outside of existence, the Hegelian forgets who (even *what*) he is, a forgetting that makes him both a hypocrite and a fool (both classic figures for the actor). At best, the Hegelian philosopher is the proverbial absent-minded professor: "Modern speculative thought . . . has not a false presupposition but a comic presupposition, occasioned by its having forgotten in a kind of world-historical absent-mindedness what it means to be a human being" (*SKS* 7:116 / *CUP* 1:120).

At his worst, the Hegelian philosopher is, as already suggested, a hypocrite—a blasphemous one at that. The world-historical point of view is a perspective for God alone, not the human: "But who, then, is this systematic thinker? Well, it is he who himself is outside existence and yet in existence. . . . It is God" (*SKS* 7:115 / *CUP* 1:119). The Hegelian who pretends to see things from the God's-eye view commits—indeed, becomes—a lie. He is, as Climacus later suggests, like a hypocrite who "follows his inclination to put on an act [*skabe sig*] and first transforms himself [*skabe sig om*] into a superrational something, just as alchemists and sorcerers bedizen themselves fantastically" (*SKS* 7:175 / *CUP* 1:191). As a result of his costumed quackery and blasphemy, Hegel, according to whom "truth is the continuous world-historical process," makes himself guilty of hypocrisy—both "charlatanry [*Charlatanerie*]" and "deceptive [*svigefuld*]" appearances (*SKS* 7:39–40 / *CUP* 1:33). To the point here, the Hegelian hypocrite also makes herself theatrically "comic [*Comiske*]" (*SKS* 7:40 / *CUP* 1:34).

Theater's Conclusiveness

Finally, Climacus also uses theatrical metaphors to expose the naïveté of the Hegelian system's pretense toward closure. What makes Hegelian philosophers theatrical—and, more than that, hypocritical—is not just their tendency to pretend to see things from God's spectatorial point of view. They also have a related tendency to act as if they can see things in their fullness and completion. On the contrary, they ought to admit that their view of existence is limited to their own finite perspective and their own finite existence, which is ongoing—at least, as long as they live to consider it. In opposition to this Hegelian tendency, Climacus remarks, "In the system and in the fifth act of the drama, one has a positive conclusiveness speculatively-fantastically and esthetically-fantastically, but such a conclusiveness is only for fantastic beings" (*SKS* 7:117 / *CUP* 1:121). According to Climacus, the Hegelian system, like the classic five-act play, has a certain order, predictability, and (most damningly) a certain totality about it. Yet, just as the classic five-act play is a fiction, incapable of doing (perfect) justice to the depth, the complexity, the chaos, and the reality of our actual lives, so too, the Hegelian system is also fictional and deficient. Such theatrical fictions are fitting, Climacus says, "only for fantastic beings" (*SKS* 7:117 / *CUP* 1:121). They are fitting, one is tempted to add, for liars and hypocrites.

In place of this unrealistic conclusiveness (seen in the simplistic resolutions of the deus ex machina of classical drama or, closer to Kierkegaard's own day, in the finale to Eugène Scribe's "well-made play"), "continued striving is the expression of the existing subject's life-view" (*SKS* 7:117 / *CUP* 1:121–22).[13] Climacus applies this antitheatrical inconclusiveness to the religious, specifically Christian domain when he writes, "Suppose that Christianity was and wants to be a mystery, an utter mystery, not a theatrical [*theatralsk*] mystery that is revealed in the fifth act, although the clever spectator [*Tilskuer*] already sees through [*gennemskue*] it in the course of the exposition" (*SKS* 7:195 / *CUP* 1:213). The appeal of Christianity to the paradox of the God-man is, for Climacus, the surest sign that it "does not at all want to be understood" but instead wants to require from its passionate adherent a never-ending— and, so, in some sense, a thoroughly *un*theatrical—striving (*SKS* 7:196 / *CUP* 1:214). Ours is not a life from which one can step back and observe how things worked out. There is no conclusion, no well-worked-out final denoue- ment to be observed—at least, not on this side of the grave. Yet, Climacus insinuates, that pretentious, blasphemous grasping at the whole is precisely what systematic, Hegelian philosophy characteristically attempts.

Consequently, Hegelian objective philosophy bears more than a little resemblance to the theater: (1) Unlike Climacus's subjective thinker, the Hegelian focuses on illusions rather than the lived reality of actual existence. (2) What's worse, he relates to those illusions in a spectatorial way by exam- ining existence aesthetically as if it did not require his own actual, ethical involvement. (3) By failing to recognize his own existence as an actual, finite, ethically responsible individual, the Hegelian resembles the actor or, worse, the hypocrite, who pretends to be what he is not. (4) In the most hypocriti- cal move of all, the objective Hegelian plays God and presumes to construct a conclusive system though even her own life is not yet concluded. In effect, Hegel's thought is essentially theatrical. In terms provided by Eric Bentley's famous definition of theater—"The theatrical situation, reduced to a min- imum, is that A impersonates B while C looks on"—Climacus insinuates that the Hegelian hypocritically and comically impersonates God, while the reader looks on.[14]

With this thoroughgoing rejection of theater in mind, one would expect Climacus to adopt anything but a theatrical approach to his own thought. Yet, as the next section demonstrates, Climacus does just that, employing a subtler, admittedly different, but thoroughly theatrical paradigm for his own philosophy.

Climacus's Philosophy of the Actor

Theater's Action Orientation

Having denounced the theatrical Hegelian subject, Climacus introduces, however surprisingly, his own theatrical metaphor for "becoming subjective" (*SKS* 7:121 / *CUP* 1:129). "Permit me by way of metaphor," he notes, "to call to mind more graphically the difference between the ethical and the world-historical, the difference between the ethical relation of the individual to God and the relation of the world-historical to God" (*SKS* 7:146 / *CUP* 1:157). Teasing out that metaphor, Climacus compares the ethical life to a private performance: "A king sometimes has a royal theater [*kongeligt Theater*] solely for himself, but this difference, which excludes the ordinary citizens, is accidental. Not so when we speak of God and the royal theater he has for himself. Accordingly, the individual's ethical development is the little private theater [*Privat-Theater*] where God certainly is the spectator [*Tilskuer*], but where on occasion the individual also is himself a spectator, although essentially he is supposed to be an actor [*Skuespilleren*], not, however, one who deceives [*bedrager*] but one who discloses" (*SKS* 7:146 / *CUP* 1:157). Again, however surprisingly, Hegelian objectivity is not distinguished from ethical-existential subjectivity by contrasting Hegelian theatricality with Climacean *non*theatricality. Rather, Climacus offers his readers a remarkably different kind of theater, but a *theater* nonetheless.

Unlike Hegel's world-historical spectacle, Climacus's "little private theater" of ethical development is not open to the onlooking gaze of (other) human spectators. Strange as it may sound, ethical development and the related internal effort constitute an insistently invisible performance, viewed by God certainly, and by oneself occasionally. However, the individual agent does not primarily relate to that performance as a detached spectator might, but instead as its actor would—"essentially he is supposed to be an actor." In the theater of the ethical-existential, the human moral agent is just that: an *agent*, one who *acts* (albeit inwardly), not one who merely watches or contemplates. Just as important, this inward theatrical performance has been (largely) purified of theater's hypocrisy, since the self, acting here, is decidedly not "one who deceives, but one who discloses" (*SKS* 7:146 / *CUP* 1:157).

True, the Hegelian world-historical stage remains. In stark opposition to the Hegelian formulation, however, Climacus insists that God is its only true spectator: "But to God, world history is the royal stage where he, not accidentally but essentially, is the only spectator [*Tilskuer*]" (*SKS* 7:146 / *CUP* 1:158). Consequently, "admission to this theater is not open to any existing spirit" (*SKS* 7:146 / *CUP* 1:158). The "existing" individual (including the would-be "objective" philosopher) is, therefore, out of line when pretending to be a spectator in the *theatrum mundi*. An individual, "if he fancies himself a spectator there . . . is simply forgetting that he himself is supposed to be the actor in that little theater and is to leave it to that royal spectator and poet [*Tilskuer og Digter*] how he wants to use him in that royal drama" (*SKS* 7:146 / *CUP* 1:158). While God remains both spectator and providential playwright of the world-historical spectacle, the ethical individual should concentrate instead on his or her own private performance and leave it to God to decide what to do with the "Drama Dramatum" (or "drama of dramas"; *SKS* 7:146 / *CUP* 1:158).

Theater's Strenuousness and Inconclusiveness

This de-emphasis on the visible spectacle and the corresponding emphasis on the internal effort of the actor find Climacus's additional support just a few pages later when, in a consideration of the act of praying and the difficulty of "becoming subjective," Climacus compares the subject to a constantly striving actor: "So one could almost think that to pray is just as difficult as to play the role of Hamlet [*spille Hamlet*], of which the greatest actor [*Skuespiller*] is supposed to have said that only once had he been close to playing it well [*spille den godt*]; nevertheless he would devote all his ability and his entire life to the continued study of this role. Should not praying be almost as important and significant?" (*SKS* 7:151 / *CUP* 1:163). While theatricality is typically synonymous with external, public performance, the internal, private efforts of the actor (either in private rehearsal or in the internal, subjective struggle to learn one's part) are all-important to that theatricality. What matters is not the onstage external show but the offstage (or, at least, internal) striving.

Climacus's particular theatrical allusion here seems especially apt, since Hamlet's part is not only a difficult one; it is also one of a subject desperately trying to figure out how to play his own life. Thus, the "To be or not to be" speech provides Climacus the opportunity to reflect on his own philosophy of subjective existence. Hamlet's passionate struggle indicates, at its core, that "existence and nonexistence have only subjective significance," a view contrary to "the way of objective reflection" and "abstract thinking" (*SKS* 7:177 / *CUP* 1:193). Hamlet is, by that account, as anti-Hegelian as Climacus himself. The Hegelian philosopher promotes a totalizing objectivity that denies the contrasts at the heart of the ethical. In contrast, real "personality," as Kierkegaard notes in his journal, "will for all eternity protest against the idea that absolute contradictions are susceptible of mediation . . . [and] it will for all eternity repeat its *immortal* dilemma: to be or not to be, that is the question. (Hamlet.)" (*SKS* 18:35, EE:93, June 14, 1839 / *KJN* 2:30). In other words, the Kierkegaardian subject who plays his part well, as something other than a mere aesthetic part, has more than a little in common with Shakespeare's prince of Denmark; both confront the life-and-death decisions of existence.

Suffice it to say that, if Hegel's theatricality was rejected not for its theatricality per se but rather for its emphasis on the spectacular and its corresponding "mask," then an alternative theatricality recommends itself here because of its emphasis on what lies behind the mask—namely, the truer, unobservable actor who acts inwardly. Consequently, though Climacus's denigration of Hegelianism invites a nonspectatorial philosophical form, it need not preclude theatrical forms altogether. In lieu of a philosophy of masks and spectators, one finds an inward philosophy of the actor, an approach reinforced by what Climacus says in his concluding appendix, "An Understanding with the Reader."

In this postscript to *Postscript*, Climacus imagines the whole work as a private, internal performance free of spectators. It is, as he says, both a "private enterprise" and "one of life's . . . quiet joys" (*SKS* 7:562 / *CUP* 1:619–20). It does not "in the remotest manner make an attempt or a gesture of wanting to oblige one single actual person to be the reader" (*SKS* 7:562 / *CUP* 1:620). Instead, Climacus claims to indulge in the "secret fiction," the "private enjoyment" of writing for an "imagined reader" (*SKS* 7:563 / *CUP* 1:621). Indeed, because having an imagined reader is only "permissible" for "the author who has no *actual* reader" (*SKS* 7:563 / *CUP* 1:620), the text poses as an utterly neglected, wholly private meditation on the inwardness of subjectivity. Consequently, Climacus's performance lacks the unattractive externality, the potential hypocrisy, and the aesthetic, unethical spectators of Hegelianism. In fact, because it has always already been revoked—"the understanding with him [the imagined reader] as the sole reader is indeed the revocation of the book" (*SKS* 7:563 / *CUP* 1:621)—*Postscript* also avoids the hypocritical conclusiveness of the pretentious Hegelian system. Insofar as it is revoked, Climacus's work is anything but a *concluding* postscript. By that light, Climacus's work bears little resemblance to the Hegelian philosophy of the spectacle and poses instead as the Climacian private performance before God and self.

To state the obvious, though, Climacus's work is no private performance. And *Postscript* is no drama. Unlike Kierkegaard's earliest attempt at anti-Hegelian satire, his play from his university days, "The Conflict between the Old and New Soap-Cellar" (*SKS* 17:280–97, DD:208, n.d. 1837 / *KJN* 1:273–89), *Postscript* lacks the usual markers of a stage-play (acts, scenes, stage directions, dialogue, and a history of public performance). It is hard to imagine how one could ever perform such a monumental work (over five hundred pages in most editions). Consequently, one might protest that Climacus's work is a unique, unprecedented formal innovation—one whose formal peculiarity suits the "single individual" it considers. Nevertheless, *Postscript* repeatedly signals its theatricality. Long before the private theater metaphor for the subject, Climacus hints at *Postscript*'s theatrical side in the subtitle to the work: "A Mimical-Pathetical-Dialectical Combination: An Existential Contribution." With that self-description, the work announces its affinities with three separate genres or, more to the point, with three separate forms of drama: (1) ancient mime (e.g., those of Sophron),[15] (2) Platonic dialogue (influenced by Sophron's mimes),[16] and (3) tragedy (characterized, in Aristotle's famous analysis, by its focus on *pathos*; *Poetics* 11.1452b, *CWA* 2:2324). To anyone familiar with Kierkegaard's earlier anti-Hegelian drama, *Postscript*'s subtitle also bears some resemblance to the hyper-hyphenated subtitle to "The Conflict between the Old and New Soap-Cellar: A Heroic-Patriotic-Cosmopolitan-Philanthropic-Fatalistic Drama in Several Scenes." To anyone familiar with Shakespeare's dramatic work about another enigmatic, philosophical Dane (himself responsible for another influential treatise on existence and nonexistence),[17] both hyphenated subtitles recall something Polonius says to Hamlet about the form of drama to be performed by a group of itinerant players on their way to court. They are, in Polonius's words, "the best actors in the world, either for tragedy, comedy, history, pastoral, pastoral-comical, historical-pastoral, tragical-historical, tragical-comical-historical-pastoral, scene individable, or poem unlimited" (*Hamlet* 2.2.391–94).[18]

One way or another, *Postscript* implies, an individual will play a part in the theater of the world. Moreover, one way or another, a philosophy of the subject will take on a theatrical form. The crucial decision comes when one chooses between the options available: on the one hand, the hypocritical spectacle of Hegelian philosophy; on the other, the Climacian private, inner performance before God and self.

Kierkegaard's Philosophy of the Mask

To be fair, the most theatrical feature of *Postscript* is not the work's subtitle or Climacus's theatrical allusions. *Postscript*'s most theatrical feature is Climacus himself. The work is, after all, a dramatic monologue, a soliloquy (not unlike Hamlet's better-known aside on existence and nonexistence), or, in light of the subtitle, a philosophical mime, ventriloquized through a pseudonymous persona.[19] Recalling this fact gives Climacus's anti-Hegelian philosophy of the actor an unexpected twist. As it turns out, this lengthy diatribe against hypocritical spectacle has been, not a private inward performance of an actual existing subject (as "An Understanding with the Reader" insinuates) but, instead, a hypocritical (or, at least, thoroughly theatrical) spectacle before a public audience, a fact S. Kierkegaard's own postscript to *Postscript* makes explicit. In "A First and Last Explanation" (which follows Climacus's "Understanding"), Kierkegaard describes his pseudonymous philosophical works, including *Postscript*, in markedly theatrical terms—no surprise, perhaps, from a writer who spent much of his time (and much of his money) frequenting the Royal Theater of Denmark.[20]

In this final addendum to *Postscript*, "S. Kierkegaard" acknowledges that his literary-philosophical technique has a hypertheatrical side: "What has been written [in the pseudonymous works], then, is mine, but only insofar as

I, by means of audible lines, have placed the life-view of the crea*ting*, poeti-cally actual individuality in his mouth, for my relation is even more remote than that of a poet [*Digters*], who *poetizes* [*digter*] characters [*Personer*] and yet in the preface is *himself* the *author*" (*SKS* 7:569 / *CUP* 1:625). Because the noun *Digter*, the verb *digter*, and the plural noun *Personer* might just as easily read "dramatist," "dramatizes," and "dramatic personae," respectively (a consequence of the longstanding prominence of verse drama), Kierke-gaard's analogy is not simply artistic or poetic but *theatrical*. Thus, this passage admits a parallel between *Postscript* and Hegel's own philosophy of the spectacle. Kierkegaard's pseudonymous work may even outdo Hegel's by embodying a more overtly theatrical philosophy of the mask, a term evoked here (for Kierkegaard and his classically educated audience, at least) by the Danish *Personer* (from the Latin *persona*, "mask").

Even more explicitly theatrical is something Kierkegaard says a line later, when he characterizes himself as a *souffleur*, or dramatic prompter who "whispers" forgotten lines to the onstage actor (*SKS* 7:569 / *CUP* 1:625).[21] If Climacus, the pseudonymous persona, is the onstage masked actor before *Postscript*'s audience, then Kierkegaard himself is the stage manager feeding him his lines and cues from the wings. By that account, Kierkegaard's work is, again, perhaps more theatrical and more "spectacular" than that of Hegel himself. Whereas Hegel's work (e.g., *Lectures on the Philosophy of History*) imagines its content (the world-historical) in theatrical terms, Kierkegaard's pseudonymous work adopts a theatrical form for treating its subject (the single individual). Notwithstanding any pretensions Hegel might have to speak for Spirit or "Mind" itself (e.g., in his *Phänomenologie des Geistes*, sometimes known as *The Phenomenology of Mind*), the "mind" on display in Hegel's works is more or less Hegel's own.[22] In contrast, if we take this final postscript to *Postscript* at its word, "in the pseudonymous books there is not a single word by" Kierkegaard himself (*SKS* 7:570 / *CUP* 1:626).

What's more, *Postscript* may be even more theatrical than actual dramatic works composed by playwrights for the stage. In contrast to Shakespeare (or Denmark's Johan Ludvig Heiberg), who remains himself in preface and title page, Kierkegaard dramatizes a persona who speaks every line, including those on the title page itself. He explains, "My relation is even more remote than that of a poet [playwright], who *poetizes* characters and yet in the pref-ace is *himself* the *author*" (*SKS* 7:569 / *CUP* 1:625). Kierkegaard's work is as thoroughly theatrical as Shakespeare's would have been had Shakespeare claimed *Hamlet* was written by Hamlet himself—or, at least, by the friend who survives him, Horatio.

The main problem for the present essay, however, is that Kierkegaard's theatrical technique (apparently) conflicts with Climacus's antitheatrical sen-timents. *Postscript* employs a mask in its discussion about the problems with (philosophical) masks. What I now conclude, though, is that this seeming contradiction suits the work's treatment of subjectivity especially well. While

Climacus's deep and persistent criticisms of the Hegelian philosophy of the spectator might incline us to think that *Postscript* would need an alternative form for writing a philosophy of the subject, that inclination makes a notable mistake; it wrongly assumes that philosophy has access to nonspectacular forms of communication. In short, it assumes that a philosophy of subjectivity can be written without slipping into objectivity. On the contrary, insofar as a philosophical publication always entails a more or less external communication of abstract thoughts for a detached group of onlookers, a philosophy of subjectivity (including this one by Johannes Climacus) is bound to resemble the Hegelian spectacle.

Nevertheless, the Kierkegaardian spectacle differs from its Hegelian counterpart in at least one crucial respect: *Postscript* admits its own theatricality. As a result, *Postscript* is not just antitheatrical or pro-theatrical; it is, more importantly, *meta*theatrical. What makes Hegelianism so offensive—indeed, what makes it a philosophy of the *hypocrite* as well as the spectacle—is its *unconfessed* theatricality. In other words, what makes the Hegelian account of the subject so disturbing is the fact that it pretends to involve no pretense at all. As Climacus repeatedly complains, it pretends to offer a fundamentally transparent, aesthetic view of the subject, even though actual subjects defy easy externalization. What Hegel offers readers, then, is not just a masked performance (what all philosophies of the subject must offer) but a masked performance that pretends to be mask-less. In yet another attack on "The [Hegelian] System," Kierkegaard complains in one of his journals, "This was the swindle. It was just as if an actor wanted to say: It is I who am speaking, these are my words—and then, the second the prompter [*Souffleuren*] falls silent, he does not have one single word to say" (*SKS* 24:192, NB22:161, n.d. 1851 / *KJN* 8:191). Like an actor who pretends he is no actor at all, the Hegelian philosopher and hypocrite pretends to be something he is not. More, like the actor who denies the animating role of the offstage prompter, the Hegelian thinker also denies that which remains offstage and hidden from view—namely, the actuality and inwardness of the self, which are (somewhat) incommensurable with appearance, thought, and language.

Postscript, on the other hand, is guilty of no such denial. In his final confession and curtain call (originally meant to be his last as an author), Kierkegaard steps from behind the curtain to highlight his role as prompter and playwright. In doing so, he reminds the reader that his has been no transparent revelation of the subject either. Rather, the subject on display here, Johannes Climacus, has always been more shadow than self. In pointing out that fact, however, *Postscript* adopts a form of communication especially apt for handling the subject. Specifically, the metatheatrical conclusion to *Postscript* comes as close as any text can to externalizing the unexternalizable: the inexpressibly inward subject. Through its metatheatricality, *Postscript* acknowledges that the best a published philosophy of the subject can do is to point beyond itself, toward the ever-elusive subject.[23] If pointing toward the subject seems still too much to ask, a work like *Postscript* can, at least, confess its own inadequacy as a representation of that subject.

Little could be both more *and* less theatrical than the moment an onstage actor admits to being, in fact, an actor on the stage; accordingly, Kierkegaard's final metatheatrical confession is both the height of *Postscript*'s theatricality and also the closest it ever comes to genuine sincerity. By pointing out the theatricality within its own treatment of the subject, *Postscript* both confesses and atones for that theatricality. Kierkegaard makes clear in another journal entry, "In the theater, if one notices the prompter [*Souffleuren*], the illusion is disturbed" (*SKS* 24:252, NB23:88, n.d. 1851 / *KJN* 8:251). Thus, by uncovering its own reliance on persona and prompter, *Postscript* both acknowledges its own similarity to a hypocritical Hegelian illusion and simultaneously protects itself against that similarity. Like a self-effacing, metatheatrical Brechtian drama, *Postscript* exposes its own theatricality, drawing attention to the wires and masks that might otherwise deceive us. In doing so, however, it cautions the reader against mistaking Climacus's lengthy account of the subject for the fully transparent subject itself. In effect, it alerts the reader to the theatricality and potential hypocrisy that necessarily attach themselves to all external and public accounts of the essentially inward subject (including this one). More than that, by anticipating the metatheatrical Brechtian *Verfremdungseffekt* (alienation effect), *Postscript* awakens its readers to the challenges posed by their own inward subjectivity. By reminding its readers that Climacus's lengthy portrayal of the subject has been more drama than reality, *Postscript* directs each of us through the exit at the back of the playhouse, back home to the central, inward task of becoming actual, and active, individuals. Through its ambivalent theatricality and, even more so, through its metatheatricality, *Postscript* ultimately directs its readers to a performance not so much before or behind but, better yet, beyond the mask.

Notes

1. See Edward F. Mooney, "*Postscript* Ethics: Putting Personality on Stage," in *Ethics, Love, and Faith in Kierkegaard,* ed. Edward F. Mooney (Bloomington: Indiana University Press, 2008), 39–47. My present essay aims, in part, to tie Mooney's insights to *Postscript*'s own theatrical rhetoric.

2. Jon Stewart argues explicitly for Kierkegaard's favorable appreciation of Hegel. Jon Stewart, *Kierkegaard's Relations to Hegel Reconsidered* (Cambridge, U.K.: Cambridge University Press, 2003). For contrary views, see Niels Thulstrup, *Kierkegaard's Relation to Hegel,* trans. George L. Stengren (Princeton, N.J.: Princeton University Press, 1980); and, more recently, Merold Westphal, "Climacus on Subjectivity and the System," in *Kierkegaard's "Concluding Unscientific Postscript": A Critical Guide,* ed. Rick Furtak (Cambridge, U.K.: Cambridge University Press, 2010), 132.

3. Kierkegaard makes repeated use of Hegel's *Philosophy of History* in his dissertation on irony, also alluding to it on occasion in *Postscript* (*SKS* 17:124 / *CUP* 1:133).

4. G. W. F. Hegel, *Vorlesungen über die Philosophie der Geschchichte*, in *GWFHW* 9, ed. Eduard Gans (1837): 20; *Lectures on the Philosophy of History*, trans. J. Sibree (London: Henry G. Bohn, 1857), 17, my emphasis. Sibree's translation is uncommonly good at capturing Hegel's theatrical motifs.

5. *GWFHW* 9:52, 97, 323; *Lectures on the Philosophy of History*, 57, 103–4, 324.

6. *GWFHW* 9:25; *Lectures on the Philosophy of History*, 22.

7. *GWFHW* 9:24; *Lectures on the Philosophy of History*, 21.

8. For a discussion of the analogy's theatricality, see Samuel Weber, *Theatricality as Medium* (New York: Fordham University Press, 2004), 3–10; Asli Gocer, "The Puppet Theater in Plato's Parable of the Cave," *Classical Journal* 95, no. 2 (1999): 119–29.

9. Kierkegaard's *Repetition* (1843) acknowledges a positive side to this aesthetic contemplation of possibilities (*SKS* 4:30–31 / *R* 154–55). See Weber, *Theatricality as Medium*, 216–17. Weber also argues that the particular dramatic form influencing much of Kierkegaard's discussion of theatricality is the so-called *Posse*, or vaudevillian burlesque, a hodgepodge of musical theater. For another discussion of the *Posse* (itself as genre-bending as *Postscript*), see Joakim Garff, *Søren Kierkegaard: A Biography*, trans. Bruce H. Kirmmse (Princeton, N.J.: Princeton University Press, 2005), 235.

10. As Kierkegaard's own citation admits, the quotation is not directly from *Confessions* but rather from a secondary source on Augustine: Friedrich Böhringer, *Die Kirche Christi und ihre Zeugen*, 9 vols. in 7 (Zurich: Meyer und Zeller, 1852–58; *ASKB* 173–77), Band 1, Abt. 3, p. 110.

11. *JP*'s "spectate" better captures *betragte*'s connotations than *KJN*'s "observe" (*KJN* 5:9).

12. The connections between spectating and speculating derive in part from their shared root, *specere* (Latin for "to view"), as do the connections between theater and theory, from a Greek word meaning "a view."

13. Kierkegaard's works make regular reference to the well-made plays of both A. Eugène Scribe and the Danish Hegelian Johan Ludvig Heiberg, whose translation of Scribe's *The First Love* receives thorough attention in *Either/Or* (1843).

14. Eric Bentley, *The Life of the Drama* (New York: First Applause, 1991), 150.

15. For a related acknowledgment of the mime's theatrical connotations, see Mooney, "*Postscript* Ethics," 40. Although Sophron's mimes are unmentioned in Kierkegaard's works, Diogenes Laertius's *Lives of Eminent Philosophers* (which connects Sophron's mimes and Plato's dialogues) is regularly cited (e.g., *SKS* 7:298 / *CUP* 1:327). For a description of the ancient mime, see James H. Hordern, *Sophron's Mimes: Text, Translation, and Commentary* (Oxford: Oxford University Press, 2004).

16. As the previous note indicates, Diogenes Laertius reports the legend that Plato's dialogues were inspired by the mimes of Sophron (*Lives of Eminent Philosophers* 3.18). Aristotle also highlights their formal similarities to one another (*Poetics* 1.1447b, *CWA* 2:2316).

17. For Climacus's own appreciation of Hamlet's thoughts on subjective existence (i.e., his "To be or not to be" soliloquy), see *SKS* 7:177 / *CUP* 1:193. For another Kierkegaardian analysis of *Hamlet*, see *Stages on Life's Way* (1846).

18. William Shakespeare, *Hamlet*, ed. G. R. Hibbard (Oxford: Oxford University Press, 1998), 224. For a recent discussion of Kierkegaard's views on *Hamlet*, see Eric Ziolkowski, *The Literary Kierkegaard* (Evanston, Ill.: Northwestern University Press, 2011), 183–212.

19. Although mimes (like Platonic dialogues) presented dialogues rather than monologues, good reasons can be given for *Postscript*'s lack of an interlocutor or dialogue partner. Climacus may think it appropriate for a philosophy of the inward, private subject to be correspondingly inward and private. Then again, the work may presume its ongoing dialogue with the reader, whether implied or actual.

20. Garff, *Søren Kierkegaard*, 102.

21. In essence, both subtitle and finale alike underscore, in Martin Thust's phrase, Kierkegaard's role as "dramatist of the religious." Quoted in George Pattison, *Kierkegaard: The Aesthetic and the Religious. From the Magic Theatre to the Crucifixion of the Image* (New York: St. Martin's Press, 1992), 120.

22. G. W. F. Hegel, *Phänomenologie des Geistes*, in *GWFHW* 2, ed. Johann Schultze (1832); *The Phenomenology of Mind*, trans. J. B. Baillie (New York: Macmillan, 1910).

23. It comes as no surprise, perhaps, that Kierkegaard's metatheatricality has implications for our understanding of the self. As one critic notes (in a discussion of Ibsen and Kierkegaard, no less), metatheater has always been "not just theatrical self-awareness but also how a play's *story* makes us aware of the realities of performance in life." Larry D. Bouchard, *Theater and Integrity: Emptying Selves in Drama, Ethics, and Religion* (Evanston, Ill.: Northwestern University Press, 2011), 130.

A Theater of Ideas

Performance and Performativity
in Kierkegaard's *Repetition*

Martijn Boven

It has always been one of the tasks of philosophy to develop categories that give an intelligible form to knowledge. This is no different for Kierkegaard. He has developed important categories such as repetition, the instant, anxiety, despair, and so forth. However, there is something odd about these categories: it is very hard to find a clear and unequivocal definition of them. In different ways, each of them is shrouded in uncertainty. This uncertainty is not the result of a lack of talent but a deliberate effect. In Kierkegaard's view, there are two types of categories: logical and existential. Logical categories can ideally exhaust their object in such a way that there is no uncertainty left. This is different in the case of existential categories. These categories will never be able ideally to exhaust their object because they are dependent on the person who is using them. Kierkegaard tries to solve this difficulty by preserving the uncertainty inherent in these categories. An example can clarify this. One of Kierkegaard's pseudonyms tells about a witty fellow who divided humankind into three classes: officers, servant girls, and chimney sweeps. "In my opinion," the pseudonym writes, "this remark is not only witty but also profound, and it would take great speculative talent to make a better classification. If a classification does not ideally exhaust its object, the accidental is preferable in every way, because it sets the imagination in motion" (*SKS* 4:37 / *R* 162). The sheer impossibility of establishing an exhaustive classification of humankind shows that it makes more sense to rely on an accidental and unessential classification than on a serious and essential one. Any classification will at best approximate the truth, without ever reaching it. But an accidental classification has the added advantage of activating the imagination and forcing the recipient to produce a creative response. This is exactly the kind of performative effect that Kierkegaard tries to achieve.

In this essay, I will argue that Kierkegaard's oeuvre can be seen as a theater of ideas.[1] This argument is developed in three steps. First, I will briefly introduce a theoretical framework for addressing the theatrical dimension of Kierkegaard's works. This framework is based on a distinction between "performative writing strategies" and "categories of performativity."[2] As a second step, I will focus on *Repetition: A Venture in Experimenting Psychology*, "by Constantin Constantius," one of the best examples of Kierkegaard's innovative way of doing philosophy. This strange and elusive book introduces the difficult and counterintuitive notion of repetition. Repetition is a category of performativity that aims to activate the subjectivity of the reader. This performative effect is achieved by confronting the reader with an "unresolved" existential problem that is not yet drawn into clarity but is staged in all its confusions and contradictions. Kierkegaard's pseudonym Constantius relies here on a performative writing strategy that is animated by a dialectic of advance and withdrawal. In the last and third step, I will analyze Constantius's own reflection on the performative dimension of his text. Constantius has left several clues behind, each of which suggests that he deliberately developed a performative writing strategy.

Theoretical Framework: Performance and Performativity

Many interpreters of Kierkegaard have studied his poetics of indirect communication as a maieutic practice that takes place on the borderline between philosophy and literature. Without denying the influence of literature on Kierkegaard's works, I will focus on a different discipline of art: the theater.[3] It is well known that Kierkegaard was an ardent lover of theater and could often be found in the Royal Theater in Copenhagen. He composed several minor writings about theater and remained fascinated with the subject to the end of his life. Although these minor writings have never received much attention, they can shed some light on the performative dimension of Kierkegaard's works.[4] "Phister as Captain Scipio" is exemplary in this respect. In this short essay, the pseudonym Procul analyzes how the Danish actor Joachim Ludvig Phister plays the role of Scipio, an alcoholic who is a captain in the Papal Police Corps.

To exploit the comic potential of this character, Phister has to make a double movement. On the one hand, he has to play Captain Scipio as someone who is constantly concealing that he is an alcoholic. On the other hand, he has to make sure that the viewer begins to develop a suspicion of this hidden condition. Nevertheless, Phister's aim is not to expose Scipio as a cheat and an alcoholic, but to hint at the contradiction between his outer appearance as an authoritative figure and the hidden condition that he tries to conceal. This contradiction is heightened when it is "his duty to clear out a pub where the people are dead drunk" (*SKS* 16:133 / "PCS" 334). Procul is so impressed with Phister's performance because he is able to keep the concealment and the disclosure in tension with each other. The way Phister conceals Captain Scipio's hidden condition betrays that something is not right. By drawing the viewer's attention to the concealment, he discloses that Captain Scipio hides something, but what he hides still has to be uncovered. In other words, the disclosure takes place *telegraphically*, in an indirect and a nonverbal way (compare *SKS* 16:139 / "PCS" 340). Throughout his oeuvre, Kierkegaard is fascinated by this tension between concealment and disclosure. Like Phister, he tries to communicate something that cannot be shown directly but can emerge only as an enigma that still has to be unraveled.

Kierkegaard develops a "theater of ideas" in which philosophical and existential problems are performed rather than represented. The performative dimension of his work ensues from his interpretation of human existence. Although Kierkegaard does not have a unified theory of the self, his pseudonyms all start from the same basic premise: the self has a temporal structure that is paradoxical in nature. It is established as a relation between several elements that cannot be synthesized with each other. This creates a fragile equilibrium that is constantly on the verge of breaking apart. An added problem is that there is a qualitative difference between the inner world of the single individual and the external and collective means of communication by which he expresses himself. Kierkegaard tries to bridge this chasm between the inner and the outer by turning his oeuvre into a theater of ideas. His works not only *say* something; they also attempt *to do* something, to have a performative effect. To analyze this performative mode of communication, I will distinguish between the "categories of performativity" that can be derived from Kierkegaard's works and the "performative writing strategies" that animate them. The first concerns the conceptual content, the second, the literary form. Their distinction indicates a difference in focus rather than in substance.

On the level of conceptual content, Kierkegaard introduces several categories of performativity. These categories address a type of communication that constitutes its own reality rather than representing it after the fact. The notion of performativity indicates that this type of communication does not refer to a preexisting state of affairs that is communicated. Rather, it confronts the readers with an unresolved contradiction, the content of which still has to be unraveled. The communication has a meaningful content, but this content is neither fixed nor predefined. It emerges only after it has been actualized by the reader. This usually involves a decision that discloses the view of the reader rather than that of the communicator. It was J. L. Austin who first introduced the notion of performativity. His main argument was that language is not just descriptive and reflective but can actually perform an action. (When I give an order, I am not describing that action, but I am performing it.) In a similar way, a category of performativity signifies a performative act that communicates something (analogous to Austin's locution), but what it communicates is a contradiction that aims to activate the subjectivity of readers (analogous to the illocutionary force) by forcing them to respond in such a way that they disclose their own views on the matter (analogous to the perlocutionary effect).[5]

Kierkegaard develops a whole series of categories of performativity. These categories not only precede Austin's analyses of performativity; they also add to the tradition that emerged in his wake. Each of them is an original invention that is developed in reaction to a specific existential problem. In *Practice in Christianity*, for example, Kierkegaard's pseudonym Anti-Climacus analyzes the performative context in which Christ, as the God-man, operates (*SKS* 12:81–151 / *PC* 69–144). To make this analysis possible he introduces several categories of performativity, such as "the incognito that demands faith" and "offense." If God would appear in all his glory without an incognito to hide his divinity, he would become an idol that can be identified and known with certainty. This would cancel out the role of subjectivity. For that reason, Anti-Climacus argues, Christ hides himself behind the incognito of a lowly human being. By deliberately creating a contradiction between his ordinary appearance and his claim of being God, Christ makes himself offensive. In this way he turns himself into an object of faith and forces the recipient to make a choice that will disclose whether he or she believes in him. Notions like incognito and offense are introduced to address the unusual performative structure of the God-man.[6]

Kierkegaard's categories of performativity are interesting in their own right. However, they will also be helpful for understanding the performative writing strategies underlying his works. We find these performative writing strategies on the level of literary form. The aim of these writing strategies is to confront the reader with an unresolved existential problem that is not drawn into clarity yet but is staged in all its confusions and contradictions. In other words, Kierkegaard does not represent a solution in which the problem has already been overcome; instead, he tries to make the reader aware of the problem and let him or her struggle with it. By performing ideas as unresolved problems rather than representing them as clear and well-defined solutions, Kierkegaard breaks with the Aristotelian tradition of mimetic representation. His pseudonym Frater Taciturnus, for instance, introduces the notion of a psychological experiment to find a performative writing strategy that no longer relies on representation (compare *SKS* 6:173–454 / *SLW* 185–494). Hence Taciturnus no longer relies on Aristotelian catharsis as a purification of emotion through a process of identification. Instead, he introduces an alternative catharsis that purifies by activating the subjectivity of the reader. This is done by dramatizing an unresolved problem without providing a way out. A fictional protagonist becomes entangled in a contradiction between actuality and ideality that is simultaneously essentially comic and essentially tragic. The reader has to decide which of these moods prevails.[7] It would be a mistake, however, to view this performative writing strategy as a kind of postmodern "empty play" that destroys meaning rather than creating it. The unresolved problems are not meaningless. Rather, they imply an excess of meaning that has to be narrowed down by the reader. Other pseudonyms, such as Johannes de Silentio, Climacus, Anti-Climacus, and Vigilius

Haufniensis, develop similar performative writing strategies. In fact, one might even argue that—at least to some extent—Kierkegaard also relies on these strategies when he writes under his own name as veronymous author.

Repetition as a Category of Performativity

Repetition is not a philosophical treatise in the traditional sense. It introduces repetition as one of the most important categories of modern philosophy, without clearly explaining how this category should be understood. On the contrary, Kierkegaard ensures that its precise meaning remains constantly in dispute. This is illustrative for the changing role of categories in his work. Instead of providing well-defined concepts that can be applied outside of the concrete contexts in which they are introduced, Kierkegaard develops categories of performativity that remain unfinished as long as the reader does not put them into action. If these categories are too hastily detached from the setting in which they emerge, they will become meaningless.

In its ordinary sense, repetition refers to an event that occurs for a second, a third, or any other time. This implies a repetition of the same. Examples of this ordinary repetition include a rehearsal (i.e., repeated practice to get something firmly in one's head), a relapse (i.e., return to a previous undesirable state), and a reprise (i.e., restaging an earlier production), as well as Constantius's own attempt to repeat his earlier trip to Berlin. Kierkegaard is not interested in these ordinary repetitions but tries to address a very different type of repetition that is existential rather than ordinary. In contrast to its ordinary counterpart, an existential repetition will always emerge as a unique event. In order to persist, this unique event has to be repeated. However, it does not remain the same as it was throughout this repetition but undergoes a transition that makes it unique again. There is no "first time" that repeats itself a "second time" (as with a touchdown that is repeated in the replay). On the contrary, the "first time" repeats itself in another "first time." According to Kierkegaard, this is how subjectivity is structured. Subjectivity is repetition, but the main characteristic of this repetition is that it is always new. It is no longer a repetition of the same but is a repetition of difference. Kierkegaard thus develops an existential philosophy in which subjectivity is no longer defined by an essential core that remains the same throughout change; instead, subjectivity is now seen as a continuous repetition of difference. As such, he is one of the first philosophers to redefine the concept of identity. Later philosophers, such as Nietzsche, Heidegger, and Deleuze, will follow him in this respect, although they will give a slightly different twist to it.

Repetition is structured in such a way that the two manifestations of repetition—ordinary and existential—are constantly confused with each other. Initially the reader will enter the text as a passive spectator who looks from a distance at the events that happen to the protagonists; however, the confusions and misunderstandings will force the reader to become an active participant. Constantius achieves this effect by means of a dialectic of advance and withdrawal. At several points, a real understanding of existential repetition is reached. In these moments the category of repetition is advanced. However, each time the text will eventually switch back to ordinary repetition, as if the two manifestations of repetition are the same. At these moments the category of repetition is withdrawn again. In this way, the understanding of repetition is always taken one step forward and two steps back. The aim of this dialectic of advance and withdrawal is to activate the subjectivity of the reader. In the case of *Repetition*, this is done by embodying repetition in the lives of two protagonists.

The first protagonist is Constantin Constantius, the author-narrator of the book who sees himself as a "secret agent in a higher service" whose task it is to expose what is hidden (*SKS* 4:12 / *R* 135). The second protagonist is a young man who has entered into a love relationship with a girl but now slowly discovers that he cannot go through with it. Both these protagonists become entangled in a discrepancy between the ordinary and the existential manifestation of repetition. On a theoretical level, Constantius seems to understand what existential repetition entails (advance), but when he tries to bring it into practice it becomes clear that he has confused it with repetition in the ordinary sense (withdrawal). In the case of the young man, the opposite happens. He faces the problem of subjectivity and freedom in practice and seeks refuge in the category of existential repetition (advance). However, because he lacks a proper understanding of this category, he is satisfied with an ordinary repetition (withdrawal). It is the task of the reader to reconstitute the category of repetition by taking up the advances and by separating them from the withdrawals.

The dialectic of advance and withdrawal can be illustrated by highlighting each of its two moments separately. A good example of a withdrawal can be found in the Berlin episode, halfway through the first part of the book. Instead of analyzing the category of repetition in a systematic way, Constantius decides to conduct an experiment in order "to test the possibility and meaning of repetition" (*SKS* 4:26–27 / *R* 150). He does this by undertaking an "investigative journey [*Opdagelses-Reise*]" to Berlin (*SKS* 4:26 / *R* 150). In his own words: "When I was occupied for some time, at least on occasion, with the question of repetition—whether or not it is possible, what importance it has, whether something gains or loses in being repeated—I suddenly had the thought: You can, after all, take a trip to Berlin; you have been there once before, and now you can prove to yourself whether a repetition is possible and what importance it has" (*SKS* 4:9 / *R* 131). After many unsuccessful attempts to relive his previous experience of the journey to Berlin, Constantius concludes that there is no repetition. This makes him feel ashamed for his big words; it seems to him that they "were only a dream from which I awoke to have life unremittingly and treacherously *retake* everything [*tage Alt igjen*; literally 'take everything back'] it had given without providing a *repetition*" (*SKS* 4:45 / *R* 172). In Constantius's view, repetition should imply a "giving again," whereas the experiment shows that life "takes everything back." That is why Constantius is forced to conclude, "There is no repetition, and my earlier conception of life was victorious" (*SKS* 4:45 / *R* 171).

The experiment fails, and the category of repetition is abandoned. The reader will not be surprised to learn about this failure. The whole effort seemed ludicrous to begin with. How could Constantius even think that it would be possible to relive his earlier experiences? What is going on here? Has he lost his mind? Or is he trying to make a fool of the reader? The sheer absurdity of his experiment already indicates that it cannot be accepted at face value. The experiment is doomed to fail from the beginning because it is the result of a deliberate misunderstanding. This misunderstanding is never explicated in the text. It is only in a later, unpublished note of 1843–44 that Constantius identifies it as such.[8] He writes there, "The most interior problem of the possibility of repetition is expressed externally, as if repetition, if it were possible, were to be found outside the individual when in fact it must be found within the individual" (*SKS* 15:69 / *R*, Suppl., 304). The external means by which the experiment is conducted are in direct conflict with the existential and inward nature of repetition. By animating this conflict rather than resolving it, Constantius forces his readers to decide the issue for themselves.

As a category of performativity, repetition can emerge only in the middle of confusions and misunderstandings. This does not mean, however, that the reader is left completely in the dark. On the contrary, the reader can fall back on the advances that have already been made by Constantius and the young man. In order to get a better grasp of existential repetition, I will highlight several of these advances. A first series of advances is made when Constantius opposes the worldview of the ancient Greeks to that of the moderns. According to him, the ancient Greeks relied on recollection, whereas modern philosophy turns toward repetition as "the new category that will be discovered" (*SKS* 4:25 / *R* 148). This category is not available yet but still has to be discovered. In fact, as a category of performativity, repetition will always remain a discovery in the making. When Constantius refers to the Greek worldview, he is thinking especially of Plato, who believed that the truth lies in the past but can be retrieved with the help of recollection. By situating truth in an originary and prior realm, Plato gives it a universal and eternal character. Constantius, on the other hand, introduces a new concept of truth. For him the truth is always something yet to come rather than a lost origin that has to be retrieved. This truth is not universal and eternal but is connected to a fleeting instant that constantly has to be repeated. As Constantius remarks, "Repetition and recollection are the same movement, except in opposite directions, for what is recollected has been, is repeated backward, whereas genuine repetition is recollected forward" (*SKS* 4:9 / *R* 131). From the metaphysical perspective of the ancient Greeks, the truth of the individual is understood as a movement that is directed toward the past. This truth does not emerge within the individual's own existence but must be conceived as an essence that precedes the individual's existence. According to Constantius, however, this essence is not the truth but is rather the untruth of the individual.

Despite the fact that modern philosophy turns toward repetition, it has not been able to grasp repetition fully. According to Constantius, this is largely due to Hegel and his followers. By reducing repetition to mediation, they transferred the problem of subjectivity and freedom from the realm of existence to the realm of logic. Constantius rejects this transfer. In his view, existence will never comply with the laws of logic. In contrast to the Hegelian conception of logical development, Constantius relies on an Aristotelian conception of existential movement. In the aforementioned unpublished note, he points out that "when Aristotle long ago said that the transition from possibility to actuality is a κίνησις [motion, change], he was not speaking about the possibility and actuality of logic, but about [the possibility and actuality] of freedom, and therefore he properly posits movement" (*SKS* 15:74 / *R*, Suppl., 310).[9] In Constantius's reading, κίνησις should not be understood as a mediated progression toward a predetermined goal but as a transition that implies a qualitative change. Repetition is the result of such a transition. As Constantius remarks, "The dialectic of repetition is easy, for that which is repeated has been—otherwise it could not be repeated—but the very fact that it has been makes the repetition into something new" (*SKS* 4:25 / *R* 149). Rather than a return to what was, repetition implies a transition to a new state. In this way it ensures that subjectivity comes into existence again.

The young man, the second protagonist of *Repetition*, also makes some advance in understanding repetition by focusing on the biblical figure of Job. In his reading, Job truly embodies repetition. Not because he "has received everything *double*" (*SKS* 4:79 / *R* 212), as the young man eventually concludes, but because he "qualifies as an exception" (*SKS* 4:75 / *R* 207). Job lost his whole family and everything he had, and still he is able to say "the Lord gave and the Lord took away." More important, Job does not despair over what has happened to him. He is able to say this without losing his faith in God and without accepting that God has been punishing him for his sins. Despite everything, Job continues to believe that he is in the right. According to the young man, it is Job who gives evidence of "the noble, human, bold confidence that knows what a human being is, knows that despite his being frail, despite his swift withering away like the flower, that in freedom he still has something of greatness, has a consciousness that even God cannot wrest from him even though he gave it to him" (*SKS* 4:76 / *R* 208). Because of his freedom, Job is able to resist his friends' suggestion that his misfortune is a punishment from God. At the same time, he is also able to withstand the ordeal that God has imposed upon him as a test. Neither God nor the human being is able to take subjectivity and freedom away from him. For the young man this extraordinary manifestation of subjectivity becomes the paradigm case of repetition. Nevertheless, despite his advance in understanding, the young man proves unable to live up to the standard that is set by Job. Instead, when he tries to achieve repetition in his own life, he unintentionally turns it into a banality.

The dialectic of advance and withdrawal ensures that the reader has to struggle through a series of confusions and misunderstandings. In this way, Constantius has turned *Repetition* into an enigma. This enigma will become fruitful only when the reader first identifies the confusions and misunderstandings and then starts to develop the emerging category of repetition on his or her own. The outcome of the book becomes the reader's responsibility. This does not mean that Constantius is simply throwing his readers into an abyss of ambiguity and uncertainty. To make them aware of the performative structure of his text, he has left a few clues. With the help of these clues it becomes possible to reconstruct Constantius's own thoughts about the performative writing strategy that is employed in *Repetition.*

Repetition as Philosophical Theater: Constantius's Thoughts on His Performative Writing Strategy

Although Constantius has not directly addressed the dialectic of advance and withdrawal, he has left certain clues in which this performative writing strategy is announced. I will focus on three of these clues. The first clue is already apparent in the subtitle of the book, *A Venture in Experimenting Psychology.* By calling his book a "venture," Constantius suggests that the outcome of the book cannot be known in advance but will emerge only gradually. The notion of "experimenting psychology" indicates that Constantius does not want to represent a real-life situation but that he tries to open up an experimental realm in which a psychological problem is put on the stage. Rather than studying repetition from the perspective of an uninvolved outsider, Constantius tries to transform it into something inward that has to be taken up by the reader. As he later remarks in a note of 1843–44, "I wanted to depict and make visible psychologically and esthetically; in the Greek sense, I wanted to let the concept come into being in the individuality and the situation, working itself forward through all sorts of misunderstandings" (*SKS* 15:68 / *R*, Suppl., 302). The venture in experimenting psychology thus becomes a philosophical theater in which ideas and categories are performed in a state of confusion.

Constantius finds an earlier example of this philosophical theater in a well-known anecdote about Diogenes the Cynic: "When the Eleatics denied motion, Diogenes, as everyone knows, came forward [*optraadte*] as an opponent. He literally did come forward [*optraadte*], because he did not say a word but merely paced back and forth a few times, thereby assuming that he had sufficiently refuted them" (*SKS* 4:9 / *R* 131). The Danish verb that is used here, *optræde*, has a clear theatrical connotation. Literally it means "stepping up" or "coming forward," but it also refers to the moment an actor "makes an appearance" by entering the scene and giving a performance. In the anecdote, Diogenes sees no need to debate whether movement is possible. Instead, he simply paces back and forth. This little performance sufficiently shows that existence does not comply with logic. By pacing back and forth, Diogenes performed the physical movement for which he was arguing. Constantius tries to achieve a similar effect by performing existential repetition as a movement that ultimately has to be concluded by the reader.

A second clue can be found in Constantius's concluding letter "to Mr. X. Esq., the real reader of this book" (*SKS* 4:89 / *R* 223). The letter opens with a few remarks about the art of reading. Constantius indicates that he is looking for a type of reader who is willing to make an effort in understanding the book, despite being completely bewildered by it. He follows the dictum of Clement of Alexandria, who is said to have written in such a way "that the heretics [were] unable to understand it" (*SKS* 4:91 / *R* 225). The term "heretics" here refers to superficial readers who fail to uncover the deliberate misunderstandings in which the protagonists become entangled. For such heretics the category of repetition will remain a strange and hazy notion.

In line with his remark about heretics, Constantius predicts that reviewers, who will try to measure the book on the basis of certain fixed standards, will not get anything out of it. The expectations of these reviewers will be frustrated because the composition of *Repetition* differs from that of most books. Constantius develops the story in such a way that the course of events "is inverse" (*SKS* 4:92 / *R* 226). Inverse? This is an odd expression. Inverse in what sense? Does Constantius mean that the book is turned upside down? Or is he referring to unexpected turning points or strange revisions? It is not entirely clear what he intends, but the context suggests that he is juxtaposing two types of compositions: teleological and paradoxical.[10] Teleological compositions are initially set in motion by a contradiction, but then progress toward a higher unity (the Hegelian 1, 2, 3). Constantius is not interested in these teleological compositions. In his view, they privilege the universal (logic) over the individual and the exception (existence). That is why Constantius has developed a new type of composition that is no longer teleological but is paradoxical in nature. This principle behind this paradoxical composition is aptly captured in the phrase "to kill a man and let him live" (*SKS* 4:92 / *R* 226). When the same man is killed and left alive, any attempt at reconciliation will run aground. In other words, the paradoxical composition ensures that the contradictions in the text cannot be overcome. The idea of a paradoxical composition already indicates how the dialectic of advance and withdrawal is generated. Taking one step forward and two steps back, the paradoxical composition generates a circulating movement that echoes Diogenes's pacing back and forth.

The third and most important clue can be found in the digression that forms the heart of the Berlin episode. This digression is best understood as an extensive mise en abyme, a story within a story that tells us how to perform the book we are reading. It deals with two examples of kitsch. The first example concerns a cheap and sentimental type of painting that Constantius calls a Nürnberg print.[11] He describes this as follows: "There one sees a landscape depicting a rural area in general. This abstraction cannot be artistically executed. Therefore the whole thing is achieved by contrast, namely, by an accidental concretion. And yet I ask everyone if from such a landscape he does not get the impression of a rural area in general" (*SKS* 4:33 / *R* 158). Two elements are of importance here. The effect is achieved "by contrast" and with the help of "an accidental concretion." To understand what Constantius means by this, it will be helpful to explicate the distinction he makes between art and kitsch. According to Constantius, art derives its perfection from the way it balances the actual and the ideal. This balance can be achieved by giving a faithful representation of an exceptional panorama or by elevating a nondescript tableau in an ideal reproduction. In both cases, the painter has made sure that the depicted landscape (actuality) is worthy of being transformed into art (ideality). Kitsch, on the other hand, is always based on a contradiction between actuality and ideality. Although the rural area that is depicted in a Nürnberg print is nothing special (actuality), it is still immortalized by being painted (ideality). This creates a contrast that defies the aesthetic categories of the educated art critic.

Constantius sees in kitsch a model of artistic production that no longer relies on representation but is based on a principle of "accidental concretion." To my mind, "concretion" should be understood here in the geological sense. Like a fossil, the Nürnberg print can be viewed as petrifaction of the accidental. It generates enormous and universal categories like "the rural area in general," even though these categories emerge only in a singular and accidental form. Constantius compares this to a child who cuts "out of a piece of paper a man and a woman who were man and woman in general in a more rigorous sense than Adam and Eve were" (*SKS* 4:33 / *R* 158).

A second and more extensive example of kitsch can be found in a specific type of popular play, the sole purpose of which is to incite laughter. In Danish and German this type of popular play is called *Posse*. Its closest English equivalents are farce, burlesque, and vaudeville. As Constantius suggests, a farce is not based on a plot that unifies the actions into a meaningful whole but relies on accidental instances, the effects of which are wholly dependent on the mood of the spectator. Constantius seems to view farce as a paradigm of subjectivity. He writes, "Its impact depends largely on self-activity and the viewer's improvisation, the particular individuality comes to assert himself in a very individual way and in his enjoyment is emancipated from all esthetic obligations to admire, to laugh, to be moved, etc. in the traditional way" (*SKS* 4:34 / *R* 159). In the same way as a Nürnberg print, a farce no longer complies with the aesthetic categories of the educated public and does not rely on the "commensurables of the artistic" (*SKS* 4:38 / *R* 163). On the contrary, a farce demands an incommensurable response that cannot be shared with others but solely depends on the individual viewer.

According to Constantius, a farce "must include two, at most three, very talented actors or, more correctly, generative geniuses" (*SKS* 4:36 / *R* 161). These geniuses do not rely on reflection and deliberation but achieve their goal by lyrical improvisation. Their talent is exceptional only insofar as they "have the courage to venture what the individual makes bold to do only when alone, what the mentally deranged do in the presence of everybody" (*SKS* 4:36 / *R* 161). Constantius illustrates this talent with a remarkable description of how Friedrich Beckmann, the leading actor at the Königstädter Theater in Berlin, enters the stage: "What Baggesen says of Sara Nickels, that she comes rushing on stage with a rustic scene in tow, is true of B[eckmann] in the positive sense, except that he comes walking [*komme gaaende*]. . . . He is not only able to walk [*gaae*], but he is also able to *come walking* [*komme gaaende*]" (*SKS* 4:38 / *R* 163). A distinction is drawn here between two types of dramatic action. Ordinary actors just walk onto the stage. Beckmann, on the other hand, "is able to *come walking*." What is the difference between these two types of movement? To understand this we have to look more closely at the Danish phrase *komme gaaende*. This phrase, which is repeated no fewer than five times, literally means something like "coming while going."[12] This ambiguous movement goes in two directions at once. On the one hand, Beckmann is arriving; on the other, he is already leaving. Constantius seems to indicate here that Beckmann does not represent a particular intentional action but embodies movement as such. That is why Beckmann can play the role of an apprentice without representing him in any way. Instead of fully developing this role, he uses it as an incognito. Behind this incognito "dwells the lunatic demon of comedy, who quickly extricates himself and carries everything away in sheer abandonment" (*SKS* 4:38 / *R* 164). The phrase "coming while going" echoes the instant of transition on which existential repetition is based. However, Beckmann embodies this ambiguous movement of repetition merely in an external way. By letting the meaningful world vanish, he gives an impetus to subjectivity. As such, he covers only one half of the transition. The other half of the transition has to be carried through by the viewer.

The performance of a farce relies on two or three geniuses like Beckmann who have a lyrical talent for invoking laughter. The rest of the cast can consist of minor actors who do not need to have any special talent. Constantius describes these minor characters in terms similar to those in which he described the Nürnberg print. According to him, "the minor characters have their effect through that abstract category 'in general' and achieve it by an accidental concretion" (*SKS* 4:37 / *R* 163). We already saw that an accidental concretion is comparable to a fossil, something unimportant and ordinary that is immortalized. In the case of a farce, the accidental concretion makes "a claim to be the ideal, which it does by stepping onto the artificial world of the stage" (*SKS* 4:37 / *R* 163). In this way, the farce defies the laws of serious theater. Instead of developing concrete characters that are thoroughly carried out in ideality, the farce remains stuck in accidental situations by highlighting something unessential. In serious theater a concrete actuality is translated into an abstract ideality by showing something essential that is not only valid for the character in question but applies to everybody. In this way, it generates universal templates of action that indicate how a courageous or chivalrous person is supposed to behave. Farce, on the other hand, moves from the abstract to the concrete. An abstract person in general is embodied by highlighting something unimportant that is completely accidental. This ensures that a farce never reaches ideality but gets stuck in actuality. By putting the accidental on the stage, the farce achieves a comic effect that destroys universal templates of action rather than creating them. Instead, it activates the viewers' own productivity and forces them to develop their own template of action.

I have analyzed three clues in which the dialectic of advance and withdrawal is announced as a deliberate writing strategy that is based on performance rather than representation. The first clue indicated that *Repetition* opens up an experimental realm that functions as a theater of ideas. A second clue was found in Constantius's suggestion that he relies on a paradoxical composition in which two irreconcilable tendencies are placed in tension with each other without providing a way out. These first two clues culminated in a digression on two forms of kitsch. This digression can be read as a mise en abyme. As such it is exemplary for the performative structure of *Repetition* as a whole. Constantius introduced two important notions there: "accidental concretion" and "coming while going." As we saw, an accidental concretion concerns the tension between actuality and ideality. This reveals something about Kierkegaard's categories of performativity. The intention of these categories is also to resist ideality by letting the reader get stuck in actuality. The notion of "coming while going," on the other hand, tells us something about the role of performance in Kierkegaard's theater of ideas. It embodies the ambiguous movement of a simultaneous advance and withdrawal.

To conclude, in this essay I have argued that Constantius invents a new way of doing philosophy in *Repetition*. This allows him to introduce existential repetition as a category of performativity. Rather than clarifying what existential repetition is, he lets it emerge in a series of confusions and misunderstandings. In this way, the category is advanced and withdrawn at the same time. It is the task of the reader to make this dialectic of advance and withdrawal fruitful. This performative demand turns *Repetition* into a theater of ideas.

Rather than representing an already finished argument, Constantius performs a problem that still has to be unraveled. In this process he provides several clues, suggesting that the dialectic of advance and withdrawal is a deliberate writing strategy that can take on several forms.

Notes

1. This essay expands upon and adds to ideas introduced in an earlier essay of mine that was published in Dutch, "De herhaling van het onherhaalbare: Constantin Constantius over vrijheid en subjectiviteit," *Wijsgerig Perspectief* 53, no. 2 (2013): 30–37.

2. My approach is inspired by and indebted to three important studies on Kierkegaard: Sylviane Agacinski, *Aparté: Conceptions and Deaths of Søren Kierkegaard*, trans. Kevin Newmark (Tallahassee: Florida State University Press, 1988); Samuel Weber, "Kierkegaard's 'Posse,'" in *Theatricality as Medium* (New York: Fordham University Press, 2004), 200–228; Gilles Deleuze, *Difference and Repetition*, trans. Paul Patton (New York: Continuum, 2001), 5–11.

3. Other scholars also have attempted to read Kierkegaard from the perspective of theater and performance. Joseph Westfall, for instance, argues "that Kierkegaardian authorship is performative, or that the Kierkegaardian author might best be understood as a kind of performer." Westfall therefore focuses on "the person, persona or personae to whom authorship of the work is ascribed (*authoring*)." *The Kierkegaardian Author: Authorship and Performance in Kierkegaard's Literary and Dramatic Criticism* (Berlin: Walter de Gruyter, 2007), 145, 146. Although I do not disagree with this approach, I will not be focusing on the issue of authorship. Instead, I focus on the existential problems that Kierkegaard performs and on the categories of performativity that he invents in the process.

4. Minor writings on theater addressing "categories of performativity" include "The Crisis and the Crisis in the Life of an Actress" (*SKS* 14:93–107/ *CCLA* 301–26), "Phister as Captain Scipio" (*SKS* 16:125–43 / "PCS" 327–44), and selections from the first part of *Either/Or* (*SKS* 2 / *EO* 1). (On these writings by Kierkegaard about the theater, and also on his avidness as a theatergoer, see also George Pattison's essay in this volume.—Ed.)

5. J. L. Austin, who first conceptualized "performativity," introduced a by now famous distinction between three aspects of performative communication: the locutionary meaning, the illocutionary force, and the perlocutionary effect. The locutionary meaning is the sense and reference of an utterance. The illocutionary force is the function that the utterance performs when it is being said. For example, the phrase "I now pronounce you man and wife" constitutes reality as such; it does not refer to a preexisting state of affairs but creates these states of affairs; it is self-referential. The perlocutionary effect is the response of the listener or reader as a consequence of what is said to him or her, for example, anger or fear in response to a threat. This threefold distinction will shed some light on the complex movement that is implied in many of Kierkegaard's performative categories. However, Austin's distinction is too general and too linguistic to explain the structure and the intended effect of this complex movement. For

instance, this movement is not rule-governed in the limited sense of Austin, and it includes fictional statements. Compare J. L. Austin, *How to Do Things with Words*, 2nd ed. (Oxford: Clarendon Press, 1975); Austin, *Philosophical Papers*, 3rd ed. (Oxford: Oxford University Press, 1979).

6. For more on the notion of incognito see my article "Incognito," in *Kierkegaard's Concepts*, Tome 3: *Envy to Incognito*, ed. Steven M. Emmanuel, William McDonald, and Jon Stewart, Kierkegaard Research: Sources, Reception and Resources, vol. 15 (Farnham, U.K.: Ashgate, 2014), 231–38.

7. I have analyzed Taciturnus's theory of the psychological experiment more extensively in my article "Psychological Experiment," in *Kierkegaard's Concepts*, Tome 5: *Objectivity to Sacrifice*, ed. Steven M. Emmanuel, William McDonald, and Jon Stewart, Kierkegaard Research: Sources, Reception and Resources, vol. 15 (Farnham, U.K.: Ashgate, 2015), 159–66.

8. This note is part of several sketches (*SKS* 15:61–88 / *R*, Suppl., 283–324) in which Kierkegaard lets Constantius develop a response to J. L. Heiberg's article "Det astronomiske Aar" (1843, "The Astronomical Year"), which discusses *Repetition* at some length. These sketches were written between December 1843 and March 1844 but never published by Kierkegaard.

9. I have slightly modified the English rendering of this sentence to eradicate an ungrammaticality that is present in the Danish original and that is preserved in the Hongs' translation.

10. For an interesting but different account of the notion of "inverse," see Arne Melberg, "Repetition (in the Kierkegaardian Sense of the Term)," *Diacritics* 20, no. 3 (1990): 71–87.

11. For a discussion of the many references to Nürnberg prints in Kierkegaard's writings, see Ragni Linnet's essay in the present volume. Linnet finds that the particular Nürnberg print described by Constantius approximates one of the *Entombment*, inspired by Raphael.—Ed.

12. Agacinski (*Aparté*, 165) and Weber ("Kierkegaard's 'Posse,' " 221–23) have also analyzed this particular phrase.

Kierkegaard's Notions of Drama and Opera

Molière's *Don Juan*, Mozart's *Don Giovanni*, and the Question of Music and Sensuousness

Nils Holger Petersen

In a recent article, George Pattison discusses Kierkegaard's theatrical criticism in relation to the particular Danish literary and theatrical context in the first half of the nineteenth century. The dominant figure in theater criticism in this period was Johan Ludvig Heiberg (1791–1860), dramatist, poet, critic (inspired by Hegel), as well as editor of literary journals and, late in his life, director of the Royal Theater in Copenhagen. Heiberg had been helpful and encouraging to the very young Kierkegaard and, as Pattison demonstrates, Kierkegaard in his theater criticism at least up to and including 1845 remained influenced by Heiberg and his notion of correspondence between idea and form, although in many other respects he turned against Heiberg (and Hegelian criticism).[1] Pattison discusses examples of Kierkegaard's criticism concerning opera and comedy mainly through texts from *Either/Or* (1843): the essay on Mozart's *Don Giovanni* (in Danish German culture of the time usually referred to as *Don Juan*), which I will also discuss, and the one on Scribe's play *The First Love* in Heiberg's translation (*Den første Kjærlighed*), supplemented by a few other texts from the years 1840–45. Pattison summarizes Kierkegaard's aesthetic position as "the life-view of the reflecteur who deliberately maintains a critical distance from the immediate object of consciousness in order to judge this object in the light of its relationship to ideality." At the same time, Pattison makes clear that Kierkegaard accepts this attitude only within a sphere of aesthetics, but not "its application to the personal life."[2]

In this essay I shall pursue the question of Kierkegaard's theatrical aesthetics and attempt to come to terms with his treatise on Mozart's opera *Don Giovanni* and to understand it in relation to broader questions of worldview.[3] As is well known, in the treatise "The Immediate Erotic Stages or The Musical-Erotic" in part 1 of *Either/Or*, Kierkegaard's aesthetic pseudonym "A" discusses Mozart and *Don Giovanni*, his main object of analysis; he also discusses the musical medium as such and further uses his understanding of the character of the musical medium to discuss different aesthetic criteria he sets up for opera and spoken theater in connection with the Don Juan theme. This discussion is carried out not least by reference to Molière's *Don Juan* (1665) in K. L. Rahbek's Danish translation (1813) as well as the free Danish version, which Heiberg wrote in 1812 and published (probably in a revised form) in 1814 (*SKS* K2–3:131–32). In the first part of this essay I shall primarily focus on the understanding of the musical medium as "A" develops it in "The Immediate Erotic Stages" as a basis for his distinctions and aesthetic criteria for music drama and spoken theater. In the second part, I shall consider some consequences of this view with respect to its possible meaning in a broad context of cultural history and life view.[4]

Drama and the Medium of Music

In his piece "Other Versions of Don Juan Considered in Relation to the Musical Interpretation," which constitutes section 2 of the treatise "The Immediate Erotic Stages or The Musical-Erotic" (*SKS* 2:107–18 / *EO* 1:103–15), "A" takes up a claim launched from the very beginning of the treatise for a more thorough discussion of the relationship between music drama and spoken theater. The assertion is that Mozart's version of the Don Juan myth captures the essence of this myth precisely because of the musical medium—in combination, of course, with Mozart's command of this medium. The main question elaborated in different ways all through "A's" treatise concerns the relationship between music and language, on the one hand, and between sensuousness and spirit, on the other, and how these two pairs are interconnected.

Early in the treatise, "A" uses the idea of Faust, with its rich literary tradition, as a backdrop for his understanding of the idea of Don Juan, which he considers to be more abstract and universal. Don Juan is the firstborn of the kingdom of sensuousness, a kingdom expressed in the medieval idea of Mount Venus, where sensuousness has its home. Language, however, has no home here. "A" argues that for this reason the Don Juan myth has not been the object of literary treatment in the same way as Faust has. It is a main idea of "A" to associate Faust with language and reflection, and Don Juan with music. "A" sees both as demonic, but "Faust is the expression for the demonic qualified as the spiritual that the Christian spirit excludes," whereas "Don Juan . . . is the expression for the demonic qualified as the sensuous." It is only when reflection sets in that the realm of the sensuous is identified as sinful, "but then Don Juan has been slain, then the music stops" (*SKS* 2:95 / *EO* 1:90).

Even earlier in the treatise, "A" remarks that "*Faust* has language as its medium, and since it is a much more concrete medium, for that reason, too, many works of the same kind are conceivable" (*SKS* 2:64 / *EO* 1:57). When this idea is brought up again in the section on other versions of Don Juan, "A" emphasizes that his discussion of such other versions "is done not for their own sake . . . but only in order to illuminate the significance of the musical interpretation more fully" (*SKS* 2:109 / *EO* 1:105–6). The focus is on what music can achieve as opposed to words. It is important to have in mind, however, that the relationship between the two media, language and music, is dialectic: one sets the limits for the other, as will become clear. "An interpretation of Faust can merit being called perfect, and yet a later generation will give rise to a new Faust, whereas Don Juan, because of the abstract character of the idea, lives on forever, in every age, and to wish to produce a Don Juan after Mozart will always be like wanting to write an *Ilias post Homerum* [*Iliad* after Homer] in a sense even more profound than is the case with Homer" (*SKS* 2:108 / *EO* 1:105). This, on the other hand, does not suggest that "a particular gifted nature should not have attempted to interpret Don Juan in some other way" (*SKS* 2:108 / *EO* 1:105). Here "A" brings in Molière, claiming that "not everyone may have noticed that the model for all other interpretations is essentially Molière's *Don Juan*." "A" does, however, find an exception in Heiberg's version, judging it to have "a great advantage over Molière's." While praising Heiberg for his "sure esthetic eye," he also argues that Heiberg may have been indirectly inspired by Mozart to see "how Don Juan must be interpreted as soon as music is not made its proper expression or he is placed in completely different esthetic categories" (*SKS* 2:109 / *EO* 1:105).

The main point for "A's" dichotomy between a literary and dramatic (i.e., spoken dramatic) treatment of Don Juan and a musical one is made clear in the following way: "As soon as he [Don Juan] is given spoken lines, everything is changed. That is, the reflection that motivates the lines reflects him out of the vagueness in which he is only musically audible" (*SKS* 2:109 / *EO* 1:106).[5] The vagueness, or perhaps rather the obscurity of a musical representation of Don Juan is something "A" discusses much earlier in his treatise; in his view, vagueness is an important characteristic for musical representations altogether. In a sense, this is the main thread running through the whole discussion of *Don Giovanni*. "A" claims *Don Giovanni* to (be the only one of Mozart's works to) make Mozart a "classic composer" (*SKS* 2:58 / *EO* 1:51), an epithet that goes far beyond delight or admiration: "With his *Don Giovanni*, Mozart enters the rank of those immortals, of those visibly transfigured ones, whom no cloud takes away from the eyes of men; with *Don Giovanni* he stands supreme among them" (*SKS* 2:59 / *EO* 1:51). "A's" panegyric statements about Mozart and *Don Giovanni* in the beginning of the treatise, including the expression just cited, are based on enthusiasm for the music Mozart wrote for this opera but just as much on an aesthetic notion of correspondence between idea and form—and, we might add, medium—as well as on "A's" general conception of music. It is in order to demonstrate that Mozart's *Don Giovanni* truly is a classic work that "A" establishes this correspondence.

First, "A" claims that the "sensuous in its elemental originality [*den sandselige Genialitet*]" is the most abstract idea conceivable. Asking, "But through which medium can it be presented?," he immediately gives his answer: "Only through music" (*SKS* 2:64 / *EO* 1:56). His argument for this assertion lies, first, in the relationship between language and music, to which I shall turn in a moment; second, in the broader historical idea that it is "first by Christianity" that "sensuality is posited as a principle, as a power, as an independent system"; and third, in a formulation that leads into the discussion of the relationship between language and music, that "sensuality was placed under the qualification of spirit first by Christianity." However, sensuality is posited in such a way as to be excluded, "but precisely because it is to be excluded it is defined as a principle" (*SKS* 2:68 / *EO* 1:61).

In his discussion of media, "A" insists that "language, regarded as medium, is the medium absolutely qualified by spirit, and it is therefore the authentic medium of the idea," and further that, as opposed to other media, "in language, the sensuous as medium is reduced to a mere instrument and is continually negated." The point here seems to be that what is important in the use of language is the message that language conveys, not the sounds it employs: "If a person spoke in such a way that we heard the flapping of his tongue etc., he would be speaking poorly" (*SKS* 2:74 / *EO* 1:67). "A" goes on to say that "language is the perfect medium precisely when everything sensuous in it is negated" (*SKS* 2:74 / *EO* 1:68). The continuation of this sentence appears slightly surprising, since the general point "A" is about to establish concerns music as the medium for presenting the sensuous: "That is also the case with music; that which is really supposed to be heard is continually disengaging itself from the sensuous" (*SKS* 2:74 / *EO* 1:68). I shall return to this point later. For now, however, "A's" main point must be established: his argument for why music is the medium through which sensuous immediacy can be expressed.

On the whole, "A" describes music in its contrast with language, although, as just pointed out, music also has a common ground with language; indeed, "A" emphasizes, more than once (including the sequel to the just cited statement), that music is also a kind of language. His comparison of music and language begins with the admission that language is the only medium that occurs in time. However, he again admits that this is true also for music, except that the musical "occurrence in time is in turn a negation of the feelings dependent upon the senses" (*SKS* 2:75 / *EO* 1:68).[6] This last remark must be read in the context of "A's" following claim of music's ephemerality. The immediacy of music may be understood to betray the feelings to which the music gives rise: "Music does not exist except in the moment it is performed, for even if a person can read notes ever so well and has an ever so vivid imagination, he still cannot deny that only in a figurative sense does music exist when it is being read. It actually exists only when it is being performed" (*SKS* 2:75 / *EO* 1:68). His attempt at explaining the basic relation between language and music begins with the assumption that prose language is the least musical, while already the rhetorical delivery of an oration "in the sonorous construction of its periods" provides an "echo of the musical." In such ways he can proceed through poetic declamation, metrical constructions, and rhyme until "language leaves off and everything becomes music." However, he also encounters music when moving in the opposite direction from prose language, which is "permeated by the concept," to sheer interjections "which in turn are musical, just as a child's first babbling is musical" (*SKS* 2:75–76 / *EO* 1:69).

Summing up so far: music is close to language; indeed, "language is bounded by music on all sides" (*SKS* 2:76 / *EO* 1:69). This claim connects music to the sensuous qualities of language on either side of its reflective semantic uses, the sophisticated sonorous qualities of poetry on the one hand and the spontaneous sound of exclamations, screaming, babbling, and so forth on the other. Music in this view, then, is less precise and reflective than language. In my trying to come to terms with "A's" account, I have so far avoided commenting on his often confusing ranking of language and music. It is a recurring, apparently important point for him to state that music is, in the end, inferior to language as a medium. This may to some extent be part of a polemic against the early Romantics, for whom music was the highest of the arts, an art form that, foremost in music without words (or experienced as "pure" music apart from words), could transcend this world and move the listener to a higher or a deeper world, as for instance described by the young poet Wilhelm Heinrich Wackenroder (1773–1798) in his *Herzensergießungen eines Kunstliebenden Klosterbruders* (1797, known in English as *Confessions from the Heart of an Art-loving Friar* or [*Heart-felt*] *Outpourings of an Art-Loving Friar*), unfinished at the author's early death, edited (and finalized) by his friend, the poet Ludwig Tieck in 1799.

This work constitutes, among other things, an early example of the new Romantic aesthetics of music, surfacing for instance in a fictional letter from a young painter to a friend describing an experience of music during a mass in Rome. Here "the full Latin song, rising and falling through swelling musical tones like ships sailing through the waves of the sea, raised my mind ever higher," and a moment later, "trombones and I do not know which almighty tones blared and thundered a sublime devotion through all limbs."[7] Albeit in a more academic style, a similar approach to music is found in E. T. A. Hoffmann's statement "Mozart leads us into the deep layers of the spiritual realm. . . . In a similar way Beethoven's instrumental music opens the realm of the immense and immeasurable."[8] Altogether, statements to such effects about music as transcending the worldly and as the highest art form are common among the Romantics.[9]

The idea that music can express what words are not able to convey has deep roots in Western Christian traditions and was possibly first formulated by Augustine in his *Expositions of the Psalms* when explaining and appropriating theologically the notion of *iubilus*, or jubilation. The spiritual side of the musical medium in Augustine's view seems to parallel the no longer explicitly theological idea in Romantic aesthetics.[10] What I suggest is an indirect polemic against such Romantic views in "A's" account comes to the fore in his comparison between language and music. Describing the movement from language to music in a poetic direction, as quoted above, "A" contends "that language leaves off and everything becomes music." He continues, "Indeed, this is a pet phrase poets use to indicate that they, as it were, abandon the idea; it disappears for them, and everything ends in music. This might seem to imply that music is even closer to perfection as a medium than language. But this is one of those sentimental misconceptions that sprout only in empty heads" (*SKS* 2:75 / *EO* 1:69). Instead, "A" wants to establish a distinction between language and music based on music's inferiority to language when it comes to reflection and precision. As already pointed out, "A" maintains that one arrives at music from language by way of moving away from ideas and reflection, either by way of poetic rhetorical devices or by way of the movement from conceptual formulation to the mentioned interjections, like the child's babbling: "Here the point certainly cannot be that music is closer to perfection as a medium than language, or that music is a richer medium than language, unless it is assumed that saying 'Uh' is more valuable than a complete thought" (*SKS* 2:76 / *EO* 1:69). What music can do is express "the immediate in its immediacy." However, for "A," this primarily shows the limitation of music as a medium in relation to language. On the other hand, in the case of "sensuousness in its elemental originality," posited by Christianity outside the realm of spirit, music is the perfect medium precisely because of its limitation: "Reflection is implicit in language, and therefore language cannot express the immediate. Reflection is fatal to the immediate, and therefore it is impossible for language to express the musical, but this apparent poverty in language is precisely its wealth. In other words, the immediate is the indeterminate, and therefore language cannot grasp it; but its indeterminacy is not its perfection but rather a defect in it" (*SKS* 2:76 / *EO* 1:70). Thus, "A" has established that music is especially suited to the subject of the sensuous in its immediacy, which is the topic of Don Juan as determined by "A" in the section "The Elementary Originality of the Sensuous Qualified as Seduction" (*SKS* 2:92–107 / *EO* 1:87–103). Altogether this substantiates the claim that Mozart's *Don Giovanni* is a classic work—granted Mozart's musical genius—because the medium, as mastered by Mozart, is in complete correspondence with the idea that the work expresses: "In Mozart's *Don Giovanni*, we have the perfect unity of this idea and its corresponding form. But precisely because the idea is so very abstract and because the medium also is abstract, there is no probability that Mozart will ever have a competitor. Mozart's good fortune is that he has found a subject matter that is intrinsically altogether musical, and if any other composer were to compete with Mozart, there would be nothing for him to do except to compose *Don Giovanni* all over again" (*SKS* 2:64 / *EO* 1:57).[11]

The conceptualization of music established by "A" lies behind the discussion of Molière's *Don Juan* and of Heiberg's free version of that play. The main point, again, is that spoken lines and the reflection behind them change Don Juan into a concrete individual, thus removing him from the ideality "A" attributes to him (*SKS* 2:109 / *EO* 1:106). This point is repeated in the context of the discussion of Molière and Heiberg. Whereas a musical Don Juan is a seducer without strategy and does not need any particular means to be victorious in his sexual conquests (*SKS* 2:112 / *EO* 1:109), a reflective Don Juan loses this immediacy:

> The musical Don Juan enjoys the satisfaction; the reflective Don Juan enjoys the deception, enjoys the craftiness. The immediate pleasure is past, and reflection on the enjoyment is enjoyed more. In this respect there is a little hint in Molière's interpretation, except that this can by no means be developed, because all the remainder of the interpretation is a hindrance. Don Juan's desire is aroused because he sees a girl happy in her relation to the one she loves; he begins to be jealous. This is an interest that in the opera would not occupy us at all, simply because Don Juan is not a reflective individual. As soon as Don Juan is interpreted as a reflective individual, an ideality corresponding to the musical ideality can be attained only when the matter is shifted into the psychological realm. (*SKS* 2:111 / *EO* 1:108)

In this context "A" emphasizes the comic effect that can be obtained by denying Don Juan the means, thus constructing an incongruence; this is partly so in Molière's piece, but "A" makes a point of claiming that Heiberg is more consistent in the comical and more "correct" (*SKS* 2:112–13 / *EO* 1:109–10). Two important examples discussed by "A," however, apply to both Molière's piece and Heiberg's version. One, which "A" acknowledges is a true comical and fitting scene in a spoken Don Juan play, is the scene where Don Juan's creditor M. Dimanche—Hr. Paaske in Heiberg's version—visits Don Juan in order to get his money but is elegantly, politely, and comically diverted. This scene makes him lose the ideality he has in the opera with a comical effect. This scene would not do in an opera (*SKS* 2:112–13 / *EO* 1:109–10).[12]

The other example concerns the judgment scene where the Commander as a statue comes to fetch Don Juan. "A" makes the point that this scene is "a stumbling block from a dramatic point of view." If Don Juan is interpreted in the ideal way, that is, not as an individual but "as power, as passion"—as the idea of the sensuous—"then heaven itself must intervene." If Don Juan is seen as an individual character, it would make much more sense to let him confront the juridical system: "It is far more practical for Mr. Paaske to have Don Juan put into the debtor's prison." "A" suggests that it would be much more convincing to let Don Juan "know the commonplace bounds of actuality" (*SKS* 2:115 / *EO* 1:112).

Modern interpreters such as Ivan Nagel have made a similar point about opera in Mozart's time, referring to two different musical dramatic genres:

opera seria and *opera buffa*. The first of these belongs to the traditional court opera of absolutism, with grace as its most fundamental notion, whereas the second belongs to the more recently emergent bourgeois opera of Enlightenment in which conflicts are resolved rationally. For Nagel, Mozart's *Don Giovanni* can be understood as a play between the two operatic genres.[13] Whereas the same point concerning absolute power versus rational governance could easily be made concerning spoken theater as for musical theater of similarly different social contexts, this, for "A" (who, like Kierkegaard, must be assumed to be a child of an absolute monarchy), is a question of the musical medium:

> In the opera, it is entirely appropriate to have the Commendatore [i.e., the term used for the Commander in the Italian libretto of Mozart's opera] come again, but, after all, his conduct has ideal truth. The music immediately makes the Commendatore more than a particular individual; his voice is enlarged to the voice of a spirit. Therefore, just as Don Juan in the opera is interpreted with esthetic earnestness, so also is the Commendatore. In Molière, he comes with an ethical solemnity and heaviness that make him almost ludicrous; in the opera, he comes with esthetic lightness and metaphysical truth. No power in the play, no power on earth, has been able to constrain Don Juan; only a spirit, an apparition, is able to do that. Understood correctly, this in turn will illuminate the interpretation of Don Juan. A spirit, an apparition, is reproduction; this is the secret implicit in the coming again. But Don Juan is capable of everything, can withstand everything, except the reproduction of life, precisely because he is immediate, sensate life, of which spirit is the negation. (*SKS* 2:115 / *EO* 1:112–13)

In the following section, where "A" discusses the individual characters in Mozart's opera, he also summarizes his view on the dramatic differences between an opera and a drama (spoken theater). The main difference emphasized is closely connected to the discussion of the musical medium and its capacity in relation to language. "A" demands that a drama should leave a total impact that should "be less a mood than a thought, an idea." Nothing should be left over "of the mood from which the drama emerges, that is, nothing of the mood *qua* mood, but everything is converted into the dramatic sacred coin: action and situation." Reflection transfigures mood into action. If the mood predominates, the drama becomes lyrical, which "is a defect, but . . . is by no means a defect in an opera" (*SKS* 2:119–20 / *EO* 1:117). In an opera there must be a dominant tone that produces the unity of mood while maintaining the plurality of voices within this unity. "Opera does not have so much character delineation and action as its immanent objective; it is not sufficiently reflective for that." Rather, "unreflective, substantial passion"

(*SKS* 2:120 / *EO* 1:118) is expressed. Therefore the opera does not have the same urgency toward action as a drama must have. Instead, "it is characterized by a kind of tarrying, a kind of self-extension in time and space. . . . The action in an opera can be only immediate action" (*SKS* 2:121 / *EO* 1:118).

The descriptions and discussions of the various figures in *Don Giovanni* in agreement with this view emphasize the dependency of all these figures, except the Commendatore, on the protagonist Don Giovanni. For all these other characters, then, the point is less the action as such than the lyrical expression of these dependencies. But the Commendatore is precisely the counterpower to Don Juan, the power of spirit or consciousness against which Don Juan rebels in vain:

> The Commendatore appears only two times. The first time it is night; it is in the background of the theater; we cannot see him, but we hear him fall before Don Giovanni's rapier. Already at the very outset his earnestness, which is made all the more manifest by Don Giovanni's caricaturing mockery, something Mozart has superbly expressed in music—already at the very outset his earnestness is too profound to be human; before he dies, he is spirit. The second time he appears as spirit, and the thundering voice of heaven sounds in his earnest, solemn voice. But just as he himself is transfigured, so his voice is transfigured into something more than a human voice; he no longer speaks, he passes judgment. (*SKS* 2:126 / *EO* 1:124)

It is well known that "A's" account does not completely fit the opera as it was actually written by Mozart and Da Ponte (1787) and generally performed. The Commendatore actually appears three times in the opera, not two. In his account, Kierkegaard let "A" omit the rather central churchyard scene where Don Giovanni invites the statue to dinner. Many scholars have commented on the relationship between "A's" account and the opera, often pointing out that "A's" account has its own purpose and inner logic presenting a literary rewriting of Mozart's opera rather than being a straightforward analysis of the opera; at the same time it is obviously inspired by and relating to the opera.[14]

The correspondence between idea and form,[15] and medium as well, clearly appears as the important criterion in "A's" theatrical evaluations, in agreement with what was shown by Pattison at the beginning of this essay. The appraisal of Heiberg for his improvement of Molière's piece, possibly through the indirect inspiration of Mozart's opera, also confirms Heiberg's crucial bearing on Kierkegaard's aesthetics—or, at least, "A's" aesthetics. However, the construction of "A's" aesthetic universe, and not least the intensity in the constant deliberations about the musical medium and the relationship between spirit and sensuousness, language, and music, seem to me to reveal "A" to be a figure quite different from the "reflecteur" who always maintains his critical distance, as Pattison summarized Kierkegaard's aesthetic position.

"A" is more than a critic, although "The Immediate Erotic Stages" is seemingly all about aesthetics. In particular the situation of the musical aesthetics and of the figure of Don Juan in relation to Christianity may be read as pointing to a grander but also more dangerous perspective.

Music and Existence in "A's" Treatise

Ettore Rocca has read "The Immediate Erotic Stages" as a Christian text claiming that what Christianity in "A's" discourse posits and excludes is the idea of the sensuous, but not therefore necessarily also the medium of sensuousness. In addition, regarding a statement about music in "A's" treatise, Rocca observes that it does not follow—in "A's" words—"that one must regard it [music] as the devil's work," although it "is an imperfect medium and . . . consequently it cannot have its absolute theme in the immediately spiritual qualified as spirit" (*SKS* 2:79 / *EO* 1:73). Rocca's argument is based on "A's" discussion of how Christianity first posited the idea of the sensuous by excluding it. As we have seen, "A" claims that the medium in which the sensuous can be expressed in its immediacy is music, and he therefore understands *Don Giovanni* as a classic work. In this context, Rocca points to the following formulation by "A":

> If the elemental originality of the sensuous-erotic in all its immediacy
> insists on expression, then the question arises as to which medium is
> the most suitable for this. . . . In its immediacy, it can be expressed
> only in music. . . . The significance of music thereby appears in its
> full validity, and in a stricter sense it appears as a Christian art or,
> more correctly, as the art Christianity posits in excluding it from
> itself, as the medium for that which Christianity excludes from itself
> and thereby posits. In other words, music is the demonic. In elemental sensuous-erotic originality, music has its absolute theme. This, of
> course, does not mean that music cannot express anything else, but
> nevertheless this is its theme proper. (*SKS* 2:71 / *EO* 1:64–65)[16]

Rocca's conclusion is that "music can properly express sensuality . . . only by presupposing spirit, only by presenting it from the point of view of spirit or Christianity. . . . Music in its perfection will tell about sensuality, but the agent who *uses* this medium is spirit, as it were."[17] Whether this makes "A's" treatise Christian, I am not sure, but it is important to point out that music, in "A's" construction, fulfills a role in a Christian context, although, as the last quotation from "A's" treatise also makes clear, music, in "A's" view, is indeed excluded from Christianity.

In this connection, one might recall the surprising analogy drawn by "A" between music and language, which was cited early in this essay in connection with the comparison between language and music more generally. Although the general context was one in which language and music were contrasted, language being reflective as opposed to the immediacy of music, "A" asserts that "language is the perfect medium precisely when everything sensuous in it is negated." He adds, "That is also the case with music; that which is really supposed to be heard is continually disengaging itself from the sensuous" (*SKS* 2:74 / *EO* 1:68). Possibly this may support Rocca's contention that the function of music—considered in the larger, spiritual context necessary for music to be posited as the medium of the sensuous immediacy—is to act under the power of the spirit. The quotation certainly seems to be in agreement with the ephemerality of existence, which "A" attributes to music: quite physically, by being ephemeral, music disengages itself from itself and leaves the stage, as it were, to the spirit.

The same function attributable to music must also be attributable to Mozart's opera as a whole in view of the intimate correspondence between the idea and the form of this work. This correspondence comes to the fore in "A's" discussion of the struggle between the powers of the Commendatore and Don Juan in his account of the overture (*SKS* 2:127–31 / *EO* 1:125–30). Here he describes the emergence of Don Juan's power, which is born in anxiety: "There is an anxiety in him, but this anxiety is his energy" (*SKS* 2:131 / *EO* 1:129). He sees, or rather hears, and, as I have submitted elsewhere, "A's" ears must have been Kierkegaard's ears, and it is easy to see in the description of the overture, through "A's" nontechnical, literary descriptions, exactly what in the music has made Kierkegaard hear this anxiety, although this musical element may be interpreted very differently from the way "A" interprets it.[18] In the overture, "A" claims, someone familiar with the opera will hear the "forces he has learned to identify in the opera move with a primitive power, where they wrestle with one another with all their might." The power of the Commendatore, however, is the victor, even before the battle, and the power of Don Juan flees, "but this flight is precisely its passion, its burning restlessness in its brief joy of life" (*SKS* 2:129 / *EO* 1:127).

It is the struggle between the spirit, the Commendatore, who, as pointed out earlier, is spirit from the outset of the opera, even before he dies (killed by Don Giovanni in the very first scene of the opera), and Don Juan who embodies the idea of the sensuous in its immediacy. For "A," it is important to claim "that the interest of the opera is Don Giovanni, not Don Giovanni and the Commendatore" (*SKS* 2:129 / *EO* 1:127). This is connected to the (distorted) assertion, already mentioned, that the Commendatore appears only twice. "The Commendatore is the vigorous antecedent clause and the outspoken consequent clause, between which lies Don Giovanni's intermediate clause, but the rich content of this intermediate clause is the substance of the opera" (*SKS* 2:126 / *EO* 1:124). And this again must be so, in "A's" account, because the music precisely is able to express Don Juan's life even as "he dances over the abyss, jubilating during his brief span" (*SKS* 2:131 / *EO*

1:130), connected again to his claim "The more the Commendatore would be drawn to the foreground, the more the opera would cease to be absolutely musical" (*SKS* 2:126 / *EO* 1:124). As spirit and consciousness, "A" claims the Commendatore lies outside the musical medium's central theme. This is a difficulty in "A's" presentation of the opera, and therefore he cannot do justice to the musical setting of the lines of the Commendatore, nor mention the churchyard scene where the Commendatore warns Don Giovanni in music that associates strongly with church music.[19]

If the earlier quoted statement—in connection with the comparison of Molière's and Mozart's uses of the statue—that "Don Juan . . . can withstand everything, except the reproduction of life, because he is immediate, sensate life" is contextualized with the statement, also quoted earlier, that music exists only while being performed, then it seems that "A's" understanding of music is one that does not allow for musical memory because music is the medium of sensuous immediacy. One obviously needs to be careful about drawing overly strict musical-philosophical implications out of a treatise that, after all, is written in a literary, associative style rather than based on a consistent theoretical construction. Still, it seems to make sense to think of "A's" musical understanding (and Kierkegaard's?) as being based on notions of ephemerality and of music being silenced by reflection and memory. What the statue brings is the memory of what Don Giovanni has done in his dance over the abyss, the humans he has hurt or killed or disregarded. This is what the opera seems to be about when it is considered in the context of its original dramatic history from the first (known) Don Juan play by Tirso de Molina in the early seventeenth century, through Molière, to Mozart and Da Ponte, not to mention the many others along the way, including the numerous operas on this subject written before Mozart's *Don Giovanni* in the eighteenth century.[20] This is what the opera seems to be about when the Commendatore is not considered to be outside its main interest.

But if the opera is considered as "A" considers it, then it must vanish like its own idea, and like Don Giovanni, into the abyss, so that all that is left is the deep voice of the spirit, of the Commendatore, who is not absolutely musical. If music is understood radically to be the medium of sensuous immediacy, it seems to be contradictory to repeat it, to perform it. The thrice-repeated "hear" in "A's" famous appraisal and exhortation to listen to Mozart's *Don Giovanni* seems to expose an inherent contradiction in "A's" overall construction of the opera as a musical work expressing what cannot be retained: the immediate, ephemeral, and nonrepeatable sensuousness of the moment. In this way, possibly by the author's intention, the whole treatise annihilates itself in order to leave the stage to reflection: "Listen to the beginning of his life; just as the lightning is discharged from the darkness of the thunderclouds, so he bursts out of the abyss of earnestness, swifter than the lightning's flash, more capricious than lightning and yet just as measured. Hear how he plunges down into the multiplicity of life, how he breaks against its solid embankment. Hear these light, dancing violin notes, hear the intimation of joy . . . hear the whisper of temptation, hear the vortex of seduction, hear the stillness of the moment—hear, hear, hear Mozart's Don Giovanni" (*SKS* 2:106–7 / *EO* 1:103). But what is the treatise itself, if not reflection? And can music exist at all without memory (and repetition)?[21]

In book 11 of his *Confessions*, Augustine discusses the notion of time and how to measure it through an example in which he imagines that he is about to sing a song which at that point is still fully contained in the future, as he has not yet started singing. As he sings, Augustine describes how the song gradually moves through the singer and how, as the song is finished, it belongs completely to the past. During the singing, some of the song belongs to the past, some to the future, and only one short part, the tone being sung in the moment, belongs to the now. What is important in this context is, first, how Augustine deconstructs the idea of the "now" by pointing out that even the tone he is singing in the moment can be divided up so that he has already sung some of it, while some of it still belongs to the future, and only a small part even of that tone is in the "now" or present moment. Because he can go on in this way (similar, actually, to the way infinitesimal calculus was invented some 1,200 years later) the "now" cannot be seen to have any duration. It is the ultra-short moment between the past and the future. Augustine must conclude that the only way he can measure time is through memory, since any time period to be measured must be said mostly not to exist: part of it lies in the past, which no longer exists; part of it, in the future, which does not yet exist; while only the ultra-brief present moment exists, ever so fleetingly.[22] For Augustine, all of this concerns the notion of time and how to measure it.

The modern Danish philosopher and theologian K. E. Løgstrup (1905–81), however, has used Augustine's philosophy of time with a different purpose in mind while drawing also upon Heidegger and Husserl, and especially employing the notion of retention—specifically retention through memory, the attempt at holding on to what is disappearing into the nonexistence of the past. In his *Skabelse og Tilintetgørelse* (1978, *Creation and Annihilation*),[23] using Augustine's thought as his basis, Løgstrup argues that perception of time arises by comparison with at least temporarily unaltered objects, against which the passing of time can be experienced. Such objects are spatial, and that is how we can experience them as unchanged in time. In this way time and space are connected. Løgstrup further argues that even an object purely of time can be retained in what he calls a fictional space. Here he takes up Augustine's example of the melody, claiming that the way we remember a melody is by its shape, its structure, its "character." These are timeless characteristics. "For a melody," writes Løgstrup, "it is necessary not only that its parts follow in the right order; also its character is necessary. But time cannot grant character to a progress in time; only space can do that."[24] For this reason, Løgstrup speaks about the fictional space of the melody, in which it is preserved for our memory, as a "timeless" structure.

Many questions arise out of this construction, and most fall outside the scope of this essay.[25] Even the notion of a melody in itself is problematic if it is not historicized. However, in the context here I need only to apply it to the situation in "A's" construction of music and of Mozart's *Don Giovanni*. In this context, the notion of melody is unproblematic and is certainly used in many places by "A." If one accepts Løgstrup's philosophical construction, or even just Augustine's, how can the melody that is sung be perceived as a melody if there is no musical memory? Take, for instance, a lyrical scene "A" describes poetically: Don Giovanni is singing his so-called champagne aria in the first act. "A's" description is convincing, even touching, with its image of Don Giovanni "intoxicated, so to speak, with himself":

> If all the girls in the world encircled him at this moment, he would not be dangerous to them, for he is, as it were, too strong to want to infatuate them; even the most multifarious pleasures of actuality are too little for him compared with what he enjoys in himself.
>
> What it means to say—that Don Giovanni's essential nature is music—is clearly apparent here. He dissolves, as it were, in music for us; he unfurls in a world of sounds. . . . What we must see especially is that it does not stand in an accidental relation to Don Giovanni. Such is his life, effervescing like champagne. And just as the beads in this wine, as it simmers with an internal heat, sonorous with its own melody, rise and continue to rise, just so the lust for enjoyment resonates in the elemental boiling that is his life. Therefore, the dramatic significance of this aria comes not from the situation but from this, that here the opera's dominant tone sounds and resonates in itself. (*SKS* 2:135–36 / *EO* 1:134)

But what about this melody? In "A's" view, if taken at face value, as discussed earlier, it would have to dissolve into nothing in order to be consistent with the character of music as a medium for the immediacy of sensuousness. To remember the melody, to repeat it and to describe its lyrical character, seems to contradict the construction of the opera and of the musical medium in "A's" treatise. Apparently Kierkegaard, if not "A," went to hear (if not see) the opera many times,[26] but "Don Juan . . . can withstand everything, except the reproduction of life, because he is immediate, sensate life" (*SKS* 2:115 / *EO* 1:113). Since in "A's" construction, Don Juan is killed by such repetition, also the retention of a melody expressive of him, and indeed the retention of the whole opera, the very classic work of music drama that celebrates him becomes problematic.

Evident here is the same kind of contradiction that would eventually emerge in the modernism of the mid-twentieth century, where Adorno in his *Philosophy of Modern Music* (*Philosophie der neuen Musik*, 1949) wrote that "music, compressed into a moment, is valid as an eruptive revelation of negative experience."[27] This idea of music as knowledge, and as true suffering condensed into a moment, was part of a rather revolutionary understanding of music's condition in the modern world, seen and understood especially through the twelve-tone system of Schoenberg and Webern. The inherent contradiction between the idea of artworks and the idea of real suffering condensed into a moment was captured and appropriated in Thomas Mann's novel *Doktor Faustus* (written in 1943–46; published in 1947), recontextualizing Adorno's contemporary understanding of music and culture into his own large-scale historical view in which Schoenberg's twelve-tone system was adapted (in a somewhat changed perspective) and resignified as a Faust pact.[28] All this falls outside the scope of this essay, except that precisely this Faust pact was made with explicit reference to "A's" identification of music as excluded from Christianity, as stated by the devil in his offer of the pact to the composer-protagonist Adrian Leverkühn: "He [the author of the Don Juan treatise in *Either/Or*] knew and understood my particular relation to this beautiful art—the most Christian of all arts, he finds—but Christian in reverse, as it were: introduced and developed by Christianity indeed, but then rejected and banned as the Devil's Kingdom—so there you are. A highly theological business, music—the way sin is, the way I am."[29]

To conclude, I wish to suggest that the music philosophy of "A" collapses if one takes it seriously in detail. His is a brilliant essay, brilliant in provoking readers to discuss the meaning of *Don Giovanni*, and, much more than that, the meaning of music as such and of existence seen through the intensity of music and drama that engage those who listen, read, and watch. The essay is far more than music or theater criticism; just as Mann much later was able to use the politicocultural aesthetics of Adorno in a large-scale existential confrontation with long-established traditions of Western culture, Kierkegaard's "A" formulated provocative statements to the effect that music would seem no longer a harmless, pleasant entertainment but rather something that potentially could threaten bourgeois life as well as spiritual life. In doing so, he formulated a theory that collapses if one takes its actual statements at face value. I believe, however, that one needs to do so in order to get to the point where this becomes clear.

Notes

Kierkegaard, as was previously the norm in Danish, refers consistently to Don Juan, not Don Giovanni. In modern times, however, the opera and its protagonist are always referred to as Don Giovanni. In order to avoid confusion, I have consistently used Giovanni whenever I refer explicitly to the opera and only the opera, but Juan whenever I refer more generally to the figure. The same seems to be true for the English translation in *EO 1*.

1. George Pattison, "Søren Kierkegaard: A Theatre Critic of the Heiberg School," in *Kierkegaard and His Contemporaries: The Culture of Golden Age Denmark*, ed. Jon Stewart, Kierkegaard Studies, Monograph Series, vol.10 (Berlin: Walter de Gruyter, 2003), 319–29. See also the discussion of Kierkegaard's relationship to the Heiberg circle in Henning Fenger, "Kierkegaard: A Literary Approach," in Stewart, *Kierkegaard and His Contemporaries*, 301–18.

2. Pattison, "Søren Kierkegaard," 329.

3. For another approach to "A's" treatment of Mozart's opera, see the essay by Peder Jothen in this volume.—Ed.

4. A recent essay by Shao Kai Tseng, "Kierkegaard and Music in Paradox? Bringing Mozart's Don Giovanni to Terms with Kierkegaard's Religious Life-View," *Literature and Theology* 28, no. 4 (2014): 411–24, published after the original submission of this essay, has some main points in common with this one. Tseng argues that Kierkegaard deliberately used "A's" distortion of Mozart's *Don Giovanni* ironically as a satire against a certain trend in Romantic aesthetics. While my interpretation takes a different path, it points in the same overall direction as Tseng's. See also Nils Holger Petersen, "Søren Kierkegaard's Aestheticist and Mozart's *Don Giovanni*," in *Interart Poetics: Essays on the Interrelations of the Arts and Media*, ed. Ulla-Britta Lagerroth, Hans Lund, and Erik Hedling (Amsterdam: Rodopi, 1997), 167–76.

5. "Vagueness" here renders the Danish word *Dunkelhed*, which could also be translated as "obscurity" or even "darkness."

6. The translator's "a negation of the feelings dependent upon the senses" seems to be a gloss on the original Danish text, which gives only "en Negation af det Sandselige" (a negation of the sensuous).

7. My translation. Wilhelm Heinrich Wackenroder and Ludwig Tieck, *Herzensergießungen eines kunstliebenden Klosterbruders* (Stuttgart: Reclam, 1994): "Der volle lateinische Gesang, der sich steigend und fallend durch die schwellenden Töne der Musik durchdrängte, gleich wie Schiffe, die durch Wellen des Meeres segeln, hob mein Gemüt immer höher empor" (84); "Posaunen, und ich weiß selbst nicht was für allmächtige Töne, schmetterten und dröhnten eine erhabene Andacht durch alles Gebein" (85).

8. My translation. E. T. A. Hoffmann, "Beethovens Instrumental-Musik," in *Fantasiestücke in Callot's Manier: Werke 1814*, in *Sämtliche Werke in sechs Bänden*, ed. Hartmut Steinecke et al. (Frankfurt a.M.: Deutscher Klassiker, 1985–), vol. 2, pt. 1 (1993), 53–54: "In die Tiefen des Geisterreichs führt uns Mozart. . . . So öffnet uns auch Beethovens Instrumental-Musik das Reich des Ungeheuern und Unermeßlichen."

9. See Carl Dahlhaus, *The Idea of Absolute Music* [orig. German 1978], trans. Roger Lustig (Chicago: University of Chicago Press, 1989), esp. 58–77; Eyolf Østrem, "'The Ineffable': Affinities between Christian and Secular Concepts of Art," in *Signs of Change: Transformations of Christian Traditions and Their Representation in the Arts, 1000–2000*, ed. Nils Holger Petersen, Claus Clüver, and Nicolas Bell (Amsterdam: Rodopi, 2004), 265–92.

10. See Østrem, "'The Ineffable,'" 279–83.

11. The notion of form in this quotation should undoubtedly be understood as a general reference to the overall design of the drama, not in the specific musicological sense of musical form from music analysis from the nineteenth century onward.

12. There is no such scene in Mozart's *Don Giovanni*. "A's" remark is ambiguous: "The famous comic scene in Molière . . . should, of course, never be included in the opera, where it has a totally disturbing effect" (*SKS* 2:112–13 / *EO* 1:109–10). This has led the translators to point out (*EO* 1:620n77) that such a scene is not included in the Danish libretto that Kierkegaard knew. It should be emphasized that there is also no such scene in the original Italian libretto by Lorenzo da Ponte.

13. Ivan Nagel, *Autonomie und Gnade: Über Mozarts Opern* (1988; Kassel: Bärenreiter, 1991), 39–47. See also the discussion in Nils Holger Petersen, "Seduction or Truth in Music? Mozart's *Don Giovanni* and Søren Kierkegaard's *Either/Or*," in *Kierkegaard Studies Yearbook 2008*, ed. Niels Jørgen Cappelørn, Hermann Deuser, and K. Brian Söderquist (Berlin: Walter de Gruyter, 2008), 109–28; see 113.

14. Most recently, Tseng, "Kierkegaard and Music in Paradox?" See also Peter Tschuggnall, *Sören Kierkegaards Mozart-Rezeption: Analyse einer philosophisch-literarischen Deutung von Musik im context des Zusammenspiels der Künste* (Frankfurt a.M.: Peter Lang, 1992), esp. 135n12 and 152; Elisabete M. de Sousa, "Kierkegaard's Musical Recollections," in Cappelørn et al., *Kierkegaard Studies Yearbook 2008*, 85–108. De Sousa suggests that "A's" treatise also relates to contemporary music culture and music performances, and not least that it seems to be an indirect tribute to Liszt's fantasy for the piano after Mozart's opera, *Réminiscences de Don Juan*, composed and already widely performed in 1841. See further Ettore Rocca, "'The Immediate Erotic Stages' in *Either/Or* as Christian Writing," in Cappelørn et al., *Kierkegaard Studies Yearbook 2008*, 129–40; Petersen, "Søren Kierkegaard's Aestheticist and Mozart's *Don Giovanni*"; Petersen, "Seduction or Truth in Music?"; Nils Holger Petersen, "Mozart und das Jüngste Gericht: Der Komtur, die Posaune Gottes und . . . Søren Kierkegaard," in *Mozart und die Religion*, ed. by Peter Tschuggnall (Salzburg: Mueller-Speiser, 2010), 191–205.

15. I use the same notion of form as in n. 11 above.

16. See Rocca, "'The Immediate Erotic Stages' in *Either/Or* as Christian Writing," 132–33.

17. Ibid., 133.

18. See Petersen, "Søren Kierkegaard's Aestheticist and Mozart's *Don Giovanni*," 168–71.

19. See Petersen, "Seduction or Truth in Music?" and Petersen, "Mozart und das Jüngste Gericht," with many further references to studies of the opera.

20. See, for instance, Stefan Kunze, *Don Giovanni vor Mozart: Die Tradition der Don-Giovanni-Opern im italienischen Buffa-Theater des 18. Jahrhunderts* (Munich: Fink, 1972).

21. See also a forthcoming essay by Christian Verdoner Larsen, "The Musical Problem of Modern Existence: Perspectives on Kierkegaard's Philosophy of Music in *Either/Or* (1843) and the Demonic Dialectic of Don Juan and Faust," in *Transfiguration: Nordic Journal of Religion and the Arts* (Copenhagen: Museum Tusculanum Press, 2017), in which the author develops the question of repetition and music in Kierkegaard in the context of a performer's perspective, drawing also on the second part of *Either/Or* and Kierkegaard's *The Repetition* (1843).

22. Augustine, *Confessions* 11.27.34–36; Latin text and English commentary, 3 vols., ed. James J. O'Donnell (Oxford: Clarendon Press, 1992), 1:161–62; *Confessions*, trans. R. S. Pine-Coffin (Harmondsworth, U.K.: Penguin, 1961), 275–77.

23. K. E. Løgstrup, *Skabelse og Tilintetgørelse: Metafysik IV* (Copenhagen: Gyldendal, 1978), 11–45.

24. Ibid., 38–39, my translation.

25. I deal with this in much greater detail in "Time and Space in W. A. Mozart's *Ave verum corpus* (1791): The Fictive Space of the Musical Work and Transcendence," in *Transcendence and Sensoriness: Perceptions, Revelation, and the Arts*, ed. Svein Aage Christoffersen et al., Studies in Religion and the Arts, vol. 10 (Leiden: Brill, 2015), 287–325, esp. 303–17.

26. Joakim Garff, *SAK: Søren Aabye Kierkegaard. En biografi* (Copenhagen: Gyldendal, 2000), 109.

27. Theodor W. Adorno, "Musik, zum Augenblick geschrumpft, ist wahr als Ausschlag negativer Erfahrung," in *Philosophie der neuen Musik*, vol. 12 of *Gesammelte Schriften*, ed. Rolf Tiedemann (Frankfurt a.M.: Suhrkamp, 1975), 43; as rendered in *Philosophy of Modern Music*, trans. Anne G. Mitchell and Wesley V. Blomster (London: Sheed and Ward, 1987), 37.

28. Mann had read the finished parts of Adorno's work about Schoenberg and Webern that were written during the Second World War. See Nils Holger Petersen, "Introduction: Transformations of Christian Traditions and Their Representation in the Arts, 1000–2000," in Petersen et al., *Signs of Change*, 1–23, esp. 9–16.

29. Thomas Mann, *Doctor Faustus*, trans. H. T. Lowe-Porter (London: Everyman's Library, 1992), 246. "Der wußte Bescheid und verstand sich auf mein besondres Verhältnis zu dieser schönen Kunst,—der allerchristlichsten Kunst, wie er findet,—mit negativem Vorzeichen natürlich, vom Christentum zwar eingesetzt und entwickelt, aber verneint und ausgeschlossen als dämonisches Bereich,— und da hast du es denn. Eine hochteologische Angelegenheit, die Musik—wie die Sünde es ist, wie ich es bin." Thomas Mann, *Doktor Faustus: Das Leben des deutschen Tonsetzers Adrian Leverkühn erzählt von einem Freunde* (Berlin: Fischer Verlag, 1963), 260.

"Let No One Invite Me, for I Do Not Dance"

Kierkegaard's Attitudes toward Dance

Anne Margrete Fiskvik

Søren Kierkegaard was a man concerned with many types of artistic expressions and social practices, dance being one of them. He made references to dance and movement in several of his writings.[1] He was concerned with dance both as an art form and as a social practice, commenting on these in different ways. Kierkegaard and certain pseudonyms of his often use dance as a metaphor or allusion to enrich their philosophical discourses and fine points. They often employ dancing images in a didactic manner. They talk about the *dancer*, the ballroom dancer as well as the ballet dancer. They contrast the female with the male dancer. Kierkegaard refers to the *ballet master* and the *dancing master*, the person who choreographs and designs the ballet. He was also interested in the *expressionistic nature of dance*, to what degree a ballet can render true human emotions. He was preoccupied with what can be expressed in *ballet plots*, and with what *subjects* can be deemed suitable for a ballet.

Even if the references to dance by Kierkegaard and his pseudonyms are less extensive than those to other art forms, such as music, he was evidently intrigued by the way dance images activate the imagination and deeper reflection of the reader. The twisted body, the tightrope dancer, the ballet leap—all of these have literal meanings while at the same time evoking images and meanings beyond the actual dance or dancing. They give the reader wonderful images to ponder, and numerous scholars have discussed some of the better known images—for instance, the "twisted dancer."

This essay does not aim to offer a philosophical interpretation of the dance images and allusions in Kierkegaard's writings. Rather, I am concerned with the different ways Kierkegaard and his pseudonyms appeal to dance. I aim to contextualize and interpret their references to and comments on dance. I do not attempt to catalogue all the mentions of dance or dancing in Kierkegaard's writings, but I do try to bring into focus most of these references, both those that are well known and some that are less well known. My perspective is that of the dance scholar, and rather than offering philosophical or religious interpretations, my main aim is to offer the reader some ideas on what could have shaped Kierkegaard's thoughts and attitudes toward dance.

The dance references in his writings have not, to my knowledge, previously been studied in the broad manner I attempt in this essay. A few dance scholars have been intrigued by the dance references, and I draw upon several of their works, for instance, Nathaniel Kramer's "August Bournonville: Kierkegaard's Leap of Faith and the 'Noble Art of Terpsichore'" and Kimerer LaMothe's "The Poet and the Dancer."[2]

Kierkegaard often betrays ambivalence in his attitude toward dancing. He admired the art form but considered it limited in its artistic possibilities. This ambivalence, which he expresses rather didactically, will be revealed in different ways in the three main parts of the essay. The first part, on Kierkegaard and dance as an art form, deals with his thoughts on dance as theatrical practice and his relationship to the ballet master August Bournonville. The second part examines his metaphors, and the third, on Kierkegaard and the ballroom dancer, deals with his thoughts on dance as social practice.[3]

Kierkegaard and Dance as an Art Form

Kierkegaard lived in an era that saw rich developments in several artistic expressions, not least in classical ballet. The Romantic era in ballet began in the early 1830s, somewhat belatedly compared to music and literature but lasting more or less to the end of the century. The Romantic ballet was epitomized by two types of female ballerina, one of them cherished for her light, eerie, and elevated way of moving, and the other appreciated for her sensual, down-to-earth dancing. The role of the male dancer, in contrast, was scaled down in the European ballet and often reduced the male to a supporter and enabler of the ballerina's steps. However, in Denmark, the dancer and ballet master August Bournonville valued the male dancer as equal to the ballerina, and it is to Kierkegaard's relation to this preeminent male Danish dancer of his time that we now shall turn.

Kierkegaard and the "Ballet Poet" Bournonville

In Kierkegaard's home country, Denmark, lived and worked one of the most significant figures of Romantic ballet, August Bournonville (1805–1879). The son of the dancer and ballet master Antoine Bournonville, August was born into a family of dancers. He started his ballet training at an early age, and his extraordinary talent was soon discovered. Bournonville took classes with Vincenzo Galeotti (1773–1813), the Italian ballet master who led and developed the Danish Royal Ballet for many years. He also studied with well-known ballet masters in Paris, such as Auguste Vestris (1760–1842), and quickly developed into a premiere dancer at the Paris Opera. Upon his return to Denmark, he started working at the Royal Danish Ballet and soon became the main ballet choreographer and leader of the ensemble. Except for some years during which he was expelled from the Royal Danish Theater (in 1841) or working in Stockholm or at the Paris Opera, Bournonville ruled the Royal Danish Ballet with a firm hand from 1830 to 1877.[4]

The effort of Bournonville in building the Danish Royal Ballet was of great importance to the ballet world, and even though his legacy has grown retrospectively, he was already a respected ballet master, choreographer, and dancer around 1840. Bournonville lived and worked at the height of the Romantic era in ballet, but in contrast to many of his contemporary ballet choreographers, he kept up the importance of the male dancer. He cherished the male dancer in Denmark when the male dancer's importance was diminished in the rest of Europe.[5]

Bournonville had been the leader of the Royal Danish Ballet for several years and was a well-known figure in Copenhagen by 1843, the year Kierkegaard published *Either/Or* (on February 20), *Repetition*, and *Fear and Trembling* (both of the latter two on October 16), as well as two sets of *Upbuilding Discourses* (on May 16 and October 16). Kierkegaard and Bournonville were acquaintances but not close friends.[6] Kierkegaard refers to Bournonville explicitly in a couple of places in his writings as well as indirectly. Bournonville, for his own part, admitted his fascination with Kierkegaard's use of irony retrospectively at a farewell party he held in 1861 on the occasion of his departure to accept a new position in Stockholm. In an unpublished speech, he revealed that the two of them took walks together, contemplating matters such as the concept of irony: "An excellent Danish philosopher has written a lengthy dissertation on the concept of Irony. I admit with modesty that I have not yet read it, since I have only pursued and digested very little of the aforesaid author. On the other hand I enjoyed the great happiness of often walking with him and refreshing myself with his insatiable fount of knowledge and perspicacity."[7] Despite Bornonville's claim that he had not read much, if any, of Kierkegaard's work, there is evidence of the contrary: several of Kierkegaard's books were in Bournonville's substantial library, books that are still part of Bournonville's legacy. However, later in life, after Kierkegaard's attack on Bishop Mynster and the Danish state church, Bournonville took a less favorable attitude toward him.[8] Bournonville was indeed a very well-read man who kept up with the literary trends and discussed these with contemporary writers. Moreover, he saw himself as a "Balletdigter"—a ballet poet.[9]

It is not totally clear during which periods Bournonville and Kierkegaard walked together, but according to the Bournonville expert Knud Arne Jürgensen, the walks would most likely have taken place in the years before and after Bournonville was exiled for half a year in 1841, from March 14, for having offended the Danish king. Bournonville returned in September 1841. On October 25 (two weeks after having broken off his engagement with Regine Olsen), Kierkegaard departed for Berlin, where he remained for four months, returning to Copenhagen on March 6, 1842. On May 8 the following year, he again left Copenhagen, this time for a shorter visit to Berlin. This is noteworthy because, according to Jürgensen, Kierkegaard's walks with Bournonville were over by 1843.[10] Nor is it clear how these walks began, since the two men seem unlikely walking companions. Yet Kierkegaard enjoyed his walking tours along the streets of Copenhagen with many of the city's eminent figures, as Kramer points out.[11] Bournonville was at this point one of the highly respected, "eminent" persons in Copenhagen, a man with strong opinions and the courage to speak against the authorities. This might have attracted Kierkegaard to Bournonville, who was clearly drawn to Kierkegaard's existentialist outlook. He points out that his walks with Kierkegaard helped to clarify his own attitudes toward the use of irony: "One thing I did discover, that irony is not identical with ridiculousness, mockery or bitterness, but is on the contrary an important element in our spiritual existence—the fortification with alcohol that takes away the sickly sweetness of wine's grapes, the jet of cold water that dampens a fever, in short the smile through tears that prevents us from becoming lachrymose."[12] Bournonville's plots were not constructed to be ironic, and therefore this quotation is highly relevant, because Kierkegaard would criticize Bournonville for his lack of refined libretti. Bournonville himself seems to have been aware that his outlook on life and art was rather naive compared to Kierkegaard's, and yet he explains and defends his position: "I will not claim that all friends here gathered know me to my inner being, but their acquaintance with me is sufficient to realise that it is more feeling than irony that plays the main rôle in my life. I and my art belong properly to a sentimental time and direction, I have unceasingly lived in a battle with the *external* influence of irony; and I will not deny that it has dominated me so much that I have often felt strange and embarrassed in the middle of its atmosphere of self-parody."[13]

Bournonville shied away from using irony actively in his own work, but through conversations with Kierkegaard he at least felt more at ease with the concept: "Today for the first time I have realised its [irony's] true worth. . . . It is certain that after our standards I possess too little irony, but that supply which I have been able to collect in so many years of this ingredient will now be to my benefit."[14] Also, as Jürgensen points out in his discussion of Bournonville's philosophical outlook, he "could certainly be called an existentialist *ante litteram*. He based his life on artistic ideals, but moved with moral and muscular immediacy both in his art and in many other social contexts outside of the theatre."[15] Thus Bournonville openly revealed that he had clear ideals for his own works and that he went for the more straightforward plots that contextualized his choreography, weaving solos, pas de deux, and corps de ballet sequences naturally into the story of the ballet. He was a prolific choreographer, creating a variety of ballets with stories situated in different countries. He was able to convey great happiness, sorrow, and pain through movement. Moreover, he was deeply religious and often brought up the conflict of good versus evil in his ballets. The plots often have a moral component to them, and most often the stories end happily: God triumphs over evil, for instance in *Napoli or The Fisherman and His Bride* (*Napoli eller Fiskeren og hans Brud*, 1842), in which the heroine, Teresina, captivated by an evil sea king, regains her memory and sense by touching the cross she wears on a necklace.[16]

Despite the admiration in which Bournonville held Kierkegaard, there is also evidence of his criticizing the philosopher. In an entry of December 29, 1854, in his unpublished diary, he wrote of an evening party he attended where the theater director Frederik Ludvig Høedt defended Kierkegaard against Bishop Mynster: "We had a pleasant time, but Høedt displeases me by defending Søren Kjerkegaard's vile attack on Münster."[17] Bournonville was thus guided by his deep religious convictions and clearly took a stance against Kierkegaard in the Mynster debate.

Kierkegaard's Views on Balletic Plots

By 1843, when *Fear and Trembling* was published, Bournonville had created the ballets *Faust*, *La Sylphide*, and *Napoli*, all typical of his choreographic style and conveying clear moral messages.[18] Kierkegaard, although he admired Bournonville as a performer, was critical of his libretti and would mock Bournonville for his simpleminded plots, either openly or in more discreet ways. His manner of expression was also quite didactic. In *Fear and Trembling*, speaking through his pseudonym Johannes de Silentio, Kierkegaard mentions dance in several places. In his discussion of the rivalry between aesthetics and ethics, he makes a derogatory remark about the limited capacity of ballet subjects when discussing the relationship between Queen Elizabeth I and her lover Essex. Johannes de Silentio finds this overly dramatic story suitable for ballet and ironically writes, "This would be a subject for a poet who knew how to pry secrets out of people; otherwise, it can best be used by a ballet master, with whom the poet frequently confounds himself these days" (*SKS* 4:183 / *FT* 94). Elizabeth's dilemma and dramatic decisions are not worthy of being elaborated upon by a real poet, but are suitable themes for a ballet master. With this claim Johannes de Silentio is implying that movements and gestures cannot replace real words. He also states that ballet masters mistakenly think of themselves as poets, referring to Bournonville, who called himself a "ballet poet" in several of his writings. He once explained, "After my return to my fatherland (in 1830) I occupied myself almost wholly with my ballet programmes, which concerning literature gave only a grievous scanty yield. For if a ballet poet allows himself to be tempted to give these outlines a touch of explanatory colouring, he risks promising more than he can deliver."[19] Jürgensen points out that Bournonville by no means was against the writing of extensive scenarios and that he often provided meticulous programs for his ballets.[20] Also, it is important to note that Bournonville had secret aspirations to be a poet. Over the years he wrote a large number of poems and songs, most of which he published anonymously. He collected them in a handwritten volume that he labeled "Poetic attempts."[21]

But to the complicated thinker Kierkegaard/Johannes de Silentio, Bournonville's plots appeared rather too naive: Kierkegaard himself would ponder questions of moral nuance and deceit over and over again in several volumes, scrutinizing topics from different angles. There were no clear-cut or easy solutions for Kierkegaard.[22] Hints of two different literary positions can be seen here as well: Kierkegaard admired the thoughts and ideas of the French dramatist Eugène Scribe, who advocated plots that could be easily told and expressed but who rather superficially described human nature.[23] Bournonville was interested in human nature and took a more personal approach to his characterizations.[24]

Even if Kierkegaard did not appreciate Bournonville's poetic effort, he clearly admired Bournonville as a performer. He probably saw him dance several times. It is known for a fact that he was present when Bournonville danced the role of Mephistopheles in his *Faust* (1832) when it was restaged in 1842.[25] Kierkegaard's pseudonym Vigilius Haufniensis comments positively on Bournonville's fantastic leap in *The Concept of Anxiety* (*SKS* 4:432 / *CA* 131). In a journal entry of 1843, Kierkegaard makes direct reference to Bournonville, admiring his diabolical leap in *Faust*: "It's a merit of *Bournonville*'s portrayal of Mephistopheles, that leap with which he always appears and jumps into a plastic [*plastisk*, i.e., carefully poised] pose. This leap is a moment that should be noted in understanding the demonic. For the demonic is the *sudden*" (*SKS* 18:172–73, JJ:104 / *KJN* 2:160, emphases in original). Bournonville danced the role of Mephistopheles from June 10, 1842, until March 1843, and it is probably his interpretation that Kierkegaard is referring to as being demonic and thus interesting. In fact, the concept of a leap intrigued Kierkegaard, and he returns to it in *Fear and Trembling*, where he uses it metaphorically. He saw the ability to leap well as something agreeable and admirable, and Bournonville was indeed known as a great jumper. In fact his entire ballet technique was built around speed and elevation.[26] Kierkegaard appreciated his ability to leap forward into a plastic position. The spring of Bournonville was sudden, and implicitly powerful, and, for Kierkegaard, this feature stands in contrast to another side of the demonic: the boring.

When choreographing *Faust*, Bournonville followed typical French ballet conventions; for example, male dancers often would leap through an open window when making an entrance. Although such leaps were quite common in many ballets of the time, Kramer suggests that Kierkegaard was unaware of this standard practice of leaping onto the stage and that he therefore misinterpreted Bournonville's initial motivation and portrayal of a demonic personality.[27] This might be so, but one must not forget that Bournonville was an excellent jumper and widely known for his powerful leaps. His leaps would probably have astonished his audience. Nevertheless, for Kierkegaard, this particular leap came across as powerful enough that it conjured images of the demonic.[28] Bournonville as dancer and performer doubtlessly gained more respect from Kierkegaard than did Bournonville the choreographer. Whereas he found Bournonville's plot boring and unimaginative, Bournonville's dancing conjured powerful images to which Kierkegaard's writings later alluded.

Aside from his admiration for Bournonville the dancer, we are once again reminded that Kierkegaard found Bournonville's choreographic works, and also ballet in general as an art form, limited in its expressiveness. This is seen in some undated notes of 1844 labeled "Begrepet Angest" (Concept of Anxiety). There he discusses the expressive nature of dance even more extensively and elaborates on what can and cannot be expressed in ballet. He writes once more about the development of the demonic, and he refers to what he previously wrote about the development of the demonic either as sudden or as boring, without continuity. Making notes to himself, using keywords rather than complete sentences, he states, "The mimetic is the best expression for the demonic. Bournonville. Without content. (Elverpigen)" (*Pap.* V B 58, my translation). As if to remind himself of his line of thought, Kierkegaard is indicating that he has Bournonville in mind when jotting this down. He again is implying that Bournonville as a dancer can portray the demonic, which is something positive. "Elverpigen" (elf maiden) is most likely another word for one of the characters of the ballet *Undine*, which Bournonville choreographed in 1842.[29] Kierkegaard found this five-act ballet, based on a dramatic fairy tale, to be "without content." Again, we see that he was not happy with this kind of naive and simple plot.

Don Juan *as Ballet*

Kierkegaard's preoccupation with the figure of Don Juan as a "protest against the ethical claim of Christianity," and hence as a "character . . . possible only within Christianity,"[30] is well known, and sure enough, he also had ideas about Don Juan in relation to ballet. In *Either/Or*, Kierkegaard's pseudonym "A" spends some time discussing what can be lost and what can be gained through the use of movement. As he is pondering various plays that tell the story of Don Juan, he points out that as soon as Don Juan is given lines to speak, everything changes in his character and makes him come across as less vague (see *SKS* 2:109 / *EO* 1:106). "A" then surprisingly admits that perhaps the best way of portraying this play is by staging it as a ballet, at least in the final scene. But again he changes his opinion: "That is, the reflection that motivates the lines reflects him out of the vagueness in which he is only musically audible. This being so, it might seem that Don Juan could be interpreted best as ballet. It is indeed well known that he has been interpreted in this way. Yet this interpretation must be commended for having known its powers, and for this reason it has limited itself to the final scene, where the passion in Don Juan would be most readily visible in the pantomimic play of muscles" (*SKS* 2:109 / *EO* 1:106). The previous interpretation that "A" is referring to is probably the version of the play *Don Juan ou Le Festin de Pierre* (*Don Juan, or the Stone Guest's Banquet*), which had been choreographed in 1761 by the Italian ballet master Gasparo Angiolini (1731–1803) to the music of Christoph Willibald von Gluck (1714–1787). Contemporary audiences found Angiolini's version of this ballet too expressive; they especially considered the scene where Don Juan is tortured on his way to Hades too literal in its expressiveness.[31] Kierkegaard was likely aware of this old controversy, thus admitting that the very last scene of *Don Juan* could be suitable for dance. He is letting "A" argue didactically about the "pantomimic play of muscles," and he is willing to admit that certain passages can be revealed through movement but that the real strength of the rendering lies in the music. Kierkegaard could have seen other balletic versions of *Don Juan*, but it is unclear which version "A" is referring to when he states that the true nature of Don Juan's inner life cannot be sufficiently portrayed in dance. Only the outwardly dramatic can be presented, "whereas the ballet presents almost nothing more than the torments of despair, the expression of which, since it has to be solely in pantomime, he shares with many others who are in despair. What is essential in Don Juan cannot be presented in ballet, and everyone readily feels how ludicrous it would be to watch Don Juan infatuating a girl by means of dance steps and ingenious gesticulations. Don Juan is an inner qualification and thus cannot become visible or appear in bodily configurations and movements or in molded harmony" (*SKS* 2:109 / *EO* 1:106).[32] "A" obviously feels that the deepest and most profound thoughts of humans cannot be portrayed through bodily movement. Note the didactic manner in which Kierkegaard lets "A" present his argument: his claim that "everyone readily feels" is didactic on the verge of being manipulative. It is a way of making the reader who would think otherwise feel insecure for having thoughts about the ability of the body to portray inner emotions in dance and movement. The didactic writing style is typical of Kierkegaard, and of course especially prominent in *Either/Or*, where the purpose of the book is to let the perspectives of multiple characters be presented and analyzed. However, none of the other characters in *Either/Or* argues against "A," nor is an alternative view offered on *Don Juan* as ballet. Kierkegaard purposefully is advocating more extreme aesthetic attitudes in order to "awaken" the reader. The general aim of the book, taken as a whole, is to place the reader in a position of having to choose for himself or herself between the "either" and the "or." Thus the reader is made to contemplate balletic plots and the usefulness of bodily movement and dance as aesthetic expressions.

Kierkegaard and Ballet as Art Form

As we saw, Kierkegaard enjoyed watching dance but discerned no literary skill or qualities in ballet plots. He admired Bournonville as a dancer, but he and the pseudonymous author of *Either/Or*'s first part are less respectful regarding Bournonville's choreographic ability and the dramatic possibilities of ballet. Interestingly, such opinions seem to be contradicted in other writings of Kierkegaard, where either he or one of his pseudonyms expresses thoughts through dance metaphors. When Johannes de Silentio describes the knight's ability to move and to render emotions through dance in *Fear and Trembling*, Kierkegaard seems to have forgotten his "prejudice." In *Fear and Trembling*, Johannes de Silentio has full faith in the power of bodily movements and dancing. Again Kierkegaard is showing that his interest in dance comes from the multiple meanings the expressive body can be interpreted as bearing. Also, in other places in Kierkegaard's writings where dance and dancing are used metaphorically, he relies on their expressiveness.

Kierkegaard and His Dancing Metaphors

Metaphors of Mortal and Working Life

As I suggested, Kierkegaard sometimes uses images of dancing to explain his thoughts, to help readers understand what he is trying to convey. Perhaps he used such images when other words seemed to fail him, or perhaps dance metaphors expressed his points more precisely. This is curious because he clearly was ambivalent toward the physical art of dancing. But the *image* of dancing was powerful to him. For instance, he appealed to it when describing human loneliness. In his *Philosophical Fragments*, which was probably written between 1842 and 1843 and was published in its complete, current form in 1844, Kierkegaard's pseudonym Johannes Climacus goes as far as to liken himself to a dancer, treading lightly in life, but at the same time rejecting the dance itself. Again we see the ambivalence. When pondering his own opinions, Climacus states, "To have an opinion is to me both too much and too little; it presupposes a security and well-being in existence akin to having a wife and children in this mortal life" (*SKS* 4:217 / *PF* 7). Climacus, by choice, is not leading this kind of life. In the mortal, everyday life, he lives alone because a family life is unsuitable to his existence, as he is up and about night and day with no fixed income. He is dedicated to the spiritual life, which must be understood as his inner spiritual world, in which he has trained himself "always to be able to dance lightly in the service of thought, as far as possible to the honor of the god and for my own enjoyment, renouncing domestic bliss and civic esteem" (*SKS* 4:217 / *PF* 7).

When reading this, one detects the underlying loneliness of Climacus. Yes, he is able to let his thoughts dance about without earthly restrictions, but this also means that the ties to earthly life are more fragile. When facing difficult times, Climacus is even free to ponder death. He is worried about dancing in real life, and in the text dancing is used as a metaphor for getting involved with someone, probably both mentally and physically:

> All I have is my life, which I promptly stake every time a difficulty appears. Then it is easy to dance, for the thought of death is a good dancing partner, my dancing partner. Every human being is too heavy for me, and therefore I plead, *per deos obsecro* [I swear by the gods]: Let no one invite me, for I do not dance.
>
> J.C. (*SKS* 4:217 / *PF* 8)

This is one of the most beautiful and at the same time ambivalent exclamations about dance in Kierkegaard's writings. "Let no one invite me, for I do not dance": in this sentence are encompassed the loneliness and perhaps also the fear of getting hurt that Kierkegaard himself struggled with in his own life. The metaphor is strikingly effective and powerful, and even more so when considered in connection with his great ambivalence toward dance. On a more speculative note, the quotation could hint at Kierkegaard's own physical body, including his crooked back, which could have made him awkward on the dance floor, making him feel insecure as dancer. Johannes de Silentio in *Fear and Trembling* also addresses the issue of dancing or not dancing: "Most people live completely absorbed in worldly joys and sorrows; they are benchwarmers who do not take part in the dance" (*SKS* 4:135 / *FT* 41). He is clearly using the metaphor of not taking part in the dancing as an example of human beings not really being present in their own lives but instead just going through the motions. This is a concept with great relevance in today's busy society. On a more personal level, as Eric Ziolkowski has suggested,[33] this idea of *not* taking part in the dance could be reflective of Kierkegaard's own experiences, even though he certainly does, in a metaphorical sense, take part in the dance—that is, the dance of the spirit that Johannes de Silentio has in mind. Kierkegaard seemed to have enjoyed participating in ballroom activities, but more as an observer than as participant.

Another of Kierkegaard's more direct dance allusions is inscribed in the margin of the *Works of Love* manuscript. There, he comments on the efforts of human beings and how they are not meant to be seen by others: "In our work, which frequently has been beyond a human being's powers but, God be praised, never without his support, we have striven to comply with the beautiful rule that one never must detect on a dancer that he is panting. We are convinced that, in their judging, people do not follow this rule, because if they do not see him pant or hear him groan they have no idea at all that he is dancing" (*Pap.* VIII² B 73:133, n.d. 1847 / *WL*, Suppl., 457). Kierkegaard is commenting on the fact that people need to show their efforts in their work in order to be recognized as hardworking. But more beautiful to Kierkegaard is the effort one makes and the hardship one suffers but does not show.

He invokes the balletic ideal that a dancer's effort should not be heard or detected; rather, the dancer should come across as moving effortlessly and with no audible trace of panting. Indeed, inside the balletic tradition there has developed an ideal of the almost supernatural dancer who breathes and moves with seeming effortlessness. Always the dancer should conceal all signs of his or her exertion, but in real life, Kierkegaard notes, people still tend to make loud efforts when working. He shows his social concern when he goes on to discuss how, in a small society like Denmark's, people form groups that exclude human beings who are different in some way. As a matter of fact, throughout the entire passage, Kierkegaard is talking about his work as an author in Denmark, comparing his concealment of his extraordinary efforts as an author to the dancer's concealment of his or her efforts. He is thus revealing that the ideal and quiet, hardworking man or woman is a tough one (*Pap.* VIII^2 B 73:134–36, n.d. 1847 / *WL*, Suppl., 457–60). Engaging in a more didactic mode, Kierkegaard uses the quadrille as metaphor for the mastering of basic skills. In *Fear and Trembling*, Johannes de Silentio discusses the need of every man and woman to create his or her own life and educational path (*SKS* 4:140 / *FT* 45–46). When pointing out that it is not wise to start with difficult tasks, he suggests that one must first master the basics. To illustrate this point, he makes a reference to learning to dance the quadrille: "But in our age people are less concerned about making pure movements. If someone who wanted to learn to dance were to say: For centuries, one generation after the other has learned the positions, and it is high time that I take advantage of this and promptly begin with the quadrille—people would probably laugh a little at him, but in the world of spirit this is very plausible" (*SKS* 4:140 / *FT* 46). The quadrille (French: *quadrille de contredanses*) is a lively dance for four couples, arranged in the shape of a square, with each couple facing the center of that square.[34] It first appeared around 1750, and by 1820 it was danced among the upper classes and the bourgeoisie. The period of its greatest popularity coincided with the later period of Kierkegaard's life, as it was one of the most popular dance forms around 1840–50. However, the tours of the quadrille could sometimes be quite complicated, and would-be dancers needed to learn and practice them in order not to make a fool of themselves in the ballroom. Thus the message is clear: a person must master the basics before engaging in the more complicated. This is the way it goes with all education. Clearly, Kierkegaard saw the process of learning the basics as crucial for becoming a civilized person. We find him, through Johannes de Silentio, again pursuing his more didactic style: the pseudonym explains that education is the course the individual goes through in order to refine himself, and this is not being helped by being born into the most enlightened age. The dancing metaphor appears to allow Johannes de Silentio a way of delving more deeply into problems at hand and of suggesting that one must learn to master the problems of life step by step.

The Knight of Faith's Metaphors: The Twisted
Image of the Tightrope Dancer

Some of Kierkegaard's powerful—and also the best-known and most often discussed—dancing metaphors are conveyed through Johannes de Silentio in *Fear and Trembling*, some of them also revealing ambivalence toward dance. Pondering the dialectics of faith, Johannes de Silentio speaks of movement and dancing metaphorically, pondering how it is possible to jump back and forth in time. He disputes the common supposition that faith has nothing to do with art but that it is "a coarse and boorish piece of work" (*SKS* 4:131 / *FT* 36). He sees faith as something that is in constant flux, moving like a tightrope dancer back and forth: "The dialectic of faith is the finest and the most extraordinary of all; it has an elevation of which I can certainly form a conception, but no more than that. I can make the mighty trampoline leap [*Tramplin-Spring*] whereby I cross over into infinity; my back is like a tight-rope dancer's [*en Liniedandsers*], twisted in my childhood, and therefore it is easy for me. One, two, three—I can walk upside down in existence, but I cannot make the next movement, for the marvelous I cannot do—I can only be amazed at it" (*SKS* 4:131 / *FT* 36). What a wealth of images is contained in this quote! Johannes de Silentio's self-conception as a tightrope dancer represents an interesting metaphor. Tightrope dancing was a popular form of entertainment during Kierkegaard's lifetime. Thus the description of the agile and traditionally itinerant tightrope dancer would have been suggestive of somebody highly skilled but also evasive.

Dancing on ropes or wires, either slack ones or tight, has long and deep roots in Europe. The practice was associated with numerous itinerant artists who traveled around Europe up through the nineteenth century. These artists specialized in performances that entertained "the people." According to the dancing master Andrea Gallini, these technically demanding styles were designed to entertain the audience by showing difficult stunts. The dancing was not targeted for the aristocracy. Thus tightrope dancing often carried connotations of popular and even less respectable entertainment.[35] Many artists traveled because of the difficulty of obtaining performance privileges in some European countries. The dance historian Marian Hanna Winter, describing the period between 1700 and 1830 in particular, notes that those official theaters that had obtained privileges from the king or state, or from both, were few and highly competitive: "Out on the continent, the theatre companies that enjoyed 'official patronage' jealously watched their smaller rivals, even down to the eeriest company of marionettes. The patented or government-sponsored theatres might also be called the 'over-privileged,' and all others the 'under-privileged.' The former were allocated complete rights for exploitation of certain types of entertainment and prosecuted infringements mercilessly."[36] Traveling artists, according to Winter, would be categorized as underprivileged, because it was difficult, if not impossible, for them to be accepted into the privileged theaters.

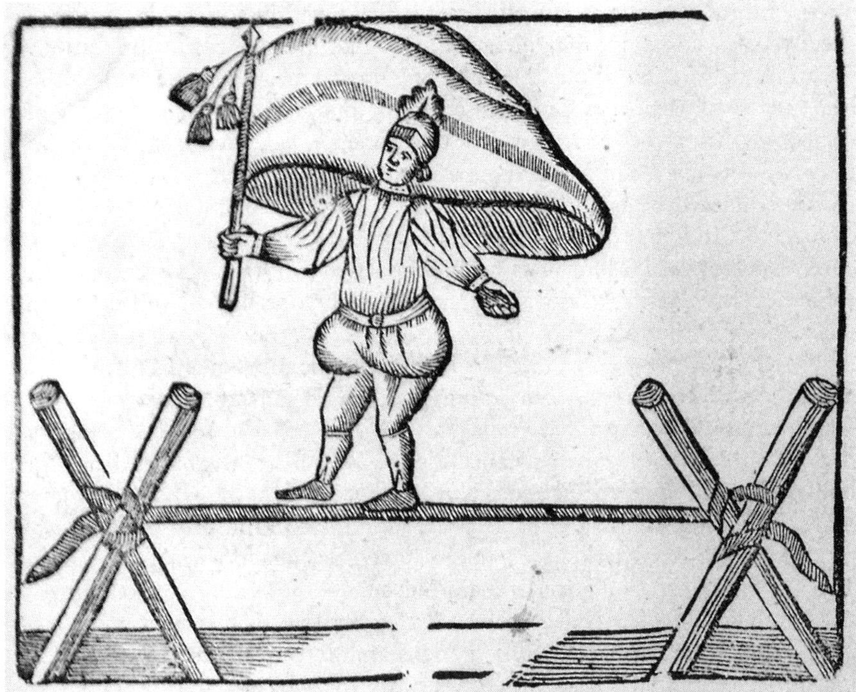

Figure 1. Tightrope dancing with balancing prop from Trondheim, 1751. Detail from a poster by *De kinesiske kunstnere* (The Chinese artists), 1751. State Archives of Trondheim: Poster/plakat, Statsarkivet, Magistraten B, bd 3, Offentlige skuespill & forestillinger.

Established European theaters would seldom hire an artist who was not within their closed circuit, and consequently, many ensembles had to move regularly in order to find work. Some probably preferred this, but others likely went in search of a safer or more stable work environment.

My research into these practices has revealed that several artists would have had to apply to local authorities in order to get permission to perform. Typically they would get the permission if they promised to give away to the poor the income from their last performances. Source material also shows that itinerant artists were admired for their skills. They were often highly technically capable, able to twist and turn their bodies, having superb ability to balance themselves on the slack or tight rope. In addition to rope or wire dancing, they typically performed acrobatics.

Tightrope dancers could in principle perform anywhere; they could tie their rope between two trees or poles at a marketplace in a given city and start dancing (see Figure 1). In short, they were not sophisticated ballet dancers but danced more in the comic or grotesque style, using acrobatic tricks alongside dancing steps in order to thrill their audiences.[37]

Itinerant artists were typically not well received in society. From the perspective of a contemporary dance scholar like me, the earlier quotation of Johannes de Silentio about the tightrope dancer bears associations with an itinerant, restless nature. It hints at a person unable or unwilling to settle into society. By using the metaphor of a tightrope dancer, Kierkegaard's pseudonym is conjuring the image of a person technically capable but whose artistic nature is unsettled. The itinerant nature of the tightrope dancer makes him changeable and adaptable, since he will have to go to a new place when the current performance space has been exhausted. Working with these images, Johannes de Silentio is suggesting that the tightrope dancer can thus easily move into another existence and in a few seconds be able to see the world with new eyes. Still, the dancer is unreliable in his movement. The metaphor makes sense as a referral to something flexible but unstable.

Johannes de Silentio's reference to the dancer's twisted back supports this interpretation: tightrope dancers were very flexible, able to bend their bodies in all kinds of directions. Nordic sources describe what an itinerant performance would have looked like around 1770 and give indications of performances that Kierkegaard might have seen outdoors at marketplaces. The Nordic tightrope dancer Martin Nürenbach, for example, performed at the Humlegården, a park in Stockholm. According to the newspaper *Hvad Nytt, Hvad Nytt*, he did equilibrist tricks and acrobatic stunts while balancing on a narrow steel tightrope.[38] Another of Nürenbach's specialties was his dance with a ladder, which stood perpendicular as he walked up it, then he moved or wormed backward, headfirst, through all of its rungs.[39] We can imagine the agility and strength needed for Nürenbach to be able to twist his body in such a way.

Johannes de Silentio's words evoke even more images. First, the tightrope dancer's back is twisted. In contrast to the idealized tightrope dancer, Johannes de Silentio sees himself as being unable to make a real movement, for he is unable to make a real decision and can only be stuck in the here and now, roaming about in some kind of mental existence. The genius of the metaphor lies in how it elicits powerful images for the reader, expressing spiritual and religious dimensions that otherwise could not so easily be described.

A little further on in *Fear and Trembling* there is a long passage where Johannes de Silentio again uses dance as a metaphor, this time for infinity. Here, it is not a tightrope dancer but rather a ballet dancer that he refers to: "It is supposed to be the most difficult feat for a ballet dancer to leap into a specific posture in such a way that he never once strains for the posture but in the very leap assumes the posture. Perhaps there is no ballet dancer who can do it— but this knight does it" (*SKS* 4:135 / *FT* 41). Once again, Kierkegaard is alluding to the flexibility of dancers that makes it possible for them to move in all directions. But only the knight of faith can make the perfect leap; not even the knights of infinitude are free of wavering when landing: "The knights of infinity are ballet dancers and have elevation. They make the upward movement and come down again, and this, too, is not an unhappy diversion and is not unlovely to see. But every time they come down, they are unable to assume the posture immediately, they waver for a moment, and this wavering shows that they are aliens in the world. It is more or less conspicuous according to their skill, but even the most skillful of these knights cannot hide this wavering" (*SKS* 4:135–36 / *FT* 41). Johannes de Silentio is referring to one of the most typical and, as he himself states, difficult tasks of a ballet dancer: to be able to do difficult leaps and to land elegantly and effortlessly. Following the leap into the air, the landing often involves this moment of a dancer's wavering that causes a slight impression of instability. A ballet dancer, when doing elevated jumps and leaps, typically lands in what is called the fifth position, which helps to secure maximum stability. But not only the landing but also the ability to *continue effortlessly*, not to waver but to go on is the sign of a real professional. As Johannes de Silentio points out, the knight of faith can do this: "But to be able to come down in such a way that instantaneously one seems to stand and to walk, to change the leap into life into walking, absolutely to express the sublime in the pedestrian—only that knight can do it, and this is the one and only marvel" (*SKS* 4:136 / *FT* 41). It is a sign of good and stable technique when a dancer is able to land as effortlessly as possible, with a minimum of wavering, and this can be read as a metaphor both for being able to continue in life and not to be rooted in previous ways, and for being able to rethink a situation and change direction.

With metaphors such as these, Kierkegaard/Johannes de Silentio reveals some knowledge about ballet. Kierkegaard must have observed ballet dancers and recognized the fine-tuning of their bodies into positions in order to describe them so well. Even though in the above quotation he does not give the specific name for the landing position (the fifth position), in other writings he does mention specific ballet steps. For instance, Constantin Constantius in *Repetition* talks about the entrechat, a technically difficult jump.

This again suggests that he was well versed in ballet, albeit perhaps no real connoisseur. It could also be that when Johannes de Silentio refers to a ballet master, he has Bournonville in mind. As mentioned earlier, Bournonville was widely known for his elevation as a dancer, as he could execute various leaps and jumps without wavering, and difficult jumps were part of his choreographic style. He would certainly have served as role model for a perfect "leap of faith."

Metaphors of Bodily Movements, Hardships, and Frustrations

Some interesting allusions to dance in *Repetition* will serve to show Kierkegaard's ability to communicate the hardships and frustrations of life through dance metaphors. In *Repetition*, Kierkegaard's pseudonym Constantin Constantius ponders the power of bodily movement, as well as dance itself, as a possible outlet of frustration as well as of happiness: "There probably is no person who has not gone through a period when no richness of language, no passion of interjection was adequate, since no expression, no gesture sufficed, since nothing satisfied him other than breaking into the strangest leaps and somersaults [*besynderligste Spring og Kolbytter*]" (*SKS* 4:33 / *R* 158). Disorderly somersaults and leaps inhibit the body when words fail. But the discipline of dance and of ballet could also be needed: "Perhaps the same individual learned to dance. Perhaps he went frequently to the ballet and admired the art of the dancer. Perhaps there came a time when ballet no longer stirred him, and yet he had moments when he could return to his room and, indulging himself, find indescribably humorous relief in standing on one leg in a picturesque pose or, giving not a damn for the world, settle everything with an *entrechat*" (*SKS* 4:33–34 / *R* 158). This passage has many layers of meaning, pertaining both to dancers and to viewers of the dance. The problem discussed in *Repetition* is to what degree repetition is possible or even meaningful. Learning to dance means disciplining oneself and developing one's technical skills by practicing them over and over again. A human being learns to obey the rules of ballet (society), but nevertheless, after a while an emptiness sets in, and the strong interests the dancer once could express more freely with somersaults and jumps now come under tight control. Anxiety sets in but can be controlled by repeating the same entrechat as always. The dullness of the mundane also serves to calm anxiety. The dancing metaphors may also be seen as a form of playing and living on the surface of life, that is, of not being able to root oneself in reality. Constantin Constantius, prior to making that statement quoted above, talks about "a depressed person I once knew [who] went through life as a dancer and deceived everyone, myself included" (*SKS* 4:17 / *R* 139). According to Constantius, the person was going through his everyday motions but without really being present. He was repeating himself, suffering from unrequited love.[40] Dancing here becomes a metaphor for going in circles, not being present in real life, not making an effort to deal with the problem at hand.

Dancing as Metaphor of the Unrepeatable

Toward the end of *Repetition*, Constantin Constantius describes the wonderful movements of the actor Friedrich Beckmann (1803–1866), whom he observed at the Königstädter Theater in Berlin.[41] Constantius even likens Beckmann's performance to that of an "incomparable dance," stating, "He has sung his couplet, and now the dance begins." Again, using dance as a metaphor becomes an interesting way of describing "Mr. B's" (Beckmann's) motions and acting, which Constantius thoroughly admires (*SKS* 4:37–39 / *R* 163–65). Later, when Constantius revisits the theater, he finds himself deeply disappointed in Beckmann's performance: "Beckmann could not make me laugh. I endured it for half an hour and then left the theater, thinking: There is no repetition at all" (*SKS* 4:43 / *R* 169). Disappointed, he makes yet another attempt, but this one too is futile: "The next evening I went to the König-städter Theater. The only repetition was the impossibility of a repetition. . . . No matter how I turned and shifted, all was futile. The little dancer who last time had enchanted me with her gracefulness, who, so to speak, was on the verge of a leap, had already made the leap" (*SKS* 4:44 / *R* 170). The dance he had seen performed by the ballerina earlier could not be repeated satisfactorily; she had already leaped forward. A dancer will not be able to give an identical experience to the viewer. Again we see Kierkegaard's preoccupation with the leap as a powerful metaphor, this time indicating that once the leap has been performed, it can never be seen the same way again. Thus movements and dance are useful for making Climacus's points: nothing can ever be repeated.

Metaphors of Love and Loss

Sometimes Kierkegaard speaks with less ambivalence and gives dance more literal meanings. In the "Second Series" of *Works of Love* is a section called "Recollecting One Who Is Dead," where Kierkegaard is writing about what it is like to mourn somebody who is dead. He points out the pure expressiveness of the human body: "If you could manage to see someone shadowboxing in dead earnest, or if you could prevail upon a dancer to dance solo the dance he customarily dances with another, you would be able to observe his motions best, better than if he were boxing with another actual person or if he were dancing with another actual person" (*SKS* 9:341 / *WL* 347). When alone, without his partner, the dancer is more expressive and clear and more easily interpreted and observed. It could also be that the sorrow of having to dance alone sharpens the bodily movements and makes them clearer. Interestingly, in this situation Kierkegaard sees the body as expressive, able to reveal and signify profound loss and grief. It is perhaps expressive because it is genuine. He would probably not think the same expressiveness could be revealed in a ballet plot.

In the section called "Love Abides" (from 1 Cor. 13:13), Kierkegaard is concerned with the strength of love and uses the dancing of two people together as a metaphor of lost love: "Does the dance end because one of the dancers has gone away? In a certain sense. But if the other remains standing in the position that expresses bowing toward the one who is not seen, and if you know nothing about the past, you will say, 'The dance will surely begin just as soon as the other one, who is awaited, comes'" (*SKS* 9:305 / *WL* 307). The beauty and power of this metaphor becomes evident when we try to interpret it, as the words then come across as much more banal than the metaphor itself: when a person has left a relationship, the person remaining stands there, frozen in the moment, unable to continue. Anticipation and longing are reflected in the body language of the person who is left; the person is no longer himself or herself. The person seems to be waiting

for the lost partner to complete the dance. Maybe the quotation also betrays
Kierkegaard's own longing "to start a dance"—that is, his longing for a lost
partner.

Kierkegaard and His Dancing Metaphors

Kierkegaard skillfully used dance metaphors of many kinds. They engage the
reader and evoke vivid images that help to convey his (or his pseudonym's)
message. At the same time, the metaphors seem sometimes ambivalent, creating room for different interpretations, which certainly must have been one
of the goals of Kierkegaard, who so much loved to ponder the nuances of
life. The didactic nature of his writing style also becomes less obvious when
he engages in dancing metaphors; instead, he becomes poetic, offering the
reader wonderful and beautiful ideas to ponder: he offers suggestions that
may lead the reader's mind to wander; he engages his reader in creative dialogue. As we saw, through his and his pseudonyms' use of dance metaphors
in both *Repetition* and *Fear and Trembling*, he even hints at his own ambivalence as a dancer in social settings.

Kierkegaard and the Ballroom

The Seductive Nature of Ballroom Dancing

So far, I have discussed Kierkegaard's thoughts on dance as a theatrical art
form—that is, on ballet, ballet masters, and ballet plots, as well as his many
powerful images of dancers and dancing. Kierkegaard and his pseudonyms
were also concerned with the social aspects of dance, such as the kind of
dancing that takes place in the ballroom. Some of the references are metaphorical; others are more concrete. Most of them are also rather didactic.

The didactic approach is taken, for example, in a comment on the seductive nature of ballroom dancing in the section called "The Seducer's Diary,"
signed by one "Johannes," in *Either/Or*'s first part. There, Johannes the
Seducer reveals, "There are certain times when I admittedly would not want
to be deprived of a ballroom, deprived of its expensive luxury, its priceless
overabundance of youth and beauty, its multiple play of powers, but I do not
enjoy it as much as I revel in possibility" (*SKS* 2:320 / *EO* 1:331). The possibilities for social interaction thrill Johannes, as he appreciates the excitement
of meeting women and the possibilities of making contact. He is making a
social comment: traditionally, the ballroom was one of the few places where
men and women could make contact and where those in love could have a
few moments together. However, these social interactions were governed by
rules of appropriate conduct. The dancing itself was only a part of a package
of skills needed to be able to function in middle- and upper-class society.

Being able to perform the dances well or at least satisfactorily was also something required of men and women of the middle and upper classes. Further into the "Diary," Johannes reveals that even he acquired certain skills when falling in love with a woman: "For the sake of the first girl, I learned to dance; for the sake of the little dancer, I learned to speak French" (*SKS* 2:335/ *EO* 1:346). Apparently, the woman with whom he was in love could dance well, and in order to be with her, he felt the need to achieve some of the same skills. He forgets to tell us to what degree he was successful in this part of the diary. But Johannes begins to reveal a sort of helplessness when dealing with a dancing woman, who is also playing with him. He assumes an even more philosophical and metaphorical tone when describing his longing for his idealized Cordelia. He feels as though he is part of a dance and that she is perhaps playing with him, sometimes acknowledging him and at other times ignoring him: "My relationship to her is like a dance that is supposed to be danced by two people but is danced by only one. That is, I am the other dancer, but invisible. She moves as in a dream, and yet she is dancing with another, and I am that other one who, insofar as I am visibly present, and insofar as I am invisible, is visible" (*SKS* 2:368–69 / *EO* 1:380). If one reads Johannes's statement as somewhat autobiographical of Kierkegaard, the insecurities of a man who perhaps does not dance well or does not dare to dance, shines through in this passage, as well as the impassiveness he feels when confronted with the beautiful but unattainable Cordelia: "The movements require another. She bows to him; she stretches out her hand to him. She recedes; she approaches again. I take her hand; I complete her thought, which nevertheless is completed within itself. She moves to the melody in her own soul: I am merely the occasion for her moving. I am not erotic; that would only arouse her; I am flexible, supple, impersonal, almost like a mood" (*SKS* 2:369 / *EO* 1:380). Movements are used as metaphors for a relationship. This quotation beautifully describes the dance of love. Cordelia is moving to the melody of her own soul; Johannes is observing her movements, and he does so while standing still, but with a flexible mind, trying to be as objective as possible, alone on the side. This idealization of love, with Kierkegaard as observer of an unobtainable (nonexisting) dream women, can be also be seen in other of Kierkegaard's writings. As Ziolkowski points out, Kierkegaard felt "an existential, spiritual affinity" with antiheroes such as Cervantes's Don Quixote: "Like the outspokenly chaste Manchegan knight, he never married, possibly remained a lifelong virgin, and had an unhappy relationship with his own Dulcinea, a young woman he transformed into an unattainable ideal."[42]

Unlike the impulsive, activist Don Quixote, however, Kierkegaard seems to have preferred remaining on the side, analyzing the actions of other persons. This can be seen in an interesting dance-related anecdote he relates in a journal entry of 1838, the year after he met Regine Olsen. There he records an encounter he had one morning with a pair of girls who were dancing to the flute music of two boys, and this leads him to identify playfully with the lovesick knight: "I came close to dancing along with them—so there is still poetry of that sort in the world.—If I encounter more phenomena of this sort I will surely become a D. Quixote who will see such things everywhere" (*SKS* 18:101, FF:137 / *KJN* 2:93). Again, Kierkegaard remains the analytical observer, not daring to participate, but with great ability to render the poetic nuances of a dancing body in the ballroom.

The Gentleman as Ballroom Dancer

Kierkegaard had clear opinions on the male dancer in the ballroom. In a passage removed from the final draft of "The Seducer's Diary," while admitting that a good dancer has certain advantages, the narrator also points out that the freedom of dance is rather conventional and somewhat limited for men: "The best thing at a dance is all the small advantages the dancers enjoy. The conventional freedoms do not signify much precisely because they are conventional and because a male dancer ordinarily does not have anything special in his favor, and ordinarily it is a very ambiguous compliment to a man when a girl says he is a good dancer" (*Pap.* III B 56:2, n.d. 1841–42 / *EO* 1, Suppl., 563). Kierkegaard's didactic approach shines through: he appreciates the freedom in the ballroom, but at the same time he warns that it is an "ambiguous compliment" for a man to be called "a good dancer." Any reader who might think otherwise is forced to rethink. Kierkegaard's thoughts on male dancers were probably typical of his time. Both in the theater and in the ballroom the male dancer was second in importance to the women, even though, in Denmark, the male ballet dancer was cultivated and appreciated to a much higher degree than in other places in Europe, thanks to Bournonville.[43] To what degree these attitudes toward the professional male ballet dancer are linked to those found in ballroom dancing is harder to decipher. It is clear, however, that above all, a gentleman must not be perceived as a professional: society dictated that a man should dance well, but not too well. This was because of puritanical opposition and the idea that to dance too well suggested the mark of a professional rather than a gentleman. This notion is illustrated by the following quotation of 1881 from an English dancing society: "For my own part, I do not like to see a gentleman dance *too* well: he does not want to be taken for a dancing master. It is enough if he dance *like a gentleman*."[44] The dancing masters, who trained bourgeois men and women, advocated the need for such a social accomplishment as dancing, but even they drew a distinction between the professional and the amateur. The dance scholar Theresa Buckland points out that there was a decline in the performance of gentlemanly masculinity during the nineteenth century. This would mean that by the middle of the century, ballroom dancing had become somewhat simplified and less complicated.[45] Kierkegaard's thoughts on and behavior in the ballroom could have been colored by similar views about the male dancer in Copenhagen society. The importance of dancing fluctuated with fashion and politics.[46] Probably men and male dancing would have been easily influenced by such changes. Dance would have been seen differently in different circles and classes of Danish society, so Kierkegaard's comments might refer to the attitudes pertaining to his own social class, where the ideals likely would be similar to those outlined in the following observation by Buckland: "The true gentleman, the aristocrat, attired in fashionable yet unostentatious dress, was identifiable by his posture and gait, ideally characterized by quiet elegance and grace. Early in life he had learned how to distinguish his movement range and energy from that of his female partner, and how to treat her publicly in a chivalrous yet unaffected manner."[47] Kierkegaard certainly seems to have been occupied with treating female dancing partners with chivalry. One final point to be made on this issue is related to his obsession with *Don Juan*. Kierkegaard undoubtedly read, in German translation, Lord Byron's oft-quoted description of his hero's dancing prowess in *Don Juan*:

> He danced without theatrical pretence,
> Not like a ballet-master in the van
> Of his drill'd nymphs, but like a gentleman.[48]

Byron emphasizes that all unnecessary affectations should be left out of the dancing. The quotation above could also have formed some of Kierkegaard's attitudes toward Bournonville. Too much theatricality would come across as dandy-like and flamboyant, traits that were fairly common in the social ballroom up to the beginning of the nineteenth century but that gradually disappeared: "A man could be graceful, but with minimal efforts being displayed."[49] It seems that Kierkegaard adhered to these rules of social conduct.

Kierkegaard as a Social Dancer

Whatever the influence, Kierkegaard was not interested in disobeying the rules of the social ballroom. It is curious that he, who in matters of the intellect would not shy away from voicing very unpopular attitudes and views, had no interest in challenging the social conventions of the ballroom. Perhaps this was because the interaction between men and women was confined to the ballroom, where the social norms were reflected. The rules of etiquette and manners were strict, even if unspoken. To be a sharp thinker and critic made Kierkegaard an intellectual rebel, but his rebelliousness did not extend into the social realm of the ballroom. He thus didactically advises his reader to behave according to the unspoken rules and, above all, not to behave like a professional ballet dancer. A gentleman should dance well, but not too well.

Kierkegaard writes about dance in metaphorical terms and discusses the nature and usefulness of dance more directly. His often dialectical way of thinking is also evident in his discussion of dance and dancing. Therefore he (or some of his pseudonyms) must frequently, perhaps always, be understood as speaking in an indirect mode when making more concrete references and allusions. This is, however, less true for several of the allusions he made to dance, where he instead creates powerful images for the reader to ponder.

Kierkegaard's thoughts on dance as a social and theatrical practice often contradicted those he revealed when so richly describing the dancer's ability to be expressive in more metaphorical terms. He was ambivalent in his attitude toward dancing. In fact, his remark "Let no one invite me, for I do not dance" is indicative of Kierkegaard's ambivalence: he wants to dance, but cannot or will not let himself be free to do so.

Kierkegaard also displays pure admiration for the creative aspect of dancing, as in *Fear and Trembling*, where Johannes de Silentio admires the dancer for his ability to go places and do things with his body that nobody else can.

Throughout his writing, regardless of whether he or a pseudonym speaks positively or negatively about dance and dancers, Kierkegaard never shows indifference. His use of metaphorically exciting images and his somewhat condescending descriptions of the art of ballet are never boring, and for this reason they can be read and reread, interpreted and reinterpreted, again and again. This is part of what makes Kierkegaard timeless and relevant not only for today's dancer and dance scholar. His comments and metaphors on dance and dancers give all readers pause to think and to ponder issues of human life.

Notes

1. There are allusions to dance and dancers in both parts of *Either/Or*, as well as in *Fear and Trembling*, *Philosophical Fragments*, *Concept of Anxiety*, and *Works of Love*.

2. Nathaniel Kramer, "August Bournonville: Kierkegaard's Leap of Faith and the 'Noble Art of Terpsichore,'" in *Kierkegaard and His Danish Contemporaries*, Tome 1: *Literature, Drama and Aesthetics*, ed. Jon Stewart, Kierkegaard Research: Sources, Reception and Resources, vol. 7 (Farnham, U.K.: Ashgate, 2009), 67–82; Kimerer L. LaMothe, "The Poet and the Dancer: Søren Kierkegaard," in *Between Dancing and Writing: The Practice of Religious Studies* (New York: Fordham University Press 2004), 85–101.

3. Theatrical dance practices include dance primarily seen and performed onstage, and in this essay classical ballet is the dance form discussed. Classical ballet evolved gradually as an art form from the theatrical practices of the Renaissance and Baroque courts in Italy and France. By the beginning of the eighteenth century, it had become codified and looked for the most part like the classical ballet of today. Technical brilliance and artistic expression were valued in the dancers. My concern with social dance practice in this essay is confined mainly to ballroom dancing. For more information on how the two dance practices evolved as one and then split apart, see Ingrid Brainard, "Court and Social

Dance before 1800," in *International Encyclopedia of Dance*, 6 vols., ed. Selma Jeanne Cohen (1998; New York: Oxford University Press, 2004), 2:619–23.

4. For an extensive overview of Bournonville's life, see vol. 1 of Knud Arne Jürgensen, *The Bournonville Tradition*, 2 vols. (London: Dance Books, 1997).

5. Bournonville choreographed ballets in the Romantic realm, such as his version of *La Sylphide* (*The Sylph*), which premiered in 1836. *La Sylphide* was originally choreographed by Filippo Taglioni in 1832 for the Paris Opera Ballet, with the ballerina Marie Taglioni interpreting the role of the Sylph. Among his numerous other well-known works are *Napoli* (1842) and *Et Folkesagn* (1854, *A Folk Tale*).

6. For an informative article on Bournonville and Kierkegaard, see Kramer's "August Bournonville."

7. Quoted in Jürgensen, *The Bournonville Tradition*, 1:66. Bournonville is here referring to Kierkegaard. The original manuscript is among Bournonville's papers in the collection of handwritten material in Stockholm's Royal Library, Kongelige Bibiliotket, Håndskriftssamlingen (hereafter KBHA), NkS 3285, 4^0. The passage is also quoted in a slightly different English rendering in Bruce H. Kirmmse, ed., *Encounters with Kierkegaard: A Life as Seen by His Contemporaries*, trans. B. H. Kirmmse and Virginia Laursen (Princeton, N.J.: Princeton University Press, 1996), 90.

8. Bournonville's changing views of Kierkegaard are also pointed out by Kramer, "August Bournonville," 68.

9. Jürgensen, *The Bournonville Tradition*, 1:41.

10. Knud Arne Jürgensen, email, July 3–4, 2013.

11. Kramer, "August Bournonville," 68.

12. Quoted in Jürgensen, *The Bournonville Tradition*, 1:66.

13. Bournonville, quoted in ibid., 1:67.

14. Bournonville, quoted in ibid.

15. Ibid., 1:66.

16. Bournonville's *La Sylphide*, with its tragic ending, is one of the few exceptions to Bournonville's otherwise generally happy endings.

17. The quotation is from one of Bournonville's unpublished diaries in the Copenhagen Royal Library (KBHA NkS 747, 8^0, Dagbøger, bind 13). The passage is quoted in Kirmmse, *Encounters with Kierkegaard*, 101. There is also correspondence between Bournonville and Hans Christian Andersen about Kierkegaard's burial, where Andersen defends Kierkegaard. See Kirmmse, *Encounters with Kierkegaard*, 136.

18. For instance, the themes of *La Sylphide* are love, faithfulness, and deception, and it carries a clear moral message, typical of both the Romantic spirit and Bournonville's own standards: You shall not aim for what you cannot have; deception and unfaithfulness in love strips you of all dignity and hope. Bournonville's version was based on the original choreographed by Filippo Taglioni in 1832, but because Bournonville could not afford to pay for the rights to the music by Jean-Madeleine Schneitzhoeffer, he choreographed and staged his own version, which premiered in 1836, with music by Herman Severin Løvenskiold.

19. Quoted in Jürgensen, *The Bournonville Tradition*, 1:85. The passage is from an unpublished article by Bournonville dealing with his literary production between 1830 and 1860, written most likely around 1861 for the planned

second volume (1865) of his memoirs: August Bournonville, *Mit theaterliv*, 5 vols. in 2 (Copenhagen: C. A. Reitzel, 1848–78), later issued in an annotated English translation by Patricia N. McAndrew, *My Theatre Life* (Middletown, Conn.: Wesleyan University Press, 1979). These memoirs undoubtedly represent Bournonville's towering achievement as a writer.

20. Jürgensen, *The Bournonville Tradition*, 1:85.

21. Ibid., 1:41.

22. A most obvious example is *Fear and Trembling*, which, in debating the moral dilemma of Abraham when he was being asked to sacrifice his own son, scrutinizes all its different angles.

23. It could also be that Kierkegaard is referring to the poet and critic Théophile Gautier (1811–1872), Scribe's rival, who wrote ballet plots, including the ultimate Romantic ballet, *Giselle*, which premiered in 1841 in Paris.

24. For a discussion of the place of Scribe and other literary figures at the Royal Danish Opera and Theater, see Erik Aschengreen, Marianne Hallar, and Jørgen Heiner, eds., *Perspektiv på Bournonville* (Copenhagen: Nyt nordisk, 1980), 54–58.

25. Bournonville choreographed *Faust* in 1832, two years after he was appointed principal dancer and artistic director of the Royal Danish Ballet.

26. Jürgensen, *The Bournonville Tradition*, 1:31–39. See also Allan Fredericia, "Bournonvilles koreografi," in Aschengreen et al., *Perspektiv på Bournonville*, 160–89.

27. Kramer, "August Bournonville," 77. After 1841, Bournonville's choreographic style became more "Danish," thus departing from the French style. See Jürgensen, *The Bournonville Tradition*, 1:81–84.

28. Mephistopheles's entrance, according to Haufniensis, is not just a dramatic moment among others in the ballet but a "very profound thought" (*SKS* 4:433 / *CA* 132). As Kramer points out, "Whatever Kierkegaard knew or did not know about ballet and French conventions, its impact on him is apparent" ("August Bournonville," 77).

29. *Undine* premiered in 1842 and was performed for the last time in 1844. It was set to music by Adolph Adam and I. P. E. Hartman. See Jürgensen, *The Bournonville Tradition*, 2:76–77.

30. Gregor Malantschuk, comment in *JP*, vol. 1, p. 526, s.v. "Don Juan." See also Ronald Grimsley, "The Don Juan Theme in Molière and Kierkegaard," *Comparative Literature* 6, no. 4 (1954): 316–34; Eric Ziolkowski, *The Literary Kierkegaard* (Evanston, Ill.: Northwestern University Press, 2011), 5, 19, 35, and intermittently thereafter. (In addition, see the essays by Nils Holger Petersen and Peder Jothen in this volume.—Ed.)

31. Angiolini's *Don Juan* was based on Molière's play of 1665. The first performance of Angiolini's ballet was in Vienna, in 1761, at the Theater am Kärntnertor. The ballet follows the legend of Don Juan and his descent into hell. It was composed according to the new, emerging ideas of the *ballet d'action*, which were advocated by Angiolini as well as by his rival Jean-Georges Noverre (1727–1810). The ideal of the *ballet d'action* was a ballet that was more believable and natural to the audience. The *ballet d'action* also emphasized more unity of dance, music, scenery, and costume and less use of artificial pantomime. In addition, Angiolini regarded music and dance as two separate components that dancers were required

to unite in their bodies, and he succeeded extraordinarily well in his effort. Gluck's expressive music was designed to aid in portraying the action. For more information on this groundbreaking ballet, see Charles C Russell, "Libertine Restored: *Don Juan* by Gluck and Angiolini," *Music & Letters* 65, no. 1 (1984): 17–27.

32. Nonetheless, as quoted in Nils Holger Petersen's essay in this volume, "A" himself characterizes Don Juan as "danc[ing] over the abyss." See also Petersen's discussion of "A's" contention that music is the sole form of art suitable for representing Don Juan.—Ed.

33. Personal communication.

34. One pair was called the head couple, the other pairs, the side couples. A dance figure was often performed, first by the head couple, and then repeated by the side couples. See Theresa Jill Buckland, *Society Dancing: Fashionable Bodies in England, 1870–1920* (London: Palgrave Macmillan, 2013), 10; Mary Clarke, *The History of Dance* (New York: Crown, 1981), 81–88.

35. Giovanni-Andrea Gallini, *A Treatise on the Art of Dancing 1762* (London: R. Dodsley, 1762), 84–86.

36. Marian Hanna Winter, *The Pre-Romantic Ballet* (London: Pitman, 1974), 30.

37. For more information on traveling dancers and tightrope dancers, see Anne Margrete Fiskvik, "Where Highbrow Taste Met Itinerant Dance in Eighteenth-Century Scandinavia: The Dance Entrepreneur Martin Nürenbach," in *Sjuttonhundratal: Nordic Yearbook for Eighteenth-Century Studies*, vol. 13 (2016), 83–107. See also Anne Margrete Fiskvik, "Information udi Dands i Christiania 1769–1773," in *Lidenskap eller levebrød: Utøvende kunst i endring rundt 1800*, ed. Randi Margrete Selvik, Ellen Karoline Gjervan, and Svein Gladsø (Bergen: Fagbokforlaget, 2015), 287–314.

38. [Anon.], "Utdrag af Bref" [Excerpt from Letters], *Hvad Nytt? Hvad Nytt?*, November 6, 1771, [p. 1].

39. Fiskvik, "Highbrow Taste Meets Itinerant Dance," 10. Ladder tricks were part of the slapstick antics of the *lazzi*, which was derived from the commedia dell'arte and figured prominently in dances belonging to both the comic and grotesque styles (ibid.).

40. Continuing this discussion, Climacus explains that he met up with the depressed young man who is hopelessly in love and tried to sort out his love problems (*SV*[1] 3:180–84 / R 139–42).

41. Kierkegaard spent time in Berlin in 1841 and attended many different performances, but especially took to the Königstädter Theater.

42. Ziolkowski, *The Literary Kierkegaard*, 131.

43. In classical ballet, the male dancer was discriminated against in France and Italy, where the female dancer, the ballerina, was much idealized. The male dancer was reduced to being a support of the female, somebody who put her on display. The early 1840s were the age of the ballerina, especially on the Continent. Bournonville, however, developed highly technically skilled male ballet dancers.

44. "The Lounger in society" [pseud.], *The Glass of Fashion: A Universal Handbook of Social Etiquette and Home Cultures for Ladies and Gentlemen* (London: John Hogg, 1881), 164, quoted in Buckland, *Society Dancing*, 118. For a thorough discussion of the male dancer in nineteenth-century England, see Buckland's chapter "Where Are Our Men?," 118–27.

45. Buckland, *Society Dancing*, 118. By the 1840s, social dancing had become much more pedestrian than at the beginning of the century, when there had been a vogue for introducing balletic steps into, for instance, the quadrilles. For an account of how to dance the ballroom dances of the day, see Buckland, *Society Dancing*, 10–11, 46–49; Henri Cellarius, *The Drawing-Room Dances* (London: E. Churton, 1847).

46. This point is made by Buckland, *Society Dancing*, analyzing the situation in London around 1900, and by Jean-Michel Guilcher, *La contredanse et les renouvellements de la danse française* (Paris: Mouton, 1969), examining the situation in France around 1800.

47. Buckland, *Society Dancing*, 119.

48. George Gordon Byron, *Don Juan*, canto 14, stanza 38, lines 6–8, in *The Poetical Works of Lord Byron* (1904; London: Oxford University Press, 1945), 825. Kierkegaard owned *Lord Byron's sämmtliche Werke: Nach den Anforderungen unserer Zeit neu übersetzt von Mehreren*, 10 vols. (Stuttgart: Hoffmann, 1839); *ASKB* 1868–70.

49. Buckland, *Society Dancing*, 119–21.

Part III

✦

Visual Arts and Film

Painting with Words

Kierkegaard and the Aesthetics of the Icon

Christopher B. Barnett

Søren Kierkegaard's dubious relation to aesthetics is, in one sense, one of the great ironies of Western intellectual history. After all, Kierkegaard was not only a lover of the arts—famously, he was said to have never missed a performance of Mozart's *Don Giovanni* at Copenhagen's Royal Theater[1]—but he is widely held to be the finest prose stylist of the Danish language. As Joakim Garff puts it, "What Danish writer had ever produced anything so fertile and prodigious?"[2] And this is to say nothing of Kierkegaard's remarkable impact on twentieth-century art, from the films of Carl Theodor Dreyer to the music of Samuel Barber and the paintings of Mark Rothko. W. H. Auden, the outstanding English poet, himself an admirer of Kierkegaard, once acclaimed the "brilliantly poetic" nature of Kierkegaard's writings, though he quickly added that Kierkegaard was not so much a poet as a "preacher, an expounder and defender of Christian doctrine and Christian conduct."[3] In this distinction lies much of the controversy regarding Kierkegaard's relation to aesthetics.

Here "aesthetics" is meant in a general sense—namely, as the study of and/ or reflection on objects of perception. Indeed, the word "aesthetics" itself comes from the Greek term *aisthanesthai* (to perceive), although, through Plato and others, it has taken on the additional significance of dealing with perceptions that are particularly beautiful or sublime. Kierkegaard adopts both usages. For him, aesthetics concerns what one can see, touch, hear, and so on, just as "the aesthetic" (*det Æsthetiske*) refers to a life oriented to the senses. On the one hand, these sensory perceptions are simply part of the data that make up human life. As Kierkegaard writes in *Either/Or*, "The esthetic is not evil but the indifferent" (*SKS* 3:165 / *EO* 2:169). On the other hand, such perceptions, especially beautiful and pleasing ones, can wield an influence over one's life, drawing one to this or to that end. It is in this sense that, for Kierkegaard, the aesthetic can be dangerous or beneficial. This tension is reflected in Auden's suggestion that Kierkegaard's poetic sensibilities ultimately yield to a more severe Christian vein. Kierkegaard's religious commitments appear to have effected a rupture from his aesthetic ones—a point of view that finds plenty of corroboration in the secondary literature.

A well-known example of this tendency lies in the work of George Pattison, who traces the rift back to Kierkegaard's 1846 treatise, *A Literary Review*. In that work, Kierkegaard chides "the present age" for its embrace of reflection—its tendency to reject authority and tradition in favor of a disposition critical of everything but the individual's self-interest. Consequently, in Kierkegaard's view, social institutions and relations have been reduced to instruments of utility. What once stirred the passions of people, whether God or country or love, have become objectively meaningless. According to Pattison, this insight compels Kierkegaard to divorce the religious from the aesthetic, even as both emerge as potential escapes from the abyss of modernity. For the redemption of art is nothing more than a whimsy, especially in an epoch of reflection, when the aesthetic preoccupation with *form* has been detached from any meaningful *content*. Thus art, too, has succumbed to the present age: it titillates but does not elevate. As Pattison goes on to explain, "The aesthetic may no longer be regarded as a legitimate stage on the path to a religious awakening. To stay with the aesthetic is to refuse the religious. . . . Although reflection has in one sense destroyed the possibility of great art, an age that fails to choose faith with the decisiveness of inward passion is . . . an 'aesthetic' age. The aesthetic has become the inauthentic."[4] The only hope for the individual, then, is to seek "the religious in the absolute interiority of the self."[5] Even concrete ethical striving in the world has become unrecognizable, *form-less*.

Pattison tenders his reading with somber understanding, adding that Kierkegaard's critique of modern art has served to shape the consciousness of modern art. In fact, as Pattison sees it, the "death of art" has come to give an almost religious mission to the contemporary artist.[6] Other commentators, however, are not as sympathetic with Kierkegaard's vision. Perhaps the sharpest critique of this sort was issued by the eminent Swiss Catholic thinker Hans Urs von Balthasar (1905–1988). Critical of the preoccupation of modern theologians with logic and ethics at the expense of beauty, Balthasar commenced one of the breakthrough theological projects of the twentieth century: his seven-volume work, *The Glory of the Lord* (*Herrlichkeit*, 1961–69). Its aim, taken as a whole, is "to complement the vision of the true and the good with that of the beautiful" and, in turn, to "show how impoverished Christian thinking has been by the growing loss of this perspective which once strongly informed theology." For Balthasar, this is an urgent task. Today, he says, beauty has become "a mere appearance" in a "world of interests," and thus its fate is to be either exploited or forgotten. But beauty's loss is also humanity's. As Balthasar goes on to explain, "In a world without beauty . . . the good also loses its attractiveness, the self-evidence of why it must be carried out. Man stands before the good and asks himself why *it* must be done and not rather its alternative, evil." This diagnosis bears a theological prescription—namely, a return to the *form* of divine revelation. For it is only through form that beauty shines, and "the ray of the Unconditional breaks through, casting a person down to adoration and transforming him into a believer and a follower."[7]

With this concern established, Balthasar turns to a genealogical account of how beauty was torn from the fabric of Western society. It is, for him, a theological story, which has its origins in the Protestant Reformation in general and in Martin Luther's teaching in particular. For Balthasar, Luther's insistence on "God's absolute veiledness"—an emphasis derived from his distaste for Neo-Platonic and Thomist versions of the *analogia entis*—results in a rejection of "every form which man tries to impose on revelation in order to achieve an overview that makes comprehension possible."[8] One can no longer look at a created form—say, a sunset or a sleeping child—and ascertain a likeness to the divine. In this way, Luther sunders nature and grace and, with it, the aesthetic and the religious.

It is at this point that Balthasar begins to attend to Kierkegaard, who, in his view, reaps what Luther had sown several centuries before. By the nineteenth century, art had been all but totally uncoupled from its relationship with theology, freeing the Romantics to deem aesthetics the "supreme value of any worldview." From there it was but a short step to the aesthetic nihilism of Nietzsche—a development that, according to Balthasar, Kierkegaard foresaw and opposed. Realizing that modern aesthetics was "frivolous, merely curious and self-indulgent," Kierkegaard fired back with an emphasis on "inwardness and religious subjectivity." But this response lacked comprehensiveness, and it led Kierkegaard to deepen—rather than to overcome—the chasm between aesthetics and religion. According to Balthasar, "Kierkegaard can no longer achieve a meeting of religion and aesthetics. He is impelled to use the concept of 'the aesthetic' to stake out and define a basic attitude which, for the Christian, is unacceptable . . . thereby eradicating from theology all traces of an aesthetic attitude. . . . This enthusiastic disjunction robs man, as it were from within, of all joy in the aesthetic." Thus Kierkegaard stands as both an accomplice to and a victim of Luther's theology. Even worse, the Dane's influence on twentieth-century ideas worked to popularize Lutheran thinking. "The Kierkegaard revival," as Balthasar puts it, "in various ways had an anti-aesthetic effect on theology."[9]

In light of Pattison's and Balthasar's analyses, it would seem unlikely that a positive appraisal of aesthetics can be developed from Kierkegaard's oeuvre. The opposition that he ostensibly establishes between the aesthetic and the religious, not to mention the fact that he himself never penned a proper treatise on the subject, appears to quell any such enterprise. In this essay, however, I will argue to the contrary. Specifically, I will show that an "aesthetics of the icon" is implicit in Kierkegaard's own copious employment of aesthetic imagery. Rather than rupturing the two spheres, he has a dialectical view of the matter: aesthetic imagery can function either in the manner of icons or in that of idols.

I will establish this point in three ways. First, I will explore the concept of "image" or "picture" (*Billede*) in Kierkegaard's authorship. As will be seen,

Kierkegaard uses this term in a variety of contexts, imbuing it with both negative and positive significance. Next I will argue that this dialectical usage of *Billede* informs his orientation toward the aesthetic in general. An aesthetic image either can draw one into its own ambit, or it can deflect one to something higher—indeed, to godliness. The upshot of this dialectic is a potential integration of the aesthetic and the religious in Kierkegaard's thinking. For inasmuch as the aesthetic brings one to seek the religious in one's concrete existence, Kierkegaard not only applauds the aesthetic but *employs* it. Finally, I will attempt to illustrate Kierkegaard's understanding of the relationship between aesthetics and religion by way of the thought of the French philosopher Jean-Luc Marion. In particular, I will point out that Marion's distinction between the idol and the icon—whereby the former aims to absorb the gaze of the observer, the latter to redirect it—can shed light on the multitude of "pictures" populating Kierkegaard's writings. This last section is not meant to serve as a comprehensive explication of how Kierkegaard and Marion stand in relation to one another; rather, it is an attempt to show, however provisionally, that Kierkegaard's approach to aesthetics bears a resemblance to that of other prominent thinkers—in this case, Marion.

To be sure, as Marion has forcefully argued, human beings are confronted by idols in both image and idea. Yet, with characters such as the woman who was a sinner (*Synderinden*) in Luke 7:37–50, Kierkegaard also fashions *icons* of faith. In this way, and with a measure of irony, he actually fulfills Balthasar's demand for attention to the form of Christian existence.

The Concept of *Billede* in Kierkegaard's Authorship

The term *Billede* occurs with regularity in Kierkegaard's authorship. In one form or another, it appears more than three hundred times, published as well as unpublished. Moreover, its usage spans his corpus, turning up as early as 1838 in *From the Papers of One Still Living* and as late as 1855 in articles in *Fædrelandet*. An exhaustive analysis of *Billede*, then, is neither possible nor desirable here. Instead, I will examine a few representative instances of the term, showing how Kierkegaard employs it in a variety of contexts and senses.

An early and striking example of Kierkegaard's use of *Billede* occurs in the first part of *Either/Or*, in its final section, "The Seducer's Diary." The story's antihero, the aptly named Johannes the Seducer, has followed his *objet d'amour* into a Copenhagen shop. Her name is Cordelia, a mere girl at seventeen years of age. Johannes watches as she makes her way through the store, fondling the items for sale with blissful caprice. In order to remain unnoticed, he stands across the room, eyeing Cordelia in a large mirror mounted on a wall. The mirror, he notes, is at once his rival and collaborator. Its seizure of her image is akin to contemplation, to devotion. However, it cannot keep her image all to itself; rather, it must deliver it to others, who are not so unfortunately constituted: "Unhappy mirror, which assuredly can grasp her image [*Billede*] but not her; unhappy mirror, which cannot secretly hide her image in itself, hide it from the whole world, but can only disclose it to others as it now does to me. What torture if a human being were fashioned that way" (*SKS* 2:305 / *EO* 1:315). Indeed, Johannes is not fashioned that way. He compares Cordelia's figure to the voluptuousness of a piece of fruit. He can, he says, *feel* her with his eyes. And, accordingly, he aims to consume her. As he puts it, "Everything will be relished in slow mouthfuls; she is picked out, she will be gathered" (*SKS* 2:306 / *EO* 1:317, my translation).

It is noteworthy that Johannes, the aesthete, interacts only with an *image* of Cordelia. Kierkegaard makes this point especially clear by using the mirror as a mediator between the two characters. He relates to her not as a three-dimensional human being but rather as a two-dimensional reflection. And this reflection, as it were, sucks him in. It consumes him as much as he wants to consume it—a detail that hints at why Pattison calls Johannes a "pitiable creature" despite his blatant exploitation of others. For "he is incapable of a real meeting, a real encounter with another person, incapable of dealing with a situation of mutual responsibility."[10] In this sense, Johannes is an antiquated, but no less authentic, version of a pornography addict. For him, image and reality have been confused; more precisely, the aesthetic as such has become his life. Even when he acts within the continuum of the real world, he remains imprisoned in his own world of fantasies, for only fantasies are capable of arousing and gratifying him (*SKS* 2:296 / *EO* 1:306). Pattison sums up Kierkegaard's point nicely: "What he is showing is what happens when one tries to base life on an 'image.'"[11]

The Seducer's aesthetic attitude terminates in sexual abuse, but elsewhere Kierkegaard points out that the lure of the image can corrupt in different ways. Insofar as it effects a break with the real world, aestheticism is like a mold that spoils whatever it touches, be it sex, politics, or religion. Kierkegaard highlights this point in his 1850 work, *Practice in Christianity*, particularly in the sixth exposition of the section entitled "From on High He Will Draw All to Himself." There Kierkegaard's pseudonym Anti-Climacus explores the ambiguity of "observing" an object, as when "one shows a painting to a person and asks him to observe [*betragte*] it" (*SKS* 12:227 / *PC* 233). On the one hand, he notes, the observer must come close to the object of observation so as to get a better look at it. On the other hand, the observer must also remain "infinitely distant" from it since "by observing I go into the object (I become objective) but I leave myself or go away from myself (I cease to be subjective)" (*SKS* 12:227–28 / *PC* 233–34). For Anti-Climacus, this dialectic captures precisely what is wrong with Christendom in the present age. The preacher stands in the pulpit and makes "observations"—a rather unsubtle reference to Bishop Mynster's book, *Observations on the Doctrines of the Christian Faith* (*Betragtninger over de christelige Troeslærdomme,*

1833)[12]—but neglects to emphasize that "it is Christian truth that is observing me, whether I am doing what it says I should do" (*SKS* 12:228 / *PC* 234).

This is also, Anti-Climacus says, the danger with Christian art. Although he admits that he cannot "pass judgment" on all artists, he gives two main reasons why he could never paint "the image" (*Billedet*)[13] of Jesus Christ (*SKS* 12:246–47 / *PC* 254–55). First, in order to paint Christ's image, he would have to secure a certain amount of "leisure" (*Ro*; *SKS* 12:246 / *PC* 255, my translation), which would allow him to shirk what Christ asks of his day-to-day life so that, instead, he could paint a picture. Second, he worries that the finished product—the painting of Christ as such—would distort the meaning of the religious life. For in the painting "the artist admired himself, and everybody admired the artist" (*SKS* 12:247 / *PC* 255). In this scenario, the person reflected in the image has been forgotten, eclipsed by the image itself. Anti-Climacus explains, "The beholder looked at the picture [*Billedet*] in the role of an art expert: whether it is a success, whether it is a masterpiece, whether the play of colors is right, and the shadows, whether blood looks like that, whether the suffering expression is artistically true—but the invitation to imitation he did not find" (*SKS* 12:247–48 / *PC* 255–56). Here Anti-Climacus reiterates the trouble with Johannes the Seducer, albeit in a Christian context. The person who views Christ's image as an end in itself, who allows the *picture* to occupy him or her more than the real thing, has abstracted the aesthetic from the religious and, in turn, transformed it into an idol.

Significantly, this critique is not limited to artists or to the bourgeois aesthetes of Christendom. In an 1850 journal entry, Kierkegaard chides the Moravian Brethren—a major Pietist group, with whom he had both familial ties and theological affinities[14]—for "gazing at Christ's suffering" rather than accentuating the "imitation" of Christ (*SKS* 23:438, NB20:78, n.d. 1850 / *JP* 2:1874, my translation). Thus he suggests that it is not enough to celebrate the Passion of Christ with liturgical and artistic pieces—a customary and, at times, extravagant feature of Moravian piety, perhaps best captured by *Christ Scourged* (1758),[15] a masterpiece of the great Moravian painter Johann Valentin Haidt (1700–1780). Instead, the religious in general, and Christianity in particular, are to be distinguished by their concrete realization in one's own life. For Kierkegaard, this is the last word, irrespective of where one falls on the ecclesial or theological spectrum. To put it in Anti-Climacus's terms, art may produce people who *admire* Christianity, but admiration is beside the point: "Only the imitator is the true Christian" (*SKS* 12:246, 248 / *PC* 254, 256).

It is clear, then, that Kierkegaard's writings treat *Billede* as a dangerous concept. Enticed to gaze at an image, one can, almost like Narcissus, fall in love with what is not real and die, in spirit if not in body. But elsewhere Kierkegaard takes a different tack. Particularly in his upbuilding discourses, he is inclined to describe certain biblical heroes as "images." He does not just *call* them images; he uses his pen to sketch them in rich, pictorial language.

A good early example of this tendency turns up in "Patience in Expectancy," the second address from *Two Upbuilding Discourses* (1844). There, Kierkegaard discusses Anna, the aged prophetess who witnessed the presentation of the infant Jesus to the Temple authorities in Jerusalem (Luke 2:36–38). What strikes Kierkegaard about Anna is not so much her presence at this momentous event as her many years as a widow, during which she apparently remained devoted both to her husband and to God. As he envisions it, where another might have sought solace in "multifarious expectancies" (*SKS* 5:212 / *EUD* 211), Anna has passed her long life in quiet fortitude, faithful to her husband's memory and hopeful that God will reunite them—and all things—in eternity. Kierkegaard continues, "My listener, let your thoughts dwell on this venerable woman, [who] . . . stands as the eternal's young fiancée. This tranquillity in her eyes that nevertheless is expectant, this gentleness that is reconciled to life and nevertheless is expectant . . . beyond flowering nevertheless still vigorous, forsaken nevertheless not withered, childless nevertheless not barren, bent with years and stooped nevertheless not broken—a widow, nevertheless betrothed, 'she is in silence' with her expectancy" (*SKS* 5:212 / *EUD* 211–12). Here he breaks off, adding that this "picture" (*Billede*) of Anna is "beautiful," so much so that "one could sit and grow old contemplating [it], powerless to tear oneself away from it" (*SKS* 5:212 / *EUD* 212). It is, in fact, "the object of contemplation [*Betragtningens Gjenstand*]" (*SKS* 5:213 / *EUD* 212) for those who rightly understand that life is replete with peril and disappointment but not bereft of hope. In fact, the *Billede* of Anna is more than a picture of a human being; it is a reflection of the eternal. As Kierkegaard explains, "The object of expectancy, the more glorious and precious it is, form[s] the expectant person in its own likeness, because a person resembles what he loves with his whole soul" (*SKS* 5:218 / *EUD* 219).

With his evocative prose, not to mention his mystically tinged language of "contemplation," Kierkegaard effectively treats Anna as an icon—that is to say, as an image of the sacred. Moreover, he invites his "listener" to do the same, to see in his rendering of Anna a picture of patient expectancy. But this *Billede* is not to be an end in itself. The one who properly contemplates it does so in order to reproduce Anna's virtue in his or her own life. After all, this is an *upbuilding* discourse. And it is Kierkegaard's painting of Anna that occasions the upbuilding.

Kierkegaard comes back to these themes—in even more pronounced fashion—in his upbuilding discourses on the woman who was a sinner. These writings draw on the seventh chapter of the Gospel of Luke, which tells of a woman who tearfully anoints Jesus's feet despite opposition from the Pharisees. In turn, Jesus praises the woman's love and declares her sins, "which were many" (Luke 7:47), forgiven. Kierkegaard clearly cherished this biblical story. Not only do his discourses from 1849 and 1850 return to it often, but it also appears early in his authorship, in "Love Will Hide a Multitude of Sins" (1843). What drew him to the text was its compressed treatment of several

Christian themes, from the mercy of Christ to the hostility of the world. Yet, more than anything else, the figure of the sinful woman herself moved him: "She has forgotten speech and language and the restlessness of thoughts, has forgotten what is even greater restlessness, this self, has forgotten herself— she, the lost woman, who is now lost in her Savior, who, lost in him, rests at his feet—like a picture [*Billede*]. It is almost as if the Savior himself momentarily looked at her and the situation that way, as if she were not an actual person but a picture" (*SKS* 11:277 / *WA* 141). What Kierkegaard sees in this moment is an image of the eternal in history. As he clarifies in an 1850 journal entry, the sinful woman appears *in effigie*—note that his Latin here means "in the form of an image"—precisely because she is "the present one [*den Nærværende*]" (*SKS* 24:74, NB21:123, n.d. 1850, my translation; compare *KJN* 8:70), wholly open to God. She is more than a human being precisely because, in that moment, she is truly a human being. "She *is* the symbol," stresses Kierkegaard, "like a picture [*Billede*]" (*SKS* 11:277 / *WA* 141).

And yet, as with Anna, Kierkegaard obviates any attempt merely to rest one's eyes on the image of the sinful woman. As he writes in *An Upbuilding Discourse* (1850), she is best seen "as a prototype of piety," as a teacher of "godliness" (*SKS* 12:263 / *WA* 149). Here the term "prototype" does a great deal of work for him: in Danish it is *Forbillede*, literally "an image that goes in front." Her image, then, is a kind of "motion picture." It invites not observation but *imitation*, calling the observer to strip himself or herself of worldly attachments in order to stand naked before God. The devotion of the sinful woman, manifested in the form of her encounter with Christ, is to be repeated in the lives of others.

For Kierkegaard, Christian faith has a kind of form. It does not issue in just any appearance but, rather, has certain contours and features. That is not to say, of course, that it is reducible to a particular manner of dress or single way of living. Nor is it to forget that even an ideal form, such as Christ's, can be approached in the wrong fashion. Nevertheless, Kierkegaard insists that the image of *worship* signifies the content of faith, including, paradoxically, the very object of faith. He writes, "In truth, to be able to worship is what makes the [human being's] invisible glory superior to the rest of creation. The pagan was not aware of God and therefore sought likeness in ruling. But the resemblance is not like that. . . . The human being and God do not look like each other directly, but inversely; only when God has infinitely become the eternal and omnipresent object of worship and the human being always the worshiper, only then do they look like each other" (*SKS* 8:290 / *UDVS* 193, my translation). To see a human being worship God is to see a reflection of God himself. This is Kierkegaard's reformulation of the ancient doctrine of *analogia entis*, which, among other things, states that human beings—as creatures—stand in a proportional relationship with their creator. They convey the divine being, but, following the Fourth Lateran Council, this similarity is nonetheless marked by an infinite dissimilarity. One of the outcomes of this teaching is just what we have seen in Kierkegaard's treatment of *Billede*: in the images of Anna and the sinful woman, it is possible, indirectly but truly, to perceive the divine. The aesthetic and the religious are not necessarily opposed.

Kierkegaard and the Dialectic between the Aesthetic and the Religious

Kierkegaardian scholarship is known for its diversity or, as some might put it, fragmentation. A quick scroll through a bibliography—or even an online bookstore—reveals as much. There are books on Kierkegaard the individualist and on Kierkegaard the social commentator, on Kierkegaard the postmodern deconstructionist and on Kierkegaard the guardian of Christian orthodoxy, just to mention a couple of fault lines. Yet, despite this interpretive range, one point seems to have achieved a wide consensus—namely, that Kierkegaard was a master *dialectician*. This, after all, was how Kierkegaard saw himself. In a lengthy 1850 journal passage, after asserting that he is neither a religious zealot nor "only a poet," Kierkegaard underlines the twin pillars of his literary career: "What, then—in addition to the main thing, that I have been helped by Governance—has helped me? The fact that I am a dialectician" (*SKS* 23:33, NB15:46, n.d. 1850 / *KJN* 7:31).

With this in mind, it is surprising that a number of commentators have neglected to see this dialectical approach as operative in Kierkegaard's analysis of the aesthetic and the religious. Consider Balthasar once again. He insists that Kierkegaard's thought inexorably leads to a chasm between beauty and faith, between art and religion. This is especially a critique of Kierkegaard's later authorship, with its increasingly strident calls for Christian obedience and suffering. But Balthasar omits examples that run counter to his thesis. There is no mention, say, of Kierkegaard's treatment of the woman who was a sinner, much less a discussion of his nuanced recognition of a "social role for art in the criticism of modern culture."[16] As a result, Kierkegaard's warnings about the misuse of the aesthetic are transformed into categorical rejections of art and of beauty. The dialectical tension is cut, replaced by the resounding thud of his conception of the religious.

To be sure, as the previous analysis of *Billede* has made clear, Kierkegaard's approach to the aesthetic is hardly so straightforward. For one thing, there is little if any cause for thinking that Kierkegaard believes the aesthetic can somehow be expunged from human existence. As C. Stephen Evans notes, "it is a universal dimension of human life."[17] The implication here is that Kierkegaard's well-known existential "stages"—the aesthetic, the ethical, and the religious—are not mere steps on a ladder, arranged in such a way that to reach the ethical is to abandon the aesthetic and so on. Rather, these stages are permanent domains within the self, which, like a Venn diagram, overlap one another at certain key junctures. To quote Evans again, "The ethical must in some way be preserved within the religious sphere, even if it is transformed as well, just as the aesthetic must be preserved within the ethical and religious spheres."[18]

This perichoresis of the existential spheres follows from the analysis of the self in Kierkegaard's pseudonymous treatise *The Sickness unto Death* (1849). There the self is understood as a "synthesis" (*SKS* 11:129 / *SUD* 13) of a series of contrary elements: the finite and the infinite, the temporal and the eternal, necessity and freedom. As such, the self is not the bare fact that these contrasting elements are in a dialectical relationship; instead, it is "the positive third" (*SKS* 11:129 / *SUD* 13) that is capable of interacting with its constitutive attributes. In the words of Kierkegaard's pseudonym Anti-Climacus, the self is "the relation that relates itself to itself" (*SKS* 11:129 / *SUD* 13).

Much could be (and has been) made of this definition. With regard to the present discussion, the decisive point has to do with Anti-Climacus's insistence that the self's goal is not to give priority to one of its features over against the others—for that would be a "misrelation of despair" (*SKS* 11:130 / *SUD* 14)—but, rather, to will to be what it is. For example, in his analysis of despair as defined by finitude and infinitude, Anti-Climacus points out that the imaginative faculty is the medium by which persons feel, know, and will. It presents to the self its own possibilities. This is, as far as it goes, good news, because the self is free precisely to the extent that it can envision possibilities, for example, the possibility of seeking the good. But the imagination can become unhinged, leading the self into a kind of "fantasy world," wherein it prefers to associate with potentiality rather than actuality. This is the despair of infinitude. Like Johannes the Seducer, such a self is aroused by abstract images but cannot bear any *real* contact with the world. At the same time, Anti-Climacus also describes "finitude's despair," which is marked by an inability to imagine possibilities beyond everyday life. Here the self fails to envision its unique potential; it becomes a "number instead of a self" (*SKS* 11:149 / *SUD* 33). The task, then, is to avoid each of these extremes. The imagination, with its distinctive ability to create and to appreciate images and, in turn, to shape the potential of the self, is an essential component of human life. But it must neither dominate nor retreat. As Anti-Climacus explains, "To become oneself is to become concrete. But to become concrete is neither to become finite nor to become infinite, for that which is to become concrete is indeed a synthesis" (*SKS* 11:146 / *SUD* 30).

This point sheds light on the status of the aesthetic in Kierkegaard's thought. As a dialectician, he does not posit a stark choice between art and religion, imagination and reality, the infinite and the finite. In other words, the issue is not *whether* the aesthetic has a role in human life and in the development of the self. It is *how* one relates to the aesthetic that is decisive.

This conclusion again calls to mind the earlier discussion of *Billede* in Kierkegaard's authorship. As was noted, Kierkegaard cautions against the lure of the image, which can draw the self out of the real world and into its own ambit. This type of idolatry—a word that literally means "slavery to an image"—is problematic no matter one's station in life, be it that of a romantic suitor or that of a Christian disciple. On the other hand, Kierkegaard both encourages and exemplifies the use of images as a means of spurring one to existential authenticity. Here the image does not absorb one's attention but, rather, redirects it, providing the observer with an ideal that is met only through concrete appropriation. Such is the ideal of *faith*, embodied in Kierkegaard's pictures of Anna and the sinful woman, which Anti-Climacus defines as the opposite of despair (*SKS* 11:196 / *SUD* 82).

Thus Kierkegaard leaves the door open for the integration of the aesthetic and the religious and makes it a key aspect of his upbuilding literature. For him, the life of faith is beautiful, and its beauty can lead one to God. This is why, as Sylvia Walsh points out, he frequently "declares in the later journals that he is essentially a poet, and in several entries he describes himself more specifically as a 'poet of the religious' and even more narrowly as a 'Christian poet and thinker.' "[19] As such, his role might be compared to that of any religious artist. For example, the business of the painter or, in traditional terminology, "writer" of Christian icons is neither to issue dogmatic proclamations nor to compose systematic treatises on theology. On the contrary, his or her artwork is intended to orient the observer toward holiness, to establish contact between the observer and sacred events and/or lives. The iconographer, then, may draw on the doctrinal tradition—to be sure, it is doctrine, and not the writer per se, that determines the existential ideals—but his or her goal is fundamentally existential. Likewise, Kierkegaard understood his artistic task as creating a "passionate impression of expressing the ideal existentially," so that a "pathos for the pathos-filled life" is nurtured (*SKS* 22:329, 331, NB13:88, n.d. 1849 / *KJN* 6:333). An 1850 journal entry puts it in more direct terms:

> But now a poetic form will be needed in presenting the religious domain itself. This is a step forward compared to the way things are now, when insignificance and mediocrity have rlly [*sic*] taken the place of the religious, so that the poet in the more ordinary sense is even higher than the religious.
>
> In any case, it is certain that something poetic must be introduced into the religious domain simply to get hold of, to come to grips with, any existential ideals once again. (*SKS* 24:82–83, NB21:132, 1850 / *KJN* 8:78–79)

This task is implicit in Kierkegaard's *Billeder* of Anna, the sinful woman, and others. What is esteemed is not artistic representation in and of itself but its service to human flourishing and to God. To cite Walsh once more, "In Kierkegaard's view, the highest existential ideality is to be a Christian. Thus, in his religious writings, he is primarily concerned to portray, like an artist, the ideal picture of a Christian."[20]

The Idol, the Icon, and Kierkegaard

I have sought to establish two overarching points. First, by examining Kierkegaard's understanding of and approach to the concept of "image," I have shown that Kierkegaard does not posit an ultimate decision between the aesthetic and the religious but rather exemplifies their careful integration. Second, I have underlined that Kierkegaard's dialectical approach to this question correlates to the conception of the self developed in *The Sickness unto Death*, not to mention the way he viewed his task as an author. What has emerged is a kind of "aesthetics of the icon"—an aesthetics that points beyond itself, viewing art not as an end in itself but as a means toward religious and, with it, existential fulfillment.

In conclusion, I want to illustrate these findings by drawing on the work of the French thinker Jean-Luc Marion, particularly his well-known text, *God without Being* (*Dieu sans l'être*, 1982). What follows is by no means a comprehensive reading of Marion's oeuvre nor a suggestion that Kierkegaard's views are somehow identical with Marion's. The idea is more basic—namely, that Marion's reflections can shed light on the various images populating Kierkegaard's works and, in turn, on the Dane's dialectical approach to aesthetic imagery.

Marion's interest in the tension between idol and icon developed over time. In his early work on Descartes, he launched an attempt "to disconnect the link between metaphysics and the divine," arguing that metaphysics—to the extent that it "defines" a supreme being for the sake of understanding other beings—always already lapses into idolatry.[21] In *God without Being*, as Christina M. Gschwandtner points out, he "pushes his definition of idolatry further by explicating a distinction between idol and icon." Whereas Marion had earlier focused on the "specific idolatry of metaphysics," he now posited a variety of idolatries, "moving from visual to conceptual, from simple to more complex."[22] What these idols have in common is that they satisfy the intentions of those who apprehend them. For example, an image becomes an idol whenever "it suggests to the gaze where to rest."[23] This, in fact, is what makes the idol charming: it relieves the observer of the burden of seeking something beyond it. As Marion puts it, "The gaze settles only inasmuch as it rests—from the weight of upholding the sight of an aim without term, rest, or end: 'to sleep with the sleep of the earth.' " Idolatry, then, "reveals a sort of essential fatigue," and this fatigue is perilous.[24] It wants its desires fulfilled on its own terms, and for that reason it is closed off to transcendence and, finally, to true divinity. Gschwandtner sums up Marion's point this way: "The idol does indeed provide a vision of the divine, but a precise vision that is fulfilled in the gaze and thus controlled by it. The observer of the idol grasps hold of the divine."[25]

In contrast, Marion sees the icon as that which "summons the gaze to surpass itself." One never really looks *at* the icon, since the icon serves as a medium through which one's vision goes "back . . . up the infinite stream of the invisible."[26] Hence, where the idol offers a circumscribed deity that is effectively a projection of human consciousness, the icon "becomes a kind of window through which the gaze travels toward the 'unenvisageable,' that which cannot ever be contained in a human gaze."[27] This is why Marion refers to the icon as "excessive."[28] It does not so much contain its subject matter as communicate that its subject matter cannot be contained. "Idols abolish distance, while the icon preserves it."[29] With this in mind, Marion points out that, before the icon, it is actually the observer who is being observed: "The icon regards us—it *concerns* us, in that it allows the intention of the invisible to occur visibly." The challenge facing the iconographer, then, is to allow for this porous quality, to clear the way for the gaze of the invisible while simultaneously acknowledging that the invisible emerges "by its aim" alone. As Marion explains, "The icon lays out the material of wood and paint in such a way that there appears in them the intention of a transpiercing gaze emanating from them." As a result, the "aesthetics of the icon" is, in a certain sense, the absence of aesthetics. For, according to Marion, the idol "supposes an *aesthesis* that precisely imposes its measure on the idol," whereas the icon's "depth withdraws [it] from all aesthetics."[30]

Here—as in all of the above reflections—Marion walks the dialectical tightrope in a way that evokes, or illuminates, Kierkegaard's own approach to aesthetic imagery. For Kierkegaard, we recall, the danger of the image is that it will close off the observer from reality. This is true of Johannes the Seducer, who would rather fantasize about Cordelia than actually *be* in a relationship with her. But it is also true of religious persons or groups whenever they reduce the divine to an artistic or conceptual object, as opposed to a living *subject*. It is this circumscribed and attenuated perspective, so deftly portrayed by Kierkegaard, that corresponds to Marion's analysis of idolatry.

And yet, Kierkegaard also uses his pen to paint pictures of holiness. These images of holy persons such as Anna and the woman who was a sinner communicate the nature of faith—in particular, how it is a movement of dispossession, whereby the claims of the believer are renounced for the sake of divine adoration—and, in doing so, they echo the divine itself. For Kierkegaard's pictures are indeed "excessive." They convey that what they convey cannot be conveyed. Far from reducing the divine to human categories, they depict the great distance between human beings and God—a distance that is "closed" only through the paradox of worship, in which the person comes to recognize that he or she is beheld by the mysterious Other. Here, *in nuce*, is a type of Marion's notion of the icon.

In a well-known remark, Heidegger once said of the god of metaphysics, "Before the *causi sui*, man can neither fall to his knees in awe nor can he play music and dance before this god."[31] Kierkegaard would register a similar concern about art and its tendency to reproduce gods of pleasure and utility. But both in practice and theory he suggests that it need not be so. When the aesthetic engenders worship, idolatry is supplanted by doxology. This may not be an aesthetics in the classic, Western sense of the term. Rather, it is an aesthetics of the icon.

Notes

1. Joakim Garff, *Søren Kierkegaard: A Biography*, trans. Bruce H. Kirmmse (Princeton, N.J.: Princeton University Press, 2005), 121.

2. Ibid., 334.

3. W. H. Auden, "Presenting Kierkegaard," in *The Living Thoughts of Kierkegaard*, ed. W. H. Auden (Bloomington: Indiana University Press, 1952), 3.

4. George Pattison, "Art in an Age of Reflection," in *The Cambridge Companion to Kierkegaard*, ed. Alastair Hannay and Gordon D. Marino (Cambridge, U.K.: Cambridge University Press, 1998), 97.

5. Ibid., 96.

6. Ibid., 98.

7. Hans Urs von Balthasar, *The Glory of the Lord: A Theological Aesthetics*, vol. 1, trans. Erasmo Leiva-Merikakis (San Francisco: Ignatius Press, 1982), 9, 18, 19, 32, emphasis in original.

8. Ibid., 47.

9. Ibid., 49, 51, 49, 51.

10. George Pattison, *Kierkegaard and the Crisis of Faith: An Introduction to His Thought* (London: SPCK, 1997), 76.

11. Ibid.

12. Kierkegaard owned a copy of the two-volume second edition of this work (Copenhagen: Gyldendal, 1837); *ASKB* 254–55.

13. Translated as "the picture" by the Hongs.

14. I have treated this subject extensively elsewhere. See Christopher B. Barnett, *Kierkegaard, Pietism and Holiness* (Farnham, U.K.: Ashgate, 2011). (See also James Rovira's essay in the present volume.—Ed.)

15. Owned by the Moravian Historical Society, Nazareth, Pennsylvania.—Ed.

16. Sylvia Walsh, *Living Poetically: Kierkegaard's Existential Aesthetics* (University Park: Pennsylvania State University Press, 1994), 188.

17. C. Stephen Evans, *Kierkegaard: An Introduction* (Cambridge, U.K.: Cambridge University Press, 2009), 69.

18. Ibid.

19. Walsh, *Living Poetically*, 224.

20. Ibid., 226.

21. Christina M. Gschwandtner, *Reading Jean-Luc Marion: Exceeding Metaphysics* (Bloomington: Indiana University Press, 2007), 40–41.

22. Ibid., 42–43.

23. Jean-Luc Marion, *God without Being*, trans. Thomas A. Carlson (Chicago: University of Chicago Press, 1991), 12.

24. Ibid., 13.

25. Gschwandtner, *Reading Jean-Luc Marion*, 43.

26. Marion, *God without Being*, 18.

27. Gschwandtner, *Reading Jean-Luc Marion*, 132. See Marion, *God without Being*, 17.

28. Marion, *God without Being*, 21.

29. Gschwandtner, *Reading Jean-Luc Marion*, 132.

30. Marion, *God without Being*, 19, 20.

31. Martin Heidegger, *Identity and Difference*, trans. Joan Stambaugh (New York: Harper and Row, 1969), 72.

Kierkegaard's Approach to Pictorial Art, and to Specimens of Contemporary Visual Culture

Ragni Linnet

Sight and Hearing

"It may at times have occurred to you, dear reader, to doubt somewhat the accuracy of that familiar philosophical thesis that the outer is the inner and the inner is the outer" (*SKS* 2:11 / *EO* 1:3). This simple opening sentence of *Either/Or* (1843) outlines the subject of this essay: Kierkegaard's and his various pseudonyms' pinpointing of the essence and nature, and the limits and potentials, of the concrete image, because a picture, if anything, is the medium of "the outer"—that is, the external presentation of its subject. We shall see how the nature of the picture we are concerned with is decisive for Kierkegaard and the pseudonyms, because only academic, idealistic painting is measured by such congruence between the inner and the outer. Popular pictorial art, on the other hand, plays in a completely different register.

Before I proceed, a word of caution is in order. Kierkegaard would not be Kierkegaard if the different statements in his writings about the capacities of a picture were formulated in a straightforward manner. Sometimes the statements are dressed as agitated showdowns followed by creative appropriations of theories and pictures around him. In other places the assertions are made with animated irony and performative twists. And one cannot simply presume that Kierkegaard's different pseudonyms are speaking for Kierkegaard himself. They present different points of view that Kierkegaard wants us to reflect upon. It is my cautious suggestion that these points of view, considered together with Kierkegaard's own use of pictures and with the texts published under his own name, form an overall tendency in his approach to pictorial art.

The pseudonymous "editor" of *Either/Or*, Victor Eremita, who gathers the papers of "A" and "B" into two separate volumes which he brings to print, has no doubt about his own doubt with regard to the visible and to the claim that the "inner" is represented by the "outer":

I myself have always been rather heretically minded on this philosophical point and therefore early in my life developed the habit of making observations and investigations as well as possible. For guidance, I have consulted the authors whose view I shared in this respect—in brief, I have done all I could to make up for what has been left undone in the philosophical writings. Gradually, then, hearing became my most cherished sense, for just as the voice is the disclosure of inwardness incommensurable with the exterior, so the ear is the instrument that apprehends this inwardness, hearing the sense by which it is appropriated. Consequently, every time I found a contradiction between what I saw and what I heard, my doubt was confirmed and my zeal for observation increased. A priest who hears confessions is separated by a grillwork from the person making confessions; he does not see him, he only hears. As he listens, he gradually forms a picture of the other's outward appearance corresponding to what he hears; thus he finds no contradiction. It is different, however, when one sees and hears simultaneously but sees a grillwork between oneself and the speaker. (*SKS* 2:11 / *EO* 1:3)

In other words, the starting point taken by Kierkegaard/Victor Eremita in *Either/Or* and its view of the aesthetic is the assumption that hearing gives us the freedom to form our own complete pictures of the inward. Sight, on the other hand, presents a contradiction between a person's inner, hidden qualities and what appears outwardly, on the surface. Sight cannot penetrate the opaque barrier that surrounds what is internal.

Either/Or plays many variations on this theme and takes a clear position on sight and hearing. In my view, this is primarily related to the polemics of the time. The book is concerned with an excoriation of an "aesthetic" mode of existence. The first part of *Either/Or* is therefore assigned to the aesthetic universe of the senses, and the book thus draws a psychogram of Kierkegaard's times with the help of the various forms of art, the senses they each appeal to, and the ideas that convey them. The various aesthetic character types in *Either/Or* are musical and concrete images. Music is the demonic, immediately sensual aesthete, Mozart's Don Giovanni, who lives out his passion. Pictorial art, on the other hand, is the reflective aesthete, Johannes the Seducer or "A," who, ghostlike, exists by parasitically observing his own passion from afar.

The Veil of Veronica—or the Beautiful Image

According to his own premises, Kierkegaard has good reason for his challenging of academic art. His aim is to challenge both the idealistic aesthetics of the time, including the idea of what I shall call the *beautiful image* as a mimetic picture, and the harmonized (or harmonizing) and distilled pictorial art of his time. Some of his grounds seem quite unreasonable when examined in the context of contemporary (Danish) Naturalistic art, which holds far more than Kierkegaard is prepared to see.

Kierkegaard has by no means left us with a cohesive pictorial theory, and he is sparing with references to concrete works, pictures, and painters. He keeps his pictures close to his chest. One text, however, does focus on the beautiful image. This is the essay "Silhouettes" in *Either/Or*. Kierkegaard research does not abound with analyses of "Silhouettes," and a blinkered close analysis warrants a prefatory reservation. Even though assessments of pictorial art and reflection on issues of form and presentation are a recurring theme in Kierkegaard's writings and are already exposed to variations in *Either/Or*, Kierkegaard's approach to identifying the ontology of pictorial art is not based on an interest in this ontology per se. Rather, Kierkegaard is concerned with the value of art as a kind of psychogram, a schematic outline or diagram that in graphic form transmits information about psychological conditions. The academic, mimetic painting of the time is thus the bearer of everything Victor Eremita attributes to Johannes the Seducer or "A." Don Giovanni cannot be painted. "The most abstract idea conceivable is the sensuous in its elemental originality [*Genialitet*]. . . . It cannot be painted, for it cannot be caught in definite contours. In its lyricism, it is a force, a wind, impatience, passion, etc., yet in such a way that it exists not in one instant but in a succession of instants, for if it existed in one instant, it could be depicted or painted" (*SKS* 2:64 / *EO* 1:56–57). Considered as a type, the aesthete *is* a painting. With variations, *Either/Or* fundamentally states the same about the nature of mimetic pictorial art. The book describes what the idealistic picture cannot do and shows how its basic characteristics buttress the aesthete's unreal mode of existence. This image is buttressed in the second part of *Either/Or* by the descriptions of "A" offered by Judge William, and by his fatherly admonishments of him.

"Silhouettes" tells the story of the unrequited love of three Romantic female figures, but in my reading is primarily about different types of pictures: pictures "within," as pictures of the imagination, and pictures "without"— the immaterial wall silhouette, painting, or graphic print, that combines form and substance, or the daguerreotype's fixation of fleeting light. It is not obvious what "A's" intentions are with pictorial art, and with the picture in this text, which thematizes the incongruence between the inner and the outer. Why does he speak in images when his message seems to be to point to what lies beyond the picture: the veiled darkness that avoids the picture's drawing things into the light but denotes the essence, the enigmatic? The answer is, among other things, that this particular approach to the problem of representation and presentation allows Kierkegaard to present the *pro et contra* of creating a picture. What can be "pictorialized" in language? How does this relate to what the pictorializing material media can and do achieve? And how is meaning created in relation to different types of image?

The hypothesis I present is that, already in this small essay of his, "A" gives us the principal terms for reconstruction of the pictorial theory that remains by and large unchanged throughout all Kierkegaard's work: the picture's relation to time, including the past (recollection), the present (presence), and the future (self-appropriation), and to the spirit, the body, existence, the self and subjectivity, and love. With this essay by "A" we move into the core of Kierkegaard's own pictorial thought that, like a walnut, is divided into two halves over a pair of questions. One is the question of the relation between the inner and the outer and of whether the inner can be objectified in an outer, visible manifestation. The other question is that of the nature of sight. In "Silhouettes," the question about the nature of sight is answered negatively. A grillwork is set up between the inner and the outer, as in the image of the confession box in *Either/Or*'s prelude, and the outer view is assigned an objectifying and reifying nature.[1] Later in Kierkegaard's authorship there is a meditation on how outer images become set as a series of inner images, but this does not dislodge his fundamental thesis about the incommensurability of the inner with the outer. What is added is a new view of the didactic significance of pictorial art and of the relation between form and appropriation. The picture still cannot encompass the inner but affects one's own innermost being.

The three jilted women in "Silhouettes" are Marie Beaumarchais from Goethe's *Clavigo*, Donna Elvira from Mozart's *Don Giovanni*, and Margaret from Goethe's *Faust*. According to Kierkegaard/"A"/Victor Eremita, the outright sorrow that first overwhelms these women can be manifested in visible shape, but this is not the case when this sorrow becomes reflective. The question is why their reflective (or reflecting) sorrow cannot be expressed within the framework of pictorial art. The argumentation follows Lessing and Hegelian sight lines. Lessing is invoked as an authority regarding the relation of pictorial art to time and space. Pictorial art is referred to as the *stasis* of space, and thus cannot encompass reflection and the reflective sorrow that will unfold over time.

> Since the time when Lessing defined the boundaries between poetry and art in his celebrated treatise *Laokoon*, it no doubt may be regarded as a conclusion unanimously recognized by all estheticians that the distinction between them is that art is in the category of space, poetry in the category of time, that art depicts repose, poetry motion. For this reason, the subject for artistic portrayal must have a quiet transparency so that the interior rests in the corresponding exterior. The less this is the case, the more difficult becomes the task for the artist, until the distinction asserts itself and teaches him that this is no task for him at all.
>
> If we apply to the relation between sorrow and joy that which has been casually stated but not developed here, it is easy to perceive that joy is far easier to depict artistically than sorrow. By no means does this deny that grief can be depicted artistically, but it certainly does

> say that there comes a point where it is essential to posit a contrast
> between the interior and the exterior, which makes a depiction of it
> impossible for art. (*SKS* 2:167 / *EO* 1:169)

The point is that the beautiful image, whose existence for Lessing is justified
by this externalization of the inner, loses any legitimacy from a Kierkegaardian perspective.[2] On the other hand, Hegel's image-less contemporary
horizon, in which inwardness is unfolded so that it breaches the bounds of
pictorial art and can only be expressed as a concept, is an unspoken premise.
In what follows, I shall consider seven key appropriations by Kierkegaard of
pictorial art and other images transmitted to him by the history of images
and the popular traditions surrounding them. These appropriations show
Kierkegaard's mastery of displacement of meaning and his modification of
pictures and attest to the vital role played by actual visual material in his
authorship.

First Appropriation: The "Acheiropoieta" Tradition

The point when presentation becomes impossible lies in the precise inter-
face between the immediate and the reflective sorrow. The immediate sorrow
may still be "a subject for artistic portrayal" (*SKS* 2:170 / *EO* 1:172). It is,
namely, "the immediate imprint and expression of the sorrow's impression,
which, just like the picture Veronica preserved on her linen cloth, is perfectly
congruous, and sorrow's sacred lettering is stamped on the exterior, beautiful and clear and legible to all" (*SKS* 2:170 / *EO* 1:172). This image, which
in reality is a depiction of the beautiful image, is my key to "Silhouettes." It
encompasses the text's polemical matter and the ideas of the beautiful image
that it at one and the same time presents and undermines.

The image of the veil takes its significance from the idealistic idea of beautiful pictorial art, which as a symbol seamlessly binds together the inner and
the outer. Depiction is the outer imprint of the inner. If one wants to poke fun
at the aesthetics of beauty, the image of the Veil of Veronica is well chosen.
As an acheiropoieton, or an icon "made without hand," Veronica's Veil, or
sudarium (handkerchief or sweat cloth), literally bears a sweaty impression
of the inner—namely, the suffering of Christ. Like the inner, the sweat flows
out into the outer cloth (canvas). We can take this even further. In Latin,
"to sweat" or "transpire" is *trans(s)pirere*, from *trans* (through) and *spirare*
(breath) or *spiritus* (spirit). In Kierkegaard's time, this word was used as a
polite, genteel expression for perspiration, but it is not too much to imagine
that Kierkegaard's pen also held the association of "inspiring" in the sense
of "giving spirit to." Thus the (canvas) cloth literally absorbs the spirit. The
image of Veronica's Veil can be seen as a metaphor of how, in one of the
expressions of the time, beautiful art "makes the idea transparent."

The image of Veronica's Veil also serves to comment on another of the theoretical artistic ideas of Kierkegaard's time, which is related to the contemporary interpretation of the concept of mimesis. The mimetic representation "resembles" the outer, it was believed, just as the image on the veil bears a "likeness" of Christ. Furthermore, it also bears his image or impression. This perception of beautiful, mimetic art was accompanied by the belief in the ability of the mimetic representation to make the imprint present (or present-like) or proximate. The traces of sweat on the veil clearly tell us that "he was here." Yet they also seem to say "here he is." The faith in the ability of the picture to create nearness quickly becomes a sense of the picture "being alive." This was an idea that occupied many people in Kierkegaard's time and is also reflected in the popularity of the Pygmalion theme.

This is a quite innocent example from "A's" image bank. Yet "A" adds irony in two ways. By using this particular picture as a depiction of the beautiful image, "A" draws the aesthetic of beauty into the sphere of magic and superstition. The early Church said of this image that it was *acheiropoietos*, that is, created miraculously, and not by a human painter. On the other hand, he assigns the painting to the sphere of the Resurrection. The image of Veronica's Veil transcends death, since Jesus is (literally) resurrected before our eyes.

Yet Kierkegaard is double-tongued. One tongue formulates itself with an uncritical presentation of the Veil of Veronica in a symbolic-aesthetic Hegelian vocabulary, where visual art is viewed in the light of eternally objective ideas. In this presentation, what makes a picture art is that it is beautiful, and it is beautiful only if it is a reflection of spirituality. The other tongue, however, hisses lowly and ironically that this criterion can probably be fulfilled only by Veronica's magical veil, which the Catholics have purportedly preserved.

"The Interior's Good-bye"

Let us continue our reading of "Silhouettes." While the immediate grief thus moves outward, like blood flowing to the skin (or the sweat flowing out into the cloth and becoming a reverse impression of the beautiful image), the reflective sorrow flows inward, like blood fleeing from the surface: "The exterior pallor is, as it were, the interior's good-bye, and thought and imagination hurry after the fugitive, which hides in the secret recesses. . . . This sorrow cannot be depicted artistically, for the interior and the exterior are out of balance, and thus it does not lie within spatial categories" (*SKS* 2:167–68 / *EO* 1:169–70).

This sorrow is in conflict with Lessing's demarcations: "In yet another respect it cannot be depicted artistically, for it does not have inner stillness but is constantly in motion" (*SKS* 2:168 / *EO* 1:170). The experience of the reflective sorrow and what nourishes it is that it constantly seeks its object and is therefore changing continuously. If one did nonetheless seek to make an artistic representation of this sorrow, which "is never really present but is continually in the process of becoming" (*SKS* 2:170 / *EO* 1:172), and therefore—to repeat the phrase from "A's" comments on Lessing—"in the category of time," this would be in conflict with what Lessing, according to "A," has said so wisely about the forces and limits of the individual medium. If we, with Kierkegaard and his pseudonyms, assumed that the outer could actually reflect the inner and maintain the inner in each of its movements, "then there would have to be a whole series of pictures in order to portray reflective sorrow; but no particular picture would express the sorrow, and no particular picture would have real artistic value, since it would be not beautiful, but true" (*SKS* 2:175 / *EO* 1:178).

This is an ambiguous passage that makes sense only if we interpret the text's use of the concept of truth in conjunction with a scientific concept of congruence. On this basis, it can also be understood why the daguerreotype, that newly developed photographic method of Kierkegaard's time, is placed outside the sphere of art. The daguerreotype captures the play of light on the surface, but does not capture the spirit.

The Picture's Sensual Moment

"Silhouettes" provides a critique of both the pictorial and the romantic. Marie, Elvira, and Margaret are convinced that their love will last forever and that they will love their beloveds, and be loved by them, for all eternity. This awareness of eternity ennobles their love. In reality, the text tells us, they are captured by the illusions of romantic love. According to Kierkegaard's "A," this shows the three women's fate. They do not see that their love has only the "empty" time of the sensual moment at its disposal.

What connects romantic love or sensual, fleeting love with the picture's moment? They are of the same kin, so that the picture, which stops time in an eternal moment, can encapsulate sensual, or romantic, love. In Kierkegaard's description of "A" and of Johannes the Seducer, the aesthete who cultivates the senses is apparent. He is also aware of the moment, but in his sensual moments disregards the eternal—that is, the truly eternal. He is not warm-blooded but bloodless and heartless, and his sensuality and sensual moments are "mediate" and completely subject to his manipulative reflectiveness. Besides much else, "A"/ Johannes the Seducer and the painting share in common that they are both reflected sensuality without spirit.

This is an important point and part of the explanation for why "A"/ Johannes must appear as a picture and not as a sculpture or orchestrated score (like Don Juan). Whether it is a flat painting or a "spatial surface," a concrete picture is always an abstraction. It depicts a three-dimensional world in two dimensions. When an academic painting is, furthermore, as in Kierkegaard's time, arranged in a mathematically based perspective structure, the abstraction merely becomes more condensed. Painting, as Kierkegaard knew it—despite his many reductions—is a good image for a reflective treatment of intuition's sensual material.

When Kierkegaard grafts his perception of romantic love with consideration of the essence and nature of painting or picture, he is, without explicitly saying so, further embroidering Pliny, who, in his *Natural History*, relates the myth of Butades and how painting is born from love.[3] The beloved of Butades has to leave, and to preserve his memory she carves out his silhouette, or profile, in a rock. Kierkegaard comments indirectly on this narrative when he shows, with "A," how the picture replaces reality. It points to the absent and represents what is (soon) to be lost. Image formation is thus fundamentally nostalgic by nature, and "A," like Butades, is already lost in recollections in the present's image-forming moment. However, Pliny's hidden role is not thereby exhausted. "A"/Kierkegaard apparently perceives pictorial art as an art of the blind. Butades carves out an image without at the same time being able to see her model, and "A" blindly overlooks his women's own nature with his reflective *skiagraphs*.[4] Kierkegaard's view of the marriage of the sensual moment, love, recollection, and image is negative. The qualities that his Danish times draw out from Pliny in order to elevate art as a child of love are used by "A" to tarnish and denigrate art. He, in fact, seems to say that image formation is nurtured by, and nurtures, a life without love.

William's "On Time"

Let us pursue this trail, still with the relation between love, time, and image creation as our wrench. The aesthete "A" is a picture, but he is also a picture of the unloving and an active practitioner of the illusion-building of romantic love. With "B," or rather Judge William, the perspective and perception of time change. The line of sight is the ethical aspect or, in brief, the relation between the general and the individual.

Two questions are now to be pursued. First, how does William's perception of time and his view of marital love affect his view of pictures, whether they be paintings, graphics, or daguerreotypes? Second, why does he present his ethics as a critique of the pictorial? I shall add an image that highlights Kierkegaard's pictorial theory.

In 1843, Kierkegaard wrote in some notes that the first part of *Either/Or* continually gets stranded on time: "This is why the second part strongly affirms it, since it is shown in the first discussion that the esthetic is broken upon time, and in the second discussion it is shown that the meaning of finitude and temporality, is to be able to become history, to gain a history" (*Pap.* IV A 213, n.d. 1843 / *JP* 1:907).

It is also the question of time, and of the relation between inner and outer time, that leads the judge to think of marriage. He draws a clear distinction between what is interchangeably called first love, erotic and sensual (or romantic) love, and marital love. The first, erotic and sensual love *is* the momentary (*SKS* 3:30 /*EO* 2:21), and its "'mine' . . . resonates . . . in the eternity of the seductive moment . . . in the illusory eternity of imagination and idea" (*SKS* 3:64 / *EO* 2:58). It has an abstract nature, never has inner substance, nor has "the law of motion in itself" (*SKS* 3:99 / *EO* 2:96). Marital love, on the other hand, "has the possibility of an inner history and is as different from first love as the historical is from the unhistorical" (*SKS* 3:97 / *EO* 2:94). Marital love "always moves inward" (*SKS* 3:138 / *EO* 2:139) and spends itself (in the good sense) in time. The inner history, the marital history, is thus hidden. This love is realized in life, as it is lived. The outer, on the other hand, which is the romantic or sensual love, can be manifested, but only as "dead," visible signs.

As a consequence, marital love cannot be depicted in the "beautiful picture," while the romantic, sensual, and erotic love allows itself to be "admirably" depicted in the picture's moment (*SKS* 3:134 / *EO* 2:135). But an aesthetic representation always requires "a concentration in the moment [*Moment*]" (*SKS* 3:132 / *EO* 2:133). Both art and poetry "concentrate the extensive in the intensive" (*SKS* 3:132 / *EO* 2:133), but marital love is nurtured by the protraction of time and the continuity of creation. For marital love, the passage of time, the road, is the same as the goal (*SKS* 3:132–33 / *EO* 2:133). The truth of marital love is "the temporal sequence" (*SKS* 3:135 / *EO* 2:136). The relation of art to time, and to time's extent, which excludes pictorial presentations not only of marital love but also of humility and endurance, is a perfect match for William's ethical mission.

For William, pictorial art serves only to pass or to kill time, not for determining choice, which occurs in time. Pictorial art thus lies outside the sphere of the ethical, just as "A" does. Ethics are dependent upon choice and on the extended, forward-looking time of repeated actions. In other words, William's pictorial critique is not at all concerned with pictorial art and its limitations but is merely another way of saying to "A" that, because of his pictoriality, he has no ethics. Under the surface simmers the same Romantic critique as expressed by "A."

Second Appropriation: Ferdinand Piloty's *Kiss*

Judge William stands by his viewpoints with surprising tenacity. In what is putatively his own monologue, "Some Reflections on Marriage in Answer to Objections. By a Married Man," in Kierkegaard's *Stages on Life's Way* (1845), he reverts to the question of the relation between pictorial art, the love that—like the romantic—never develops, and marital love.

William's starting point is a picture of Romeo and Juliet, "an eternal picture" (*SKS* 6:156 / *SLW* 167; figure 2).[5] "The eternal element in the picture is that it portrays a pair of lovers and portrays them in an essential expression"

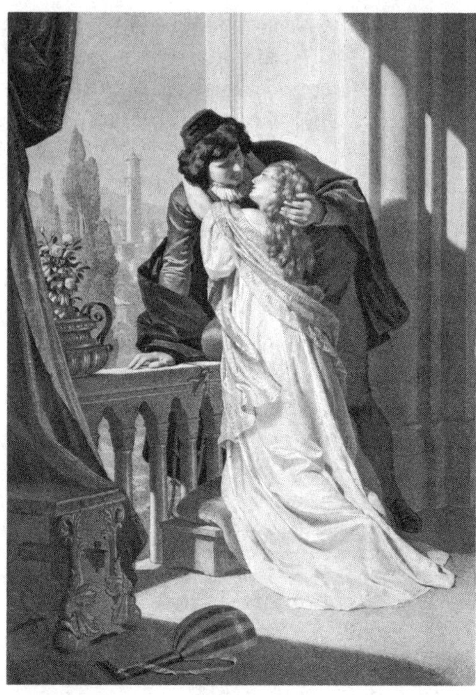

Figure 2. *Romeo and Juliet's Farewell Kiss*, lithograph by Ferdinand Piloty, from William Shakespeare, *Romeo und Julia*, trans. [to German] August Wilhelm von Schlegel (Berlin: G. Grote, 1875), facing p. 75.

(*SKS* 6:156 / *SLW* 167), namely Juliet sunk in admiration at her lover's feet. Her gaze at Romeo is filled with heavenly bliss, "but Romeo stops this look and with a kiss all the longing of erotic love is set at rest forever, for the reflection of eternity surrounds the moment with a halo, and no more than Romeo and Juliet does anyone who looks at the picture think that there will be a next moment, even if it were only to repeat the sacred seal of the kiss" (*SKS* 6:157 / *SLW* 168). The picture of Romeo and Juliet is thus "an eternal picture" as its tableau depicts an eternal moment that can never change. Yet it is also an eternal picture because it is timeless and depicts a universal ideal that transcends history: "Do not ask the lovers, for they do not hear your voice, but out in the world ask in what century this happened, in what country, at what time of the day, at what hour it was—no one replies, for it is an eternal picture" (*SKS* 6:157 / *SLW* 168). This pair of lovers is "an eternal subject for art" (*SKS* 6:157 / *SLW* 168).

This is not a married couple—and, strangely enough, the picture fades for William when he projects it into the context of marital love. The picture begins to work and move; she is "in the admiration of love" sinking in admiration at her lover's feet (and we see her sinking movement before us), but she sinks not only before him, the visible, "but before the invisible" (*SKS* 6:157 / *SLW* 168), and now his strong arm grasps her (and we "see" how it is extended to grasp her), and together they are held up by a kiss: "This is no picture, there is no repose in the artistic situation, for as one looks at her almost *sinking* in adoration, *one sees beyond this interrupted posture the necessity of a new one*, that she stands upright at his side. One has intimations of a new prototype, the authentic prototype of marriage, because married people are contiguous angles on the same base. What is it that produces that *incompleteness* in the first picture, what is being sought in this *faltering*—it is the equality of resolution; it is the higher immediacy of the religious" (*SKS* 6:157 / *SLW* 168–69, my emphases). With the introduction of movement and incompleteness, William's view of the ethical, which previously framed the image reflection, is now obviously drawn into the picture. Yet the married couple is thereby also drawn out of the picture's world.

Shadow(image)s in the Realm of Death—
or Mimesis as Negative Existential

Let us pursue this line of inquiry. When Kierkegaard's fictitious characters make explicit the connection between image and death, the disjunction of inner and outer in the materialized image becomes even clearer, as does also the indissoluble alliance of inwardness with time. Like the picture, the corpse-like "A" has no inner. The soul has departed, and there is only a de-ontologized outer shell left. This world of shells is "A's" world—that is, the world to which he wants to take his readers in "Silhouettes."

"Just as Charon took people across from the fullness of life to the shadowy land of the underworld" (*SKS* 1:277 / *CI* 236), so has "A" shipped both himself and those he addresses in "Silhouettes" to a shadow world. "A" addresses the co-deceased, the Συμπαρανεκρώμενοι (Symparanekromenoi, Fellowship of the Dead), and the silhouette appears if not in the realm of death, then on its threshold.

Kierkegaard's (and "A's" and Johannes's) use of the shadow as a metaphor of the picture is virtuosic. The shadow is bloodless, in contrast to reality's beating pulse, and belongs to a world of dreams. It is a phantom. A shadow is a sham, without flesh or a chest that moves with each breath. As Kierkegaard puts it in *Works of Love*, "The shadow is weak in comparison with the strong actuality" (*SKS* 9:108 / *WL* 104). It is merely a monochrome, diffuse reflection, stripped of any individualizing features. But the shadow is also without substance and firmness. It takes flight when you reach out for it, and slips between your fingers. A shadow cannot contain an interior element because it has nothing "inside." The shadow is pure surface. Like a mirror without depth, "a shadow" is "a reflection, a simile [in a double sense], an image [*et Billede*]" (*SKS* 5:105 / *EUD* 100).

Kierkegaard's connection of the picture with death is already hinted at with "A's" picture of Veronica's Veil. A veil is also the cloth that the Jews used to cover the face of a corpse to absorb bodily emissions. This idea is also apparent from this passage in *Either/Or*'s little interlude, "The Unhappiest One." "A" speaks to his co-deceased about Niobe:

> Is this an actual person or is it an image; is it a living person who is dying or a dead person who is living—it is Niobe. She lost every-thing all at once; she lost that to which she gave life; she lost that which gave life to her! Look up at her, dear Συμπαρανεκρώμενοι; she is standing only a little higher than the world, like a monument on a burial mound. But no hope beckons her, no future motivates her, no prospect tempts her, no hope perturbs her—hopeless she stands, turned to stone in recollection. . . . The world changes, but she knows no change, and time comes, but for her there is no future time. (*SKS* 2:220 / *EO* 1:227)

The picture is "like a dead person that is alive."[6]

Chemical Shadow Pictures

Kierkegaard and his pseudonyms use daguerreotypes to epitomize the absur-dity of the idealistic claims of a congruence of inner and outer, inwardness and outwardness, in the beautiful picture. In the essay "The Esthetic Validity of Marriage," Judge William, or "B," blames "A" for turning everything into shadow pictures (*SKS* 3:20 / *EO* 2:10) and, in the same voice, complains about "A's" fascination with daguerreotypes. "A" collects daguerreotypes and is a master of both the "study of the lighting" and "magic formulas" (*SKS* 3:20 / *EO* 2:10). He puts these shadow pictures in his pockets, so he has them within reach when he wishes to enjoy visible evidence of his conquests.

A Daguerreotype: The Sculptor Bertel Thorvaldsen

At that time, daguerreotypes, which had already come to Denmark in 1840,[7] were connected with superstition and Satanism. The creation of a daguerreo-type involves the use of mercury fumes and sodium hyposulfite, and the actual process by which the photograph was created on an iodized silver plate, or an iodized copper plate faced with a thin layer of silver, evoked associations with the alchemist's bubbling, steaming workshop. It was also feared that this perceived devilry could steal one's soul. The camera obscura "took" one's shadow (in the double sense of taking and stealing), and popular superstition maintained that the dead did not cast a shadow. While today we are photo-graphed, at that time people were "drawn off." The origins of this expression may lie in an idea from Balzac (1799–1850). He believed that the human

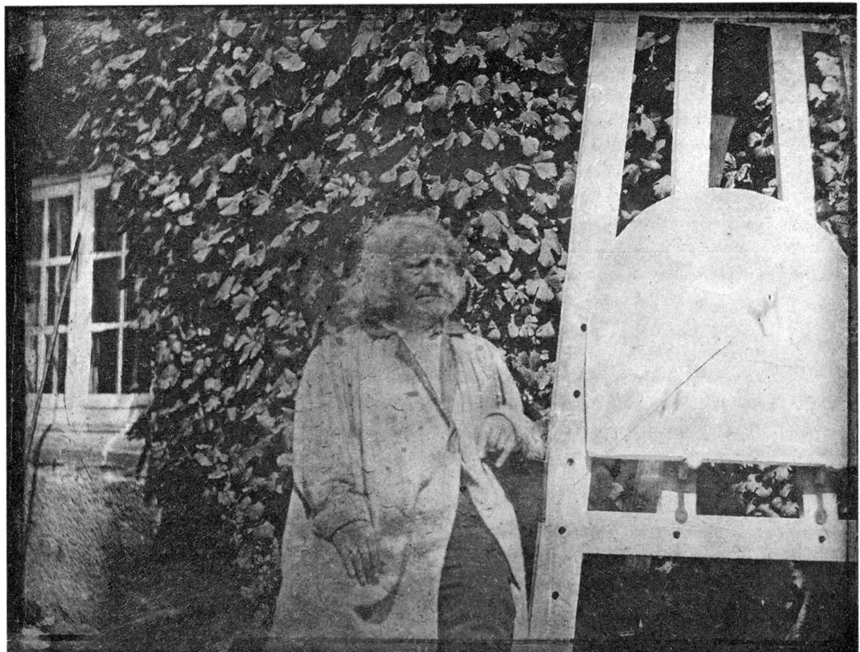

Figure 3. A. C. T. Neubourg, *Portrait of Bertel Thorvaldsen*. Whole-plate daguerreotype, 1844. Thorvaldsens Museum, Copenhagen.

body consisted of several transparent layers that were successively drawn off by the camera with each new exposure.[8] Finally, there was a risk of becoming as transparent as a ghost and, like a ghost, being left without a soul.

The camera had the evil eye, like a person who brings bad luck (Italian: *jettatore*), and could cast a spell (Latin: *fascinum*). When Bertel Thorvaldsen, who was certainly not "uneducated," was photographed in the Charlottenborg Gardens in 1844, he found it necessary to ward off Satan in the apparatus with a hand movement (the "sign of the horns"), literally to stab out its/his evil eyes (figure 3).

From the outset, the relationship between life and death in the photograph was disquieting. The daguerreotype, as the relation between the picture's frozen time and the exposure time (which "B" in *Either/Or II*'s 1843 universe determines to be half a minute; *SKS* 3:17 / *EO* 2:7), points to a human-made opportunity to freeze time. However, when time stops, our time also stops, and we die. While a living person may appear dead in his or her picture, the dead picture's depiction of a person who may now be deceased appears to be alive. The photograph, or *thanatograph* (literally a written account, or, in this case, a photograph of a dead person), blurs the border between living and dead, the dead and the living.[9]

In *Either/Or*, Kierkegaard uses the picture, painting, and daguerreotype to describe something else that bears the same characteristics: a life of insignificance, "a lifelike death," emptied of life's inner fluids, without spirit, passion, or intensity, as a superficial life, or the aesthete's "life." But he also creates another relation, which is between image formation and the demonic.

The Mirror's Image-Forming View

While "A" and the portrait he gives of himself in his papers mainly focus on the relation between inner image and outer image, this focus is somewhat displaced by the introduction of Johannes the Seducer in "The Seducer's Diary." Johannes creatively examines the equation formulated by Plato of mimetic image and mirror. The question of inner and outer still resides in the background, but it is the outward aspect that is developed. The point seems to be to present some samples of (faulty) image forming through the deployment of the metaphor of the mirror. Johannes the mirror and image former plays out Plato's ideographic rules but gives them a Romantic twist. He is but a blank mirroring surface, and his image is as devoid of existence as he himself is.

In "Silhouettes," "A" presents his fictive female images from contemporary European culture. Johannes, on the other hand, draws the picture closer, in behind the ramparts of Copenhagen. Johannes creates pictures of everything and everyone and forms them in his own image. Moreover, being a shadow himself, Johannes also describes himself as a picture. On one of the last pages of "The Seducer's Diary" we see him hurrying to the last meeting with Cordelia, "my work [*mit Værk*]" (*SKS* 2:431 / *EO* 1:445), as he confidently and delightedly calls her. Cordelia is his work. And he himself? Like his picture (Cordelia), he is himself a metaphor (*Billede*). "Everything is a metaphor [*Billede*]; I myself am a myth about myself, for is it not as a myth that I hasten to this tryst? Who I am is irrelevant; everything finite and temporal is forgotten; only the eternal remains, the power of erotic love, its longing, its bliss" (*SKS* 2:431 / *EO* 1:444). The only love that the metaphor (*Billede*) Johannes knows is rooted in the illusory, metaphorical eternity of imagination and dissemblance.

In book 6 of the *Republic*, Plato describes the picture and the mirror as one and the same thing. Johannes the Seducer further develops this union. One of his potential victims is reflected in the mirror: "There is a mirror on the opposite wall; she is not contemplating it, but the mirror is contemplating her. How faithfully it has caught her image [*Billede*], like a humble slave who shows his devotion by his faithfulness" (*SKS* 2:305 / *EO* 1:315). Yet it is an unhappy mirror, which surely dares to frame her but not to embrace her, "which assuredly can grasp her image [*Billede*] but not her" (*SKS* 2:305 / *EO* 1:315). An unhappy mirror, "which cannot secretly hide her image in itself, hide it from the whole world, but can only disclose it to others. . . . And yet are there not many people who are like that, who possess nothing except at the moment when they are showing it to others, who merely grasp the surface, not the essence, lose everything when this is going to show itself, just as this mirror would lose her image if she were to disclose her heart to it by a single breath" (*SKS* 2:305–6 / *EO* 1:315). Nor does this mirror manage to grasp the essence of existence: the inner element, the heart.

Johannes's mirror is a remarkable, "living" mirror. The mirror thinks. But "what torture if a human being were fashioned that way" (*SKS* 2:305 / *EO* 1:315). It is chilling to note that this is exactly what Johannes, the reflective seducer, is. Otherwise, the mirror is just as mirrors are. It is the nature of a mirror to remain on the surface, in visuality. The living object it mirrors, which has weight and mass before the mirror, is reflected as a "dead" surface, as a mirror image. It can grasp, but not embrace. This is a very precise description of Johannes the Seducer, since he is not actually interested in his women qua actual women. Cordelia, for example, is not fascinating as Cordelia, but only as the image he creates of her for himself.[10]

Third Appropriation: *Theseus and Ariadne*

Let me provide a very tangible example of Johannes's image-forming view. In a letter to Cordelia, the hunting trophy in "The Seducer's Diary," he describes "a painting from ancient times" (*SKS* 2:391 / *EO* 1:403) of Ariadne and Theseus, but only to create immediately his own very different image ("my picture," he writes), which better communicates his message. Kierkegaard had probably not seen "the painting from ancient times." However, in P. F. A. Nitsch's *Neues mythologisches Wörterbuch* (1821, *New Mythological Dictionary*), he could find a description of two different wall paintings from Herculaneum (figures 4 and 5), which he took the liberty to combine into one.[11]

Here is his "own" painting: "Imagine this picture; imagine it slightly changed. Cupid is not weeping and his bow is not unstrung, or would *you* then have become less beautiful, less triumphant, because *I* had gone out of my mind" (*SKS* 2:391 / *EO* 1:404, my emphasis). Note how Johannes undergoes an imperceptible metamorphosis and takes on Theseus's pictorial form. "Cupid smiles and draws the bow. Nemesis does not stand idle at *your* side; she, too, draws her bow" (*SKS* 2:391 / *EO* 1:404, my emphasis). And observe how Cordelia becomes Ariadne's image:

> In that old painting, we see on the ship a manly figure busy at his work. Presumably it is Theseus. Not so in my picture. He is standing in the stern; he is looking back longingly. He is stretching out his arms; he has repented of it or, more correctly, his madness has left him, but the ship is carrying him away. Cupid and Nemesis both aim,

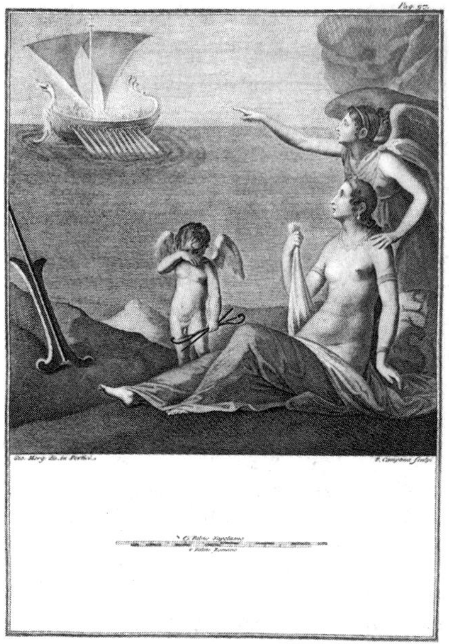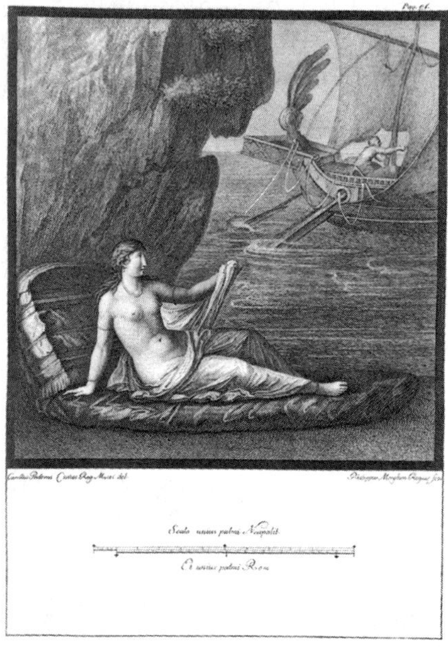

Figures 4 and 5. *Theseus and Ariadne.* Engravings. Illustrations from *Le Pitture Antiche D'Ercolano e contorni encisi con qualche spiegazione,* vol. 2 (Naples: n.p., 1760), 91, 97 (plates 14, 15).

> an arrow flies from each bow, they accurately hit the mark; we see and we understand that both have hit one spot in his heart to symbolize that his love was the nemesis that avenged. (*SKS* 2:391–92 / *EO* 1:404)

Johannes is like the painter who in reality takes residence in the world he himself has created.

What we have just considered is an example of how Johannes the aesthete weaves himself, Cordelia, and his readers into a cobweb that transforms reality into intuitions and (outer) perception into (inner) fantasy. Apparently this exercise in the art of describing the psychological profile of fictional characters indirectly and via their image-forming powers and propensities led to a search for pictures in which you cannot reside. Kierkegaard, master of style, through his pseudonyms, looked for pictures with formal characteristics that would cast out the beholder and turn the relationship between picture and beholder, outer and inner, upside down. To my mind he asked himself how the image-forming of the individual might be turned into a vehicle for authentic living. Let us begin with Anti-Climacus's description of the patterns of physical and mental movement evoked by an academic painting of the 1840s.

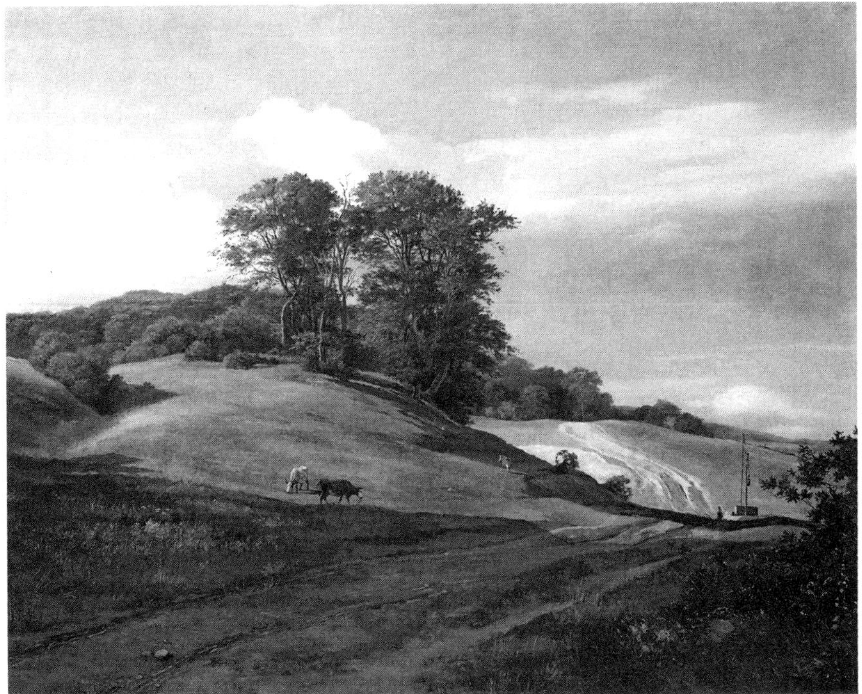

Figure 6. J. Th. Lundbye, *Søbyvang*. Oil on canvas, 1841. Ordrupgaard.

The Visual Culture's Popular Images: Performativity and Temporality

In *Practice in Christianity* (1850), Kierkegaard's pseudonym Anti-Climacus claims that the observer is subsumed when he or she observes one of the perspective-based paintings of the academic type:

> But "to observe" can mean in one sense to come very close to something, namely, to what one wishes to observe; in another sense, it signifies keeping very distant, infinitely distant, that is, personally. When one shows a painting to a person and asks him to observe it . . . he steps very close to the object . . . in short, he comes as close to the object as possible, but in this very same movement he in another sense leaves himself entirely, goes away from himself, forgets himself, and nothing reminds him of himself, since it is he, after all, who is observing the painting and the cloth and not the painting and the cloth that are observing him. In other words, by observing I go into the object (I become objective) but I leave myself or go away from myself (I cease to be subjective). (*SKS* 12:227–28 / *PC* 233–34; see figure 6)

With these words, Anti-Climacus's starting point is the image matrices available in his time and the expectations people have of them. These paintings are assessed according to whether "they are a good likeness," purify, and point upward. This pictorial universe has two roots. One is the perception of the experience of art as a disinterested pleasure. The other root is the contemporary metaphysics of presence, with the belief in the presence of the universal in the beautiful image. In relation to Danish fine arts in the 1830s and 1840s, which were governed by a striving for harmony, idealization, the "nature-like," good craftsmanship, perspective theory, and Goethe's color theory, Kierkegaard seems to wish to be at odds. It seems that his pictorial aesthetic can be reduced to a "not." Instead of harmony, for example, *Either/Or*'s "A" points to the paradox. Instead of idealization, he opts for reality; instead of "nature-like" verisimilitude, abstraction; the sketch replaces "good craftsmanship"; two-dimensionality, or a reverse perspective whereby the picture falls outward to the viewer, replaces the classical linear perspective; and the holistic Goethean palette is replaced with glaring, "striking" colors ("light green in yellow," "yellow-green," and so forth; compare, for example, the description of these in *Either/Or*'s prefatory "Diapsalmata"; *SKS* 2:31 / *EO* 1:23).[12] Kierkegaard, through "A" and some of the other pseudonyms, seems to find his alternative to Danish fine arts in contemporary folk art, whether it be the time's one-sheet prints, including the "Neuruppiner Bilderbogen" or "Nürnbergs," or as he finds it in the petit journalism of the time.[13]

Whereas academic pictorial art tends to invite a wrongly directed bodily and mental movement *outward*, that is, into the picture, along the pathway already painted for the viewer to follow, Kierkegaard (through his pseudonyms) attempts to reverse this wrong movement, so that it correctly points *inward*—that is, toward the self. Other picture types create an inverse movement whereby the half-completed picture is pushed back into the body of the observer and, enfolded in time, is completed by his or her inner, active eye. These pictures function as midwives for the observer. We find them inscribed in different elements of the works: folk-like, nonmimetic, and nonperspectivist pictorial impressions that schematize and abstract and leave it to us, the viewers, to add body to the image; trick pictures whose middle space and empty, unworked areas play a vital role; fragments, an uncompletable form, which in the picture's world are embodied as, for example, sketches or studies of fragmented details; outline drawings; and finally a permanent, provisional image expression, such as the arabesque. All of these pictorial types share a focus on how the original picture is received and on the supplementary pictures it generates—that is, the acquisition process.

In *Repetition*, Kierkegaard's pseudonym Constantin Constantius compares one of his time's cheap, template-painted, exaggerated, and very popular prints with an academic landscape—he does not name one in particular—that functions "as a true copy" or by "ideal reproduction." The example serves to show us how we are affected by the final, complete, and finished form and the incomplete attempt.

Fourth Appropriation: Raphael's *The Entombment*

At times we see the more mature individuality who satiates himself on the strong food of actuality and is not really influenced by a well-executed painting. But he can be stirred by a Nürnberg print, a picture of the kind found on the market not long ago. There one sees a landscape depicting a rural area in general. This abstraction cannot be artistically executed. Therefore the whole thing is achieved by contrast, namely, by an accidental concretion. And yet I ask everyone if from such a landscape he does not get the impression of a rural area in general, and if this category has not stayed with him from childhood. In the days of childhood, we had such enormous categories that they now almost make us dizzy, we clipped out of a piece of paper a man and a woman who were man and woman in general in a more rigorous sense than Adam and Eve were. A landscape artist, whether he strives for effect by faithful representation or by ideal reproduction, perhaps leaves the individual cold, whereas a print like that produces an indescribable effect, since we do not know whether to laugh or to cry, and the whole effect depends upon the observer's mood. (*SKS* 4:33 / *R* 158)

I am unaware of any extant Nürnberg print of "a landscape depicting a rural area in general."[14] The closest I have come, so far, to Kierkegaard's example is *The Entombment* from 1847, a mirror image copied from a German Nürnberg original, inspired by Raphael (figure 7). Note the template-like landscape in the background, where it is left to us, the observers, and our imagination, to create a landscape that we can see, feel, and smell. There are numerous references to Nürnberg prints in Kierkegaard's writings, where, in accordance with the custom of the time, the word is used as a general designation of the German woodcuts, copperplate prints, and lithographs that increasingly flooded into the Danish market in the first half of the 1800s and dominated it from around 1840. These German prints originally came from, and hence were named after, Neuruppin and Nürnberg. Their most striking aspect is the colors, which children found appealing. Sometimes, the pictures are in reverse perspective, so that the figures step out of the surface instead of moving into the picture. The picture-signs, or those elements in the pictures that are rendered as abstractions, sometimes resembling pictographs, were easily replaceable. It was only necessary to cut the block a little (if it was a woodcut, as in this case), replace the poplars with a beech or pine tree, and voilà, a new location and new images would appear. The structural lines are rough and the paint appears to be slapped on and seems almost too bright.

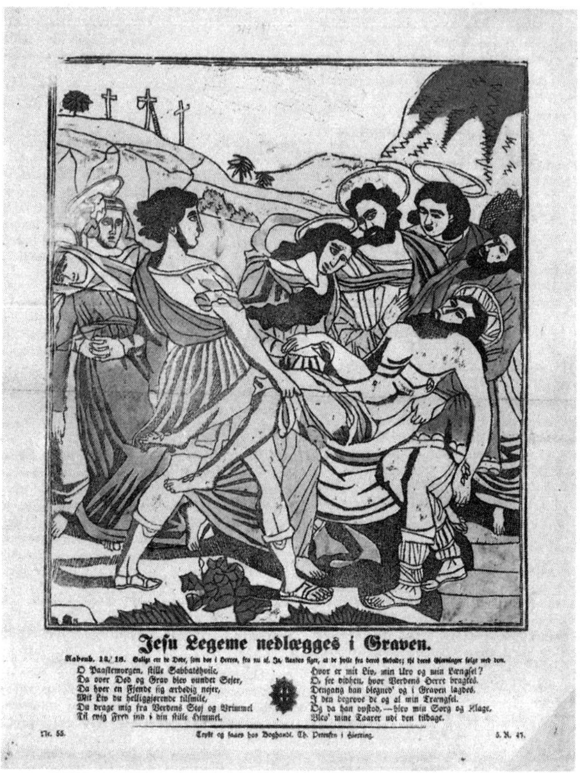

Figure 7. Laterally reversed copy of a German lithograph probably printed in Nürnberg ca. 1830. The original source is Raphael, *The Entombment*, woodcut, 1507. Printed in Denmark by Th. Petersen, ca. 1847. V. E. Clausen, Copenhagen.

The lack of shadowing contributes to flattening everything in this picture. There is no rounding—that is, no synesthetic dimension—to grasp and no space to enter. But also the relationship between image and imaged is uncertain and left to us to determine.

The connoisseur's appraising gaze, which admiringly absorbs the perfectly completed landscape painting, leaves the connoisseur cold. However, in the view of another of Kierkegaard's pseudonyms, Johannes Climacus, the Nürnberg print of "a landscape depicting a rural area in general" will "turn the observer's gaze inward into himself" (*SKS* 7:328 / *CUP* 1:359), so that it is possible for the observer to "thrust him[self] away" (*SKS* 7:328 / *CUP* 1:359) and continue to work on the half-finished or unfinished "images." With this pictorial approach, Kierkegaard in many ways anticipates what is today the common approach, which focuses on art's performative or performing dimension. The German art critic Dorothea von Hantelmann's poststructuralist and very inclusive definition of the concept is relevant to our purpose:

The notion of performativity, as I relate to it, centers around the possibilities and limits of productivity—the ability to produce a meaning, to provide an experience or to create a situation. We all know, for example, the meaning of a door: you enter or leave a room through it. But asking about the performativity of this door points to the *situation* it produces, which might be integrative, segregative or exclusive. Or towards the actions that can take place with or through this door, like slamming it and thereby performing a certain culturally coded convention of arguing. So, in a nutshell, performativity leads us towards a situational understanding of culture, to a situational aesthetics.[15]

In art history, performativity theorists focus on the "in-between" between the observer and the object of analysis, where both the work's significance and the observer's subjectivity are created. Despite all differences, it is such a middle space and such a "situational aesthetic" that Kierkegaard projects in his alternative to the beautiful image.

Irony in Art as a Controlled Element versus Socratic or Romantic Irony

In his Master of Arts dissertation, *The Concept of Irony* (1841), Kierkegaard distinguishes between Romantic and controlled irony. He reminds us several times that K. W. F. Solger, one of the standard-bearers of German Romanticism, in his *Vorlesungen über Aesthetik* (1829, *Lectures on Aesthetics*) and *Nachgelassene Schriften und Briefwechsel* (1826, *Posthumous Writings and Correspondence*), describes how any artistic creation must be ironic if it is to be art: "It has already been pointed out in the foregoing that in his lectures on esthetics Solger makes irony the condition for every artistic work" (*SKS* 1:325 / *CI* 324). Kierkegaard does not refer to Solger as an example to be followed; quite the contrary. For Kierkegaard, Romantic irony is both speculative and metaphysical.

Unfortunately, Solger does not distinguish between the individual art forms. One can ask oneself how an "irony" painting or picture from the 1840s, when Naturalism dominated, would look. Are we referring to the way the painting or picture interprets its subject or to a figure that reflects upon its own form? I choose the latter option, as does Kierkegaard.

Let us take *The Concept of Irony* in reverse order and begin where Kierkegaard ends, the section in which he describes irony as a controlled element and the truth of irony. The irony described here is the irony that we should strive for. For Kierkegaard, irony is about our approach to actuality, but thereby also to ourselves. As a controlled element, irony "limits, finitizes, and circumscribes and thereby yields truth, actuality, content; it disciplines and punishes and thereby yields balance and consistency" (*SKS* 1:355 / *CI* 326). Irony as a controlled element is also "a guide" (*SKS* 1:355 / *CI* 327) and "the way" (*SKS*

1:356 / *CI* 327), a "way" that leads to "actuality" (*SKS* 1:354 / *CI* 325). As such, irony is closely related to doubt, for the way shown by irony is not "the way whereby someone fancying himself to have the achievement comes to possess it, but the way along which the achievement deserts him" (*SKS* 1:356 / *CI* 327–28). The actuality Kierkegaard describes is the historical actuality of existence, where time is lived and people are born and die. Irony as a controlled element makes people human (*SKS* 1:357 / *CI* 329), as it teaches us "to actualize actuality" (*SKS* 1:356 / *CI* 328). When irony constitutes a controlled element, it does not cause either the ironic or actuality to be carried away.

Fifth Appropriation: *Napoleon Haunting His Grave*

The Concept of Irony, which among other things seeks to describe the difference between Plato's and Socrates's uses of irony, is concerned with the contrast between the inner and the outer, being (or noumenon, in Kant's sense of the term) and phenomenon. For Kierkegaard, furthermore, irony is determined as absolute negativity and, it can be said, "scoops out the kernel" (*SKS* 1:106 / *CI* 45). The model for Kierkegaard's "controlled irony" is Socratic irony. This is not surprising since Socrates plays a central role in all of Kierkegaard's literary works and in his perception of the nature of philosophy. A deeper understanding of Socratic irony, as Kierkegaard reads it, can be gained from familiarity with the trick picture he apparently had before him as he wrote. Socratic irony is like the picture's "Napoleon" (the empty space between the trees; see figure 8), where "'nothing' becomes almost visible" (*SKS* 1:113 / *CI* 52), a negative picture:

> The more Socrates tunneled under existence [*Existentsen*], the more deeply and inevitably each single remark had to gravitate toward an ironic totality, a spiritual condition that was infinitely bottomless, invisible, and indivisible. . . . Allow me to illustrate what I mean by a picture [*Billede*]. There is a work that represents Napoleon's grave. Two tall trees shade the grave. There is nothing else to see in the work, and the unsophisticated observer sees nothing else. Between the two trees there is an empty space; as the eye follows the outline, suddenly Napoleon himself emerges from this nothing, and now it is impossible to have him disappear again. Once the eye has seen him, it goes on seeing him with an almost alarming necessity. So also with Socrates' rejoinders. One hears his words in the same way one sees the trees; his words mean what they say, just as the trees are trees. There is not one single syllable that gives a hint of any other interpretation, just as there is not one single line that suggests Napoleon, and yet this empty space, this nothing, is what hides that which is most important. (*SKS* 1:80–81 / *CI* 19)

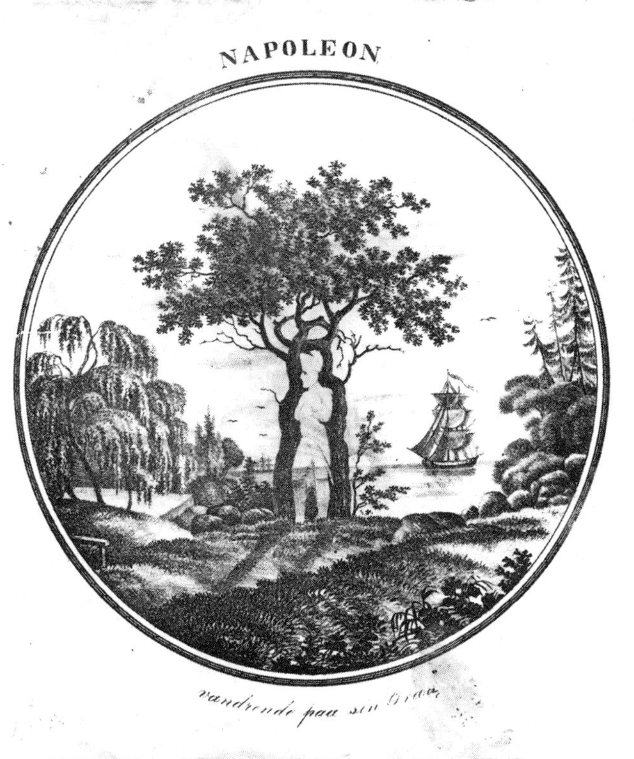

Figure 8. Anonymous, *Napoleon Haunting His Grave*, engraving, ca. 1820. Royal Library, Copenhagen.

The trick picture gives us an understanding not only of Kierkegaard's perception of Socratic irony, which reappears, reworked, in his diagnosis of controlled irony, but also of the manifestation of the relation between the dialogue partners that the controlled irony takes as its premise: co-acting, co-creating, producing, and, in brief, performing. If we transplant the traits and abilities of the trick picture, and the perception of the reception process that determines its design, there appears to be a relation between Kierkegaard's opting for the popular pictorial culture and the controlled irony.

Romantic Irony—or a Controlled Ironic Approach to a Painting Loved by Romanticism

Kierkegaard more than hints at the relation between mimetic pictorial art and Romantic irony through an association he draws while working on his dissertation's section on Plato. Unexpectedly, he suddenly draws a copperplate into his discussion. With exquisite irony, he alludes to copperplate

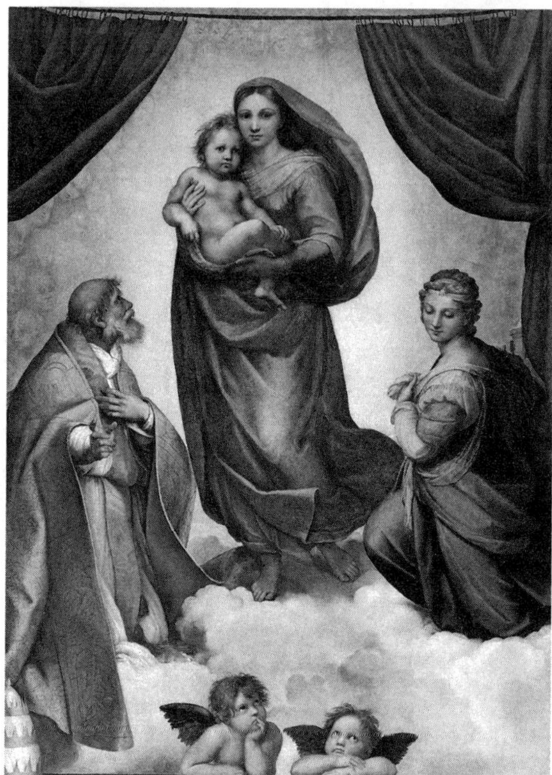

Figure 9. Raphael, *The Sistine Madonna*, oil on canvas, 270 × 201 cm., 1513–14, Gemäldegalerie, Dresden.

etchings in conjunction with a critique of Friedrich Ast's book *Platon's Leben und Schriften* (1816, *Plato's Life and Writings*), in which Ast argues that Socrates's defense is written neither by Plato nor by Socrates himself, but by someone unknown. Kierkegaard finds Ast's viewpoint absurd and— (Romantically) ironic.

Sixth Appropriation: Raphael's *Sistine Madonna*

This concerns a description of a presumably colored reproduction of Raphael's *Sistine Madonna* from 1512–14 (figure 9), one of the the most popular icons of Kierkegaard's time, reproduced, described, and copied over and over by artists both at home and abroad. The passage reads, "There is an etching of the ascension of the Madonna. In order to raise heaven as high as possible, there is drawn across the bottom a dark line, over which two angels peek up at her. Similarly, by quoting Ast's words in the text, I shall elevate his words as high as possible, and in order to heighten his pathos even more, I shall draw a line over which at times irony's roguish face will be allowed to peek" (*SKS* 1:146 / *CI* 90). The irony in relation to Ast is obvious in terms of the use of the etching and the repetition of the word "high" and images of height. Kierkegaard will "elevate his [Ast's] words" as high as possible and in order to "heighten his pathos," and so forth. It is also obvious when he turns the angels into "irony's roguish face." Kierkegaard's treatment of the picture is, to put it diplomatically, quite unimpressed and creative.

The picture presents not the Madonna's ascension but her appearance among us mortals. It would also be quite unfortunate if she were to rise to heaven with the Christ child before he could become an adult and a main protagonist in the New Testament. The painting is of the Madonna with child, and the two saints, Sixtus and Barbara. The figures stand on a bed of clouds and are framed by heavy curtains that are each pulled aside. Mary is descending from the heavenly skies and seems to continue her progress out of the picture, to enter the "actual" space in which the painting is hanging. This effect is due to the painting's focal point, Mary's left knee, which is bent as if she is walking. The attention of St. Sixtus and St. Barbara is on the faithful, who we imagine are standing in front of the balustrade raised at the lower edge of the picture. The two cherubs who are resting their arms on the balustrade are "within" or behind it, and thus in the picture's imaginary space, which is in fine harmony with their nature. There, they appear now as angels and now as cupids—that is, as creatures on the cusp between immanence and transcendence. The tiara placed on the top of the balustrade functions as a visual and symbolic link between the "actual" Church of Rome and the imaginary, transcendent space.

Kierkegaard seems at play here, like a street urchin, and it seems unlikely that he imagined he was faced with a heavenly ascension. His use of this picture almost besmirches its iconic status and Christian significance. Even though Kierkegaard was not a great scholar of the classical art history tradition, this pictorial interpretation is governed by a (controlled) ironic view.

Postscript

One of the small aphorisms that introduces *Either/Or* and gives us a first taste of "A's" psychological profile reads, "My life achievement amounts to nothing at all, a mood, a single color. My achievement resembles the painting by that artist who was supposed to paint the Israelites' crossing of the Red Sea and to that end painted the entire wall red and explained that the Israelites had walked across and that the Egyptians were drowned" (*SKS* 2:37 / *EO* 1:28). Many have sought to identify the picture for this *diapsalma*, which is based on Exodus 14:21–31, but the solution is clear. According to the record of the auctioneer who sold his library, Kierkegaard owned a copy

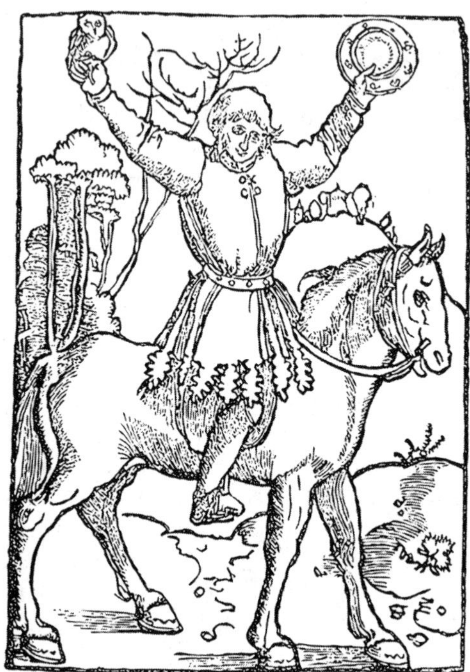

Figure 10. Anonymous, *Owlglass*, woodcut, from the 1515 edition of *Eulenspiegel*. The woodcut is printed on the front page. Presumably published by Johannes Grüninger.

of *[Underlig og selsom] Historie om Tiile Ugelspegel* (The Strange and Curious Story of Owlglass), from which the story originates.[16] *Uglspil* (Owlglass) was so popular at that time that, in a Copenhagen entertainment magazine, people could read about "the most favorable moment for the painter [*det gunstige øieblik for maleren*]," the moment that made his task easy:

A prank by Owlglass is related, that is almost too witty for him. Owlglass pretended to be a painter, and offered his services to some monks who wished to have a wall painted in one of the rooms of their monastery. They bargained with him about this, and required him to paint the Red Sea that the Children of Israel crossed with dry feet, while the Pharaoh and all of his army were drowned. Owlglass took on this task, and got to work straight away, simply by covering the entire wall with red paint. After completing the work in less than half a day, he came to demand his payment. When the monks saw the work, they were not pleased, and the Father Superior complained that one could not see the Children of Israel crossing the Red Sea, and asked why they were omitted. "There is a good reason for that," said Owlglass: "They have already crossed to the other side, so you cannot see them." "But where are the Pharaoh and his riders?" asked the monks. "You cannot see them," the painter replied, "because they are on the bottom of the sea."[17]

If we juxtapose the *diapsalma* with this version of one of Owlglass's pranks, we get a picture of "A"/Johannes!

Seventh Appropriation: *Owlglass's Owl and Mirror*

Owlglass is often depicted with an owl in one hand and a mirror in the other, which is a literal visualization of his name (in High German, Eulenspiegel). Kierkegaard may have known of editions of the book in which the prankster Eulenspiegel is seen with owl and mirror in his hands (figure 10; Strassburg edition 1515, reprinted in 1885). He may have just played with the name. At any rate, "A" and Johannes the Seducer are incarnations of both images. The reflective "A"/Johannes is the owl and the constantly image-forming "A"/ Johannes is the mimetic mirror.

Notes

1. Elsewhere in his authorship, including the works published under his own name, there is reflection on sight and the interconnectedness of the Christian message and the way we look at our neighbor and at ourselves (compare Christ's all-embracing look in *Works of Love*) and on its liberating potential to create new opportunity (compare, e.g., *The Concept of Anxiety*).

2. Lasse Horne Kjældgaard and Isak Winkel Holm have convincingly shown how Kierkegaard deliberately undermines the Lessing dictum with "animated tableaux" (my expression) that enroll movement and change in the linguistic metaphors. See Lasse Horne Kjældgaard, "Bevægelser og stillinger: Om det hvilende og det bevægelige i Kierkegaards tableauer" (Movements and Postures: On the Resting and Moving in Kierkegaard's Tableaux), in *Tableau: Det sublime øjeblik* (Tableau: The Sublime Moment), ed. Elin Andersen and Karen Klitgaard Povlsen (Aarhus: Klim, 2001), 177–94; Isak Winkel Holm, "Unpregnant Moments," unpublished paper presented at the international research-school seminar "Nonlinear Narrative in Twentieth and Twenty-first Century Artistic Practices," Goldsmiths College, University of London, 2008. However, these studies by Kjældgaard and Holm do not affect the thesis of my essay.

3. The myth was resuscitated around 1800 by the Romantics in Northern Europe and Denmark. Two paintings might illustrate this. In 1811 C. W. Eckersberg painted *Malerkunstens fødsel* (*The Birth of Painting*). The painting is reproduced in Kasper Monrad and Peter Michael Hornung, *C. W. Eckersberg: Dansk malerkunsts fader* (C. W. Eckersberg: The Father of Danish Pictorial Art) (Copenhagen: Palle Fogtdal, 2005), 92. Around 1830, Heinrich Eddelien completed his painting *Malerkunstens oprindelse* (*The Origin of Painting*), Statens

Museum for Kunst (National Gallery of Denmark), Copenhagen. The painting is reproduced in Mogens Nykjær, *Kundskabens billeder: Motiver i dansk kunst fra Eckersberg til Hammershøi* (Images of Knowledge: Subjects in Danish Art from Eckersberg to Hammershøi) (Aarhus: Aarhus University Press, 1991), 123, fig. 64. I am implying not that Kierkegaard knew these paintings but rather that the myth was part and parcel of the horizon of the Romantics and their critics.

4. This blind track (!) in my interpretation of Pliny is inspired by Jacques Derrida, *Mémoires d'aveugle: L'autoportrait et autres ruines* (Paris: Réunion des musées nationaux, 1990), 54–56; *Memoirs of the Blind: The Self-Portrait and Other Ruins*, trans. Pascale-Anne Brault and Michael Naas (Chicago: University of Chicago Press, 1993), 49–51.

5. It is very hard to say which picture this actually concerns. There are countless depictions of Romeo and Juliet (paintings, graphics, book illustrations, theater posters, pictures celebrating illustrious actors and actresses playing the loving couple, *bilderbogen*, etc.). A review of the (German) works of Shakespeare owned by Kierkegaard (see *ASKB*) has not yielded any result. The work catalogued as *ASKB* 1882, namely, *Vierzig Kunstblätter zu Shakespeare's dramatischen Werken (in Stahl grawirt)* (Forty Art Sheets to Shakespeare's Dramatic Works [Engraved in Steel]) (Stuttgart, 1840), which does not register anywhere, must be *Nachträge zu Shakspeare's Werken von Schlegel und Tieck: mit 40 Stahlstichen zu Shakspeare's Werken* (Postscript to Shakespeare's Works by Schlegel and Tieck: With Forty Engravings to Shakespeare's Works), 4 vols., ed. Ernst Ortlepp (Stuttgart: L. J. Rieger, 1840). The only scene from *Romeo and Juliet* depicted in the *Nachträge* is the one that takes place in the burial vault, represented in outline. It has been suggested by some (e.g., Howard and Edna Hong) that the lithograph Kierkegaard refers to is Ferdinand Piloty's (1786–1844) *The Kiss*; see *SLW* 703n129. The Hongs mention the picture without source and do not reproduce it. Fortunately, Eric Ziolkowski has followed up on their suggestion and referred me to his book *The Literary Kierkegaard* (Evanston, Ill.: Northwestern University Press, 2011), where he reproduces *The Kiss* as the frontispiece. It was originally reproduced in *Shakespeare's Romeo und Julia* (Shakespeare's Romeo and Juliet), ed. A. W. Schlegel (Berlin: G. Grote 1875), facing p. 75 (new edition 1889, facing p. 75). We have no knowledge of how this picture circulated in Kierkegaard's lifetime. He might have encountered it in Copenhagen or Berlin—or he might not. Although it must be a conjecture that Kierkegaard is writing about exactly this picture, it perfectly fits his description and helps us understand how Kierkegaard enlivens and freezes his pictures because, to paraphrase Goethe, he looks with a touching eye and a seeing hand; see J. W. Goethe, *Römische Elegien* (Roman Elegies) (1788; Frankfurt a.M.: Insel, 1980), 6:93.

6. Kierkegaard is not alone in associating the picture with death. The family resemblance is also apparent from Blanchot, for example, and in a way that, notwithstanding all the differences, resembles Kierkegaard's. For Blanchot the comparison serves to "de-ontologize" the picture; see Maurice Blanchot, "Les deux versions de l'imaginaire," in *L'Espace littéraire* (Paris: Gallimard, 1955), 345–59; "The Two Versions of the Imaginary," in *The Space of Literature*, trans. Ann Smock (Lincoln: University of Nebraska Press, 1982), 254–63.

7. The commentary in *SKS* K3:245 also states that in 1842 there were two "photo" studios in Copenhagen: the Austrian portrait painter Joseph Weninger's

in Bredgade and M. Alstrup's in a pavilion in Kongens Have. At the opening of Tivoli in 1844, one more studio was established. About this and the Bertel Thorvaldsen daguerreotype portrait, see, e.g., Marie Louise Berner, *Bertel Thorvaldsen: A Daguerreotype Portrait from 1840* (Copenhagen: Museum Tusculanums Press, 2005).

8. See Mette Mortensen, "Kampen om ansigtet: Fotografi og identification" (The Battle Surrounding the Face: Photography and Identification), Ph.D. dissertation, University of Copenhagen, 2006, 51. Balzac's conceptions of the daguerreotype are developed in his novel from 1847, *Le cousin Pons* (Paris: Booking International, 1993), 144. Felix Nadar in 1899 described Balzac's attitudes toward daguerreotypes in *Quand j'etais photographe* (When I Was a Photographer) (Paris: Seuil, 1994), 9–18.

9. There is a vast body of literature on the nature of photography as the boundary between life and death, presence and absence. Here, reference is solely made to Roland Barthes's now classic *La chambre claire: Note sur la photographie* (Paris: Gallimard, 1980); *Camera Lucida: Reflections on Photography*, trans. Richard Howard (New York: Hill and Wang, 1981); and to David Freedberg's study of the fear of the vitalizing look, the "living" images, and the picture's demonic powers, *The Power of Images: Studies in the History and Theory of Response* (Chicago: University of Chicago Press, 1991).

10. The parallels between Kierkegaard's "making Regine an image," as shown by the correspondence retained from the engagement period, and "A"/Johannes the Seducer are a trail I cannot pursue here.

11. See P. F. A. Nitsch, *Neues mythologisches Wörterbuch für studirende Jünglinge, angehende Künstler und jeden Gebildeten überhaupt* (New Mythological Dictionary for Studying Young People, Future Artists and Every Educated Man), 2nd ed., 2 vols. (Leipzig: F. Fleischer, 1821), 1:310. Kierkegaard probably writes on the basis of the description alone. I have found the illustrations in *Le pitture antiche d'Ercolano e contorni incise con qualche spiegazione* (The Ancient Paintings of Herculaneum and Engraved Outlines with Some Explanation), 5 vols. (Naples: Regia Stamperia, 1757–79), 2 (1760): 91, 97 (plates 14, 15). (The British Museum Catalog and WorldCat identify Ottavio Antonio Baiardi [1694–1764] and Pasquale Carcani [1721–83] as the editors of *Le pitture antiche d'Ercolano.*—Ed.) Unfortunately, the *SKS* commentary volume to *Either/ Or* includes only one of the ekphrasis's two (model) pictures.

12. Kierkegaard's indisputable fascination with children's and folk art's predilection for the bright unmixed primary colors—red, yellow, and blue—might also be one of his many ways to get at Hegel. In his *Aesthetics*, Hegel writes about the choice of colors among "barbarians": "Barbarians in general take their pleasure in simple and vivid colours like red and blue etc." G. W. F. Hegel, *Vorlesungen über die Ästhetik*, 3 vols. (Frankfurt a.M.: Suhrkamp, 1986), 3:85; *A* 2:851. For Hegel, to bring forth the shimmer (*das Schein*) of live spirituality, the colors need to be mixed either on the palette or by using glazed colors that fuse with the refraction of light. As Hegel sees it, the use of primary colors symbolizes a bygone stage in the history of art and is a thing of the barbaric past.

13. Quite remarkably, we see how pictorial artists are concerned with folk art and its bright, glaring colors (often primary colors: blue, red, and yellow); with its resemblance to the synthesizing, flattened, and simplified expression of a child's

drawing (how large is the most important, no matter how large in reality); and with the eye folk art has for materiality and texture—that is, for the visual and tactile rather than the intellectual. See Meyer Schapiro, "Courbet and Popular Imagery: An Essay on Realism and Naïveté," in *Modern Art: 19th and 20th Centuries* (London: Chatto and Windus, 1978), 47–85. In Denmark, a professor at the Royal Danish Academy of Fine Arts, C. W. Eckersberg, in a popular engraved sheet, chooses a loud yellow to fill out a scene before a lottery booth. See Monrad and Hornung, *C. W. Eckersberg* (n. 3 above).

14. See also the essay by Martijn Boven in the present volume, where this same Nürnberg print is discussed as an example of kitsch.—Ed.

15. Quoted by Camilla Jalving, *Værk som handling: Performativitet, kunst og metode* (The Work of Art as Action: Performativity, Art and Method) (Copenhagen: Museum Tusculanums Forlag, 2011), 54. (See also the discussion of Kierkegaard and performativity in Boven's essay in this volume.—Ed.)

16. Cf. *ASKB* 1469. The sales record does not identify any publisher or publishing house but does state that the book was probably published between 1812 and 1842. The work is known in about twenty editions from the nineteenth century, of which a number are from the first half of the century. It is thus not possible to state which edition Kierkegaard used.

17. "The Most Favorable Moment for the Painter" ("Det gunstige Øieblik for Maleren"), *Kiøbenhavns Moerskabsblad indeholdende Alvor og Skjemt* (Copenhagen Amusement Magazine on Serious and Jesting Matters), no. 84 (1831): 335.

Kierkegaard's Concept of Inherited Sin

A Cinematic Illustration

Ronald M. Green

The doctrine of hereditary sin is not one of the more fashionable Christian teachings today. Modern people find it hard to believe that we can inherit sin and guilt from our ancestors all the way back to Adam and Eve, the parents of the human race. They find it even harder to believe that such sin can be transmitted from our forebears to us through sexual intercourse, as some classical Christian theologians have held.

Nevertheless, aspects of a doctrine of hereditary sin were strongly defended in the nineteenth century by Søren Kierkegaard. In what follows I want to do two things. First, I want to offer a brief overview of Kierkegaard's position. This is developed in several of his writings, notably in sections of his early work *Either/Or* (1843) and his subsequent book *The Concept of Anxiety* (1844). Second, I want to provide a very modern illustration, and defense, of some of Kierkegaard's key points. I will do this by looking closely at scenes from the 2010 Academy Award nominee for best foreign language film, *Incendies*, by the Quebec director Denis Villeneuve.[1] *Incendies* (Fires) is based on an extraordinary play of the same title by the Lebanese playwright Wajdi Mouawad,[2] but Villeneuve's film version is a work of art in its own right.

Here I must issue a spoiler alert. *Incendies* is a surprising, shocking film. As I discuss scenes from the film, I am going to give away some of these surprises, so if you wish to see the film in its entirety, please stop reading now and return after viewing the film.

Let me begin by summarizing the main ideas conveyed by the penetrating analyses of hereditary sin and guilt by several of Kierkegaard's pseudonyms.[3]

First, there is the idea that none of us is born without a deep relationship to our past. Although we are free to choose our paths in life, we do not do so in a vacuum. We are "situated freedoms," unavoidably shaped by the deeds of those who went before us: our parents, other family members, our communities, even the whole human race. As Vigilius Haufniensis, the pseudonymous author of *The Concept of Anxiety*, puts it, "Each individual begins in an historical nexus" (*SKS* 4:376 / *CA* 73).[4] Vanessa Rumble is thus right when she says of Kierkegaard, "The 'father of existentialism,' while affirming the importance of the individual's decisions, not only dismissed the notion of a *liberum arbitrium* but also displayed an overweening interest in those aspects of personality and milieu which may prove fateful for the individual."[5] Drawing on an observation by Gregor Malantschuk, Rumble adds, "The task facing humans is not to withdraw themselves from the historically determined conditions of heredity or environment but somehow to accept those conditions in freedom and thus bring them under the domain of human responsibility."[6]

This understanding is more intensively expressed in *Either/Or* by Judge William, one of the work's leading figures, who urges his protégé, an aesthetically inclined young man, to abandon his drifting, moody existence and "choose himself." But even as the judge calls the young man to exercise his freedom to define a life course, he reminds him that he is not absolutely free to become the person he would like to be. Each of us inherits from our forebears many things that define us and condition our choice. Let me quote the judge as he describes someone choosing himself:

> Now he discovers that the self he chooses has a boundless multiplicity within itself inasmuch as it has a history, a history in which he acknowledges identity with himself. This history is of a different kind, for in this history he stands in relation to other individuals in the race and to the whole race, and this history contains painful things, and yet he is the person he is only through this history. That is why it takes courage to choose oneself, for at the same time as he seems to be isolating himself most radically he is most radically sinking himself into the root by which he is bound up with the whole. (*SKS* 3:207 / *EO* 2:216)

For the judge, this painful element in the choice of oneself as a situated being stems from the fact that we are in some ways implicated in and responsible for the deeds of our parents and ancestors. We benefit from their courage and their achievements, but we also enjoy the fruits of their misdeeds and wrongful acts. We cannot ignore the misdeeds of those before us because those misdeeds, as well as their positive accomplishments, have made us what we are. Thus, we must become aware of their misdeeds and be prepared to accept some measure of responsibility for them. Using religious terminology, Judge William makes this point as he continues to describe the process by which a person chooses himself:

> When the passion of freedom is aroused in him . . . he chooses himself and struggles for this possession as for his salvation, and it is his salvation. He can give up nothing of all this, not the most painful, not the hardest, and yet the expression for this struggle, for this acquiring, is—repentance. He repents himself back into himself, back into

the family, back into the race, until he finds himself in God. Only on this condition can he choose himself. . . .

And even though it was the father's guilt that was passed on to the son by inheritance, he repents of this, too, for only in this way can he choose himself, choose himself absolutely. (*SKS* 3:207–8 / *EO* 2:216–17)

What Judge William is trying to say here about participating in our parents' and forebears' guilt and repenting for their sins is given even more focused attention in a long essay in the first part of *Either/Or*, an essay ostensibly written by another one of Kierkegaard's pseudonymous authors, the aesthete "A." This essay is entitled "The Tragic in Ancient Drama Reflected in the Tragic in Modern Drama" (*SKS* 2:137–62 / *EO* 1:137–64).

The essay focuses largely on Sophocles's drama *Antigone*. To the heroine of that drama, whom he terms the "Greek" Antigone, "A" juxtaposes a heroine shaped by Christian culture. He calls this second heroine the "modern" Antigone. The Greek Antigone is a tragic figure. She belongs to an ill-fated lineage, being the fruit of the union of Oedipus and his mother Jocasta, whom Oedipus has wed after killing his father. Because of Antigone's ancestors' deeds and her own choices, she is fated to sorrow and suffer. In "A's" words, the Greek Antigone suffers partly as a result of her father's guilt, but for her this guilt is an "external fact." She is not personally involved with it. It is, as "A" interjects in Latin, "quod non volvit in pectore [something she does not turn over in her heart]" (*SKS* 2:159 / *EO* 1:160).

"But for our [modern] Antigone," the essay writer continues, "it is different." Oedipus is dead, but "even when he was alive, Antigone knew this [family] secret but did not have the courage to confide in her father. By her father's death, she is deprived of the only means of being liberated from her secret" (*SKS* 2:159 / *EO* 1:161). The essayist continues, "She loves her father with all her soul, and this love draws her out of herself into her father's guilt. As the fruit of such a love, she feels alien to humankind. She feels her guilt the more she loves her father; only with him can she find rest; as equally guilty, they would sorrow with each other" (*SKS* 2:161 / *EO* 1:161). Some Kierkegaard scholars may see here shadows of Kierkegaard's own relation to the sexual transgressions of his father. But we need not go into Kierkegaard's biography to appreciate his essayist's point: parents and children are connected, through guilt and blame. Emotionally and morally charged silences permeate their relationships.

None of this means that we are fated or determined in our life choices by our familial inheritances. Kierkegaard and his pseudonyms avoid any deterministic interpretation of the classic Christian idea of inherited sin, and he rejects the idea that we are predestined to sin (*SKS* 4:332 / *CA* 62). Adam and Eve's free choice of sin may be the prototype of all sinning, "the first sin" (*SKS* 4:297–306 / *CA* 25–34), but each of us participates in the sinfulness of our forebears only by freely replicating their choices.

Kierkegaard's third and final point about hereditary sin is that it is intimately connected with our nature as sexual beings. Sexuality evidences our tense positioning between embodiment and finite creatureliness on the one hand, and our transcendent spiritual possibilities on the other. In *The Concept of Anxiety*, Vigilius Haufniensis tells us that sexuality and procreation express the tension between the finite and transcendent aspects of our natures, between the "physical" and "psychical" components of our being. The challenge of "spirit" is to unite these, but this challenge is a source of anxiety, and anxiety furnishes the opportunity for sin. "Anxiety," says Vigilius Haufniensis, "is the dizziness of freedom, which emerges when the spirit wants to posit the synthesis and freedom looks down into its own possibility, laying hold of finiteness to support itself" (*SKS* 4:331 / *CA* 61).

Vigilius Haufniensis is clear that sensuousness and sexuality per se are not sinful: "Sensuousness is not sinfulness but an unexplained riddle that causes anxiety" (*SKS* 4:335 / *CA* 65). While he says that conception and childbirth are moments "furthest away" from spirit, Kierkegaard is not repeating the centuries-old Christian disparagement of sex. His point instead is that human physical existence, which sexuality epitomizes, creates the existential tension that, with anxiety as its first expression, provides the ground for the free but wrongful choices that are sin.

Drawing on and developing Kierkegaard's insights, we can see that sexuality is a realm where anxiety can easily become sinfulness through the use of other persons, where love can lie close to cruelty, where gender roles can become an excuse for domination or self-abandonment, and where our most private and intimate acts express themselves concretely in the creation of another human being. No wonder, then, that hereditary sin as the sin of family lines most readily evidences itself in connection with our sexual and gendered lives.

I have launched a barrage of difficult and challenging ideas. I could continue developing each of them, but I want to devote the remainder of this discussion to intensively illustrating their meaning by exploring their presence in the film *Incendies*.

I should note that it is entirely fitting that a film be used to illustrate Kierkegaard's ideas. Kierkegaard was a pioneer in the use of fictional materials, including operas, plays, and novels, for the development of philosophical and theological ideas. The first part of *Either/Or* offers four extended essays dealing with fictional or theatrical pieces: "The Immediate Erotic Stages or the Musical Erotic," which focuses on Mozart's *Don Giovanni*; "The First Love," a treatment of Scribe's play of the same name; "Silhouettes," which deals with several different fictional pieces, including Goethe's *Faust*; and our present concern, "The Tragic in Ancient Drama Reflected in the Tragic in Modern Drama." At a deeper level, many of Kierkegaard's writings, from "The Seducer's Diary" in *Either/Or* to the lengthy *Stages on Life's Way*, have a deliberate fictional or theatrical quality, while other works, such as *Repetition*, actively muse about the meaning of theater for human existence.[7] Kierkegaard was a thinker for whom fiction was often a medium for dense philosophical and religious reflection. Indeed, this is one of the more distinguishing features of his authorship that he handed on to later existentialist writers such as Sartre, Beauvoir, and Camus. If Kierkegaard were alive today, there is no doubt in my mind that he would be entranced with contemporary cinema and that *Incendies*, if he viewed it, would be among the creative works that would draw his interest.

Before turning to *Incendies*, let me briefly recapitulate the three major points that Kierkegaard's writings make about hereditary sin. One is the idea that we are situated freedoms. Though we are always free to shape our own destiny, in choosing ourselves we are inevitably influenced by our past and by the choices of those who went before us. Second, we participate in and are responsible for the deeds and misdeeds of our forebears. In choosing ourselves, therefore, we must acknowledge and repent for the wrongs they have done. Third and finally, our moral and psychological ties to our parents and forebears are unavoidably intertwined with sexuality. Although sexuality is not itself sinful, it is a domain that expresses the deep tensions in our physical and psychical nature. Our forebears' life choices were intensively expressed in their sexual conduct and their gendered self-understandings. We are the result of that conduct and those self-understandings, which we are prone to replicate in our own sexual choices and gendered behaviors.

Now, *Incendies*.

The film begins with four central characters. The first is Nawal Marwan, an aging woman who is an immigrant to Montreal from an unnamed Middle Eastern nation (based on Lebanon) and who has worked as a secretary in a notary's office. The next two are her two adult children, the twins Jeanne and Simon. Finally there is the notary Jean Lebel, Nawal's employer and family friend. In French-speaking cultures like Quebec, notaries are almost the equivalent of lawyers.[8]

As the film begins, Nawal visits a public swimming pool with Jeanne. When Jeanne emerges from the pool, she finds her mother seated in a chair, catatonic. Nawal's apparent stroke soon leads to her death, but before dying she manages to dictate a will to her employer and friend, Jean Lebel.

Lebel summons Jeanne and Simon to his office to read them their mother's will. The will begins with Nawal's request that she be buried naked, face down, with no prayers and no name on the stone marking her grave. "No epitaph," she says, "for those who don't keep their promises." The will continues with her further requests.

Lebel hands the twins two sealed envelopes. He explains that one is to be delivered to their father, whom the twins up to then believed had died long ago in their mother's home country. The second is to be delivered to their brother. They never knew that they had another sibling.

From its start, the film keeps shifting between the present-day world of Nawal's two children as they try to fulfill their mother's strange requests and the events of Nawal's youth in the tumultuous civil war in her home country during the 1970s.

After Lebel reads the conditions of Nawal's will to the twins, an angry Simon stalks out, declaring, "I'll bury my mother normally. For once in her life she'll have acted normally. End of discussion." As Jeanne regards her mother's youthful photo in an old passport that was among her papers, Lebel tells her, "I know it's very unusual. But your mother wasn't crazy, Jeanne."

Outside in the street Simon continues fulminating. He quips, "We're a big family now. She ever mention a dog? Big families always have a dog. Do we have to find it now, too?" His mother, he says, is "fucking crazy," and he wants nothing to do with her request. He will talk to Lebel about burying her normally. "You feel guilty about everything," he tells Jeanne. "I don't feel guilty." Jeanne shouts back, "Do you realize what we just heard?" Simon replies, "She's gone, Christ! It's over. Peace at last." Angrily kicking the side of his pickup truck, he shouts, "I feel so fucking peaceful." Throughout the film, unless pressed, Simon repeatedly resists cooperating with his sister in this quest.

The film now shifts back in time to the unnamed Middle Eastern country in late 1969 and to a rocky, tree-marked hillside beneath a small Christian village. A young Nawal runs to meet her lover, a Muslim (perhaps Palestinian) refugee, named Wahab, but their meeting is abruptly interrupted by two of Nawal's brothers. One shoots Wahab dead and is about to shoot Nawal for "staining" the family honor by being with a Muslim, when their grandmother's voice interrupts from the village to save Nawal's life.

Back in the house Nawal reveals to her grandmother that she is pregnant. The grandmother wails that Nawal has cast the family into "blackness." She asks Nawal to promise that after the child is born, she will leave the village and get an education in order to escape their condition of misery.

Months later, Nawal delivers the child. She watches as her grandmother tattoos three small spots, one on top of the other, on the boy's heel. Just before the child is taken away from her to an orphanage, Nawal holds him and says, "I will find you again one day, I promise you, my love."

Nawal leaves for studies in Daresh (a fictional city in the north of the country), where she has an uncle who runs a progressive newspaper.

The film shifts back to today. Jeanne travels to Daresh, carrying a photo from Nawal's university years. Writing on the wall behind Nawal in the photo permits an older professor to identify it as taken at Kfar Ryat, a prison "in the south."

The scene shifts back again to the events of what we can presume to be the Lebanese civil war that raged for fifteen years beginning in the mid-1970s. We see Nawal as a university student. At the start of a bloody conflict between right-wing Christian Nationalist militias and Muslim refugees in the south, the militias shut down the university. Although Nawal is a Christian, she opposes the war.

Nawal is now desperate to find her son. She journeys south, negotiating roadblocks, hitchhiking, and proceeding on foot to the orphanage of Kfar Khout, where her son had been sent, but she finds it burned to the ground, the children gone, perhaps taken to a Muslim refugee camp farther south. Concealing the cross she wears on a necklace and donning a shawl to cover her head like a Muslim woman, Nawal boards a southbound bus. The scene that follows gives the film its name.

Boarding the bus, Nawal seats herself across from a young mother who is holding her child in her lap. Nawal falls asleep, only to be awakened when the bus is stopped by a contingent of Christian militia. When the driver tries to persuade them to let the bus continue he is shot dead and a volley of bullets riddles the bus, killing many of the passengers. Amid the bodies, Nawal and the young Muslim woman and her child cower on the floor. When a militiaman climbs to the top of the bus and begins pouring gasoline through the ceiling hatches, a terrified Nawal crawls to the door, holds out her cross and cries, "I'm Christian, I'm Christian." A militiaman signals her to come out. Looking back, she sees the Muslim mother and her child at the bus door. She turns, and after an instant in which the two women exchange a glance, she takes the child from the woman's arms. But the child won't cooperate. As Nawal runs from the bus, the child wriggles in her arms and, looking backward, screams "Mama, Mama." A militiaman wrenches the child from Nawal, and as the child runs back to the bus she is felled by a single bullet. Another volley aimed at the bus causes it to burst into flames. The scene closes when the militiamen drive away, and a stunned Nawal, on her hands and knees, stares at the conflagration.

We shift back to the present. Jeanne locates her mother's childhood village. Meeting with female relatives to explain her visit, she identifies herself as the daughter of Nawal Marwan and is abruptly told that she is not welcome there.

Back amid the civil war, Nawal continues her search for her son. Traveling south to the Muslim refugee camp, she finds nothing but devastation and pools of blood. Traumatized by the vicious behavior of the Christian militias she has witnessed, she offers her assistance to a Muslim warlord, Chamseddine, explaining to one of his aides that she has abandoned her previous pacifist position and wants to teach her enemy, the Christian Nationalists, what life has taught her. She adds that she has "nothing to lose."

At Chamseddine's behest, Nawal gains access to the family of the leader of the Christian Nationalist movement by serving as a French tutor for his children. Concealing a gun in her briefcase, she assassinates him. Brutally dragged off to the Kfar Ryat prison, she undergoes fifteen years of torture at the hands of her coreligionists.

Back in the present, Jeanne, with her mother's photo in hand, travels to Kfar Ryat. No one at the prison recognizes the woman in the photo, but

Jeanne is directed to an elderly custodian in a hillside grade school not far away. She shows him the picture, but he remains silent. When she tells him that the woman in the picture is her mother, he speaks: "She is 'La femme qui chante' [the Woman Who Sings], 'Number 72.'"

The custodian explains that he had watched this woman for thirteen of her fifteen years in prison. He says that they did everything to break her, but she looked them straight in the eye and "never bent." Finally, they sent in Abou Tarek, a specialist in torture. He repeatedly tortured and raped her. Nawal became pregnant by him, and after giving birth she was released. The janitor says that the midwife who delivered Nawal now lives in Daresh. Jeanne phones Simon in Montreal, insisting that he join her now in the search for their brother, this child of rape, and Simon reluctantly agrees. Lebel joins him.

Along with Lebel and a local notary friend who serves as translator, the twins visit the hospital where the midwife lies gravely ill. She speaks in Arabic, only part of which is translated. The scene is one of the more remarkable ones in the film. The midwife is awakened. A nurse introduces them as coming from Canada and as the children of Nawal Marwan. The midwife pulls herself up in the bed, excitedly gestures to the twins to come to her, and repeatedly calls out to them, "Sarwan, Janaan, Alhamdulillah [Thank God]!" Not comprehending, Simon says, "Madame, we're looking for the child she had in jail, can you help us?" The midwife continues her excited talking as the nurse translates. "She worked in Kfar Ryat prison. She assisted the Woman Who Sings during her delivery. She safeguarded the babies, and returned them to her on her release." The scene ends with the midwife once again reaching out to Jeanne and Simon, crying "Sarwan! Janaan!" as the nurse, with the camera on the stunned faces of Simon and Jeanne, adds, "Nawal Marwan had twins."

Simon and Jeanne have learned that they are the offspring of torture and rape and that their father is the torturer Abou Tarek. But they still don't know who their brother is and what has become of him. At Label's urging they continue their search. The Lebanese notary has found records indicating that a child was born to Nawal in May 1970 and was taken to the orphanage of Kfar Khout, which was burned down by the Muslim warlord Chamseddine. The child was given the name Nihad of May. The notary believes that Chamseddine may know what happened to the boy. In scenes from those years, we learn that Nihad was raised by the warlord's men and during the war became a pitiless sniper, often killing other children.

Because the world to the south is so patriarchal, it is now up to Simon to take the lead. He must travel to a Muslim refugee camp in search of his brother. He is finally taken, blindfolded, to a meeting with the aged warlord Chamseddine.

The warlord confirms that he had spared Nihad and the other Christian children when, after a revenge attack on the Christian foes, he burned down the orphanage of Kfar Khout. He had raised Nihad to be a fighter in their cause, and Nihad became a "fou de guerre," crazed with war. Above all, Nihad wanted to find his mother, at one point offering to become a martyr in the hope that his mother would see his picture on walls across the country. Chamseddine refused this request. When "the enemy" invaded the country, Nihad was captured, but only after killing seven of the foes. He was turned once again and sent to the Kfar Ryat prison—as a torturer. Simon asks, "With my father?" "No," Chamseddine replies, "he didn't work with Abou Tarek, your father." As the camera moves from the face-to-face exchange of the two men to scan a dark and twisted forest scene, Chamseddine's voice-over explanation continues. "When he became a torturer, your brother changed names. He became Abou Tarek. Nihad of May is Abou Tarek." Chamseddine concludes by saying that Abou Tarek eventually moved to Canada, where he is living under the name of Nihad Harmanni.

Put yourself for a moment in the shoes of either Jeanne or Simon. They have learned that they are not only the fruit of rape and torture, but of incest. Like Antigone, they are the offspring of a union between their mother and her own son.[9]

We return to the public swimming pool in Montreal prior to Nawal's stroke. We see Nawal swimming to the edge of the pool. A man's heel looms before her. On it is a tattoo with three rising dots, the same tattoo inscribed on the heel of her infant child. Climbing out of the pool, she approaches the man she knows is her son. He is Abou Tarek, her torturer. This identification—or, as Aristotle might say regarding Greek tragedy, this recognition (*anagnorisis*)—causes the stroke and Nawal's death, with which the film began.

So here we have the very "modern tragedy" of which Kierkegaard speaks. The twins issue from a primal deed of incest and violence. This misdeed hangs like a dark cloud over their present. But unlike the Greek Antigone, who merely suffers her fate and sorrows over it, the twins, like Kierkegaard's "modern Antigone," must regard themselves as culpably involved, as somehow tragically complicit in this dreadful family history.

Consider. The twins know that they bear within them—in their blood and DNA—traits of their torturer father. Here we see a literal sharing of family characteristics that can be a source of profound psychological discomfort and anxiety. To what extent, for example, are Simon's truculence, his anger at his mother, and his resistance to respecting her will a continuation of the misogynistic brutality of his biological father? Although neither Simon nor Jeanne can be blamed for their inherited characteristics, these characteristics are a source of psychological unease—the anxiety of which Kierkegaard speaks—and they become a source of guilt if they are allowed to shape an individual's choices.

And then there are the behaviors and choices for which the twins must clearly feel both responsibility and guilt. To what extent is their ignorance about their mother's past a wrongful ignorance? Did they ever ask her about her past? Were they even interested? All their lives, the twins relied on and took for granted their mother's love, without imagining, without even think-ing to suspect the agony that their very presence in the world may have caused her. And now Nawal is dead, beyond any solace they might offer her, beyond any plea they might make for understanding or forgiveness. As is true in the case of Kierkegaard's modern Antigone, culpable silence permeates this family drama. Compared to the Greek Antigone, the twins' sorrow is less, but their pain is greater. It is a pain sharpened by their own willed involvement and by a family history that looks back to an unpremeditated incestuous act and a willed history of torture and rape.

Incendies, of course, depicts an extreme situation. But in some ways, it also depicts the universal human condition. Its background is the Christian-Muslim violence of Lebanon's civil war and the Middle East in general, where groups of ethnically similar people—literally brothers and sisters, mothers and fathers—have tortured, raped, and slaughtered one another for generations. Abou Tarek's crime, and Nawal's experience, are our human experience. We must all ask to what extent, by accepting, affirming, and sexually reproducing our identities within warring families, ethnicities, and communities, we are complicit in the crimes of our ancestors. This, I think, is one of Kierkegaard's basic points in his exploration of hereditary sin.

But it is not Kierkegaard's final point. Kierkegaard does not believe that sin is the last word on our human condition. That last word is love: our love for one another and God's love for us despite our sinfulness. In a journal entry of February 16, 1839, Kierkegaard writes, "Fear and trembling . . . is [*sic*] not the *primus motor* [the prime mover or primary driving force] in the Chr. [Chris-tian] life." That primary force, he says, is love (*SKS* 18:14, EE:25 / *KJN* 2:9).

This, too, is the message of *Incendies*. I want to direct attention to the very end of the film. The twins have located their father-brother, Nihad Harmanni, in Montreal, where he is working at a menial job. They approach him on the street outside his apartment and hand him an envelope containing both letters.

Harmanni retreats into the hall of the building and opens the first letter. It begins, "I'm shaking as I write. I recognized you. You didn't recognize me. It's magnificent, a miracle. I am your number 72." The letter continues, "Our children will deliver this. You won't recognize them for they are beautiful, but they know who you are." Harmanni runs out to the street, but the twins are gone. Returning to the hallway he continues reading. "Through them, I want to tell you that you are still alive. Soon you'll turn silent . . . I know. For all are silent before the truth. Signed, Whore 72."

Harmanni retreats to the privacy of his apartment. Hands shaking, he opens the second letter:

> I speak to the son, not to the torturer. Whatever happens, I'll always love you, I promised you that when you were born, my son. Whatever happens, I'll always love you. I looked for you all my life. I found

you. You couldn't recognize me. You've a tattoo on your right heel. I saw it. I recognized you. You are beautiful. I wrap you in tenderness, my love. Take solace, for nothing means more than being together. You were born of love. So your brother and sister were born of love, too. Nothing means more than being together. Your mother, Nawal Marwan, Prisoner No. 72.

The scene now shifts to Lebel's office, where the notary informs the twins of their mother's wish now that "the silence will be broken, a promise kept," that a stone be placed on her grave and on it her name engraved in the sun. He hands the twins a letter addressed to them: "My loves, where does your story begin? At your birth? If so, it begins in horror. At the birth of your father? Then it begins in a great love story. But I say your story begins with a promise to break the chain of anger. Thanks to you, today I have finally kept it. The chain is broken. Finally I can take the time to cradle you, to gently sing a lullaby to console you. Nothing means more than being together. I love you. Your mother, Nawal."

As the final music of the film sounds, we see a graveyard and Nawal's stone. Standing before it, head bowed, is Harmanni/Abou Tarek.

"Nothing means more than being together."

This remark that weaves throughout the film is Nawal's reply to the brutal fratricide that scarred her life and the lives of those before her for count-less generations. She tells her children, "Your story begins with a promise to break the chain of anger." That chain is broken by a mother's love.

I think Kierkegaard understood this. For him, as for this film, hereditary sin is only the first part of the human story. The full story includes and is concluded by God's love, the overarching and unconditional love of which a mother's love is an expression.

It may seem odd to bring Kierkegaard's religious sensibility into connection with the themes of *Incendies*, because on the surface *Incendies* does not seem to be a religious film at all. The primary role religion plays in the narrative is as a source of hatred and division. However, one moment in the film suggests something else. As Nawal takes her seat in the bus in the scene leading to the conflagration that gives the movie its name, she looks across the aisle to the mother and to the child whose life she ultimately fails to save. The Muslim woman wears a diaphanous headscarf. Cradling the child against her bosom, the image is that of a traditional portrait of the Madonna. The film thus signals the religious importance of maternal love. It is precisely here that we find the unconditional and unwavering love that Christian faith always attributed to God, to God's son, and to Mary, the mother of God. Remarkably, the Maronite (Lebanese) Christian Church to which Nawal pre-sumably belongs has always claimed a special devotion to Mary, who is also the patron saint of Lebanon.[10] Thus, religiously understood, maternal love permeates *Incendies*. It can even be said that Nawal Marwan is the modern suffering Madonna of her own Christian tradition. (In tragic counterpoint, a Christian militiaman who sprays the bus with gunfire and sets it alight is shown to bear a small iconic portrait of Mary on the stock of his gun.)[11]

Of course, Kierkegaard as a Lutheran had little interest in the importance of Marian devotion, and, as a nineteenth-century male, he also had as little regard for the religious or spiritual significance of women and women's experience. In a journal entry, he explicitly rejects maternal love as a suitable expression of selfless Christian love. "Maternal love," he states, "is simply self-love raised to a higher power, and thus the animals also have it." At the same time, however, he adds that maternal love has qualities that render it a "beautiful metaphor" for divine love (*SKS* 22:192, NB12:92, n.d. 1849 / *KJN* 6:192). In *Works of Love*, he comments on the "strength" of maternal love and its willingness to "endure all things" for the beloved child (*SKS* 9:213 / *WL* 221).

Understanding maternal love not as Christian love per se, which for Kierkegaard always exhibits selflessness, but as a "figure" or metaphor for God's love allows us to value a mother's intense and unconditional bonding with her child at birth, as is the case for Nawal. Certainly, Nawal's love for her child is the force that breaks the cycle of hatred and violence. Thus, close attention to *Incendies* may help us update and sharpen Kierkegaard's own accounts of hereditary sin. If sexuality and procreation can be an important medium for perpetuating and accentuating human sin, they also provide us unique insights into the possibility of overcoming sin through unconditional love.

Kierkegaard's writings and this remarkable film are explorations of the ways in which, as embodied, familial, and sexual beings, we alienate and mutilate one another across generations. However, both the film and Kierkegaard's writings also point to the spiritual resources and insights that we must call on to break the chain of human anger and mutual destruction. Above all, they point to the understanding that we are not foes but members of one family; not hostile strangers, but brothers and sisters, fathers and mothers.

Notes

1. Released in 2011 by Sony Pictures Classics. Directed by Denis Villeneuve and starring Lubna Azabal and Mélissa Désormeaux-Poulin, with supporting roles by Maxim Gaudette and Rémy Girard.

2. Wajdi Mouawad, *Incendies: Le Sang des Promesses* (Quebec: Babel Leméac, 2009). For a discussion of some of the differences in the film version of *Incendies*, see Mary Jean Green, "Denis Villeneuve's *Incendies*: From Word to Film," *Quebec Studies* 54 (Fall 2012): 103–10.

3. The term Kierkegaard uses is *Arvesynd*, which is best translated as "hereditary sin."

4. For a discussion of the role that historical context and "distorted social structures," what he calls "objectified anxiety," play in enabling each individual's free choice of sinful deeds, see Gregory R. Beaubout, "Does Anxiety Explain Hereditary Sin?," *Faith and Philosophy* 11, no. 1 (1994): 117–24.

5. Vanessa Rumble, "The Oracle's Ambiguity: Freedom and Original Sin in Kierkegaard's *The Concept of Anxiety*," *Soundings* 75, no. 4 (1992): 605–25, quote at 606.

6. Ibid., 621.

7. See George Pattison, "The Magic of Theater: Drama and Existence in Kierkegaard's *Repetition* and Hesse's *Steppenwolf*," in *International Kierkegaard Commentary: "Fear and Trembling" and "Repetition,"* ed. Robert L. Perkins (Macon, Ga.: Mercer University Press, 1993), 359–77. (On the important bearing of the theater on Kierkegaard's writings, see also the essays by George Pattison and Martijn Boven in the present volume.—Ed.)

8. The importance of the notary in the film version of *Incendies* is signaled by Green in her "Denis Villeneuve's *Incendies*," 107–9.

9. The parallel to Sophocles's play is noted by Lisa Kennedy, "Movie Review: Daughter Uncovers Her Immigrant Mother's Complicated Past in 'Incendies,'" *Denver Post*, May 12, 2011, http://www.denverpost.com/movies /ci_18050704#ixzz2FtkJ74HX.

10. Margaret Ghosn, "Saints in the Maronite Tradition," Our Lady of Lebanon Maronite Catholic Parish, http://www.olol.org.au/cypc/17-about-us /tradition/29-saints-in-the-maronite-tradition.

11. I am indebted to my student Benjamin H. Jenkins for his keen observation of this detail.

Part IV

✦

Comparisons

The Moravian Origins of Kierkegaard's and Blake's Socratic Literature

James Rovira

Alastair Hannay asserts in his introduction to *Kierkegaard and Philosophy*, "Not everyone looks for philosophy in Kierkegaard, let alone arguments. And if they do look, especially if they are philosophers like me trained in the Anglo-American analytic tradition, they will be hard put to find either."[1] Kierkegaard's "psychological acuity" and "huge literary talent" are to blame in Hannay's account, as he wryly apologizes for discussing Kierkegaard in a philosophical context before explaining his own project. Hannay's difficulties originate of course in the demands of the analytic tradition, for Kierkegaard's literary qualities come from the Socratic nature of his philosophical task, which favors dialogic contemplation of significant questions over the systematic, discursive presentation of conceptual truths. More advanced forms of a Socratic methodology represent philosophical points of view in characters who embody them, which requires not only dialogue but character development as well. This essay attempts to illuminate the significance of the literary qualities of Kierkegaard's authorship by comparing him to the English poet and printmaker William Blake (1757–1827), who was similarly engaged in a Socratic project, and then demonstrates how their view of Socrates was particularly inflected by Moravianism through Zinzendorf. This comparison of both authors' approach to Socrates via their Moravian backgrounds accounts for many details of their deeply ambivalent relationships both with Plato's works and with their own state churches.

Kierkegaard's books (as opposed to his letters or journals and papers) are typically divided into two groups: works that he signed with his own name, such as *Concept of Irony* and *Works of Love*, and works attributed to pseudonyms, such as *Either/Or*, *Concept of Anxiety*, *Philosophical Fragments*, *Concluding Unscientific Postscript*, *The Sickness unto Death*, *Repetition*, and *Fear and Trembling*. These pseudonymous works are conceptually sophisticated and often linguistically dense prose considerations of philosophical subjects, so it may seem odd to refer to them as "literature" rather than "philosophy." However, Kierkegaard himself very often referred to these works as forming his "poetic" authorship, primarily because he does not identify himself as their author. Employing an older definition of "poetic" that is closer in meaning to the word "fictional" today, he presents himself instead as having created fictional characters representing different points of view, and these fictional characters are the authors of these works. And since later works draw from, critique, and develop ideas in earlier works, all of them together form an extensive Socratic dialogue in which different characters are speaking to one another, but only one of them is Kierkegaard. It is in this sense that Kierkegaard's pseudonymous authorship might be thought of as "literature" comparable to the poetry and mythology of Blake, a point I will develop in more detail.

In addition to sharing literary form, the two authors shared literary influence. Any elaboration of Blake's and Kierkegaard's shared intellectual history could emphasize Kierkegaard's engagement with European Romanticism in general and English Romanticism particularly, which may well have included Blake. Blake could not have been familiar with Kierkegaard, who had only turned fourteen the year of Blake's death, but Crabb Robinson's brief essay about Blake, accompanied by a selection of Blake's poetry, had been available to German audiences since 1811. Unfortunately, there is no indication in Kierkegaard's writings that he was familiar with Blake's works. He seems not to have encountered Robinson's translation during his time in Germany, or if he did, it did not make enough of an impression for him to comment on it. Kierkegaard had read Shakespeare, Byron, Shelley, and Edward Young in German translations, the last being particularly significant because Blake illustrated an edition of Young's *Night Thoughts*, so Kierkegaard did find British literature appealing and fertile. The figure of Socrates and the writings of Plato are, however, much more important to both Blake and Kierkegaard than were any of Blake's Romantic contemporaries or literary predecessors.

Blake and Kierkegaard are mutually illuminating figures not only because they similarly appropriated Socratic thought but also because their works respond to very similar, and mutually influential, cultural milieux.[2] Because both were raised by Moravian parents, it is likely that their views of the figure of Socrates are partially if not profoundly influenced by the founder of the modern configuration of the Moravian Church, Nikolaus Ludwig von Zinzendorf (1700–1760),[3] who fashioned himself a Socratic figure in a series of early pamphlets. So after situating Zinzendorf within the history of Moravian religion, I will describe the conception of the figure of Socrates that emerges from his pamphlets and extend this history to the connections that both Blake's and Kierkegaard's families had to the Moravian Church. However, our understanding of each author's approach to Socrates must be nuanced by the observation that their religious backgrounds also resulted in some ambivalence about the figure of Socrates, an ambivalence that I will later define as a form of Kierkegaardian anxiety.

Understanding each author's Moravian background, therefore, is necessary to understanding the religious component of each author's thought as well as the profile of Socrates in their thinking.

Kierkegaard, Blake, and the Moravian Church

The Moravian Church, in brief, traditionally divides its history into three eras: the "'Ancient Church,' from the year 1457 to 1656 . . . that of the 'Hidden Seed' . . . from the year 1656 to 1722 . . . [and] the 'Renewed Church' from the year 1722 to the present."[4] J. Taylor Hamilton, however, in his account of Moravian Church history for the introduction to third edition of *The Moravian Manual*, begins in 863 C.E. with Prince Ratislaw's request of Emperor Michael to send for Cyril and Methodius of Constantinople to preach the Gospel in Moravia. In 871 Boriwoj, the Prince of Bohemia, and his wife, Ludmilla, visited the Moravian court and converted to Christianity as well. Cyril and Methodius spent some time preaching around Moravia and Bohemia, developing local rituals and, most important, translating the Bible into Slavonic. This early missionary work established regionally specific forms of Christianity that were significant predecessors to the Protestant Reformation and resistant to Roman Catholic impositions of uniformity even though the area became officially Roman Catholic in 1080. Jan Hus (1369–1415) originated in southern Bohemia; his religious consciousness was formed in part by this social and religious milieu.

However, divisions among these local Christianities soon forced the Brethren to practice their faith secretly, alongside and within state-recognized churches. The followers of Hus divided into two groups: the Calixtines, who eventually won legal recognition after their acceptance of the Council of Basel in 1431, and the Taborites, who rejected the Council of Basel. The Calixtines came to constitute the national church of Bohemia. In 1457, reform-minded followers of Hus from both groups composed a formal declaration of principles, establishing an association called the Unitas Fratrum, or Unity of the Brethren, often shortened to "the Brethren."[5] They did not seek at that time to establish a separate church but rather to "form a society within the National Church,"[6] one dedicated to reform and to an emphasis on Scripture as the principal guide for faith and practice over twenty years before the birth of Martin Luther. As early as 1461, however, persecutions against the Brethren began, but they managed to thrive until the Smalcaldic wars (1546–47), when persecution became more intensely targeted against those who were neither Roman Catholic nor Calixtine. The rise of Counter-Reformation activity in this area specifically targeted evangelical groups, so that by 1627 "the evangelical party in Moravia and Bohemia ceased to exist."[7]

The Brethren found another opportunity to surface publicly with the rise of Philipp Jakob Spener in Germany, who as the author of *Pia Desideria* (1675) is often identified as the father of the Pietist movement. This movement was not initially separatist but rather viewed its members as "little churches within the church,"[8] specifically the Evangelical Church of Germany. Spener emphasized an orientation against intellectualism in religious belief and practice, criticism of the state church, and sincere faith defined by an inwardness that is manifested in action and decision. One of Spener's disciples was the Baroness von Gersdorf, who married Count von Zinzendorf, giving birth to Nikolaus Ludwig in May 1700. Nikolaus Ludwig became the Zinzendorf who, working with like-minded clergyman, resuscitated the Brethren when he agreed to donate part of his estate in Berthelsdorf to a settlement of Brethren. These Brethren had been gathered together by a working-class Moravian evangelist named Christian David when he converted from Roman Catholicism to pietist Christianity. That settlement grew into Herrnhut; within five years, over three hundred people occupied it. Internal divisions in the new community led Zinzendorf to retire from court, acquire documents and literature from a more active period of the Brethren's history, and then settle disputes by meeting with community leaders and drawing up statutes. By the age of twenty-seven, Zinzendorf was the figurehead and leader of the revived Unitas Fratrum.

George Forell calls Zinzendorf the "most influential German theologian between Luther and Schleiermacher."[9] Similar in stature to John and Charles Wesley in England or Grundtvig in Denmark, Zinzendorf helped revive and eventually lead the movement that was continuous with a nine-hundred-year tradition of Christianity at the borderlands of traditional structures, sometimes practicing freely, sometimes working within existing structures, and sometimes suppressed by them, but never comfortable and often adopting a stance of principled critique and reform from within. Zinzendorf's followers in both England and Denmark, like those of the Wesleys in England (who helped establish the first Moravian mission in England), were encouraged to practice their religion both as members of the Unitas Fratrum and as members of state-recognized congregations.

Joakim Garff explains that Kierkegaard's family had been associated with a congregation of Brethren at Stormgade in Copenhagen that was established in 1739, following Zinzendorf's Herrnhut model.[10] Michael Pedersen Kierkegaard, Kierkegaard's father, had a leading role in rebuilding the meeting hall to accommodate the congregation's growth in the early nineteenth century. The Moravian community in Denmark lived the same history there that it did elsewhere, existing outside the state church and occasionally suffering persecution. However, Kierkegaard's family, again consistent with Moravian patterns, participated simultaneously in Moravian and state-recognized Danish Lutheran religious services. Bruce Kirmmse explains that Michael Pedersen, "while retaining his rural pietist connection to the Herrnhut Congregation of Brothers," also "made Jacob Peter Mynster his pastor."[11] Mynster eventually rose to the position of Bishop and became the leading figure for the socially mobile Danish Lutheran rationalism of the day. Kirmmse observes that by "attending the Herrnhut congregation for evening prayer during the week and Mynster's Church of Our Lady on Sunday mornings, Michael Pedersen expressed the tension between independent peasant religiousness and respectable Copenhagen piety."[12]

Kirmmse elsewhere describes this tension as "a tension in the religious life—and certainly in the social self-understanding as well—of the Kierkegaard family, a tension between rural and urban religion, between peasant pietism and Golden Age oratory."[13] Johannes Climacus, the pseudonymous author of Kierkegaard's *Concluding Unscientific Postscript*, reflects this division as he considers his audience: "What is developed here by no means pertains to the simple folk, whom the god will preserve in their lovable simplicity (although they sense the pressure of life another way), the simplicity that feels no great need for any other kind of understanding, or, insofar as it is felt, humbly becomes a sigh over the misery of this life, while this sigh humbly finds comfort in the thought that life's happiness does not consist in being a person of knowledge" (*SKS* 7:158n1 / *CUP* 1:170n). Climacus (and most likely Kierkegaard) did not consider the reflective complexity of his work relevant to Denmark's rural population; instead, he leveled his critique at urban Copenhageners who imbibed Danish Hegelianism from pulpits and periodicals and who were therefore alienated from their roots of rural simplicity. But Climacus's description of his audience is rife with tensions. At the same time that a simple faith is being idealized, it is treated condescendingly (as a "lovable simplicity"). Furthermore, this dichotomy between urban and rural subjectivity is not the whole issue. Kierkegaard extends A. G. Rudelbach's contention that the state church contributed to the rise of the modern proletariat in a moral direction: "What is unchristian and ungodly is to base the state on a substratum of people whom one totally ignores, denying all kinship with them—even if on Sundays there are moving sermons about loving 'the neighbor' " (*SKS* 22:217–18, NB12:124 / *KJN* 6:124). It is not coincidental that Kierkegaard used the language of kinship in this passage, which was written in the year of Denmark's transition to a constitutional monarchy, as these divisions existed within the home of his birth.

Blake's Moravian background follows many of the same patterns. Keri Davies and Marsha Keith Schuchard have succinctly summarized previous assumptions about Blake's religious background and the history of and evidence for the actual Moravian background of Blake's family.[14] Both Schuchard and Davies took Nancy Bogan's 1968 suggestion that "Blake and his family were Anglicans and at the same time maintained a connection with the Moravian Church"[15] seriously enough to seek out archival support for this claim, which they found. Schuchard and Davies report that the Moravian Church in England in the late eighteenth and early nineteenth century occupied an unusual position, being "recognized by an Act of Parliament as an episcopal church and therefore a sister of the church of England" but still "required to have their places of worship licensed as Dissenting chapels," so that they both "*were* and then again *were not* Dissenters."[16]

The Moravian Church in England, furthermore, encouraged its members to maintain their Anglican membership and identity while still participating in Moravian services, so that "one could be an Anglican and a Moravian at the same time—and it turns out that a majority of the English Brethren were and remained loyal members of the Church of England."[17] Schuchard's and Davies's archival work reveals that Blake's mother and her first husband were members of the same Fetter Lane church in London that Zinzendorf visited on more than one occasion, their petition to join falling between Zinzendorf's visits of the late 1830s and early 1850s. Schuchard later asserts that their attendance extended through the 1850s, during at least one of Zinzendorf's visits. She explains in a follow-up to her 2004 article that while Blake's mother was married to her first husband, Thomas Armitage, it is very likely she knew John and James Blake, who were William Blake's uncle and his father, respectively, as James eventually became Catherine's second husband. Because they also attended Fetter Lane at the same time, both sides of William Blake's family had connections with the Moravian Church in London and were directly influenced by Zinzendorf.[18]

It is not difficult to imagine the place that the figure of Socrates might take among Brethren familiar with him, for both critiqued the social structures within which they lived, sometimes gathering a following and sometimes suffering persecution. Zinzendorf's own appropriation of the figure of Socrates took place in a series of biweekly pamphlets first published under the name "The Socrates of Dresden" and then gathered into book form, more ambitiously, under the title *The German Socrates*.[19] Over thirty of these pamphlets were originally distributed in 1725–26, around the time that Zinzendorf first welcomed the earliest community of the Brethren onto his estate. Zinzendorf envisions a Socratic figure engaged in socially provocative polemic designed to lead his readers and listeners to self-examination. According to August Gottlieb Spangenberg's biography of Zinzendorf, "the Count's object in the publication of this periodical work was (to use his own words) 'to bring, like Socrates, his fellow-citizens to reflect upon themselves, and by his example to show them the way to the attainment of real and lasting contentment.' "[20] Harold Steffe asserts that both "authors [Kierkegaard and Zinzendorf] harness Socrates to inquire into whether and how Christianity and philosophy can be united, and into the meaning of passion for the understanding,"[21] and in this union we should observe an emphasis on existential self-reflection. Both Zinzendorf and Kierkegaard also share an early publication history in which they concealed their authorship, Zinzendorf initially leaving his pamphlets unsigned just as Kierkegaard published his most important early philosophical works pseudonymously.

While Spangenberg claims that Zinzendorf's pamphlets avoid satire and irony—that Zinzendorf merely spoke "freely"—they still provoked a rather hostile response. By the third issue, according to Spangenberg, "Some were enraged at it, and caused the confiscation of the third Number; the reason assigned for which was, that the author's name was not given; until the Count at length avowed himself as the author. He continued this publication till the thirty-fourth Number."[22] After the last issue, Zinzendorf collected the pamphlets and republished them in book form. Kierkegaard felt similarly compelled to step forward and identify himself as the author of his pseudonymous philosophical works prior to and including *Concluding Unscientific Postscript* in a signed but unpaginated appendix attached to that book, which again warrants a comparison to Zinzendorf's unpaginated introduction to *The German Socrates.*

However, the most important parallels to Kierkegaard's thought relate to the pseudonymous authorship itself, which comprises a Socratic dialogue among different characters around the topics of faith and inwardness. Similarly, Blake's mythological works, especially the later ones, are not so much narrative as dialogue among mythological characters representative of different points of view. Both writers' commitment to dialogue rather than to a systematic presentation of conceptual truths, as we might find in analytic philosophy, commits them likewise to specific literary forms emphasizing either character development or, at least, characters engaging one another in some type of conflict. Both authors hope to serve maieutic purposes in their works, believing that the development of their fictional or mythological characters will be paralleled in their readers, bringing to birth a new "soul" in their readers, a psychology that de-emphasizes environmental and social influence in favor of what Kierkegaard's Vigilius Haufniensis calls in *The Concept of Anxiety* an "acquired originality."

Furthermore, Christopher Barnett describes Zinzendorf's pamphlets as seeking "to interrogate a new generation of philosophers, whose elevation of reason threatened to reduce Christianity to a series of rational principles."[23] This task resonates with both Blake's and Kierkegaard's critique of the effects of rationalism upon Christianity. Thus, the literary form of each author's work is integral to his philosophical task and inherent to its nature. Both authors sought to combat intellectual abstractions with personalities embodied in literary dialogues, and perhaps most of all to frustrate reason itself with the sheer complexity of their projects, a goal consistent with Spener's marginalization of intellect.[24]

"Socrates," however, is not necessarily a single entity for either of these authors. Kierkegaard came to the Socratic tradition and its variants through his own theological study and his reading in the German Romantics, in German philosophy, and in a number of different traditions from the early medieval period to his own day, while Blake read a number of figures who were themselves influenced by Plato's writings. Eric Ziolkowski's *The Literary Kierkegaard* begins his review of Kierkegaard and literature with the figure of Socrates, reminding his readers that Kierkegaard's dissertation, *The Concept of Irony*, carefully and complexly negotiates the conflicting portraits of Socrates presented by Aristophanes, Plato, and Xenophon. The presence of options means that the figure of Socrates invoked or suggested by Blake's and Kierkegaard's works is a matter of conscious decision: they not only chose to engage in a Socratic task, but they also needed to choose which

Socrates to emulate. The nature of this choice will be made apparent in the ensuing, brief review of the position that Socrates and Plato's writings have in Blake's and Kierkegaard's respective corpuses.

Kierkegaard, Blake, and Socrates

Any review of how each author perceived his Socratic task perhaps best begins with Plato's Seventh Letter, where he describes feeling compelled to revisit Sicily to instruct its ruler, Dionysius, in philosophy.[25] Dionysius's character, such as it was, would not take no for an answer to his requests that Plato return to Sicily. Plato describes Dionysius as a vain character who "made it absolutely a point of honor that no one should ever suppose that I had a poor opinion of his natural gifts" (Letter 7, 338e–339a, *CDP* 1586). Plato further questions the motives behind Dionysius's desire for instruction in philosophy and comports himself accordingly, hoping to see whether Dionysius truly loved philosophy or was instead "stuffed with secondhand opinions," having "only a superficial tinge of doctrine" (340b, *CDP* 1588).

Plato's account of Dionysius is hardly flattering, especially as he demeans Dionysius for composing a philosophical "handbook of his own" (341b, *CDP* 1588) following Plato's first visit. In Plato's opinion, those who systematically organize the philosophy of others into written handbooks have "no real acquaintance with the subject [of philosophy]" (341c, *CDP* 1589) because the insights provided by philosophy cannot be communicated directly through language. Only after "a long period of attendance on the subject" does acquaintance with the insights of philosophy ignite "like a blaze kindled by a leaping spark [which] is generated in the soul and at once becomes self-sustaining" (341d, *CDP* 1589). This process is necessary, Plato argues, because of the fundamental difference between any reality and the words or images used to describe it. Direct instruction presents words and images to the learner but can never present the reality itself. At best, instruction can only be the occasion through which individuals perceive the truth for themselves after a long period of their own contemplation and reflection. Plato therefore idealizes a dialectical and dialogic philosophical method rather than a systematic and expository one. The dialogue communicates philosophical truth indirectly by articulating several points of view without being exclusively devoted to any single one, prompting reflection and engagement on the part of the listener.

But perhaps the most significant aspect of Plato's Seventh Letter is that he defines the personality of Dionysius by his engagement with a text: those who seek to produce systematic expositions are vain and shallow, while those who inwardly contemplate are truly philosophical. Plato's Seventh Letter develops ideas considered by Socrates in the *Phaedo*, in which he defines the goal of philosophy as separation of the soul from the body, drawing a sharp distinction between those who "regard the body with the greatest indifference and spend their lives in philosophy" (68c, *CDP* 51) and those incapable of philosophy, whose souls are "permeated by the corporeal, which fellowship and intercourse with the body will have ingrained in its very nature through constant association and long practice" (81c, *CDP* 64). Plato believes that Dionysius's vanity drives his misunderstanding of philosophy, as his thinking seems to proceed from a bodily incursion upon the soul rather than a philosophically attained freedom from the body. The bodily person in Plato's thought believes that truth lies in the text; the philosophical person finds truth within her soul. The text may prompt the philosopher's discovery of soul truth but cannot instruct the soul directly.

By the time of Origen (ca. 185–254), the ideas circulating in Plato's dialogues and letters had developed into an informal taxonomy of personality types intimately associated with hermeneutic strategies, a development Origen reflects in book 4 of *On First Principles* (ca. 215 C.E.): "One must therefore pourtray [*sic*] the meaning of the sacred writings in a threefold way upon one's own soul, so that the simple man may be edified by what we may call the flesh of the scripture, this name being given to the obvious interpretation; while the man who has made some progress may be edified by its soul, as it were; and the man who is perfect . . . may be edified by the spiritual law. . . . For just as man consists of body, soul and spirit, so in the same way does the scripture."[26] If human beings exist as body, soul, and spirit, so does Scripture, therefore an interpreter's hermeneutics reflect the state of his or her soul in its preference for one approach to a text rather than another. Socrates makes a similar but less differentiated judgment in the *Phaedrus*, advising Phaedrus to have a "discernment of the nature of the soul, discover the type of speech appropriate to each nature, and order and arrange your discourse accordingly, addressing a variegated soul in a variegated style that ranges over the whole gamut of tones, and a simple soul in a simple style" (277c, *CDP* 523).

One might see this progression in Plato's allegory of the cave in a movement from a bodily existence whose knowledge is compared to the sight of shadows on a wall, to a soulish existence whose light is represented by a humanly generated fire, and finally to a spiritual existence whose light is represented by the sun (*Republic* 7.514a–520e, *CDP* 747–52). And one might see the same progression in the *Symposium* in Diotima's description of the different ways men seek immortality—through the body (procreation), through the soul (social institutions and one's place in community), and through the spirit (the self alone before God; 206e–212a, *CDP* 558–63). More important, the body, soul, and spirit relationship in this tradition does not imply a fixed self but rather makes possible different phenomenologies, some oriented toward the body, some toward soul, and some toward spirit. These phenomenologies give rise to potentially conflicting hermeneutics that in Origen become distinct markers of one's spiritual development. Origen associates literal or obvious interpretations with the body and spiritual interpretations with spirit, placing between them a soulish interpretation.[27]

Kierkegaard appropriated this model, with all of its assumptions, start-ing with the two parts of *Either/Or* and its two basic personality types, the Socratic-ethical and the Romantic-aesthetic. As he proceeded through his career, he published his best-known philosophical works under pseudonyms representing a variety of personality types and points of view, each author quoting, engaging, and exceeding the next. Kierkegaard's model of existential development begins when the author of *Either/Or I*, an aesthetic personal-ity identified only as "A" within the text, suggests a developmental pattern within aesthetic personalities in an essay titled "The Immediate Erotic Stages." Clearly influenced by Hegelian and other German Idealist models, this essay divides the aesthetic sphere of existence into "immediate" and "reflective" poles, developing the characteristics of each pole in some detail. "A's" reader, the ethical personality "B," or Judge William, "reads" "A's" work and, in true Hegelian fashion, "goes beyond" him. *Either/Or II* is his response, in which he argues that there is something more than the aesthetic: the ethical. The ethical contains the aesthetic but is higher than it, as the judge argues for the aesthetic validity of an ethical relationship: marriage. Following a pattern derived from Hegel's *Science of Logic* (*Wissenschaft der Logik*, 1812–16), the judge sees the ethical as a synthesis comprising the "negation of the first immediate," which in this case is the aesthetic.

Sometime the following year, Vigilius Haufniensis "read" *Either/Or I* and *II*, like many other Copenhagen intellectuals, and felt the need to explain how a transition from the innocence of the aesthetic sphere to the guilt con-sciousness of the ethical sphere is possible, casting the question in terms of a theological reflection upon the sinlessness of Adam and Eve and their subse-quent fall, suggesting a psychological answer for this dilemma. He "writes" *The Concept of Anxiety* in response and "publishes" it in 1844. Kierkegaard's Johannes Climacus, encompassing the insights of "A," "B," and Haufniensis in his reconsideration of his own previous (pseudonymous) work, *Philo-sophical Fragments*, completes the work they began in his own *Concluding Unscientific Postscript* by adding a religious sphere, which he divides into religiousness A and B. In addition to this pseudonymous activity, Kierke-gaard published other works bearing his signature at the same time, so that his major philosophical works and his signed religious works comprise a vast dialogue among his pseudonymous authors in which he himself is engaged. This dialogue also illustrates his debt to Hegel, for each author synthesizes the insights of the previous ones into a new thesis.

Kierkegaard's use of a Hegelian model, combined with his attention to classical thought, leads his major philosophical works to present a series of developmental stages consisting of sequential differentiations of the self from its natural environment (or bodily existence), its social environment ("the crowd," or ethical existence), and then facets of its mental environment produced by the first two. Kierkegaard calls these stages the aesthetic, the ethical (like Schiller), and the religious. Religiousness A is the subjectivity of allegory, seeing through nature to the infinite beyond it, while religiousness B is an anagogical subjectivity, or a self that stands alone before the Divine. These are existential stances, however, not simple classifications of religious thought or hermeneutic strategies: it is possible to identify oneself as a Christian in belief and upbringing but still be an aesthetic, ethical, or religiousness A personality.

The indebtedness of Blake to the Socratic-medieval tradition most clearly surfaces in his anagogical study of innocence and experience as states of the human soul.[28] Blake's notion of innocence corresponds to Kierkegaard's aesthetic stage, as his innocent characters tend to have bodily and environmentally determined subjectivities, such as Thel. Blake's experience corresponds to Kierkegaard's ethical stage, as experienced characters have developed a social consciousness and an ethical ideal and have subsequently become bitter, as is the case with Blake's chimney sweep of *The Songs of Experience*. Blake's visionary subjectivity compares well to features of Kierkegaard's religiousness A and B, though primarily A: when Blake sees the world in a grain of sand, he reveals a religiousness A subjectivity. To illustrate better how important the classical tradition was to Blake's thought, I will examine the complex profile Plato's works have in Blake's authorship through his direct statements about them, recalling also that in Origen hermeneutic strategies were closely linked to spiritual maturation and personality development.

At times, Blake seems to validate Platonic idealism with few qualifications, as in "A Vision of the Last Judgment," which presents an explicit condemnation of nature as well as Blake's strongest affirmation of idealism: "This World <of Imagination> is Infinite & Eternal whereas the world of Generation or Vegetation is Finite & [*for a small moment*] Temporal There Exist in that Eternal World the Permanent Realities of Every Thing which we see reflected in this Vegetable Glass of Nature."[29] It is very easy to read a Platonic idealism into these words: everything has a dual existence, one in the world of imaginative vision and the other in the world of generation in which all living things experience birth, growth, death, and decay. The "Eternal Image & Individuality" of a living thing never dies while its physical form does,[30] requiring that imagination or vision serve as the capacities by which the artist sees everything in its eternal form. In addition to his affinities with idealist thought, Blake seems to validate Plato's use of dialogue in his letter to the Rev. John Trusler of August 23, 1799, saying, "The wisest of the Ancients considered what is not too Explicit as the fittest for Instruction because it rouzes the faculties to act. I name Moses Solomon Esop Homer Plato."[31] Like Plato, Blake is not so much concerned with a simple presentation of the truth as he is with rousing his readers to apprehend the truth for themselves after doing the work of reflection.

Blake's mythology often takes the form of a series of narrative dialogues among subjectivities representative of components of human personality, so it has a great deal in common with both Plato's method as explained in the Seventh Letter and Kierkegaard's indirect communication, described above. *The Book of Thel, The Marriage of Heaven and Hell, Visions of the Daughters of Albion, The Four Zoas, Milton a Poem,* and *Jerusalem* could be described as primarily dialogic works in that a significant proportion of their content depicts characters engaged in self-defining dialogue with one another. *America a Prophecy* and *Europe a Prophecy* might be viewed as mixed narrative and dialogic works, while *The [First] Book of Urizen, The Song of Los, The Book of Los,* and other prophecies might be considered primarily narrative mythologies. Even in these cases, however, a single speaker often ejaculates a cry of suffering or domination. *The Songs of Innocence and of Experience* at times take on a dialogic nature, "The Tyger" and possibly "The Fly" responding to "The Lamb," "The Blossom" possibly being answered by "The Sick Rose," in addition to the presence of both innocence and experience versions of the poems "Holy Thursday" and "The Chimney Sweeper."

As S. Foster Damon explains, Blake organizes his mythology around a fourfold view of the human person: "Blake identified [the four Zoas] with the four fundamental aspects of man: his body (Tharmas—west); his reason (Urizen—south); his emotions (Luvah—east); and his imagination (Urthona—north)."[32] Blake's divisions represent body, soul, and spirit, emphasizing soul as emotion (on the east-west axis with body) and spirit as reason and imagination (occupying the north-south axis), mirroring the fourfold hermeneutic of the medieval period. In his letter of July 6, 1803, to Thomas Butts, Blake seems to identify his allegorizing with Plato's, saying (probably) of *Jerusalem* that he considers "it as the Grandest Poem that This World Contains. Allegory addressed to the Intellectual powers while it is altogether hidden from the Corporeal Understanding is My Definition of the Most Sublime Poetry. it [*sic*] is also somewhat in the same manner defind by Plato."[33] Blake qualifies his identification with allegory in Plato with the words "somewhat in the same manner," which signals ambivalence toward Plato. Blake feels that his allegory shares some features in common with Plato's, but he does not want to identify the mode of his work with Plato's either.

Blake, like Kierkegaard, emphasizes that Platonic knowledge is recollection and considers this knowledge inferior to the Christian or prophetic mode, so that both he and Kierkegaard are simultaneously attracted to but disagree with Plato. For example, in "A Vision of the Last Judgment," Blake explicitly critiques Platonic allegory, associating the "Hebrew Bible & the Gospel of Jesus" with "Eternal Vision or Imagination of All that Exists," while associating Greek literature with an inferior "Fable or Allegory" that is really the product of memory.[34] Plato is particularly and repeatedly condemned for his rejection of poets and prophets and his support of the "Moral Virtues."[35] Blake juxtaposes Platonic idealism against apocalyptic convention in the vein of Ezekiel and Revelation, clearly and consistently associating himself with the latter in "A Vision of the Last Judgment" and elsewhere.

A pattern therefore emerges of a mixed or ambivalent vision of Socrates in both Blake and Kierkegaard. Blake's view of Socrates and Plato's works see them both as sublime allegory and as inferior to Christian revelation at the same time. Barnett similarly describes Kierkegaard's view of Socrates, specifically as it was influenced by Johann Georg Hamann (who was in turn influenced by Zinzendorf): "As 'the greatest humorist in the world,' Hamann brings Socratic irony to the point where it touches, but does not cross into, Christianity. Thus his efforts are commendable, even essential, but not ultimate."[36] The very works in which Kierkegaard is most engaged in his philosophic project constitute his poetic, but not Christian, authorship. This ambivalence toward Socrates closely follows the patterns of Kierkegaardian anxiety.

Conclusion: Anxiety and Literary Form

I should begin this section with further consideration of Plato's own ambivalence about literature, including his famous expulsion of poets from his ideal republic, especially Homer. Mirroring the concern of scholars over the relationship of Kierkegaard to his pseudonymous writings, one recurring question in scholarship on Plato concerns the relationship between Plato and his works. The literary form of Plato's dialogues complicates this question for contemporary scholarship in philosophy because the dialogues distribute different conceptual possibilities among different characters and, especially in the early dialogues, often leave questions unresolved. This structure makes it difficult to identify any given concept in Plato's dialogues with Plato's own position. Kierkegaard's reading of Plato and of the figure of Socrates in *The Concept of Irony* and Vigilius Haufniensis's commentary in *The Concept of Anxiety*, for example, assume that while the dialogues present a range of conceptual options they also present, intentionally or not, a range of phenomenologies associated with those conceptual structures, so that a dialogue not only articulates ideas but creates the kinds of character who would assert them. Philosophy in literary form, such as Plato's and Kierkegaard's, works out individual existential and phenomenological struggles, modeling these struggles for its readers, who, as they read along, engage in these struggles themselves. Debates about the specific philosophical concepts that are the presumed reasons for the dialogue are the stage upon which existential struggle occurs.

Richard Kraut describes Plato's relationship to his own works in his introduction to the *Cambridge Companion to Plato* in terms of two possibilities: first, Plato wanted to obscure what he believed in order to get readers to think for themselves; second, he used the dialogues to express his own beliefs, which are voiced by Socrates or other interlocutors.[37] This question can serve as a starting point for a historicized reading of Plato, as Kraut's arguments fail to consider a third possibility developed within the Seventh Letter and implied by the dialogues themselves. Readers of Plato who assume that the point of a dialogue is to work out a conceptual problem will ignore that in Plato's works acquiring truth is an activity of the soul, not just of the mind. While this claim may seem like another way of stating Kraut's first possibility, for Plato the word "soul" was not merely a metaphor, so that to understand his relationship to his works and to his own philosophy we need to take seriously his developmental model, which is based upon his tripartite view of the self, described above.

Members of Plato's own family were part of the oligarchy that briefly suspended Athenian democracy in 404 B.C.E. at the end of the Peloponnesian Wars. Reliance on democratic governance during times of war can be frightening. When the Athenian city-state under a democracy expressed a political will or committed to a course of action, it subjected each decision, including every court case, to the governing body or to a section of it that had to be convinced of the best decision in any given situation. Oratory skills therefore grew in importance under Athenian democracy, and with them the importance of language generally. In the case of Socrates, the effectiveness of oratory was literally a matter of life and death. Within this context, how might Plato be positioned in relation to his works? His *Republic*, a later dialogue that many scholars believe employs Socrates as a mouthpiece for Plato's ideas, advocates for an oligarchy in which leaders, who are called "guardians," are divested of self-interest in their governing. They are not allowed to own land, possess wealth, or even have children or families of their own, as children among the ruling class are communally raised with no clear identification of paternity. Leaders who possess great wealth and a lineage, in Socrates's opinion, resemble statues with purple eyes: purple may well be the most beautiful color, but as an eye color it is grotesque (*Republic* 4). Plato's Socrates has rejected democracy but has divested his oligarchy of self-interest, so that these new rulers may be philosopher-kings guided by reason in their pursuit of the interests of the state. Socrates's goal for his ideal republic is the attainment of the most beautiful form of the state, one in which the whole should be made harmonious and beautiful rather than just a part, so that the state is one rather than divided into the rich and the poor.

It is not difficult to read these passages in *Republic* against the background of Plato's life, however speculative that activity may be. He could be read as defending the principle of oligarchy while establishing the conditions necessary for it to work. But the most important emphasis of *Republic* is not the efficacy or implementation of such a government; it is the educational emphasis of Socrates's ideal republic and the desired outcomes of that educational emphasis: "Neither could men who are uneducated and inexperienced in truth ever adequately preside over a state" (*Republic* 7.519b–c, *CDP* 751). This passage follows the allegory of the cave, which is the primary educational allegory in the Platonic corpus and which describes education in terms of different existential orientations, each one creating a different kind of soul. In this light, the Socratic irony of Plato's early dialogues, as well as the pronouncement about Socrates made by the oracle at Delphi, may be implicit critiques of democratic governance and of oratory only to be made explicit by the later dialogues: if Socrates alone is wise because he alone is aware of his ignorance, how can we trust the judgment of a democratic body? Plato's concern for education, therefore, is implicated in his tripartite view of the self, and the two of them together are bound up in his conception of the ideal republic, all of which converge on his desire to ban poets from his ideal republic. All of these ideas seem to be heightened in importance because of the succession of two major wars and the stresses upon Athenian democracy caused by these wars.

But the place of literature itself in Athens must also be considered. To be educated during Plato's lifetime was to be taught to read Homer, who was used as a source text for a variety of subjects, such as knowledge of the gods, of government, of war, and of history. Socrates's complaints about Homer and the poets in *Republic* focus primarily on the bad behavior of Homer's gods and heroes and on their management of emotions, but to Socrates the worst element of Homer's presentation of the gods is its emphasis on feeling over reason. Socrates's argument in *Republic* therefore criticizes the erotics of literature to replace them with rational instruction provided by philosophy, as Penelope Murray argues in *Plato on Poetry*.[38] The philosopher's progression toward death in *Phaedo* consists of an increasing separation from the body that has been carried out over the course of the philosopher's entire life, while *Crito* effectively rejects public opinion as a valid repository of truth in favor of one's own rational contemplation of the subject, so that between these two dialogues body and soul are rejected in favor of rational spirit as the basis of governance. The tripartite view of the soul, therefore, serves instrumental and political purposes in Plato's works. It identifies differing elements of the individual in order to establish a hierarchy extensible to the organization of a *polis*: body, then soul (which can be defined as societally conditioned thought and feeling), should be subject to spirit (divine reason). Only philosophy finally disciplines the body and teaches its adherents to live above society to be guided only by divine light, and it is by means of this progression that persons attain full individuality. For that reason, only a community of philosophers who have subjected themselves to continual symbolic deaths in the form of the loss of possessions and of family can be trusted to govern, and only an educational system that places philosophy above literature can develop a worthy oligarchy.

Ion establishes the fundamental existential oppositions guiding reading practices in Plato against this background. Socrates closely cross-examines Ion in order to determine if Ion's recitations proceed from skill, *technē*, or only from inspiration. The dialogue concludes that Ion does not know what he is doing, so he must be reciting Homer only under a kind of divine inspiration.

Albert Rijksbaron's *Plato, "Ion," or: On the "Iliad"* suggests that *Ion* was composed around the same time as *Republic*, that Plato did not anywhere express the possibility of a *technē* of poetry, and that he believed pursuing the origins of poetic inspiration was a waste of time.[39] The real opposition here, I would argue, is between the possibility of a *technē* opposed to the erotics of poetry distributed across appetitive and rational responses to literature. If neither Socrates nor Plato desired to establish a *technē* of poetry, Aristotle's *Poetics* filled that gap, suggesting uses for the erotics of literature that go beyond mere imitation into the management of emotions themselves: both aesthetically via catharsis and then, in book 2 of *Rhetoric*, instrumentally, as a tool for functioning effectively in a democracy.

Because Plato's literary form, the dialogue, exists in a kind of tension or anxiety in relationship to literature itself, it should not be surprising that this anxiety is reflected in those influenced by his thought. *Kierkegaardian anxiety involves a simultaneous attraction and repulsion to the same object* without establishing fixed and opposite poles on a clearly defined spectrum. In Vigilius Haufniensis's words, it is "*a sympathetic antipathy* and *an antipathetic sympathy*" (*SKS* 4:348 / *CA* 42, emphasis in original). Individuals experiencing Kierkegaardian anxiety face a simultaneous attraction to and repulsion from each element of the tension, feeling repulsion within their attraction and attraction within their repulsion, leaving them in a state of "psychological ambiguity" (*SKS* 4:348 / *CA* 42). In this case, the same Christian commitments that led each author to see himself as a type of Socrates standing in critique of a state church also caused him to distance himself from the figure of Socrates, who as a pre-Christian philosopher lacked visionary insight, in Blake's terms, or the apostolic authority of revelation, in Kierkegaard's.

Anxiety arises when no clear conception of how one's life could be different is possible—when the change involves a leap into a complete unknown—so that this unknown future state is only a "possibility of possibility." We should keep in mind that the context of Vigilius Haufniensis's discussion of anxiety and its relationship to freedom in *The Concept of Anxiety* is a consideration of the psychology of the fall from innocence to experience, Adam and Eve serving both as ideal paradigms of innocence, being the only two human beings in the world with no examples of moral transgression before them yet illustrating the pattern that we all must follow. Anxiety, therefore, is a particularly heightened reaction to our ignorance of the future and of the changes the future may bring. Kierkegaard compared this feeling to the vertigo experienced while standing on the edge of an abyss. This dizziness forces decision as those experiencing it feel compelled to cling to an immediately available concrete option, something known and understood, thereby provoking a self-defining choice.

This self-defining choice in Blake's and Kierkegaard's respective cases began with the decision to pursue a Socratically defined task and then to choose an image of Socrates as the outsider within, one communicated to them through their Moravian upbringing. Anxiety, in their cases, prompted them to grasp a concrete option in the guise of literary form. However, these choices were made against the backdrop of unknown possibility in the form of a new conception of the human brought to birth by the incursion of contemporary thought upon religious faith. In Blake's case, hostile contemporary thought took the form of the mechanical philosophers—Bacon, Newton, and Locke—while in Kierkegaard's case it took the form of Danish Hegelianism. So while contemporary philosophy became either speculative or mechanical, as did the human beings who followed it, Blake's and Kierkegaard's thought became humanly concrete.

Danish Hegelianism seems an unlikely phenomenological counterpart to the mechanical philosophy in England, as it has little directly in common with the empirical sciences. One scholar of Hegel asserts that Hegel's very value lies in his critique of the mechanical philosophers, explaining that he believes "Hegel's general criticism of philosophers such as Descartes, Leibniz or Locke to be powerful and insightful; this is one reason why we are Hegelians."[40] However, Blake's and Kierkegaard's critiques of the mechanical philosophers and the Hegelians, respectively, parallel one another by showing that each system provides seemingly transcendent constructs that remove the human being to a vantage point outside human existence. In their view, transcendent philosophies, whether empirical or speculative, attempt to circumvent anxiety by falsely positing the human observer as standing outside of existence as he or she views it in its entirety through the system.

So Kierkegaard's Climacus feels compelled to assert that "existence itself is a system—for God, but it cannot be a system for any existing [*existerende*] spirit" (*SKS* 7:114 / *CUP* 1:118). Similarly, Blake's mythological works react to the social and cultural contexts that he and Kierkegaard held in common by consistently assuming the monstrosity of the new human born from these interrelated tensions as well as the monstrosity and fallenness of the mythological creator of these constructs, Urizen. This assumption is in part Blake's critique of Enlightenment conceptions of the human. In response to these tensions, both Blake and Kierkegaard appropriated models of personality derived, originally, from Plato's writings in order to counteract the effects of the new philosophies upon their contemporaries' understanding of what it meant to be a human being. Since the human being was their subject, so was the human being their object, so that their deeply philosophical responses to contemporary philosophical currents had to be expressed through characters engaged in dialogue, or literary in nature.

The influences of Plato's works, the figure of Socrates, and Moravian religion upon both Blake and Kierkegaard are complex and perhaps overdetermined: each author was influenced directly by Plato as well as by other authors who were in turn influenced by Plato, just as each author was influenced by the Moravian movement along with a variety of other religious movements and perspectives, some of them contributing to or influenced by

Moravianism. However, their respective projects are simultaneously literary and philosophical, a philosophy presented in literary form. As literature, they involve dialogue among characters representative of human faculties and developmental stages. As philosophy, they participate in a philosophical tradition that emphasizes the growth of the soul through reflection leading to enlightenment. As religious authors, they were committed to the Moravian goal of reform, a call to a return to a primal Christianity that preexists and takes precedence over state-sponsored forms of Christianity, and one that specifically invokes the figure of Socrates as a critic and reformer, the outcast within our midst who speaks to us about ourselves, showing us the way both out of and back to ourselves. These intersecting tensions drew both authors to Socrates as a leading figure and repelled them from him at the same time, and their response to this anxiety was to grasp the concrete option of literary form itself. For that reason theirs is a literary philosophy and a philosophical literature. It examines how persons define themselves by their ideas rather than explaining persons by a system of ideas—while still confronting the humanly created artifact, whether literary or philosophical, in all of its danger and its allure.

Notes

1. Alastair Hannay, *Kierkegaard and Philosophy* (London: Routledge, 2003), 1.

2. See James Rovira, *Blake and Kierkegaard: Creation and Anxiety* (London: Continuum, 2010). I observe in that book's first chapter that Blake and Kierkegaard share much in common in terms of their social, political, and intellectual histories. Tensions between and among monarchy and democracy, science and religion, and nature and artifice took much the same shape in each author's respective countries, particularly during their most productive and creative periods. These competing sociocultural elements are fairly commonplace to anyone familiar with the period, but in my bringing together of Blake and Kierkegaard they serve the function of gridlines on a playing field, defining the space within which the action takes place. The action, in this case, is psychological, and the space provided represents a range of self-defining options that provoke anxiety by their mere presence. Chapter 2 then describes each figure's relationship to Plato, and chapter 3 their appropriation of his model of personality, extending those ideas into Blake's and Kierkegaard's similar critiques of generation in chapter 4. Blake's critique of generation leads directly into creation anxiety in the figure of Enion in *The Four Zoas*, which in chapter 5's analysis of *The [First] Book of Urizen* is grounded in the cultural tensions described in chapter 1 and explained as a manifestation of Kierkegaard's concept of the demonic as found in *The Concept of Anxiety*. The book does not directly link Blake's and Kierkegaard's social and historical contexts to their Platonism, which is the work performed by this essay.

3. Zinzendorf's full name has been variously rendered in English using Nicholas, Nicolas, Nicolaus, Nikolas, Ludwig, Louis, and Lewis. Many thanks to Eric Ziolkowski for his work tracking down the spelling in German sources, which

will be the preferred spelling used throughout this paper. The spellings of Zinzendorf's name in quoted and in bibliographic material will, however, stay true to source spelling.

4. J. Taylor Hamilton, *The Moravian Manual Containing an Account of the Moravian Church, or the "Unitas Fratrum,"* 3rd ed. (Bethlehem, Pa.: Times, 1901), 9.

5. Ibid.

6. Ibid., 8.

7. Ibid., 15.

8. Ibid., 21.

9. George Forell, ed. and trans., *Nine Public Lectures on Important Subjects in Religion Preached in Fetter Lane Chapel in London in the Year 1746* (Iowa City: University of Iowa Press, 1973), vii.

10. Joakim Garff, *Søren Kierkegaard: A Biography*, trans. Bruce Kirmmse (Princeton, N.J.: Princeton University Press, 2005), 11.

11. Bruce H. Kirmmse, "'Out with It!': The Modern Breakthrough, Kierkegaard and Denmark," in *The Cambridge Companion to Kierkegaard*, ed. Alastair Hannay and Gordon D. Marino (Cambridge, U.K.: Cambridge University Press, 1998), 23.

12. Ibid.

13. Bruce. H. Kirmmse, *Kierkegaard in Golden Age Denmark* (Bloomington: Indiana University Press, 1990), 260.

14. Keri Davies and Marsha Keith Schuchard, "Recovering the Lost Moravian Background of Blake's Family," *Blake: An Illustrated Quarterly* 38, no. 1 (2004): 36–43. Robert Rix's *William Blake and the Cultures of Radical Christianity* also provides a careful exploration of the influence of Blake's Moravian origins upon his later thought. His description of the difficulty in doing so is worth considering: "How much Moravianism did Blake's mother pass on to her son? To answer this question demands that we can distinguish between strict Moravianism, the fluid mix of other religious believers who met at Fetter Lane and the more intense manifestations of evangelical mainstreams" (11). Rix identifies parallels between Moravianism and Blake's work in an emphasis upon the "immediacy of religious experience" leading to "a millennial time of peace and brotherhood" (11). To these characteristics Rix adds Moravian appreciation for the arts, especially song, which was unique among Pietist movements. Earlier commentators observed parallels between Blake's poetry and Moravian hymns. See Robert Rix, *William Blake and the Cultures of Radical Christianity* (Aldershot, U.K.: Ashgate, 2007).

15. Davies and Schuchard, "Recovering the Lost Moravian Background," 38.

16. Ibid.

17. Ibid.

18. Marsha Keith Schuchard, *William Blake's Sexual Path to Spiritual Vision* (Rochester, Vt.: Inner Traditions, 2006), 28.

19. Abbreviated title for Nikolaus Ludwig (Graf von) Zinzendorf, *Der Teutsche Socrates, Das ist: Auffrichtige Anzeige verschiedener nicht so wohl Unbekannter als vielmehr in Abfall gerathener Haupt-Wahrheiten: In den Jahren 1725 und 26. Anfänglich in der Königl. Residentz-Stadt Dreßden, Hernach aber, dem gesamten lieben Vaterland teutscher Nation zu einer guten Nachricht nach und nach*

ausgefertiget, und von dem Autore selbst mit einem kurtzen Inhalt jedes Stücks, nunmehro auch mit verschiedenen Erläuterungen, die sich in der ersten Auflage nicht befinden, und einem Anhange versehen Marchen (Leipzig: Zu finden bey Christian Gottfried Marchen, 1730).

20. August Gottleib Spangenberg, *The Life of Nicholas Louis Count Zinzendorf, Bishop and Ordinary of the United (or Moravian) Brethren,* trans. Samuel Jackson (London: Samuel Holdsworth, Amen-Corner, 1838), 63. Spangenberg was a follower of Zinzendorf, one of his traveling companions, and a leader in the Moravian Church.

21. Harold Steffes, "Kierkegaard's Socrates Sources: Eighteenth- and Nineteenth-Century Germanophone Scholarship," in *Kierkegaard and the Greek World, Tome 1: Socrates and Plato,* ed. Jon Stewart and Kaitland Nun, Kierkegaard Research: Sources, Reception and Resources, vol. 2 (Burlington, Vt.: Ashgate, 2010), 268.

22. Spangenberg, *The Life of Nicholas Louis Count Zinzendorf,* 62. Steffes, "Kierkegaard's Socrates Sources" emphasizes the suppression of this text to the extent that he believes Kierkegaard was unlikely to have read it, but he does not provide any evidence of this suppression. Spangenberg's account implies that only the third issue was suppressed and that Zinzendorf was able to publish the pamphlets freely after he stepped forward as the author. However, Spangenberg does indicate that Zinzendorf later feared retaliation against the community at Herrnhut because of the pamphlets.

23. Christopher B. Barnett, "Socrates the Pietist? Tracing the Socratic in Zinzendorf, Hamaan, and Kierkegaard," in *Kierkegaard Studies Yearbook: Kierkegaard's Late Writings,* ed. Niels Jørgen Cappelørn, Hermann Deuser, and K. Brian Söderquis (Copenhagen: University of Copenhagen, 2010), 318.

24. Rovira, *Blake and Kierkegaard,* 46–47.

25. A significant part of this section is drawn from Rovira, *Blake and Kierkegaard.* Used with permission. All quotations from the works of Plato are taken from *CDP.*

26. Origen, *Origen on First Principles: Being Koetschau's Text of the "de Principiis,"* trans. G. W. Butterworth (Gloucester, Mass.: Peter Smith, 1973), 275–56.

27. I would like to add at this point, however, that belief in a tripartite self was rejected no later than the late ninth century in the Eighth Ecumenical Council, Constantinople IV, a rejection reaffirmed by Aquinas in the *Summa Theologica,* who articulated what is Roman Catholic belief today, that the distinction between soul and spirit is an error proceeding from a misunderstanding. Nevertheless, a belief in a tripartite self persisted among some believers from Irenaeus to Erasmus and persists in minority Catholic opinion and among some Protestant groups.

Kierkegaard clearly believes in a tripartite self, as the opening pages of *The Sickness unto Death* make apparent, while Blake's devils in *The Marriage of Heaven and Hell* sound very traditionally Roman Catholic in their beliefs about the soul. For example, where the modern Catechism asserts, "The unity of soul and body is so profound that one has to consider the soul to be the 'form' of the body: i.e., it is because of its spiritual soul that the body made of matter becomes a living, human body; spirit and matter, in man, are not two natures united, but rather their union forms a single nature" (par. 365), Blake's Devil similarly asserts, "Man has no Body distinct from his Soul for that calld Body is a portion of Soul discernd by the five Senses. the chief inlets of Soul in this age." *The Marriage of Heaven and Hell*, pl. 4, in William Blake, *The Complete Poetry and Prose of William Blake*, new and rev. ed., ed. David V. Erdman, commentary by Harold Bloom (Berkeley: University of California Press, 1982), 34. All quotations from Blake's works hereafter are taken from this edition, which reproduces the idiosyncrasies of Blake's spelling and punctuation exactly. Erdman's practice continues to be conventional in Blake studies. Quotations here will do the same without comment. Erdman represented textual variants within Blake's works with the following conventions: "Italics within square brackets [*thus*] indicate words or letters deleted or erased or written over. Matter in Roman type within square brackets [thus] is supplied by the editor. Angle brackets <thus> enclose words or letters written to replace deletions, or as additions, not including words written immediately following and in the same ink or pencil as deleted matter" (xxiv).

Remnants of belief in a tripartite self persist, however, in Aquinas's hermeneutic, which reveal elements of Origen's description of interpretation based upon the body, soul, or spirit of Scripture. Aquinas divides the senses of Scripture into two broad categories, the literal and the spiritual, and then divides the spiritual into the allegorical, moral, and anagogical senses. Origen would locate the allegorical and anagogical senses in the spiritual and associate the moral with the soul. Aquinas validated a similarly tripartite approach to hermeneutics as a legitimate alternative, identifying it with Hugh of St. Victor.

28. For another recent discussion of Plato's influence on Blake in addition to my own, see Laura Quinney, *William Blake on Self and Soul* (Cambridge, Mass.: Harvard University Press, 2009).

29. Blake, *The Complete Poetry and Prose*, 555.

30. Ibid.

31. Ibid., 7.

32. S. Foster Damon and Morris Eaves, *A Blake Dictionary: The Ideas and Symbols of William Blake* (Hanover, N.H.: University Press of New England, 1988), 458.

33. Blake, *Complete Poetry and Prose*, 730. Susanne M. Sklar's *Blake's "Jerusalem" as Visionary Theatre: Entering the Divine Body*, Oxford Theological Monographs (Oxford: Oxford University Press, 2011) identifies Blake's notion of a sublime allegory with "the way of reading described by St. Augustine, who enjoins us to read Scripture on four levels: the literal, the allegorical, the moral, and the anagogical" (41).

34. Blake, *Complete Poetry and Prose*, 554.

35. Ibid., 664.

36. Barnett, "Socrates the Pietist?" 321.

37. Richard Kraut, ed., *The Cambridge Companion to Plato* (New York: Cambridge University Press, 1992), 25–30.

38. Penelope S. Murray, ed., *Plato on Poetry* (New York: Cambridge University Press, 1996).

39. Albert Rijksbaron, ed., *Plato, "Ion," or: On the Iliad*, Amsterdam Studies in Classical Philology, vol. 14 (Boston: Brill, 2007).

40. Stephen Houlgate, ed., *The Hegel Reader* (Oxford: Blackwell, 1998), 125.

Don Giovanni and *Moses and Aaron*

The Possibility of a Kierkegaardian Affirmation of Music

Peder Jothen

> The double doors were opened; the effect of the brilliant lighting,
> the coolness that flowed toward them, the spicy fascination
> of the scent, and the tasteful table setting overwhelmed the
> entering guests for a moment, and when at the same time the
> orchestra began playing the dance music from *Don Giovanni*,
> the forms of those entering were transfigured, and as if in
> deference to an invisible spirit encompassing them, they stood
> still a moment, like someone whom admiration has awakened
> and who has risen in order to admire.
> —"In Vino Veritas" (*SKS* 6:32 / *SLW* 27)

The relationship between music and religion within Western thought is, in general, an ambivalent one. Augustine, in his *Confessions*, wrote, "When [hymns] are sung these sacred words stir my mind to greater religious fervour. . . . But I ought not to allow my mind to be paralysed by the gratification of my senses, which often leads it astray."[1] Martin Luther, himself an Augustinian monk, viewed music as the second best means of revealing the gospel after preaching. Lutheran hymnody thus connected music with theological and biblical truth.[2] Though from different presuppositions, both thinkers yet understood music as a powerful artistic form that must be carefully restrained by the mind or linguistic forms of truth in order to be appropriate within Christianity.

I start this chapter on Søren Kierkegaard's musical aesthetic by referencing Augustine and Luther because in many ways, Kierkegaard's appreciation for and mistrust of music overlap Augustine's and Luther's musical ambivalence. On the one hand, Kierkegaard makes positive references to music in his journals, particularly in relation to Christian hymnody. On the other hand, notably through his pseudonym "A" in *Either/Or I*, he argues that the essence of music is sensuous and nontemporal and contradicts the permanence and repeatability of word-based, spiritual truth. Here, music has little to no place in the Christian life. But as such, like his theological ancestors, his musical aesthetic itself is thus deeply ambivalent.

This essay argues that there are two main reasons for this ambivalence. One, Kierkegaard, partially shaped by the Lutheran doctrine of *sola scriptura*, views the truths that matter for Christian selfhood as being biblically revealed and made intelligible through words. As with Luther before him, Kierkegaard's musical aesthetic then arises out of his primary concern about making Christian truth, most notably biblical truth, inwardly real for a hearer. Even in "A's" depiction of music as being merely sensuous, making the Word of God concrete is a latent presupposition. Second, Kierkegaard's critique is a component of one of the broader aims of his authorship, that of provoking his readers to a deep reflection about the form of one's selfhood. As such, rather than a sophisticated musical aesthetic, his musical critique establishes the basic contours of the aesthetic stage of existence, one exemplary type or form of selfhood. As "In Vino Veritas" relates, music has a power that can "transfigure" and lead people to admire the present moment rather than strive to become a Christian and truly hear Christian truth. His musical aesthetic is, then, less about music itself and more concerned with the role music plays in shaping desire, thought, and the overall form of one's life.

To clarify this argument, this essay makes two movements, each relating to these Kierkegaardian sensibilities. The first movement develops Kierkegaard's concept of music as an artistic genre. Famously, Kierkegaard's pseudonym "A" explores Mozart's opera *Don Giovanni*.[3] Writing as an aesthete, "A" describes music as uniting an aural, sensuous form with the existential content of natural passion. Music is then a means of communication, one that unveils sensuous, abstract immediacy to a listener rather than any clear, understandable truth. Yet, within his journals, Kierkegaard stresses the importance of music, in particular hymns, as being valuable for his own faith life when framed by the gospel and thus connected to the Christian form of life. Here, music is an ally for communicating Christian truth and thereby helpful to a listener developing a Christian self-consciousness.

The second movement uses Arnold Schoenberg's opera *Moses and Aaron* (*Moses und Aron*, first performed in the 1950s)[4] in comparison with "A's" critique of *Don Giovanni* to elucidate this ambivalence. Subverting the harmonic tradition of someone like Mozart, Schoenberg's opera uses a wide variety of nontraditional musical techniques such as *Sprechstimme* (literally, "spoken-voice") and dissonance to create an opera in which no word-based or idea of truth is ever clear or stable, whether in thought, word, or deed. In short, Schoenberg does not view human language as being able to articulate the mystery that is the divine. Both music and words fail in this task, and his opera thereby reveals the negation of words as able to contain essential truths about human existence. Thus, any certainty about a life built out of the knowledge of God is ever unstable.

The value of this comparison for understanding Kierkegaard's musical aesthetic is threefold. First, Schoenberg's playful, creative, and genre-bending use of music reveals the limited notion of the genre of music that Kierkegaard uses, notably in *Either/Or I*. Second, "A's" critique is valuable more as a treatment of the aesthetic stage than as a musical aesthetic. Third, this comparison also supports the claim that even amid the presentation of "A's" decidedly critical view of music, Kierkegaard affirms his *sola scriptura* roots. Unlike Schoenberg's negation of the power of words to contain ultimate truth, "A's" critique of music implicitly expresses Kierkegaard's trust of the foundational basis for Christian existence, the Bible. When rooted in divinely given words, human language concretizes truth. And when paired with music, these words can shape one's Christian existence, the central thrust of Kierkegaard's authorship.

Movement One: Kierkegaard, *Don Giovanni*, and Music

Kierkegaard never strove for a systematic aesthetic, meaning his conception of music expresses a jumble of attitudes about the value and purpose of music within human existence. Yet he is consistent in giving music several important characteristics. For one, in his journals, Kierkegaard relates how music can affect his emotional state. Humans are passionate beings, and music speaks to this dimension of human existence. For instance, in an entry of August 25, 1836, he writes of the romance of hearing street music: "Why is hand organ music so often appealing? It is no doubt because of the romantic involved [*sic*] in the mode of its appearance. It is, so to speak, a kind of poetry on the street corner. One does not expect music at all, and suddenly [the organist] begins to play" (*SKS* 27:144, Papir 175 / *JP* 3:3812). Music as "romantic" here relates to human emotions and sensuality; a listener experiences a surprising shift in mood in response to the appealing scene that music creates on the street. Music has a transformative power on human mood. It speaks to human passion and desire.

And it is possible for this affective power to be tethered to existential content. In particular, Kierkegaard shows an affinity for the power of hymnody. For instance, in 1850, he writes, "The 8th of September! The gospel: No one can serve two masters (my beloved gospel)! My favorite hymn: 'Commit Thy Way' [a German hymn by Paul Gerhardt, no. 42 in *Roskilde-Konvents Psalmebog*], which Kofoed-Hansen [the curate at Frelsers Church] chose today!" (*SKS* 23:478, NB20:160 / *KJN* 7:486). By implication, music, when it accompanies words, serves an important function for Kierkegaard: it can relay Christian truth to a hearer. As it did for Luther, in hymnody, human thinking about existence, grounded in words given by God, allies with music's power to affect passion and desire as a result.

The broader point here is that in both instances, Kierkegaard affirms the experiential relevance and vitality of music in human existence. On the one hand, music has a transformative power that alters one's mood; it affects desires and passions. On the other, and in relation to his own faith, music can actually help him to "hear" the gospel better. This connection between words and music, as well as between thought and passion, is thus vital to the role that Kierkegaard creates for music within the Christian life.

Yet, though Kierkegaard offers such a space for music in his own life, his pseudonym "A's" development of music as a sensuous, erotic, abstract, and immediate artistic medium in "The Immediate Erotic Stages or the Musical-Erotic" sees music as a distraction from leading an examined, intentional life.[5] Masked by his pseudonym, he provocatively develops the basic structure of the Kierkegaardian suspicion of music in the Christian life: music is the "demonic" and thus moves one away from Christian becoming. With this idea of becoming, I suggest, Kierkegaard stresses a view of human existence in which one's moral, religious, psychological, and intellectual formation is a lifelong process. His authorship thus seeks to provoke his readers to the recognition that one is never a fully integrated, true self but is always in process toward this end. Such a form or shape of selfhood is the highest task for a person, and Christianity offers each individual the means to rightly orient one's becoming toward the true, divinely given vision of human existence.

Indeed, the essential nature of music is the opposite of the spirit of Christianity, even though Christianity, ironically, divorced music from spiritual experience. Whereas in ancient Greece, music was harmoniously intertwined with sensuality and spirituality within religious expression, in Hegelian fashion, "A" argues that Christianity postulated sensuality, with music as the proper medium for its expression, as separate from spirituality. This separation establishes the concept of the spiritual, the opposite of the sensual. The spiritual has its roots in words and also makes music into essentially a sensuous mode of expression, for "A" stresses how it overwhelms words. In this positing, Christianity excludes music "from itself" as the means to emphasize God's Word as the source of spiritual truth (*SKS* 2:71 / *EO* 1:64). Foundational to this argument, music conceptually unites a sensuous form with erotic content, expresses abstract immediacy, and cannot communicate word-based truth concretely. It is this conception of music that serves as the primary locus for developing Kierkegaard's musical aesthetic, for it affirms the general outline of Kierkegaard's own view: music can be an ally to Christian selfhood when intertwined with word-based, Christian truth. Yet, without such a frame, music pulls a listener away from Christian existence.

Form and Content

As David Gouwens succinctly puts it, "Mozart, supremely in *Don Giovanni*, achieves a perfect union of form and content, wherein absolutely musical subject matter (the Don Juan myth) is united with the absolutely musical form that reflects it."[6] This perfect permeation of form and content makes certain types of artistic endeavors "classic," unable to be copied. And "A" views Mozart's *Don Giovanni* as such a musical work.[7] "The subject matter permeates the form and also . . . the form permeates the subject matter—this mutual permeation, this like-for-like in the immortal friendship of the classic" makes a work like Mozart's inimitable (*SKS* 2:60 / *EO* 1:52–53). This form and content "permeation" makes this opera a classic.

Music's form is aural sensuality. "A" argues that music is prereflective and that it uses the immediate, natural sense world as its structure. "Music always expresses the immediate in its immediacy" (*SKS* 2:76 / *EO* 1:70). It is momentary, alive only in the immediate present, full of sensuous energy that then lacks a past and has no future; it is nonrepeatable as such. This mere presentness means that it has a temporal indeterminacy, for only by having a past and a future does an artwork have a history, a trail of a legacy that lasts and a future that engenders a responsibility for its continued aliveness.

With this formal power, "A" affirms, Mozart's music is the sensual artifact par excellence. *Don Giovanni* unveils sensuality through time and sound. Because music is performed and heard, music has its own time: different performances perform the music at a particular point in time and may use different tempos, rhythms, and so forth. Music has meter and rhythm that structure sound temporally. "Music does not exist except in the moment it is performed, for even if a person can read notes ever so well and has an ever so vivid imagination, he still cannot deny that only in a figurative sense does music exist when it is being read" (*SKS* 2:75 / *EO* 1:68). But music expresses time only metaphorically as it does not take place within the strict demands of a set, ordered, clock-based chronological time; it plays with time rather than follows the strict demands of the human experience of the endless tick-tock of temporality. Music also is directed at the ear, the most sensuous of the sense organs. As heard, music, and in particular *Don Giovanni*, creates a sensual tickle within the ear as the most sensible of the human ways of perceiving.

Don Giovanni unites this sensual form with a similar content: the Don's story of seduction and erotic love. It is an existential content, as Don Giovanni's life exemplifies a natural power: erotic desire is what gives him life and vitality. He is unconcerned about both his past (i.e., a history that makes him guilty for his actions) and a future (i.e., being responsible for his present actions); he lives merely in the immediate present, guided by his never-ending desire for erotic conquest: "It is the energy of desire, the energy of sensuousness of desire" (*SKS* 2:103 / *EO* 1:100). This power can be expressed only by music: "This power in Don Giovanni, this omnipotence, this life, only music can express, and I know no other predicate to describe it than: it is exuberant gaiety" (*SKS* 2:105 / *EO* 1:101).

"A" provides examples of the development of sensuous desire. The Page in *Figaro* exemplifies the first level. The Page's desire lacks any clarity about its own desire; a dream-like consciousness, it flits about rather than intentionally focusing upon an object to possess. "Desire possesses what will become the object of its desire but possesses it without having desired it and thus does not possess it" (*SKS* 2:81 / *EO* 1:75–76). Papageno in Mozart's *The Magic Flute* exemplifies the second level. Desire in this case leads a self to intend toward an object. As "A" puts it, "This awakening in which desire awakens, this jolt, separates desire and its object, gives desire an object" (*SKS* 2:85 / *EO* 1:79). But in the process, one recognizes not one object to desire but rather a multitude of things to desire in the world.

Don Giovanni exemplifies the third and highest level. Natural, innate desire rules his life, and he fully desires an object in its particularity. Desire, rather than self-reflective thought, is the principle of action, the power that moves him to act. He then is a "downright seducer," a person who acts in the world through sensual love, a form of love that essentially is "totally faithless; it loves not one but all—that is, it seduces all. It is indeed only in the moment" (*SKS* 2:98 / *EO* 1:94). The Don expresses natural, unrestrained erotic passion that can never commit to loving one particular person. Such passion is amoral, as it is unaware of any ethical axioms because any awareness of moral codes would negate the vitality and power of desire. It cares only about the immediate present and nothing about the consequences of past acts or future possibilities. And being sensual, a passion for things in the world rather than spiritual love and the love of the unseen, it can never be oriented toward God, as such an orientation would negate its immediate, amoral character.

Mozart's opera, through its musical form, instantiates as its existential content the Don's eroticism. "In elemental sensuous-erotic originality, music has its absolute theme" (*SKS* 2:71 / *EO* 1:65).[8] This opera, in its originality, is the perfection of the sensuous union between form and content, making it "demonic." As Sylvia Walsh notes, "It is 'demonic,' being a medium for the expression of that which lies outside the realm of spirit."[9] It is demonic not in the sense of revealing demons but rather in the sense of being the opposite of the spiritual life of Christianity. Where Christianity calls one to hear and live by the Word of God, the language of the spirit, music calls one to hear and live by sensuous desire, natural inclinations, and unreflective immediacy. And it is this demonic calling that *Don Giovanni* perfects.

Idea Mediation

Another essential feature of "A's" musical critique is how well music mediates or expresses ideas. He thus develops music as a type of language. For "A," language has two distinct forms: of words and of nonwords. A language of words expresses ideas, or as "A" calls it, "reflection," in space and time: words, systematized into a language, determinately express ideas clearly and intelligibly. "A" calls this quality of determinacy "concretization." Nonverbal languages include music, which can "legitimately [be] called a language," as they also express ideas in the temporal sphere (*SKS* 2:73 / *EO* 1:67). Yet it is only words that can clearly articulate spiritual and existential ideas because word-based "language, regarded as medium, is the medium absolutely qualified by spirit, and it is therefore the authentic medium of the idea" (*SKS* 2:73 / *EO* 1:67). In short, in heavily Hegelian terms, "A" argues that words authentically mediate spiritual truth.[10] However, music revels in sensuality, which dissipates when faced with reflection and cognition. It thus lacks the formal ability to express ideas clearly; sensuality always saturates words within its own presentness, overwhelming their power to reveal any clear idea.

Underneath this view lies the conceptual distinction between abstraction and concretion. To make something "concrete" is to determine its meaning clearly. It is to make X be understood as meaning X within time (as past-present-future), space, and the human senses. And as concrete, the idea can be repeated, as "the more concrete and thus the richer the idea and likewise the medium, the greater the possibility of a repetition" (*SKS* 2:62 / *EO* 1:54). In its repeatability, a self becomes responsible for appropriating the idea; an intelligible idea accordingly expresses existential truth as understandable, one that can determine how one exists. So, like Hegel, "A" esteems word-based language as the most spiritually valuable medium as it states the idea most intelligibly.[11]

However, musical language, as typified by *Don Giovanni*, can express abstract ideas only in a prereflective, immediate language. "Reflection is fatal to the immediate," meaning, "in other words, the immediate is the indeterminate" (*SKS* 2:76 / *EO* 1:70). In its ability to convey energy, vitality, and natural desire, music itself is what it mediates: eros. Being demonic, it is itself abstract, immediate, desirous energy that bubbles forth for a listener rather than any concrete, repeatable, and intelligible spiritual truth. Although there are other types of truths that music may express, "this is its absolute theme" (*SKS* 2:77 / *EO* 1:71). Sensuous desire is the highest, truest form of music, which *Don Giovanni* instantiates as both its form and content.

Consequently, even in "A's" affirmation of sensuous music lies a presupposition about the primacy for words for clarity about one's existence. Words make ideas concrete; music only reveals abstraction. This point pushes us to recognize that at play in Kierkegaard's thought is the Lutheran theological pillar of *sola scriptura* as the determining mark for both theological and existential thinking. In Kierkegaard's wider authorship, especially his period of direct communication (1848–51), several of his texts detail the existential relevance of the Bible. For instance, *For Self-Examination* (1851) states that like a love letter from a beloved, "God's Word is just as precious to you as this letter is to the lover" (*SKS* 13:54 / *FSE* 26). We also see this in his affirmation of hymnody in his journals. Words matter, and not just any words, as "The Seducer's Diary" in *Either/Or I* demonstrates; instead, only God's love letter reveals the words that truly matter for existence.

Ever underneath "A's" aesthetic lies Kierkegaard's stress on the absolute need for clarity about the sinful yet saintly existence of being human, a clarity possible only through the Bible. Indeed, in his journals, he criticizes biblical scholarship: "We have invented scholarship in order to evade doing God's will. This much we certainly do understand—that face to face with God and his obviously understood will to say 'This I will not do'—this no one dares to do. We do not dare do it that way, so we protect ourselves by making it seem as if it were very difficult to understand and that therefore we—he must indeed be flattered by this and regard it as praiseworthy in us—study and investigate etc., that is, we protect ourselves by hiding behind big books" (*SKS* 27:620, Papir 490, n.d. 1854 / *JP* 3:3597). Words matter for who we are to become, specifically words of Christian truth.

Existence-Communication

As the perfect union of sensuous form and erotic content amid the mediation of abstract immediacy, "A's" musical aesthetic reveals to listeners a conception of existence in which ethical responsibility, moral reflection, and theological truth play no part. "A's" critique plays a part in the notion of "existence-communication" that Kierkegaard's Johannes Climacus develops in *Concluding Unscientific Postscript* (*SKS* 7:74–84 / *CUP* 70–85). Throughout his authorship, his dominant concern is to provoke each person to care about the ethical form and content of his or her life.[12] In short, what makes a person act? What does one love? What does one imagine being a "good" self might be?

"A," and *Either/Or I* as a whole, thus are vital for Kierkegaard's indirect communication of the aesthetic stage of existence. The aesthetic stage is a concept (along with the ethical and religious stages) that provides a heuristic device for a reader to reflect on the values, actions, and relations that make the reader a particular person. An aesthete is someone who is unconcerned with ethical codes and a life of faith. One lives for worldly beauty; one fears boredom, critical thought, and ethical responsibility. And music, as "A" develops it, communicates this model of existence.

As an aesthete, "A" seduces a reader into two understandings about music, both of which indirectly ask one to examine the values, commitments, and relationship within one's form of life. First, "A" describes how Don Giovanni enacts a musical seduction within the opera itself. Music, as the highest mode of immediacy, is the stage for an operatic example of erotic seduction between the characters. The music itself here exemplifies unexamined, natural desire. "A's" underlying impulse is that any listener will be captivated and become an "admirer" of the Don's life, as Kierkegaard states in "In Vino Veritas." Being accessible to anyone, "A" erotically seduces one into inhabiting the world of this sensual-erotic opera.

As a consequence, "A" seduces readers into the Don's existence. He strives to have readers connect their passion with the Don's musical desire that imaginatively asks them to fall in love with the erotic shape of the Don's way of life. "A" celebrates such sensuality and immediacy. He wants readers to imagine existing through natural passion and the vitality of sensuous desire, a form of life modeled by the Don.

"A" thus plays a vital role in developing the archetypical shape of the aesthetic stage within the Kierkegaardian corpus by presenting this erotic Don, ever ignorant of developing an ethical or faithful self-consciousness. And this existential seduction suggests that "A's" ironic concern is that someone listening to *Don Giovanni* might then realize the emptiness and abstract nature of the sensuous-erotic. Though seemingly exhilarating, erotic desire is neither repeatable nor peaceful, for sensuality has an endless supply of things to desire. There is always another Zerlina around the corner. Like musical immediacy, the Don lacks any self-integrity as he lives merely in the present moment; his desire causes him constantly to flit from one object and relationship to another. "A's" ironic aim in this musical seduction is to leave the reader wanting more, especially of a type of life in which the emptiness and endless nature of desire is reshaped (or "qualified," in "A's" words) to desire true, spiritual things.

The vacuity of "A's" depiction of the Don's life calls upon the reader to desire a more reflective, responsible life. One particularly relevant example is the ethical life developed in, among other places, Kierkegaard's *Either/ Or II*, written under the pseudonym Judge William. Indeed, "A's" argument is not a solitary critique but rather part of an either/or choice related to the existence stages: either the Don's aesthetic life or the Judge's ethical life. "A" thus links the lower, sensual life with ethical life by creating a musical juxtaposition between spirit and sensuality by arguing that music's sensuality is always qualified, always intertwined with spirit. As posited by Christianity, sensuality is always connected to the spiritual; as a body and a spirit, one is ever amid a both/and rather than an either/or (as in either a natural body or an infinite spirit). "That is, it is qualified by spirit and therefore is power, life, movement, continual unrest, continual succession. But this unrest, this succession, does not enrich it; it continually remains the same; it does not unfold but incessantly rushes forward as if in a single breath" (*SKS* 2:77 / *EO* 1:71). A listener of *Don Giovanni* hears the erotic amid a complexity of relations, and in particular between sensuality and spirituality. There is no pure sensuality as such, as even music is infused with spirit.

Yet, by implication, to hear music in the right manner requires that a listener intentionally respond to music as an existential either/or: *either* it is mere sensuality, imaginatively snatching the listener away from ethical responsibility (and into the aesthetic stage of life) *or* it is both sensuous and spiritual, requiring the listener's consciousness to "qualify" it as an existentially formative experience (and thereby to be snatched into the ethical and religious stages). When placed in this existential frame, the choice "A" presents is not *either* music *or* not-music but rather a call for the listener to hear music rightly, notably its sensuous elements, as ever intertwined with spirituality. As such, hearing rightly means hearing it as ennobling a passion for the world, becoming ethical, and affirming spiritual truth (as in rightly knowing God). But hearing it wrongly means accepting the consequences of living a life like the Don's.

Consequently, "A's" musicality overlaps with the existential either/or that Kierkegaard enacts between the two types of existence forms exemplified by the Don and the Judge. Reading *Either/Or I* is ever juxtaposed to the form of life offered by William in *Either/Or II*; the aesthete "A" is ever in conversation with William. To best understand the outlines of "A's" argument, one must read William's life, and vice versa. Through "A's" erotic seduction, Kierkegaard is thus challenging readers to a deeper consciousness about how one lives as he uses the mask of "A" to ironically affirm the sensuous-erotic life.

This view gains depth when understood in relation to several other caveats to "A's" critique. For one, Mozart's *Don Giovanni* was widely adapted and altered during Kierkegaard's lifetime. Compared to the premiere in Prague in 1787, the opera Kierkegaard heard most likely had a number of modifications. Elisabete de Sousa observes, "Besides adding dramatic material borrowed from Molière, [translator Laurids Kruse] not only suppressed all recitatives in favor of spoken dialogue, but altered the structural development of the scenes and omitted the *scene ultima*, the whole following the structural pattern of the *Singspiel*."[13] The omission of the *scene ultima* is particularly significant for "A's" view. The final scene follows the Don's fiery death and descent to hell as a result of his lack of repentance. Here, the characters sing about the consequences of sinful actions with lines such as "This is the end which befalls evildoers. And in this life scoundrels always receive their just deserts!"[14] Kruse likely omitted these scenes because he "disapproved of the use of recitatives and looked suspiciously on opera as a dramatic genre, on ethical and on aesthetical grounds."[15] Had this scene been included, "A's" argument that *Don Giovanni* reveals only sensuous desire would have been more difficult to support, to say the least, what with the ethical ending.

Additionally, Kierkegaard admits the possibility that the music could have been different. Two years before the publication of *Either/Or*, Kierkegaard writes in his journals, "Precisely because he has been presented musically, D. Giovanni's natural genius has clearly been accentuated; if one so wished, one could present a more reflective D.G. by way of recourse to the arbitrary. thus [*sic*] he seduces a girl not because he finds himself at all affected by her, but she awakens a pleasant memory; as a pastime he will see if it can be made real; or she arouses a pleasant memory,—[which will] always remain beyond his grasp" (*SKS* 19:238, Notesbog 8:41, n.d. 1841 / *KJN* 3:232). This entry implies that there could have been a more reflective, thoughtful Don; the Don could have been less erotic. But by implication, "A's" suggestion that music is essentially sensual is a false claim, a possibility that Kierkegaard does incorporate into "A's" argument, however.

Consequently, "A" writes as an aesthete in order to develop an aesthetic form of existence: the unreflective life, a life lived through natural passion and erotic desire, a life ungrounded in the spiritual. Developing a clear musical aesthetic is thus not the primary concern. Placed alongside *Either/Or II* and the ethical deliberations of Judge William, Mozart's *Don Giovanni* is the means to help readers think about how they live their lives. His view brilliantly captures in words, ironically, the sensuous and aural beauty of Mozart, but largely with an aim of moving readers into a deeper engagement with ways of being in the world. Music can then become a component of an examined life rather than just a part of life caused by the admiration and affirmation of sensuous desire.

Movement Two: Schoenberg's *Moses and Aaron*

Yet, despite these deeper presuppositions, "A's" development of an opposition between musical sensuality and the spiritual is frequently taken as reflecting Kierkegaard's view. For instance, Hans Urs von Balthasar writes that Kierkegaard, as well as Karl Barth, "warn us against overstepping the established boundaries [of music], saying that, if we attempt this nonetheless, we are doomed either to naïve banalities or to irrelevant abstractions."[16] As a result, prima facie, "A's" musical aesthetic challenges any clear affirmation of the inclusion of music within the Christian life.

Such views read Kierkegaard as using "A" to develop a musical aesthetic rather than primarily as the means to communicate one model of existence. One means by which to deepen this argument is to compare "A's" argument with another musical frame of reference. Doing so enables Kierkegaard's affirmation of the power of words to contain truth, a claim at the heart of "A's" negative critique of music as well as exemplified in his journals, to emerge more clearly. It can also then reveal the polemical yet limited idea of the nature of music that Kierkegaard works through "A" to present a model of an aesthetic existence. Schoenberg's *Moses and Aaron* is one such musical work.

Why? For one, both *Don Giovanni* and *Moses and Aaron* are operas and therefore have a connection to human words and thought as well as music. For another, both works develop their insights by focusing on the communicative power of music, especially about the effectiveness of music in clarifying word-based ideas. Finally, both see human desire as part of the content expressed in and moved by music. Yet, where this comparison is most fruitful is in the underlying concept of music. Whereas "A" sees in *Don Giovanni* the perfection of the sensual-erotic that is the essence of music, Schoenberg crafts *Moses and Aaron* to destabilize the power of words to mediate truth. Both then, though in different ways, relate to ideas about the nature of theological and ethical claims; "A" offers a playful exploration of *Don Giovanni* that is framed by Kierkegaard's work to upbuild his readers, while *Moses and Aaron* toys with the inability to articulate God and the difficulties inherent in living out such a reality. This comparison suggests that "A's" argumentative presuppositions, alongside Kierkegaard's appreciation of hymnody, can give further impetus to opening a space for a positive role for music to play in Christian becoming within his thought.

Schoenberg composed *Moses and Aaron* between 1930 and 1932. It has three acts, only loosely based on Exodus, as little attention is given to the liberation of the Israelites. Though ethnically Jewish, Schoenberg was a convert to Protestantism, so his source text was the Lutheran Bible rather than the Buber-Rosenzweig German translation of the Hebrew Bible. In the first act, God calls Moses to lead the Israelites out of Egypt, with Aaron as his tongue.[17] Moses lacks the conviction that he can truly speak for the "one, infinite, omnipresent, unperceived and unrepresentable God," the true liberator.[18] The second act details Moses's reception of the Ten Commandments as Aaron sets up a golden calf for the restless Israelites, ever desiring a visible symbol of God. The third act, for which the music was never completed, depicts a trial scene where Moses judges Aaron for his idolatry.

The primary theme of the opera is the impossibility of representing the divine in thought, word, or material object. By implication, one made most clearly in the depiction of Moses's view of the Ten Commandments as being an idol, visions of a life grounded in claims about God are also problematic. The opera instantiates this view by having Moses refuse to see in words the power to name God's being, whereas Aaron fluently uses language and external things to represent God. Doing so, as Bluma Goldstein puts it, means that "the opera attempted to resolve the communicative dilemma of language—of word, image, symbol—to transmit the idea" of God as unrepresentable.[19] Connecting the conceptual categories used in the previous section to *Moses and Aaron* shows that the opera unites a dissonant aural form with the human desire for, yet the impossibility to clarify, God's nature as the opera's content. The opera thus mediates the attempt to represent God within the finite as both an internal and an external struggle for humanity.

Form and Content

As in *Don Giovanni*, commentators note the perfection of form and content in *Moses and Aaron*. Adorno states, "The a priori impossibility of sacred art today and the problematic nature of skill regarded as something that aspires to perfection form a perfect fit in the *Moses* opera."[20] At the root of this perfection is a critique of sensuality; Schoenberg sought to free the musical form from an overemphasis on sensual harmony. He developed an "atonal" method of composition, known as serialism or twelve-tone music. Unlike the sensual, erotic harmonies and the "exuberant gaiety" of Mozart, the music is atonal and sparse. "The opera begins with a series of notes that express God's presence at the scene of the burning bush," observes Lora Batnitzky. "These opening notes are the only text-expressive idea or theme dominating the opera. However, with the communication of God's self to Moses, the notes begin to sound distorted."[21] At the formal level, Schoenberg de-sensualizes music such that it no longer has the sensual power that "A" finds so moving in *Don Giovanni*.

For instance, traditional operatic form requires that the libretto be sung, thereby intertwining the music and words. Yet, Schoenberg deconstructs this formal relationship by contrasting words that are sung with words that are spoken. Whereas Aaron sings, Moses speaks his own part in the manner known as *Sprechstimme*. In Elliot Gyger's words, "Within the norms of the operatic world, someone who speaks rather than singing is dealing with a great handicap, unable to communicate in a 'normal' way with the other characters."[22] Aaron, as the singer, is the idolater, believing that operatic words, the "normal" operatic form of expression, can concretely represent God. Schoenberg is playing with the musical form such that it breaks down because it itself has become an idol, a rigid, established set of formulaic rules.

But as such, unlike "A's" view that music is about sensual harmony and erotic desire, *Moses and Aaron*'s orchestration uses abrasive instruments and orchestration to assault the senses. For example, in the second act's orgy scene, the orchestration moves from relatively quiet strings to an agitated drum- and brass-filled explosion of wild drunkenness. The scene has no tonal, harmonic center, and like its subject material, the overall musical effect is itself of desire gone haywire, lost. Ironically, this scene would work well with "A's" linkage of music with the aesthetic stage, for it is a desire for human bodies and sensual pleasure.

Working with this thematic, Schoenberg presents humans as being desirous creatures, and, in particular, the opera suggests that they fundamentally have a desire for clarity about the nature of God. To repeat an expression from more than one earlier quotation, this is the "absolute theme" of the opera, and thus its existential content. So whereas "A" views music as an erotic power, thereby linking sensuous form with an ethical content rooted in natural passion, Schoenberg connects music's sensuous form with a negative content: the human desire for, yet the impossibility of, the articulation of a decisive foundation to know God and a life rooted in this truth.

Idea Mediation

But as a result, Schoenberg's work suggests the impossibility of concretizing truth, whether linguistically or mentally. For instance, within the libretto, which Schoenberg composed, this impossibility is enacted in the dialogue between Moses and Aaron. Whereas Moses desires but is unable to speak or to find sensual expression of the divine, Aaron speaks in order to find a sensual image. Indeed, Moses eventually destroys the tablets of the moral law after he realizes that they too are idolatrous, full of finite, vague words; even ethical ideals are unstable. The climax of the opera is at the end of act

2, when Moses says, "O word, thou word, that I lack" (*MA* 60). This utterance is in reaction to Aaron's claim, amid the creation of the golden calf, that no one can "worship what one dare not even represent" (*MA* 27). Any human expression of God, and the existential ideals rooted in knowledge of the divine, is thus abstract, only a partial truth at best. Any attempt even at delimiting a representation of God fails, what with the finite, limited nature of human speaking and thinking.

Schoenberg's musical orchestration mediates this perspective. For example, in act 1, scene 1, Moses sees God as the burning bush, but says, "My tongue is not flexible: thought is easy; speech is laborious" (*MA* 25). Although Moses finds thinking "easy," one commentator even argues that all of Moses's lines are actually thoughts and that, in the end, his thoughts shade into the realm of idolatry and impossibility. God has a full voice; Schoenberg uses singers (both adults and children), wood instruments, and speakers (both adults and children) to depict God when calling Moses through the burning bush. Musically representing God thus requires using all the forms of operatic utterance available as a means to juxtapose the transcendent divine nature with the temporal nature of humans. In opposition to this full musical expression lies Moses's attempt to express verbally the idea of God. As Gyger puts it, Moses's "opening words delimit *his* idea of God, which he will adhere to for the rest of the opera."[23] Such a delimitation is limited, merely human, and thus always a failure in relationship to any true understanding of God. Unlike "A's" underlying affirmation of the power of words to concretize truth, in Schoenberg's view, human words, thoughts, and deeds all fail to concretize God, and the vision of life that follows is thus itself unstable.

If anything, Schoenberg uses music to mediate not abstract immediacy but rather desire, truth, and impossibility. He connects human thinking with conceptual ideas, revealing the idolatrous nature of our ideas about ultimate things. The opera mixes the profane with the sacred, the sensuous with the spiritual, suggesting that there is no pure position, no confident foundation upon which to speak or think about transcendent matters. What then becomes clear is not a representation of God but a deeper insight about the human condition: the desire for precision about the truths we live by, yet the very impossibility of such truth.

It is this mediacy that offers a profound challenge to "A's" musical conception, for it speaks to the power of music to provoke self-reflection in the mind of a listener. "A," while never making an explicit claim about the divine, nonetheless stresses that words make ideas and spirit concrete. But as such, he affirms the possibility of concretizing the idea of God, something Schoenberg suggests is impossible. This comparison then gives greater depth to the claim that underneath "A's" view is Kierkegaard's affirmation of *sola scriptura*. Even for "A," words about God flow out from the clarity offered in the Word of God; there is thus a reliable foundation for thinking about God and the human-divine relationship.

Existence-Communication

The clearest difference between "A's" aesthetic and Schoenberg's work lies in the shape of the relationship between the music and listener or performer. Rather than enveloping one in a harmonious bubble of sensuous-erotic love, *Moses and Aaron* communicates the pain and frustration that comes with desiring clarity about the divine. This type of communication arises because, as Adorno puts it, Schoenberg's opera communicates an "absolute metaphysical content," one that places the opera in the realm of other great works of art that are "destroyed in the process and their broken outlines survive as the ciphers of a supreme unnamable truth."[24] The opera deals with the impossibility of naming transcendence in the finite realm; it deconstructs the possibility about being certain about the nature of God. Like Moses's recognition of the idolatry inherent even in the moral law, a life grounded in confidence in one's view of God is a form of idolatry.

In Schoenberg's hands, music expresses the impurity of human thinking when it comes to divine things, and the impossibility of the communication of God's essence. "He uses the distortion of the notes," writes Batnitzky, "which reaches its height in the character of Aron, to reflect the implicit tension that arises in the finite human's desire to know the infinite God. . . . The point is that the problem of idolatry and representation is one intrinsic to the relationship between the human and God."[25] The finite cannot contain the infinite; in *Moses and Aaron*, neither music nor words can concretize the divine. This leads another scholar to conclude, "In the end, perhaps all music is contaminated and compromised by its very audibility, its motility, its lack of changelessness."[26] Words and thought are contaminated as well. In this end, it is this frustration that the opera communicates, leading listeners into their own dialectical web of possibility and impossibility to see the failure of human words.

Consequently, *Moses and Aaron* seductively plays with both the human desire to think of God and also, nonetheless, the reflective awareness that such concretization is impossible. Words and music work together to express the desire for reflection and clarity as such, but both fail in the process. Whereas "A" sees a life based on natural desire inherent in music's sensuality, Schoenberg uses dissonance such that there is little to no pleasing harmonic sensuality. In *Moses and Aaron*, sensuality hurts the ear, and a listener is not seduced into further sensual desire but left amid the tension of saying something yet nothing about God.

In fact, rather than a seduction into sensual desire, the opera negates harmonious sensuousness as the means to confuse and frustrate the listener into an awareness about the impossibility of naming transcendence. The form of desire enacted by Schoenberg's opera is the desire to surpass human limits and to know God. But this desire in the end is futile; it fails, and like Moses, the listener must acknowledge that any and all worldly representations of

God are themselves idols. Rather than the desire for endless erotic conquests and an aesthetic life, Schoenberg's desire leads to the frustrating and painful understanding that the human desire to find certainty about the ineffable is a doomed project.

While "A" suggests that music such as *Don Giovanni* is mere immediate presentness within the temporal scheme, Schoenberg's opera makes the listener a part of the very problematic tension he is exploring. The listener is listening to an idol, experiencing the frustration of wanting to say something positive about God yet being unable to do so. As a result, here music calls one to become not an erotically driven Don Juan but a frustrated Moses.

Some Kierkegaardian Implications

This comparison clarifies a number of implications about Kierkegaard's view of music. For one, in relation to "A's" critique, Schoenberg's work is a helpful reminder of the narrow frame through which "A" defines music. "A's" explication focuses on only a *certain* kind of music, one exemplified by Mozart's opera, rather than a grand musical theory that can encompass all forms of music. "A's" view of music even runs counter to Kierkegaard's affirmation of hymnody in his journals.

Second, because of this narrow focus, when placed within Kierkegaard's broader existential authorship, "A" in reality uses this particular musical work to paint a seductive picture of the aesthetic life. His aim is to construct music as instantiating an existence driven by erotic desire and sensual immediacy. And Mozart's music expresses this sensuous, abstract desire to perfection. The words the Don sings, combined with the music, brim with eroticism rather than any spiritual truth. As a result, "A's" musical aesthetic is limited; he chooses one particular example and uses that to explore the aesthetic life rather than develop a robust conception of music itself.

Finally, and more important, considering "A" and Kierkegaard alongside of Schoenberg adds greater depth to the argument that Kierkegaard believes there is a stable foundation on which to understand God (even in the paradoxical form of Christ) as well as human life: the Bible. Music, when linked to such truths, can affirmatively impact Christian becoming. Whereas Schoenberg destabilizes word-grounded truth, "A" presents music as an alternative to verbal language, one rooted in eroticism and desire. But to do so he yet remains confident in the power of words to express truths that matter to moral formation. This claim gains further depth in recognizing that in Kierkegaard's own life, music, especially when connected to biblical truth, positively shaped his relationship to the world and his own self-development.

Don Giovanni, in "A's" presentation of it, is then an antihymn. It tears a person away from attending to the true words that matter: biblically expressed, Christian truth. It also speaks to the passionate, desirous dimensions of a self in such a way that it charms one away from concern over being intentional about the type of life one lives. Music, with its power to affect human emotions and desires, when allied with Christian truth, can positively shape a self in its growth in the Christian life. But the opposite effect is possible as well; music can thus be an ally of Christian truth; it is never an end in itself but always a dimension of becoming a Christian subject.

This essay has used the comparison between "A's" argument and *Moses and Aaron* as a means to develop a better picture of Kierkegaard's musical aesthetic. A variety of larger questions yet remain. For instance, are hymns the only type of genuinely Christian music? Can *Don Giovanni* ever be redeemed and appreciated within the Christian life? Can there ever be nonword-based Christian music? Yet, the overall shape of Kierkegaard's musical aesthetic suggests that these questions arise from an incorrect foundational assumption. Rather than a thoughtful elaboration of music itself, his attention is on how one hears and interprets music amid the highest task of existing as a Christian. Kierkegaard's overall point is that any act of listening to music must be framed or "qualified" by the divinely given words that shape Christian existence. Thus, listening to music is ever a part of one's ethical and religious development.

In fact, music, like other arts, is a relative project in the process of becoming a Christian. His authorship as a whole, full of beautiful twists and turns, offers a rhetorically beautiful example of just this aim. He uses his pen to provoke his readers to care about the type of person they are becoming. Music too is a form of "existence-communication" amid the cacophony of everyday life. And like writing, in this subjective task, music, particularly when linked to words that mediate Christian truth, can actually aid an individual in the provocative, self-reflective practices prominently featured throughout his authorship. But it can also tear one away from deeply reflecting on and enacting a higher form of existence. As a result, what matters most is how one listens to music in the never-ending process of becoming a true, Christian subject.

Notes

1. Augustine, *Confessions* 10.33.49; Latin text and English commentary, 3 vols., ed. James J. O'Donnell (Oxford: Clarendon Press, 1992), 1:138; Eng.: *Confessions*, trans. R. S. Pine-Coffin (Harmondsworth, U.K.: Penguin, 1961), 238.

2. See, e.g., a letter Luther wrote in 1524 to George Spalatin, the theologian, chaplain, and secretary to Frederick the Wise of Saxony: "We have planned to follow the example of the prophets and the church fathers and to compose German songs for the German people so that God's Word may resound in the singing of the people." Quoted by Paul Nettl, *Luther and Music*, trans. Frida Best and Ralph Wood (New York: Russell and Russell, 1967), 38–39.

3. See also the essay by Nils Holger Petersen in this volume.—Ed.

4. Act 3 incomplete; "The Dance before the Golden Calf" ("Der Tanz um das goldene Kalb"), now in act 2, first performed in concert, Darmstadt, 1951; acts 1 and 2 first performed in concert, Hamburg, 1954; acts 1 and 2 first staged, Zürich, 1957.

5. With regard to making sense of the thorny issue of the connection between Kierkegaard's thought and that of a pseudonym, I see the pseudonyms as authorial tactics that allow a reader to reflect imaginatively on the view of life presented by each pseudonym. So "A" presents a view of the aesthetic life. Yet, all of the various authorial tactics Kierkegaard uses are rooted in his aim of upbuilding his readers into a Christian existence. For more of this view, see Peder Jothen, *Kierkegaard, Aesthetics, and Selfhood: The Art of Subjectivity* (Burlington, Vt.: Ashgate, 2014), 7–46.

6. David J. Gouwens, "Mozart among the Theologians," *Modern Theology* 16, no. 4 (2000): 461–74, here 462.

7. In an October 11, 1837, journal entry, Kierkegaard affirms this "perfection" of Don Juan: "Having said previously that D. Juan is immediate musically, and thus describing the character's infinite immanence in music, that action, character, and text stand in a necessary relation to one another as in no other opera. . . . I find this corroborated in noting that in the folk legend, the demonic is essentially musical" (*SKS* 17:244, DD:69 / *KJN* 1:235).

8. Kierkegaard's original conception of the title of the essay in his journals demonstrates this view of music as lacking any reflective content. "[*For the title* 'Immediate Erotic Stages,' etc.] What Homer says is true of music: οἷον ἀκούομεν, οὐδέ τι ἴδμεν. *Iliad*, II. 486. One hears it, but he does not know it, does not understand it" (*Pap.* IV A 222, n.d. 1844 / *JP* 1:147).

9. Sylvia Walsh, *Living Poetically: Kierkegaard's Existential Aesthetics* (University Park: Pennsylvania State University Press, 1994), 73.

10. For more on the critique of music by Hegel, see his *Vorlesungen über die Aesthetik*, in *GWFHW* 10, ed. Heinrich Gustav Hotho, pt. 3 (1838): 125–219; *A* 2:888–955. These lectures, delivered in Berlin in the 1820s, were published first in 1835–38. "As his journals testify, Kierkegaard devoted himself to Hegel's aesthetics during the years 1841–42." Eric Ziolkowski, "Kierkegaard and the Aesthetic," *Literature and Theology* 6, no. 1 (1992): 33–46, here 39. *Either/Or* was published in 1843.

11. In the introduction to his lectures on aesthetics, Hegel stresses that it is philosophy (as conceptual thought expressed through words) that reveals spirit, or *Idee*, most intelligibly. Any form of art thus is always a lower form of thinking and human activity than that offered by philosophy. See Hegel, *Vorlesungen über die Aesthetik*, pt. 1 [prefatory sec.], in *GWFHW* 10, ed. Hatho, pt. 1 (1835): 136; *A* 1:104.

12. My view stresses a deep continuity throughout his authorship. This view follows, among others, Gouwens's approach, which intertwines the pseudonymous and upbuilding works into a single whole frame that strives to challenge ideas of being a Christian for a variety of readers (including philosophers, Christians by birth but not practice, etc.). See David Gouwens, *Kierkegaard as Religious Thinker* (New York: Cambridge University Press, 1996), 24–26.

13. Elisabete de Sousa, "Wolfgang Amadeus Mozart: The Love for Music and the Music of Love," in *Kierkegaard and the Renaissance and Modern Traditions,* Tome 3: *Literature, Drama and Music,* ed. Jon Stewart, Kierkegaard Research: Sources, Reception and Resources, vol. 5 (Farnham, U.K.: Ashgate, 2009), 144.

14. Wolfgang Amadeus Mozart, *Don Giovanni,* libretto by Lorenzo da Ponte, trans. William Murray, Philharmonia Chorus and Orchestra, dir. Carlo Maria Giulini, EMI Records, 2002, 253.

15. Sousa, "Wolfgang Amadeus Mozart," 144.

16. Hans Urs von Balthasar, *The Glory of the Lord: A Theological Aesthetics,* 7 vols., trans. Erasmo Leiva-Merikakas, ed. Joseph Fessio and John Riches (San Francisco: Ignatius Press, 1982–89), 1:68. George Pattison puts it more generally: "For in relation to the kind of scene shown in the image of the crucified one, the crucified image of God-in-human-form, aesthetic representation itself is judged to be a way of participating in the ongoing cruelty which characterizes the human rejection of divine love." *Kierkegaard: The Aesthetic and the Religious* (New York: St. Martin's Press, 1992), 184.

17. Though using a German Protestant Bible, he maintained the use of traditional Hebrew spellings of names like "Aron."

18. Arnold Schoenberg, *Moses und Aron,* libretto trans. Allen Forte, Chorus of De Nederlandse Opera and the Royal Concertgebouw Orchestra, dir. Pierre Boulez, Deutsche Grammophon, 1996, 24 (hereafter *MA*).

19. Bluma Goldstein, "Schoenberg's *Moses und Aron*: A Vanishing Biblical Nation," in *Political and Religious Ideas in the Works of Arnold Schoenberg,* ed. Charlotte Cross and Russell Berman (New York: Garland, 2000), 159.

20. Theodor W. Adorno, "Sacred Fragment," in *Quasi una Fantasia: Essays on Modern Music,* trans. Rodney Livingstone (New York: Verso, 1998), 239.

21. Lora Batnitzky, "Schoenberg's *Moses und Aron* and the Judaic Ban on Images," *Journal for the Study of the Old Testament* 92 (2001): 73–90, here 82.

22. Elliot Gyger, "Speech, Song, and Silence: Modes of Utterance in *Moses und Aron,*" *Opera Quarterly* 23, no. 4 (2007): 418–40, here 419.

23. Ibid., 427.

24. Adorno, "Sacred Fragment," 226.

25. Batnitzky, "Schoenberg's *Moses und Aron,*" 82.

26. Daniel Albright, "Butchering Moses," *Opera Quarterly* 23, no. 4 (2007): 441–54, here 451–52.

Kierkegaard, Dylan, and Masked and Anonymous Neighbor-Love

Jamie A. Lorentzen

Although the lyrics of Bob Dylan (b. 1941) offer evidence of his familiarity with many philosophers and poets, it is unclear if he has read any works by Søren Kierkegaard. Still, the two thinkers have more in common than thin legs, big hair, and an appreciation for the power of both sacred and profane music. Among other things, they are poets of mighty opposites, both dialectical and paradoxical. They are earnestly funny while simultaneously qualifying as unorthodox penitents. They also respect the other (the neighbor) in the development of each individual's full humanity—and they prefer to pay their respects in great part in disguise.

Regarding his respect for the neighbor, Dylan writes in 2004 about something he read in the early 1960s: "I came across one of [Arthur Rimbaud's] letters called 'Je est un autre' [I is an other]. . . . When I read those words bells went off. It made perfect sense."[1] Characteristically, Dylan does not elaborate on how the nineteenth-century French poet's words made "perfect sense" to him then. He writes about it later in his career, however, like an epiphany, like a destiny that tolled for him: "Bells went off."[2]

As a bell-ringing epiphany, "I is an other" calls home Dylan's apparently disparate body of work, particularly the lion's share of his songs that treat love in its many forms, especially romantic-erotic love, friendship, neighbor-love, and divine love. Just as Rimbaud's "I is an other" offers some direction home to Dylan's thought and vision, Kierkegaard's sense about *I* and *other* (self and neighbor) helps pave the way: "The concept 'neighbor' is actually the redoubling of your own self; 'the neighbor' is what thinkers call 'the other,' that by which the selfishness in self-love is to be tested" (*SKS* 9:29 / *WL* 21). In this context, "I is an other" is what Kierkegaard would call the Archimedean point for Dylan, or that point at which individual genius may move the world (see, e.g., *SKS* 19:200, Notesbog 6:24, n.d. 1840 / *KJN* 3:196). "I is an other" informs Dylan's corpus as a whole, bringing it all back home. The phrase alone allies seemingly antipathetic aspects of Dylan's aesthetic, ethical, and religious personae in the same way Kierkegaard's pseudonym Judge William sees how aesthetic, ethical, and religious aspects of a person must be allied to make life meaningful (*SKS* 3:145 / *EO* 2:147).

Aesthetics and Poetic Freedom

Kierkegaard speaks through hundreds of imaginative constructions he conjures by his own masked and pseudonymous voices and characters. Of his formidable pseudonymity and poet-communication, he writes that they have "not had an *accidental* basis in my *person* . . . but an *essential* basis in the *production* itself." Consequently, Kierkegaard is "impersonally or personally in the third person a *souffleur* [prompter] who has poetically produced the *authors*. . . . Thus in the pseudonymous books there is not a single word by me" (*SKS* 7:569–70 / *CUP* 1:625–26).

Similarly, "I is an other" offers Dylan aesthetic license to form narrative voices, characters, and stage personae that people his own mosaic of the world. With or without inlay of his own opinions, values, or beliefs, Dylan populates his world by first imaginatively walking in the shoes of one character or narrator after another. "I is an other" offers Dylan the means by which he may cast a kind of "infinite sweep of humanity" that he saw cast in the work of folk musician Woody Guthrie (1912–1967),[3] that is, the organizing principle to compose, with succinct words and phrases, hundreds of highly individualized characters.

With a gifted imagination and a powerful associative memory, Dylan's own poet-communication engenders a vast progeny of human portraits and voices: a girl with a leopard-skin pillbox hat, a lone pilgrim, a one-eyed midget, a politician with jogging shoes, a lonesome organ grinder crying, Charles Darwin trapped out there on Highway 5, a guilty undertaker sighing, a tambourine man, Miss Lonelies, a dreamer of St. Augustine, a not-so-dear landlord, poor immigrants, lonesome hoboes, scores of babies and sweethearts and ladies and mommas and wanted men and minstrel boys—a seemingly never-ending tour of humanity. (The peripatetic Kierkegaard equally drew a vast and multifaceted portrait of so many human beings he acutely observed on his own virtually never-ending tour of humanity along the streets and side streets of Copenhagen.)

Nor would Dylan avoid responsibly claiming his villainous, saintly, innocent, experienced offspring. You may call him Terry, Timmy, Bobby, Zimmy, R.J., Ray, Jack Fate, Whiteface, and even Lucky or Boo Wilbury, just as you may unwittingly or surreptitiously call Kierkegaard by some sixteen or so pseudonyms. No matter what you say, the responsive, responsible Dylan is gonna have to serve somebody. It may be the devil of Faustian faces or it may be the Lord of poignantly human voices, but he's gonna have to serve somebody. He knows it. He wrote the song ("Gotta Serve Somebody").

Aesthetics and Personhood

Masks also help protect Dylan from those attempting (to paraphrase from Dylan's "To Ramona") to hype him or type him or make him feel that he must be exactly like them. In this context, Dylan is not only aesthetically but also existentially solid, a man masking his personal self to reveal the authentic literary-musical self that is his renown and legacy. Of the metaphysics of personhood and the fundamental roles that appearances and masks play, Kierkegaard scholar Howard Hong has song-and-dance men like Dylan in mind:

> The Latin *persona* means a mask used by actors to identify the character represented and as an aid in projecting the voice. The word itself is derived from *per*, meaning "through" and *sonare*, "to sound." Therefore a person is the one who sounds through the mask or the various masks seen by others. The person is not the mask of function, type, class, or social-economical-political relations but is the agent, the responder, the thinker, one who acts . . . one who bears the external mask or masks that others see. The mask is indeed the person's mask but the person is not synonymous with the mask and is not exhausted by the aggregate of his masks.[4]

Kierkegaard, along with several of his pseudonyms, repeatedly cites the French statesman Talleyrand as allegedly having said "Man did not acquire speech in order to reveal his thoughts but in order to conceal them" (*SKS* 1:292 / *CI* 253; see also *SKS* 4:409–10 / *CA* 108; *SKS* 6:315 / *SLW* 339; *SKS* 18:208, JJ:212, n.d. 1844 / *KJN* 2:191; *Pap*. V B 115:2, n.d. 1844 / *JP* 3:2322; *SKS* 26:283, NB33:42, n.d. 1854 / *JP* 4:3870). Words and speech equally prove revelatory to listeners of Dylan's characters and narrators. And understanding language is, according to Hong, "our best means to get behind the masks."[5]

The artist formerly known as Robert Zimmerman thereby has, like everybody else (including the man in his "Man in the Long Black Coat"), "a face like a mask." Dylan's narrator in "Abandoned Love" makes this opacity transparent: "Everybody's wearing a disguise / To hide what they've got left behind their eyes." But his literary persona—Bob Dylan—is equally transparent: "But me, I can't cover what I am / Wherever the children go I'll follow them."[6] Wherever, that is, the progeny of his fecund imagination (his songs) go, he will follow them, for Dylan finds "the religiosity and philosophy in the music" and nowhere else. "Songs like 'Let Me Rest on a Peaceful Mountain' or 'I Saw the Light'—that's my religion. I don't adhere to rabbis, preachers, evangelists, all of that. I've learned more from the songs than I've learned from any of this kind of entity. The songs are my lexicon. I believe the songs."[7]

At the 1964 Halloween Night Carnegie Hall concert, Dylan informed the audience that he was wearing his Bob Dylan mask. Before that, the young folk singer spun creation myths of being in places he had never been (like jail) and doing things he had never done (like joining the circus).[8] The title of his 2003 film, *Masked and Anonymous*, directed by Larry Charles, confirms

Dylan's reliance over time on not so much demonic concealment but what Kierkegaard would call "pious fraud." Along with Kierkegaard, Dylan can say, "In a sense I began my activity as an author with a falsum [deception] or with pia fraus [pious fraud]" (*SKS* 21:19, including 19*m*:1–2, NB6:21, n.d. 1848 / *KJN* 5:16, including 16*m*:1). Even back then he knew his back pages: that he "who sings with his tongue on fire" must always protect it from "the rat race choir" and "society's pliers" ("It's Alright, Ma [I'm Only Bleeding]"). Not only was Dylan older then, he was younger then, too, existing in a sort of Kierkegaardian second ignorance behind and beyond his rightful time (see, e.g., *SKS* 10:37–39 / *CD* 25–27).

There is, then, reason in the rhyme of Dylan's aesthetic foundation that Kierkegaard would endorse: "An author certainly must have his private personality as everyone has, but this must be his ἄδυτον [inner sanctum] . . . as the entrance to a house is barred by stationing two soldiers with crossed bayonets" (*SKS* 8:94 / *TA* 99). By not protecting an inwardness out of which black and bright truths in song may be sung, Dylan might not know his song well before he starts singing (see "A Hard Rain's A-Gonna Fall"). His *falsum* or *pia fraus* installs footings of a healthy self-love that preserves a genius and founds a towering literary-musical edifice. Not preserving such privacy amid the world's "mixed-up confusion" could have killed at least the poet in him. "There's too many people and they're all too hard to please" ("Mixed-Up Confusion").

Ethics and Social Justice

Born Jewish in a predominantly Christian American culture, Duluth native Robert Zimmerman was heavily influenced by American folk and gospel music and their Christian themes. The songs' messages likely lay the groundwork for his late-1970s conversion to Christianity. His 1962 debut album includes arrangements of two Christian gospel songs, "In My Time of Dyin' " and "Gospel Plow." Since then, scholars have inventoried and investigated hundreds of biblical references and Christian allusions in his canon.

The period that produced Dylan's evangelical albums (*Slow Train Coming*, 1979; *Saved*, 1980; and *Shot of Love*, 1981) shows him proclaiming Christianity and the need to love God. For a convert, this proclamation reasonably responds to the first of the two love commandments on which, according to Matthew 22:34–40, hang all laws and prophets. Along the line of Kierkegaard's indirect forms of communication, however, the more nuanced pathos of Dylan's religiosity, philosophy, and ethics takes stage before and after this period. These pre- and postevangelical sets spotlight the second love commandment (love your neighbor as yourself) through lyrical expressions of so many human actions that *lack* neighbor-love amid civil unrest, restless loves, and restive mobs.

Despite (or perhaps because of) his musical upbringing and conversion, Dylan learned early that humans regularly fall short of and are in need of voices with messages that run deeper than either the longing for requited romantic love or oaths of friendship in which most pop songs find their themes—voices with messages of neighbor-love that echo the civil rights, protest, and gospel songs of Woody Guthrie and other folk artist greats. Neighbor-love especially informs many of Dylan's love songs by subordinating romantic-erotic love and friendship. It also blows the whistle on unruly crowds.

"I is an other" subsequently takes on ethical qualifications, including a compassionate and egalitarian sense of social justice that enlists the self, the *I*, to move toward *the other*, the lowly, the needy, the down-trodden, the disenfranchised, the outcast. Here, "I is an other" neither appeals to quid pro quo nor offers much room for reciprocal-based romance and friendship (i.e., preferential, like-for-like, possessive, mine-thine relationships by which the selfishness in self-love is tested). Writes Kierkegaard:

> Erotic love [*Elskov*] and friendship . . . contain no moral task. . . .
> Erotic love is defined by the object; friendship is defined by the object; only love for the neighbor is defined by love [*Kjerlighed*]. . . .
> *Love* [Kjerlighed] *is a matter of conscience and thus is not a matter of [erotic] drives and inclination, or . . . feeling.* (SKS 9:57, 73, 145 / WL 50–51, 66, 143, emphasis in original)

This is perhaps why, before abandoning a romantic love in "Abandoned Love," the narrator claims, "I march in the parade of liberty / But as long as I love you I'm not free." Such abandoned romantic-erotic love and friendship ennoble Dylan's neighbor-love message to inform songs of protest and social justice.

Ethical bells ringing for justice chime, for instance, when "I is an other" tolls with compassion for the other in Dylan's "Chimes of Freedom." Here, "majestic bells" of lightning bolts strike "shadows in the sounds" that seem "to be the chimes of freedom flashing." Such bells toll for all, including

> warriors whose strength is not to fight . . .
> refugees on the unarmed road of flight
> . . . .
> the mistreated, mateless mother, the mistitled prostitute . . .
> the misdemeanor outlaw, chased an' cheated by pursuit.

Elsewhere, in "Thunder on the Mountain," the narrator sings, "Gonna forget about myself for a while, gonna go out and see what others need." In "With God on Our Side," Dylan's song about religious self-righteousness that deigns to justify wars, the narrator's name, "it ain't nothing," and his age, "it means less." Focus is not on the needs of a singer but on the needy in the song, not on the messenger but on the message. Such narrators mold masks of anonymity from a solid ethical cast of actuality that Kierkegaard would humbly applaud: "Would that you in silence might forget yourself, what you yourself are called, your own name, the famous name, the wretched name, the insignificant name" (*SV*[1] 11:21 / *WA* 18–19).

Ethics and Romantic-Erotic Love

Kierkegaard advises the multitudes who may see themselves as prima donnas, lovers, and friends who naturally and regularly try to upstage neighbor-love at every turn: "The love commandment . . . simply says, 'You shall love your neighbor.' Just as this commandment will teach everyone how to love oneself, so it also will teach erotic love and friendship genuine love; in loving yourself, *preserve love for the neighbor*; in erotic love and friendship, *preserve love for the neighbor*" (*SKS* 9:69 / *WL* 61–62, emphases added). Similarly, Dylan's treatment of neighbor-love's attention to the unknown and disenfranchised never loses sight of attending to the known beloved in romantic-erotic love or friend in friendship. Instead of actually disowning or abandoning romantic love and friendship to take up the banner of some righteous cause, Dylan (like Kierkegaard) relegates romantic love and friendship to second fiddle. Romantic-erotic love and friendship are not ejected from the band but are directed to back up the lead, which is neighbor-love.

For instance, as much as the enmeshed, overly dependent Babe in Dylan's "It Ain't Me, Babe" wants the narrator to "die for [her] *and more*" (emphasis added), the narrator knows that such love is not real, hence his answer: "It ain't me, babe." Or when the beloved in Dylan's "Don't Think Twice, It's Alright" wants the lover's soul, Dylan's lover-narrator knows to give the beloved no more than his heart. By offering only his temporal romantic love and not his eternal being, Dylan's poet-narrator instinctively knows what Kierkegaard knows, namely, that "lovers no doubt think that in erotic love they have the highest." By knowing this, Dylan's poet-narrators on the whole shed selfish masks of romantic-erotic love and don the ethical mask of neighbor-love, for, as Kierkegaard writes, "the [romantically inclined] poet promises the lovers immortality . . . but who then is the poet, what good is his vouching, he who cannot vouch for himself?" (*SKS* 9:68 / *WL* 61).

In other Dylan love songs,[9] relationships that could blossom into erotic love or friendship are instead "abandoned" for expressions of love that are more real, expressions that do not beg for something in return. Narrators speak not to curry romantic-erotic favor but to help others understand and see through the world's deceptions and individuals' self-deceptions, to help them become more inward, human, rounded, and less porcelain, dependent, and flat. In "Trust Yourself," for instance, the narrator advises, "Don't trust me to show you love / When my love may only be lust / If you want some-body you can trust, trust yourself."

That said, Dylan *has* written touchingly romantic-erotic love songs.[10] Most if not all of these kinds of songs, however, either admit to limits or failures of romantic love and friendship, or their narrators generally see the beloved as consenting adults instead of vulnerable prey.[11]

Other responses to vicissitudes of romantic-erotic love include "Love Sick," in which the narrator is "sick of love" while concurrently under its spell (love sick). In "When the Deal Goes Down," the narrator knows "transient joys . . . are not what they seem." In two songs, Dylan hilariously de-romanticizes even Romeo and Juliet's love affair, making the invocations serve as speed bumps to possessive, impatient backseat lovers:

> In comes Romeo, he's moaning
> "You belong to me I believe"
> And someone says, "You're in the wrong place my friend
> You better leave." ("Desolation Row")

> Romeo, he said to Juliet, "You got a poor complexion
> It doesn't give your appearance a very youthful touch!"
> Juliet said back to Romeo, "Why don't you just shove off
> If it bothers you so much." ("Floater [Too Much to Ask]")

(Kierkegaard, by the way, would cheer on Dylan's sucker punches to starry-eyed romantic Romeo. According to Eric Ziolkowski, "Kierkegaard . . . suggests that these two lovers' emotions belong on stage" because such romanticized emotions have "no place in 'practical life'" [*SKS* 21:164, NB8:43, n.d. 1848 / *KJN* 5:171].)[12]

Then there are playful songs of romantic-erotic love on the brink of neighbor-love, where the beloved is loved despite obvious limitations and because of unseen possibilities. In Dylan's "Ugliest Girl in the World," the narrator does not know why he loves her, but he just can't stop loving her. (The only physically attractive thing about her is her sweet breath—suggestive, of course, of inward beauty trumping outward imperfection.) On Dylan's debut album, the first lines of his first song, "She's No Good," tell of a darkly funny romantic-love turned neighbor-love: "Well I don't know why I love ya like I do / Nobody in the world can get along with you." What arguably may be Dylan's sweetest (least possessive) love song, "Love Minus Zero / No Limit" portrays a woman impervious to being hyped or typed:

> She doesn't have to say she's faithful
> Yet she's true, like fire, like ice . . .
> Valentines can't buy her . . .
> She knows too much to argue or to judge.

Yet even this extraordinary Love is no romanticized dovelike lovebird, but "like some raven / At my window with a broken wing." "Humanly speaking," Kierkegaard would add, "the truly loving one, the sacrificing, the self-giving one who loves, totally self-denying in all things, is . . . the injured one, the most injured of all . . . by continually giving [her]self" (*SKS* 9:267 / *WL* 268).

So Dylan *writes* touching romantic-erotic love songs, too, but his narrators generally remain weary of romantic-erotic love's ephemeral qualities.

Ethics and Friendship

As for friendship, Dylan's narrator in "Buckets of Rain" says it straight: "Friends will arrive, friends will disappear." Like romantic-erotic love, friendship traffics in partisanship, preference, reciprocity, quid pro quo—not pro bono, nonpreferential neighbor-love. Arguable exceptions in the playlist include the playful desire to want just to be "friends" with a lover in "All I Really Want to Do,"[13] or suffering loss of friends in songs like "Ballad for a Friend," or the nearest thing to sentimentality in Dylan's decidedly unsentimental songbook, "Bob Dylan's Dream," in which the narrator wishes "in vain . . . to sit . . . again" amid his "first few friends."

Generally, however, friends are what Dylan's narrator in "Gates of Eden" calls "other strangers," who conceal more than reveal so as to take as much of whatever their "friends" have. Other examples include:

> You do the work of the devil, you got a million friends
> They'll be there when you got something,
>   they'll take it all in the end. ("You Changed My Life")

> My best friend, my doctor
> Won't even say what it is I've got. ("Just Like Tom Thumb's Blues")

> You got a lotta nerve
> To say you are my friend
> When I was down
> You just stood there grinning. ("Positively 4th Street")

Dylan even anticipates the worst fear of friends on Facebook and other social media:

> Now I got a friend who spends his life
> Stabbing my picture with a bowie knife
> Dreams of strangling me with a scarf
> When my name comes up he pretends to barf
> I've got a million friends! ("I Shall Be Free No. 10")

Ethics and *They*

Dylan's and Kierkegaard's critiques of romantic-erotic love and friendship, however, pale before their relentless assaults upon that which Kierkegaard calls *the crowd* or *the rabble* and Dylan calls *They*, namely, the demonic legion from which so much of an individual's sorrow stems. More than lovers or friends, *They* makes one feel that one must be exactly like *Them*. Subsequently, Dylan's antipathies toward the machinations of the mob-like *They* throw into greatest relief his sympathies toward relationally integrated and concrete individuals (*I* and *you*) whom he, like Kierkegaard (and Jewish philosopher Martin Buber),[14] champions.

Despite a shared sense of egalitarianism, Dylan and Kierkegaard are ever skeptical of groups, members of which are forever compelled to be unreflective rank-and-file partisans. Seeking accountability for wrong action from *They* is difficult, however, because *They* is an oceanic abstraction into which individuals quickly dissolve. The concept of *They* also erodes individual consciences, compelling Kierkegaard to write, "If everyone in truth loved the neighbor as himself, then perfect equality would be achieved unconditionally. . . . Everyone who, even if he confesses, as I do, that his striving is weak and imperfect, is still aware that the task is to love the neighbor. . . . I have never read in Holy Scripture this commandment: You shall love the crowd" (*SKS* 16:91 / *PV* 111). Here, Kierkegaard describes the essentially egalitarian relationship between self and neighbor and reminds the reader that the egalitarian cannot forget from whence it came, namely, the personal—lest the egalitarian turn totalitarian. Which is why in "It's Alright Ma (I'm Only Bleeding)," Dylan's narrator notes that "even the president of the United States sometimes must have to stand naked." Similarly, in Dylan's "Masters of War," demonically masked war sponsors and purveyors are singled out as individuals for purposes of indictment:

> You that hide behind walls
> You that hide behind desks
> I just want you to know
> I can see through your masks.

Kierkegaard's and Dylan's critiques of *They* subsequently have their strongest foothold in the context of an at-large culture's conflict of *They* versus *I* (society versus the individual) more than in partisan politics' conflict of *They* versus *We* (*We* merely being another variant of *They*). "For it is only a great man who speaks, not a party," Kierkegaard writes. "It is only a solitary voice, not a party voice" (*SKS* 14:43 / *Cor.* 7). If individuals who make up *They* were honest with themselves, individuals in Dylan songs like "Who Killed Davey Moore?," "Only a Pawn in Their Game," and "The Lonesome Ballad of Hattie Carroll" would have reason to bury their faces in rags and cry, for individuals know that *They* is manmade, man-killing, and *They* will stone you "when you're tryin' to be so good . . . / just a-like they said they would." And then *They* will stone you

> when you're tryin' to go home . . .
> when you're there all alone . . .
> when you're tryin' to make a buck . . .
> and then they'll say, "good luck."

And then *They* will stone you again "and they'll say that it's the end . . . / and then they'll come back again . . . / and then say you are brave." And then *They* will stone you "when you are set down in your grave" ("Rainy Day Women #12 & 35"). Despite the mayhem portrayed in what is one of Dylan's most recognizable songs, however, the *second* line of the two-line refrain—"But I would not feel so all alone / *Everybody must get stoned*"—sucks all the oxygen out of the room, rendering the song the presumptive anthem of the drug culture.

But if *Everybody must get stoned* is the song's essential message, it is also essential to recognize that the bulk of the song *critiques* the message. A casual inspection of the lyrics yields narrative concern for two dangers: the loneliness an individual faces if he or she does not give in to *They*'s daunting peer pressure, and the power wielded by *They* to make the individual be governed by an enforced insanity that incrementally and absolutely kills the song's *You* and *I*.

Instead of the narrator abdicating because he feels so all alone, what listeners might hope the narrator would say is what Dylan's narrator of "Standing in the Doorway" says: "I know I can't win, / But my heart just won't give in." This assertion at least affirms innate goodness and bravery within the individual despite knowledge of a collective force's ultimate usurpation. What listeners of "Rainy Day Women #12 & 35" instead hear, however, is the narrator's sad surrender to the crowd by disclaiming the good and the brave by at least quoting if not internalizing *They*'s message: *Everybody must get stoned*. In addition, the refrain—presumably uttered affirmatively by *You* and *I*—seems mismanaged with great skill by *They*. If *You* or *I* object—for instance, at a Dylan concert—the objection would likely be drowned out by the crowd gleefully yelling en masse the only line that registers: *Everybody must get stoned*.

What also cannot be denied is that *Everybody must get stoned* may be a masked and anonymous acoustical illusion by Dylan to show the force of *They* to the nameless faces of *They*, as if to channel to each individual face what the narrator in Dylan's "Things Have Changed" knows: "All the truth in the world adds up to one big lie." In the end, the refrain *Everybody must get stoned* exploits crowd madness that happily consigns everybody to the Final Solution: dehumanization before annihilation of the very goodness and bravery with which all individuals are endowed. *Everybody must get stoned* is the mantra for a Dr. Jekyll/Mr. Hyde version of "I is an other": out-of-body, mind-altered, lacking in deliberation and conscience. Commensurate with ethics to which Dylan subscribes throughout his canon, the twenty lines of the thirty-line "Rainy Day Women #12 & 35" that begin by essentially prosecuting *They* read like so many upbuilding Kierkegaardian thoughts that, by their indirection, ethically wound from behind (see, e.g., *SKS* 10:167–252 / *CD* 161–246). As masked and anonymous indirect communicator extraordinaire, in other words, Dylan knows that if you invite a listener to receive a message upon the message's baseline aesthetic-sensuous-immediate level, then—after the listener begins *really to hear* the meaning of the message— the listener is confronted by its ethical or ethical-religious demands.[15] At that point the listener must *either* deny and reject the message's deeper ethical meaning by yielding to the sensuous sway of the aesthetic *or* accept Dylan's unorthodox art of helping the other that has just played out on a higher ethical level.

If, as Dylan's narrator claims in "Gates of Eden," "there are no truths outside [Eden's] gates," then all communication of truth, as Kierkegaard claims, must necessarily begin with an untruth. Such communication necessarily requires a mask. "Ethical communication in character always begins with placing a 'deception' in between," Kierkegaard writes, "and the art consists in enduring everything *while remaining faithful to character in the deception and faithful to the ethical*" (*SKS* 27:411, Papir 368:10, n.d. 1847 / *JP* 1:653, p. 288, my emphasis)—which may be why the "Gates of Eden" narrator prefaces the above remark by noting, "At times I think there are no words / But these [read: masked, arcane, metaphorical words] to tell what's true."

Ethics, *They*, and *Mundus vult decipi*

"What, then, does it mean 'to deceive' [into the truth]?" Kierkegaard asks. "It means that one does not begin *directly* with what one wishes to communicate but begins by taking the other's delusion at face value" (*SKS* 16:36 / *PV* 54). Dylan, too, knows to begin by taking the crowd's delusions at face value (in the present case, illicit drugs' short-term value), then building up the individual listeners' ethical or ethical-religious imagination. "If one is truly to succeed in leading a person to a specific place, one must first and foremost take care to find him where *he* is and begin there," Kierkegaard writes. "This is the secret in the entire art of helping" (*SKS* 16:271 / *PV* 45).

That said, how is this song about getting stoned—of all songs—so ethically good?[16] Its original and most enduring audial version, after all, conjures up a carnival atmosphere in which both Dylan and his backup vocals sing amid toxic laughs. Then there is the problem of any performing artist's, even Dylan's, need to self-promote. One of Kierkegaard's (unpublished) pseudonyms writes,

"Every juggler always and immediately makes a hit, because he simply wants to deceive; thus he wants what the times demand—*Mundus vult decipi* [the world wants to be deceived]" (*Pap.* VIII² B 12 59fn. / *BA* 171fn.).

Who can thereby blame the *world*? Is it not true that everybody, as Dylan's narrator sings in "Quinn the Eskimo," is "in despair, ev'ry girl and boy"? Is it also not true that, as Dylan's narrator sings in "High Water (For Charlie Patton)," it is "tough out there . . . rough out there . . . bad out there. High water everywhere"? Even Kierkegaard's pseudonym Frater Taciturnus seems sympathetic to the world (if not cynically, ironically so): "*Mundus vult decipi*; my relationship to the environment that I must call my world can hardly be more definitely expressed. In fact, I believe that in a wider sense it is the best that has been said about the world. Thus speculators should not cudgel their brains trying to fathom what the times demand, for it has been essentially the same since time immemorial: to be tricked and bamboozled. If one just says something silly and drinks . . . with humanity *en masse*, then one comes to be . . . loved and esteemed by the whole congregation" (*SKS* 6:316 / *SLW* 340). After the smoke clears, however, other masks of Dylan and Kierkegaard reveal themselves, masks that condemn *They* for prohibiting individuals from living deliberately, reflectively, compassionately, and empathetically, alone and together. In a discourse he entitles "Becoming Sober," Kierkegaard writes, "The world *wants* to be deceived; not only is it deceived—ah, then the matter would not be so dangerous!—but it *wants* to be deceived. Intensely, more intensely, more passionately perhaps than any witness to the truth has fought for the truth, the world fights to be deceived; it most gratefully rewards with applause, money, and prestige anyone who complies with its wish to be deceived. And perhaps the world has never needed to become sober as much as it does today" (*SKS* 16:192–93 / *JFY* 139–40). Meanwhile, Dylan's narrator in "Ain't Talkin'" talks:

> The world is filled with speculation
> The whole wide world which people say is round
> They will tear your mind away from contemplation
> They will jump on your misfortune when you're down.

An authentic self thus becomes, according to Kierkegaard's pseudonym Anti-Climacus, "the last thing the world cares about and the most dangerous thing of all for a person to show signs of having" (*SV¹* 11:148 / *SUD* 32)—dangerous because it is only within such a self that the ethical and the ethical-religious find a voice. "The good person," Kierkegaard writes, "must get people separated as individuals. The same people, who as individuals are able to will the good in truth, are immediately corrupted as soon as they unite and become many, and therefore the good person will neither try to have a *crowd* for help in splitting up the *crowd* nor try to have a *crowd behind him* while he is splitting up the *crowd in front of him*" (*SKS* 8:200 / *UDVS* 96).

It is no wonder that action figures like Kierkegaard and Dylan come with masks. As with Superman, Batman, and the Lone Ranger, what more compelling means than masks do they have to "spare the defeated . . . speak to the crowd . . . preach peace to the conquered [and] tame the proud" ("Lonesome Day Blues")?

Which is where masked and anonymous *You* and *I* come in. For "the last thing I would surrender is my faith in individual human beings," Kierkegaard writes. "And this is my faith, that however much confusion and evil and contemptibleness there can be in human beings as soon as they become the irresponsible and unrepentant 'public,' 'crowd,' etc.—there is just as much truth and goodness and lovableness in them when one can get them as single individuals" (*SV*[1] 13:499 / *PV* 10–11).

Religiousness and *You* and I

In Dylan's "All Along the Watchtower," a desperate "joker," exasperated by feeling no relief from worldly chaos and a sense of worthlessness, confides in his friend—a consoling (if not humorously chastising) thief:

> "No reason to get excited," the thief he kindly spoke,
> "There are many here among us who think that life is but a joke.
> But you and I, we've been through that, and this is not our fate;
> So let us not talk falsely now, the hour is getting late."

The lines are not from the only hit song Dylan sings in apocalyptic terms.[17] Nor is it the only song in which its narrator implores the need to avoid talking falsely to oneself and others while seeking what Kierkegaard (invoking Socrates) calls an "honest distrust of oneself, to treat oneself as a suspicious character" (*SKS* 13:70 / *FSE* 44).[18]

An honest distrust of one's self means coming clean—*becoming sober*—even in the eleventh hour. Here is where the *I* begins to see the other, the neighbor identified as *You*, as essential to becoming fully human: namely, becoming *itself*, the ethically self-loving *I*, the *relational phenomenon* striving ethically to relate itself to itself, to others, and to the power that established it (see *SKS* 11:129–30 / *SUD* 13–14). Here is where the *I* sees the neighbor as "the *other you* . . . the *first you*" (*SKS* 9:60, 64 / *WL* 53, 57). Here is where the *I*'s self-love sheds the thick skins of egoism and narcissism, metamorphosing into its better angel, one that presupposes better angels in others. Here is where the stage is *really* set—with love, according to Kierkegaard, being the only thing that presupposes itself: "The one who loves presupposes that love is in the other person's heart and by this very presupposition builds up love in him" (*SKS* 9:219 / *WL* 216–17). Here is where the task of self-love is ethically "to be [critically] objective in relation to oneself and [sympathetically] subjective in relation to all others" instead of being "subjective toward [one-self] and objective toward all others" (*SKS* 20:164, NB2:57, n.d. 1847 / *KJN* 4:162). Here is where the self's meaningful relation with itself exists when the self is in an ethical relation with the other, the neighbor. Here is where moving to accept—even favor—eccentricities of the neighbor by altering one's own eccentricities requires ever more inward self-love, love that moves toward (not away from) one's better angels by routinely challenging (instead of being smugly satisfied with) one's own eccentricities. Here is where becoming human becomes more difficult, yet, for all that, more meaningful.

Great difficulty arises because moving toward that which is not naturally preferred is anathema to romantic-erotic love and friendship, both of which lead a person to embrace only what is like or similar to that person. In this context, what Dostoevsky's rational egoist Ivan Karamazov says about neighbor-love seems not so outlandish. "I must make an admission," Ivan explains to his youngest brother. "I never could understand how it's possible to love one's neighbors. In my opinion, it is precisely one's neighbors that one cannot possibly love. Perhaps if they weren't so nigh."[19] Natural instincts and acts of will based upon rational egoism to which Ivan aspires embrace only that which is like or similar to one's own self. Ethics, on the other hand, generally indicates the *opposite* as counterweight to impulsive and unreflective tribal instincts. This is why Kierkegaard calls the neighbor "the *other you*," compelling *You* to consider the neighbor as essentially more like than unlike *You*.

If becoming fully human has something to do with developing the self-as-relational-phenomenon, then becoming fully human has something to do with relating well with others, which implies ethically moving *toward* the other, the neighbor, the *other you*. Only by moving toward the neighbor (who may not be dear to *You* but who is nonetheless near to *You*) will *You* come to embody *You*. *You* must find *the other*, according to Kierkegaard, "lovable despite and with his weaknesses and defects and imperfections," for "the task is not to develop one's fastidiousness but to transform oneself and one's taste" (*SKS* 9:158–59 / *WL* 158)—all for the love of the other. Here is where becoming human becomes meaningful: *You*, choosing to love the neighbor, may be the only way *You* can love itself, can live in and with itself well. Here is where *the other* is far more like *You* than unlike *You*, no matter what *You* might say. Which is perhaps why, in "What Good Am I?," Dylan sings

> What good am I if I'm like all the rest
> If I just turn away, when I see how you're dressed
> If I shut myself off so I can't hear you cry . . . ?
>
> . . . .
>
> What good am I then to others and me
> If I've had every chance and yet still fail to see

> If my hands are tied must I not wonder within
> Who tied them and why and where must I have been?

Here is where knowing the *neighbor* as *the other you* is "I is an other" at its best. It is where "I is an other" is the Archimedean point at which the self ethically moves itself in ways that may ethically move the neighbor, the *other*, the one whom *I* cannot choose, the one who may just as well be an enemy, because "The thing that scared me most was when the enemy came close / And I saw that his face looked just like mine" ("John Brown"). And if *You* can love the enemy from within and without, then here is where *You* can move the world, for here is where neighbor-love begins, where it is ultimately up to *You*. All that is left to do is don the mask with which *You* is fundamentally endowed: the responsive and responsible mask, the authentic *persona*, neither selfish nor childish—the genuine mask of *I* that befits the genuine mask of *You*, wherein "I is an other" ultimately makes perfect bell-ringing sense.

According to Kierkegaard,

> It is a mark of childishness to say: *Me wants, me—me*; a mark of adolescence to say: *I—and I—and I*; the sign of maturity . . . is to will to understand that this *I* has no significance unless it becomes the *you* [in] . . . *you* shall, *you* shall, *you* shall. Youthfulness wants to be the only *I* in the whole world; maturity is to understand this *you* personally, even if it were not addressed to a single other person. *You* shall, *you* shall love the neighbor. O my listener, it is not *you* to whom *I* am speaking; it is *I* to whom eternity says: *You* shall. (*SKS* 9:95 / *WL* 90)

Likewise, Dylan knows that the perfect sense of "I is an other" is up to him—his mature, ethical *I*. Which is why, in his "Up to Me," Dylan is the perfect master thief of love: "The old Rounder in the iron mask slipped me the master key / Somebody had to unlock your heart, he said it was up to me."

In the end, Dylan and Kierkegaard accept the varied masks they wear outside Eden's gates, masks that emit sounds and illumine visions that lure us toward the kind of self-love that neighbor-love presupposes. Through these ethically derived and Janus-like masks, they show life forward by looking back to some forgotten home (back to the soul's gate behind and beyond which essential *Being* resides) rather than, homesick and blue, looking away and down so many lonesome roads again.

Coda: Kierkegaard on Dylan's Music (A Thought Experiment)

As mentioned at the outset, Dylan and Kierkegaard share an appreciation for the power of both sacred and profane music. Had Kierkegaard heard Dylan, how might the former (for whom music was so important to convey various dimensions of the spirit) respond to the latter's musical, compositional, and performing skills? At the least, how might a Kierkegaardian ear regard Dylan's music?[20]

In the paean to Mozart's *Don Giovanni* in Kierkegaard's *Either/Or I* ("The Immediate Erotic Stages or the Musical-Erotic"), pseudonym "A" does not claim musical expertise: "I am well aware that I do not understand music; I readily admit that I am a layman. I do not hide the fact that I do not belong to the chosen tribe of music experts, that at most I stand in the doorway as a gentile convert drawn from afar to this place by a strange, irresistible impulse—but no further" (*SV* 1:48 / *EO* 1:65). Here, "A's" disclaimer may comport with Kierkegaard's own understanding of music, although Kierkegaard might broaden his own sphere of ignorance beyond the musicological to the philosophical.[21] On the title page of his *Either/Or I* chapter on Mozart's *Don Giovanni*, for instance, Kierkegaard writes, "What Homer says of music is true: οἶον ἀκούομεν, οὐδέ τι ἴδμεν [we only hear, we know nothing]. *Iliad*, II, 468. One hears it, but he does not know it, does not understand it" (*Pap.* IV A 222, n.d., 1843 / *JP* 1:147). That said, Kierkegaard's extraordinary expositions of music, lyrical-musical voice, and the ethics of music and voice read like a fitting critique of Dylan.

Writing about the overture to *Don Giovanni*, for instance, "A" offers a compact aesthetic description of the kind of music toward which Dylan aspires: "It is powerful like a god's idea, turbulent like a world's life, harrowing in its earnestness, palpitating in its desire, crushing in its terrible wrath, animating in its full-blooded joy; it is hollow-toned in its judgment, shrill in its lust; it is ponderous, ceremonious in its awe-inspiring dignity; it is stirring, flaring, dancing in its delight" (*SKS* 2:129 / *EO* 1:127). And earlier:

> If you cannot get an idea of Don Giovanni by hearing him, then you never will. . . . Just as the lightning is discharged from the darkness of the thunderclouds, so he bursts out of the abyss of earnestness, swifter than the lightning's flash, more capricious than lightning and yet just as measured. Hear how he plunges down into the multiplicity of life, how he breaks against its solid embankment. Hear these light, dancing . . . notes, hear the intimation of joy, hear the jubilation of delight, hear the festive bliss of enjoyment. Hear his wild flight; he speeds past himself, ever faster, never pausing. Hear the unrestrained craving of passion, hear the sighing of erotic love, hear the whisper of temptation, hear the vortex of seduction, hear the stillness of the moment—hear, hear, hear. (*SKS* 2:106–7 / *EO* 1:103)

In an ethical context, Kierkegaard's abiding fascination with the medieval troubadour speaks not only to Kierkegaard's intent to shape a lyrical-ethical voice for himself but also to Dylan's own musical-ethical intent to serve as a performing artist qua modern troubadour.[22] In reading notes he made of Friedrich Diez's 1829 *Die Poesie der Troubadours* (*The Poetry of Troubadours*) under the heading "The Sirvente" (the moral or religious song of the Provençal troubadours satirizing social vices), Kierkegaard writes, "With this genre the troubd. began to influence life, making some impact upon the princes and the powerful. . . . Troubd. sang the exploits of the well-born but undertook also to reprove them for their faults" (*SKS* 17:72, BB:2, April 22, 1836 / *KJN* 1:66). Many of Dylan's musical scores speak to the song of the Sirvente that troubadours of yore sang.

In a religious context, a journal entry of October 30, 1838, by Kierkegaard may offer a critique of Dylan's ethical and ethical-religious music and musical performances, especially of concerts given during his evangelical period. In the entry, Kierkegaard imaginatively addresses "D.L." ("devout listeners" of, presumably, the sermon he sketches out in the entry), and he considers what seers and hearers of John the Baptist preaching in the desert might expect to hear and see versus what John actually offers them: "My talk shall be like wild honey—its clothing like the woolen shirt J. the Baptist wore, rough and sharp, perhaps to many a severe talk" (*SKS* 17:268*m*:22–26, DD:164 / *KJN* 1:259*m*:10–14). Here, Kierkegaard essentially claims an unvarnished if not prophetic voice that Dylan himself appropriates throughout his career, especially in so many of his ethical and ethical-religious songs. (Kierkegaard's words might also go so far as to justify what many of Dylan's more musicological sophisticates maintain as Dylan's "rough and sharp" singing voice—words that also warn that attention to the accident of physical voice should never eclipse the spirit in which the song is delivered and its lyrical meaning. Kierkegaard writes elsewhere that "everything that is said and sung in church should be true, not that it should be beautiful, great, glorious, ravishing, etc." (*SKS* 27:558, Papir 452, n.d., 1853–54 / *JP* 1:829).

In the end, what Kierkegaard's "A" says of Mozart's music might also be Kierkegaard's last word on Dylan's music (one that, in addition, may comport with most earnest and flippant Dylan fans' last words): "A" "usually passes the time humming something I do not understand" (*SKS* 2:56 / *EO* 1:49). Nevertheless, "A" knows "that if Mozart ever became entirely comprehensible to me, he would then become completely incomprehensible to me" (*SKS* 2:68 / *EO* 1:61). With Dylan's music, the same.

Notes

1. Bob Dylan, *Chronicles* (New York: Simon and Schuster, 2004), 1:288.

2. Rimbaud of course is no religionist with theological designs. That said, the overall thesis and argument of the present essay entertain how Rimbaud's famous assertion influenced Dylan, both in theological and nontheological ways—no matter if Dylan properly read or misread what Rimbaud was attempting to mean in a nontheological context.

3. Dylan, *Chronicles*, 244.

4. Howard V. Hong, "Trying to Do the Right Thing," *Reece Report* (Northfield, Minn.) 7, no. 1 (1992): 18.

5. Ibid.

6. Quotations from Dylan's songs are identified by song titles within the text and are either from his lyrics located online at bobdylan.com or from *Bob Dylan: Lyrics, 1962–2001* (New York: Simon and Schuster, 2004).

7. David Gates, "Dylan Revisited," *Newsweek*, October 7, 1997. As much as Kierkegaard loved singing hymns, the New Testament was clearly his lexicon, and he insisted that, as quoted in the closing coda to this essay, "everything that is said and sung in church should be true." That said, Kierkegaard himself (like Dylan) found it increasingly difficult to adhere to so many preachers' words, especially in Denmark's state church—an institution that became, in his increasingly strident opinion, ever more accommodating and diluted over time. See especially Kierkegaard's late writings for his brutal critique of what Dylan would call the "watered-down love" of the Church.

8. See, e.g., "My Life in a Stolen Moment" in *Studio A: The Bob Dylan Reader*, ed. Benjamin Hedin (New York: Norton, 2004), 3–7.

9. For example, "Queen Jane Approximately," "Like a Rolling Stone," "Just Like a Woman," "Trust Yourself," "Most Likely You Go Your Way and I'll Go Mine," "I'll Keep It with Mine," "She Belongs to Me," and "Abandoned Love."

10. For example, "Feel My Love," "Lay Lady Lay," "I Want You," "If Not for You," "Tomorrow Is a Long Time," "To Ramona," "Buckets of Rain," "You Gonna Make Me Lonesome When You Go," "Simple Twist of Fate," and "Girl from the North Country."

11. One exception is "Belle Isle," from Dylan's *Self-Portrait* album, although it is a Newfoundland folk song, not written by Dylan. The song highlights a pleasure-seeker crossing paths with a young maid pining for a long-lost love; the young man tells her that he is her beloved returned . . . in disguise!

12. Eric Ziolkowski, *The Literary Kierkegaard* (Evanston, Ill.: Northwestern University Press, 2011), 191–92.

13. It is hard to imagine, however, that Kierkegaard would think this song very "playful" vis-à-vis his complicated relationship with Regine Olsen—the lyrics of which include "I don't want to straight-face you / Race or chase you, track or trace you / Or disgrace you or displace you / Or define you or confine you."

14. For Buber, just as for Kierkegaard and the Jewish-born Dylan, a self is a *relational* phenomenon that recognizes the necessity of but is not limited in a strictly binary way to dual structures of the self. In addition, all three authors recognize that distinctions are to be made even as relationships are to be acknowledged between such words as *I, it, me, he, she, you* (the human *thou*, the divine *Thou*), *we, they, the world*, and *the eternal*. (Throughout the remainder of this essay, by the way, I increasingly use variant grammatical constructs that occur in Kierkegaard's and especially Buber's own lyrical thinking.) Given the limited size and scope of the present essay, it is with a special regret that I have chosen not to incorporate Buber and Judaism in a more plenary way. What follows are a few brief passages from Buber's *I and Thou* as they relate to this essay: "Primary words do not signify things, but they intimate relations. . . . There is no *I* taken in itself. . . . Every *It* is bounded by others. *It* exists only by being bounded by

others. . . . *Thou* [on the other hand] has no bounds. . . . As experience, the world belongs to the primary word *I-It*. The primary word *I-Thou* establishes the world of relation. . . . For *Thou* is more than *It* realizes. . . . I become through my relation to the *Thou*; as I become *I*, I say *Thou*. All real living is meeting. . . . In the beginning is relation. . . . Spirit is not in the *I*, but between *I* and *Thou*." Martin Buber, *I and Thou*, trans. Ronald Gregor Smith, Scribner Classics (New York: Charles Scribner, 2000), 19, 20, 21, 24, 26, 27.

15. Refrains of "Watered-Down Love" and "Property of Jesus" offer other examples.

16. To counter so many critics who have maintained over the years that the song's theme is more suspect of decadence than deserving of ethics' respect, Dylan laconically puts the matter to rest in a 2012 *Rolling Stone* interview. Interviewer: "Do you ever worry that people interpreted your work in misguided ways? For example, some people still see 'Rainy Day Women' as coded about getting high." Dylan: "It doesn't surprise me that some people would see it that way. But these are people that aren't familiar with the Book of Acts." Mikal Gilmore, "Bob Dylan: The Rolling Stone Interview," *Rolling Stone*, September 27, 2012, 45.

17. Others include "Knockin' on Heaven's Door," "I Shall Be Released," "Tryin' to Get to Heaven," "Up to Me," "Dark Eyes," "Caribbean Wind," "It's Not Dark Yet," "Highlands," and "Sugar Baby."

18. Others include "Abandoned Love," "To Ramona," "Every Grain of Sand," "Up to Me," "What Good Am I?," "Most of the Time," "Ain't No Man Righteous, No Not One," "The Disease of Conceit," and "Mississippi."

19. Fyodor Dostoevsky, *The Brothers Karamazov*, pt. 2, book 5 ("Pro and Contra"), chap. 4 ("Rebellion"), trans. Richard Pevear and Larissa Volokhonsky (London: Quartet Books, 1990), 236.

20. A few pairs of Kierkegaardian ears have made a performance artist's attempt to answer this question in their own way. A 2015 album, *Mother Tongue*, by Jonathan Byrd, in collaboration with a Danish folk-rock trio, The Sentimentals, contains songs inspired by Kierkegaard and Dylan. (The album's cover art alone—which offers, side by side, the left half of perhaps the most iconic frontal head portrait of Kierkegaard and the right half of perhaps the most iconic frontal head portrait of Dylan—is compelling.)

21. Compare the suggestion made by Nils Holger Petersen in his own essay in this volume, "that the music philosophy of 'A' collapses if one takes it seriously in detail."—Ed.

22. In their own essays elsewhere in this volume, George Pattison likewise comments on Kierkegaard's fascination with the medieval troubadours, and Marcia C. Robinson ascribes to Kierkegaard "the role of a Socratic troubadour."—Ed.

CONTRIBUTORS

Christopher B. Barnett is an associate professor in the Department of Theology and Religious Studies at Villanova University.

Martijn Boven is a Ph.D. candidate in the humanities at the University of Groningen.

Anne Margrete Fiskvik is a professor in the Department of Music and chair of the Program for Dance Studies at the Norwegian University of Science and Technology, Trondheim.

Joakim Garff is director of the Søren Kierkegaard Research Centre and an associate professor of ethics and philosophy of religion at the University of Copenhagen.

Ronald M. Green is Professor Emeritus of Religion and the Eunice and Julian Cohen Professor Emeritus for the Study of Ethics and Human Values at Dartmouth College; he has also served as director of Dartmouth's Institute for the Study of Applied and Professional Ethics, and is a member of the Department of Community and Family Medicine at Dartmouth's Geisel School of Medicine.

Peder Jothen is an assistant professor in the Religion Department at St. Olaf College.

Ragni Linnet is a *lektor* in the Department of Arts and Cultural Studies at the University of Copenhagen.

Jamie A. Lorentzen is a teacher at Tower View Alternative High School in Red Wing, Minnesota.

Edward F. Mooney is a professor emeritus of philosophy and religion at Syracuse University.

George Pattison is the 1640 chair of Divinity at the University of Glasgow.

Nils Holger Petersen is an associate professor emeritus in the Department of Church History at the University of Copenhagen.

Howard Pickett is an assistant professor of ethics and poverty studies and director of the Shepherd Program for the Interdisciplinary Study of Poverty and Human Capability at Washington and Lee University.

Marcia C. Robinson is an assistant professor of religion at Syracuse University.

James Rovira is the chair of the department and an associate professor of English at Mississippi College in Clinton, Mississippi.

Eric Ziolkowski is the Helen H. P. Manson Professor of the English Bible and head of the Department of Religious Studies at Lafayette College in Easton, Pennsylvania.

Aaron (brother of Moses): as depicted in Schoenberg's opera, 272–74. *See also* Schoenberg, Arnold

Abraham: (aborted) sacrifice of Isaac by, 59, 67n6, 90, 172n22

acheiropoieta [icons made without hand], 197–98. *See also* icon(s); Veronica's Veil

Achilles: SK likened to, 5

Adam, Adolph, 172n29

Adam and Eve, 125, 211, 223, 248, 254; choice of, 225–26

Adorno, Theodor, 19, 148n28; aesthetics of, 145; *Philosophy of Modern Music* (*Philosophie der neuen Musik*), 144–45

aesthetics (esthetics), 52n24, 78, 131; of "A," 19, 139; of Adorno, 145; of beauty, 197–98; defined, 177; of Don Juan, 140; vs. ethics, 153; etymology of, 177; of Hegel, 43–44, 278nn10–11; of icon, 21–22, 177, 179, 188–90; idealistic, 194; modern, 179; of music, 135; musical, 140; and poetic freedom, 282; and personhood, 282; and religion, 179–80; Romantic, 135–36, 146n4; situational, 213; and SK, 139, 177–90, 194; of Solger, 213; as supreme value, 179; theatrical, 18. *See also* Adorno, Theodor; beauty; Hegel, Georg Wilhelm Friedrich; Solger, Karl Wilhelm Ferdinand

Agacinski, Sylviane, 17

Alexander the Great, 34n42

Allen, Woody, 8, 25, 56; "My Philosophy," 34n45

Alstrup, Mads: photo studio of, 221n7

analogia entis, 179, 184

Andersen, Hans Christian, 40, 42; and Bournonville, 171n17; *Only a Fiddler*, 46

Andersson, Roy: *En kärlekshistoria* (*A Swedish Love Story*), 34n45

Angiolini, Gasparo: *Don Juan ou Le Festin de Pierre* (*Don Juan, or the Stone Guest's Banquet*), 156, 172n31

angst, 39

antihymn: Mozart's *Don Giovanni* as, 276

Anna (biblical prophetess), 22, 183–85; faith of, 187, 189

Antigone, 225; modern versus Greek, 231–32. *See also* Sophocles

anxiety, 14, 55, 73, 75, 77, 80, 85–86, 115, 164, 231, 251, 256; ambiguous essence of, 94; ambivalence as, 240; created by SK, 61; as Don Juan's energy, 141; and freedom, 61, 226, 254; and literary form, 251, 254–55; objectified, 235n4

apostles (of Christ): Thorvaldsen's statues of, 6, 33n42

Aquinas: *Summa Theologica*, 258–59n27

Ariadne and Theseus: painting of, 24, 207–8, 208 figures 4 and 5

Aristophanes, 8, 44, 56, 245. *See also* burlesque

Aristotle, 74; *Poetics*, 27, 102, 109, 113n16, 254; *Rhetoric*, 254

Armitage, Thomas, 244

art(s). *See* cinema/film/moving pictures; icon(s); literature; mime(s); novella(s); novel(s); painting(s); poetry; satire; sculpture; troubadours; troubadour tradition

Ast, Friedrich: *Platon's Leben und Schriften* (*Plato's Life and Writings*), 216–17

Auden, W. H., 39, 56, 177

Auerbach, Erich, 33n36